P9-EDO-716

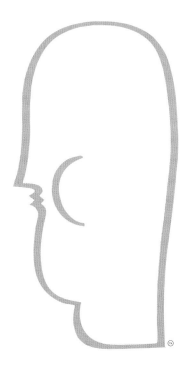

2004 Guide to DiRōNA Award Restaurants

Lebhar-Friedman Books

NEW YORK • CHICAGO • LOS ANGELES • LONDON • PARIS • TOKYO

Lebhar-Friedman Books
425 Park Avenue
New York, NY 10022

Copyright © 2003 Lebhar-Friedman Books

All rights reserved. No part of this work covered by the copyright hereon may
be reproduced or used in any form or by any means—
graphic, electronic, or mechanical, including photocopying, recording, taping,
or information storage and retrieval systems—
without the written permission of the publisher.

Published by Lebhar-Friedman Books
Lebhar-Friedman Books is a company of Lebhar-Friedman, Inc.

DiRōNA Award symbol and DiRōNA logo are registered trademarks of
Distinguished Restaurants of North America.

ISBN: 0-86730-933-4

Library of Congress Cataloging in Publication Data on file at the Library of Congress.

Project Director: Sue Moskowitz
Editor: Lisa Lindsay
Sales Coordinator and Project Manager: Paula Kaye Scheiber
Production Assistants: Gwen Jagde, Jill Rembar
Pre-Press Services: Graphic Process, Inc., Nashville, TN

Book Design: Nancy Koch, NK Design

A complete list of DiRōNA Award winning restaurants
is available at **www.dirona.com.**

Volume Discounts

This book makes a great gift and incentive.
Call (212) 756-5183 for information on volume discounts.

About the Endpaper Art: **Guy Buffet** is famous for his whimsical fantasies. He has a remarkable
ability to capture the essence of the moment and to visually articulate a sense of character and place.
He is a recognized master of such subjects as chefs, sommeliers, and wine makers. He is also widely
respected for his paintings of historical events. Corporations, private collectors, museums, and
special-events committees from around the world continue to commission his work.

Contents

Introduction		v
About DiRōNA		vi
Inspection Program		vii
How to Use This Guide		viii
DiRōNA Officers and Directors		ix
The DiRōNA Guarantee		xii
DiRōNA Sponsors		xiv

THE UNITED STATES OF AMERICA

AK	Alaska	1
AL	Alabama	3
AR	Arkansas	5
AZ	Arizona	6
CA	California	
	Northern California	11
	Southern California	42
CO	Colorado	75
CT	Connecticut	91
DC	District of Columbia	94
DE	Delaware	112
FL	Florida	113
GA	Georgia	172
HI	Hawaii	183
IA	Iowa	188
ID	Idaho	189
IL	Illinois	190
IN	Indiana	210
KY	Kentucky	211
LA	Louisiana	213
MA	Massachusetts	226
MD	Maryland	245
ME	Maine	257
MI	Michigan	259
MN	Minnesota	266
MO	Missouri	268
MS	Mississippi	279
NC	North Carolina	282

DiRōNA Fine Dining Guide

NH	New Hampshire	289
NJ	New Jersey	291
NM	New Mexico	301
NV	Nevada	305
NY	New York	321
OH	Ohio	372
OK	Oklahoma	381
OR	Oregon	382
PA	Pennsylvania	387
RI	Rhode Island	402
SC	South Carolina	405
TN	Tennessee	412
TX	Texas	423
UT	Utah	440
VA	Virginia	446
VT	Vermont	457
WA	Washington State	460
WI	Wisconsin	467
WY	Wyoming	470

CANADA

Alberta	471
British Columbia	474
Manitoba	483
Ontario	484
Quebec	498

MEXICO

Acapulco	516
Cancun	517
Cozumel	520
Cuernavaca	521
Mexico City	522
Oaxaca	527
San Miguel de Allende	528

INDEX

| INDEX OF RECIPIENTS (ALPHABETICAL) | 529 |

Introduction

Dear Distinguished Diner,

Rick Powers

Welcome to *The 2004 Guide to Distinguished Restaurants of North America (DiRōNA).* DiRōNA was established over a decade ago to serve as the authority for recognizing and promoting excellence in dining. The DiRōNA Award is given to restaurants that exemplify fine dining from the initial making of a reservation to the final presentation of the check. Created by DiRōNA, this *Guide* is representative of the great dining experiences that await you in the United States, Canada and Mexico. While the *Guide* does not include a full page listing for each DiRōNA restaurant, a complete listing of all DiRōNA restaurants is located in the index of this *Guide* and is also available on our website, www.dirona.com.

Whether you are looking for a steakhouse in Portland, a French restaurant in Montreal or an establishment specializing in regional Cajun cuisine in New Orleans, rest assured that you can rely upon DiRōNA as the premier source of fine dining restaurants across North America. Since 1992, each DiRōNA award recipient restaurant has been awarded membership in this prestigious organization by successfully passing a 75-point anonymous inspection which judges their establishment on every aspect of the fine dining experience ranging from the friendliness of the wait staff to the overall quality of the cuisine and decor.

Please take the time to familiarize yourself with the more than 750 DiRōNA award recipient restaurants across North America and prepare yourself for a wonderful dining experience.

Enjoy the *Guide,* welcome to DiRōNA and happy dining,

Rick Powers
Chairman of the Board, 2002-2003

DiRōNA Fine Dining Guide

THE AWARD
OF EXCELLENCE
FROM
DISTINGUISHED
RESTAURANTS OF
NORTH AMERICA

About DiRōNA

Distinguished Restaurants of North America (DiRōNA) is a non-profit organization which seeks to raise dining standards and promote distinguished dining throughout Canada, Mexico and the United States. The organization was founded in 1990 and is governed by an independent board of directors. The mission of Distinguished Restaurants of North America is to serve as the authority for recognizing and promoting excellence in dining.

In 1992, the DiRōNA Awards Program was launched. The founding members were the recipients of the Travel Holiday Award in 1989, which was the last year that award was presented. DiRōNA's "Award of Excellence" recognizes restaurants that exemplify the highest quality in every aspect of the dining experience, from the making of the reservation to the presentation of the check. Founding sponsors of the DiRōNA Awards Program are American Express and Allied Domecq Spirits, U.S.A.

The DiRōNA Award Inspection Program is the only independent and anonymous restaurant inspection program in North America. To qualify for the DiRōNA Award, a restaurant must be in business under the same ownership and concept for at least three years. Having met that requirement, a restaurant must pass a 75-point evaluation conducted anonymously by a specially trained independent panel of qualified professionals and distinguished dining connoisseurs. The inspection process examines the total dining experience and is supervised by the DiRōNA Council of Inspection, Evaluation and Criteria.

The DiRōNA designation remains in effect for four years, at which point the establishment is evaluated again, using the exact same criteria. If a restaurant undergoes a change in ownership or concept during the four years the Award is in effect, it forfeits the DiRōNA Award until it has fulfilled the "three years in business" requirement and passes inspection.

THE AWARD
OF EXCELLENCE
FROM
DISTINGUISHED
RESTAURANTS OF
NORTH AMERICA

DiRōNA Inspection Program

The DiRōNA Awards result from an independent and anonymous restaurant evaluation, administered by Harold Stayman, Director of Inspections since 1993. Mr. Stayman heads a team of forty inspectors, most of whom have been serving for more than seven years. They are thoroughly oriented with the seventy-five point evaluation criteria developed by Cornell University, which is the basis for all inspections. They have impeccable credentials and are very experienced in fine dining!

Dr. Morris Gaebe, Chancellor of Johnson & Wales University, heads the Inspections, Evaluation and Criteria Council working closely with Mr. Stayman. The Council provides oversight and input to the DiRōNA Board of Directors. He has met most of the Inspectors and attends workshops of the inspecting team.

Inspectors visit restaurants throughout North America, Mexico and Canada at the direction of the Director of Inspections, who monitors thousands of restaurants each year. Candidates for evaluations are identified through a multitude of resources, including requests for inspections that are submitted to DiRōNA Headquarters by operators hoping to become DiRōNA members. With the exception of the Director of Inspections, the team of Inspectors is unknown to the Board and the DiRōNA Members.

To qualify, a restaurant must be in business for three years before it is eligible for inspection, and once a restaurant earns the DiRōNA Award, it must be re-inspected within four years in order to maintain the award.

A 75-point list of criteria is used to evaluate the restaurant on quality of overall environment, cuisine, beverages and service. The physical property and décor are also evaluated, with comfort, cleanliness, room temperature and light levels observed.

Cuisine quality is the most important criterion in the decision to confer a DiRōNA Award to a restaurant. The menu is examined for accuracy, variety of items, cooking techniques, creativity and originality, as well as for health and nutrition-oriented items. The food is evaluated on temperature, appearance and quality of ingredients. Beverages offered by restaurants are evaluated on the basis of variety, availability, value and food affinity.

The service criteria evaluate guest interaction with the service staff, starting from the reservation process, greeting and seating, service throughout the meal, and assistance with departure. The staff's knowledge of the menu is tested, their friendliness, attentiveness, cleanliness and attire are appraised. Finally, the restaurant's procedures for handling the check are evaluated by verifying that the check is a consolidated bill which is accurate, legible and professionally presented.

Fine dining establishments that pass this rigorous inspection are invited to join the elite North American restaurants that proudly hold the DiRōNA Award.

How to Use This Guide

We made the *Guide to Distinguished Restaurants of North America* as user-friendly as possible. U.S. restaurants are listed alphabetically, by state and then by city. Canadian restaurants follow, listed alphabetically by province and then by city. Restaurants in Mexico, alphabetized by city, follow the Canada listings.

For each restaurant, the following information is provided:

1 A locator map

2 Address

3 Phone and fax numbers

4 Web site address
(where applicable)

5 The owner or owners

6 Type of cuisine

7 Days open

8 Pricing
a range for dinner for one, without tax, tip, or drinks

9 Dress code

10 Reservations policy

11 Parking availability

12 Distinctive features

13 Credit cards accepted

AE = American Express
VC = Visa
MC = MasterCard
CB = Carte Blanche
DC = Diners Club
ER = En Route
JCB
DS = Discover

14 Smoking area available

⬜ No smoking

New York • NY

🇺🇸

Vong

Directions

On East 54th Street just off Third Avenue, 30 min. from LaGuardia Airport

2 200 East 54th Street
New York, NY 10022

3 PH: (212) 486-9592
FAX: (212) 980-3745

4 www.jean-georges.com

5 Owners
Jean-Georges Vongerichten, Phil Suarez, Bob Giraldi

6 Cuisine
Thai-inspired French

7 Days Open
Open Mon.–Fri. for lunch, daily for dinner

8 Pricing
Dinner for one, without tax, tip, or drinks: $40-$60

9 Dress Code
Business casual

10 Reservations
Required

11 Parking
Garage nearby

12 Features
Private parties (must rent entire restaurant)

13 Credit Cards
AE, VC, MC, DC

14 ⬜

Vong is Chef Jean-Georges Vongerichten's homage to the exotic spices and flavors of the Far East. Thai-inspired French food is served amid beautiful Thai silks, red paint under gold leaf, and a Buddha altar with bowls of fragrant spices. Signature dishes include sautéed foie gras with ginger and mango, and crisp squab with egg noodle pancake and honey-ginger glazed pearl onions.

Exquisite dining room

DiRōNA
AWARD WINNER
SINCE 1998

316

Distinguished Restaurants of North America

BOARD OF DIRECTORS

EXECUTIVE COMMITTEE

CHAIRMAN
Rick Powers
Beverly's
P.O. Box 7200
Coeur d'Alene, ID
83816-1941
Tel: 208.765.4000
Fax: 208.664.7220
rpowers@cdaresort.com

PRESIDENT
John J. Arena
33 Wallace Street PH #10
Woodbridge, Ontario L4L 9L4
Canada
Tel: 905.265.0596
Fax:905.265.0597
*Chairman 1990-1991

PAST CHAIRMAN
Paul Athanas
Anthony's Pier 4
299 Salem Street
Swampscott, MA 01907
Tel: 781.599.0240
Fax: 781.598.9321
pathanas@pier4.com
*Chairman 1998-1999

VICE CHAIRMAN
David Stockman
Lawry's Restaurant, Inc.
234 E. Colorado Blvd.
Ste., #500
Pasadena, CA 91101
Tel: 626.440.5234
Fax: 626.440.5232
Dstockman@Lawrysonline.com

TREASURER
Alon Yu
Tommy Toy's Cuisine Chinoise
655 Montgomery Street
San Francisco, CA 94111
Tel: 925.283.2382
Fax: 925.283.5399
Ayu789@aol.com

PAST CHAIRMAN
John Folse
Chef John Folse &
Company
2517 S. Philippe Avenue
Gonzales, LA 70737
Tel: 225.644.6000
Fax: 225.647.0316
folse@jfolse.com
*Chairman 1999-2001

VICE CHAIRMAN
Larry Work
Sam & Harry's
1200 19th Street NW
Washington, DC 20036
Tel: 202.296.4333
Fax: 202.785.1070
larrywork@tmo.blackberry.net

IMMEDIATE
PAST CHAIRMAN
Kurt Knowles
The Manor
111 Prospect Avenue
West Orange, NJ 07052
Tel: 973.731.2360
Fax: 973.731.5168
Info@themanorrestaurant.com
*Chairman 2001-2002

PAST CHAIRMAN
Christianne R. Ricchi
i Ricchi
1220 19th Street, NW
Washington, DC 20036
Tel: 202.835.2021
Fax: 202.872.1220
crricchi@aol.com
*Chairman 1997-1998

DIRECTORS

Richard Alberini, Sr.
Alberini's
1201 Youngstown Warren
Rd. Rt. 422
Niles, OH 44446
Tel: 330.652.5895
Fax: 330.652.7041
Alberinis@aol.com

Vincent Bommarito
Tony's
410 Market Street
St. Louis, MO 63102
Tel: 314.231.7007
Fax: 314.231.4740

Vincent J. Catania
Dan'l Webster Inn
141 Falmouth Road
(Rte. 28)
Hyannis, MA 02601
Tel: 508.771.0040
Fax: 508.771.0883

Reinhard Barthel, Sr.
Café 36
22-24 Calendar Court
La Grange, IL 60046
Tel: 708.354.5722
Fax: 708.354.5042

Michael Carlevale
Prego Della Piazza
150 Bloor Street West
Toronto, Ontario M5S 2X9
Canada
Tel: 416.920.9900
Fax: 416.920.9949

Gerard Centioli
ICON, LLC
5419 N. Sheridan Road,
Suite 116
Chicago, IL 60640
Tel: 312.423.3300
Fax: 312.423.3312
gcentioli@icon.com

DIRECTORS CONTINUED

Allan H. Conseur
Oneida, Ltd.
163-181 Kenwood Avenue
Oneida, NY 13421
Tel: 315.361.3803
Fax: 315.361.3658
aconseur@oneida.com

Priscilla Cretier
Le Vichyssois
220 W. RT. 120
Lakemoor, IL 60050
Tel: 815.385.8221
Fax: 815.385.8223
Levichys@imaxx.net

Jack Czarnecki
Joel Palmer House
600 Ferry Street/P.O. Box
#594
Dayton, OR 97114
Tel: 503.864.2995
Fax: 503.864.3246
JoelPalmerhouse@onlinemac.com

Remo d'Agliano
Raffaello, Inc.
26137 Atherton Drive
Carmel, CA 93921
Tel: 831.624.9411
Fax: 831.624.9411
pedona@earthlink.net

Jordi Escofet
La Cava
S.A. de C.V. Insurgentes Sur
2465
Mexico, D.F. 01000
Tel: 011.525.616.1376
Fax: 011.525.550.3801
Lacava@prodigy.net.mx

William Hyde, Jr.
Ruth's Chris Steak House
3321 Hessmer Avenue
Metaire, LA 70002
Tel: 504.454.6560
Fax: 504.454.9067
wlh@ruthchris.com

Norbert Goldner
Café L'Europe
331 South County Road
Palm Beach, FL 33480
Tel: 561.655.4020
Fax: 561.659.6619
Norbert@cafeleurope.com

Rita Jammet
La Caravelle
33 West 55th Street
New York, NY 10019
Tel: 212.586.4252
Fax: 212.956.8269
ritaj@lacaravelle.com

Neil C. Jones
CN Tower, 360 Restaurant
301 Front Street West
Toronto, Ontario M5V 2T6
Canada
Tel: 416.601.3815
Fax: 416.601.4895
njones@cntower.ca

Wade Knowles
The Manor
111 Prospect Avenue
West Orange, NJ 07052
Tel: 973.731.2360
Fax: 973.731.5186
wwkchateau@aol.com

Joe Mannke
Rotisserie for Beef & Bird
2200 Wilcrest Street
Houston, TX 77042
Tel: 713.977.9524
Fax: 713.977.9568

Chick Marshall
Mr. Stox Restaurant
1105 E. Katella Avenue
Anaheim,CA 92805
Tel: 714.634.2994
Fax: 714.634.0561
chick@mrstox.com

Tony May
San Domenico
240 Central Park South
New York, NY 10019
Tel: 212.459.9016
Fax: 212.397.0844
Sandomny@aol.com

John Metz
Hi Life Kitchen & Cocktails
3380 Holcombe Bridge Road
Norcross, GA 30092
Tel: 770.409.0101
Fax: 770.409.1160
hilife@mingspring.com

Leonard Mirabile
Jasper's
1201 W. 103rd Street
Kansas City, MO 64114
Tel: 816.941.6600
Fax: 816.941.4346
jmirab2900@aol.com

Craig Peterson
RingSide Steakhouse
2165 West Burnside
Portland, OR 97210
Tel: 503.223.1513
Fax: 503.223.6908

Gunter Preuss
Broussard's
819 Rue Conti, Vieux,
Carré
New Orleans, LA 70122
Tel: 504.581.3866
Fax: 504.581.3873
broussrd@bellsouth.net

Andre Rochat
Andre's
401 South 6th Street
Las Vegas, NV 89101
Tel: 702.385.5016
Fax: 702.798.7175
jmirab2900@aol.com

Bob Spivak
The Grill
11661 San Vicente Blvd.
Los Angeles, CA 90049
Tel: 310.820.5559 ext. 240
Fax: 310.820.6530
bobs@thegrill.com

Alan Stillman
Smith & Wollensky
Restaurant Group
114 First Avenue, 6th Floor
New York, NY 10021
Tel: 212.838.2061 ext. 2871
Fax: 212.838.8057

Ernest Zingg
The Cellar
305 N. Harbor Blvd.
Fullerton, CA 92632
Tel: 714.525.5682
Fax: 714.525.3853
TheCellar@msn.com

Distinguished Restaurants of North America

DIRECTORS EMERITUS

Ted J. Balestreri
Sardine Factory
765 Wave Street
Monterey, CA 93940
Tel: 831.649.6690
Fax: 831.649.1864
Tbalestreri@canneryrow.com
*Chairman 1992-1994

Bert Cutino
Sardine Factory
765 Wave Street
Monterey, CA 93940
Tel: 831.649.6690
Fax: 831.649.1963
Bcutino@canneryrow.com
*Chairman 1996-1997

Tom Margittai
The Four Seasons
31 San Juan Ranch Road
Sante Fe, NM 87501
Tel: 505.986.1000
Fax: 505.986.1276
*Chairman 1991-1992

Jerry Berns
The Springs
14 East 75th Street
New York, NY 10021-2657
Tel: 212.988.1121

Ralph Evans
8340 Greensboro Drive
#801
McLean, VA 22102
Tel: 703.821.8565
Fax: 703.356.3708
ralphbevans@earthlink.net

Richard Marriott
Host Marriott Corporation
10400 Fernwood Road
Bethesda, MD 20817-1109
Tel: 301.380.1420
Fax: 301.380.6993

Ella Brennan
Commander's Palace
1403 Washington Avenue
New Orleans, LA 70130
Tel: 504.899.8231
Fax: 504.891.3242

Victor Gotti
Ernie's
3010 Pacific Avenue
San Francisco, CA 94115
Tel: 415.346.0629
Fax: 415.346.0602

THE AWARD
OF EXCELLENCE
FROM
DISTINGUISHED
RESTAURANTS OF
NORTH AMERICA

The DiRōNA Fine Dining Guarantee

Congratulations! You hold in your hands a guide to one of the most exclusive collections of fine dining establishments in the world. The Distinguished Restaurants of North America organization stands behind its award qualifications and inspection process. DiRōNA guarantees diners will have an exceptional dining experience at all DiRōNA restaurants listed in this *Guide*.

Diners who have completed the following steps may request a reimbursement of their dining bill, up to $200, if they have experienced an unsatisfactory dining experience that is not remedied to their satisfaction at a DiRōNA Award restaurant.

1. Register with DiRōNA headquarters by December 31, 2004. Include your name, address, telephone number, where you purchased this *Guide* and proof of Guide purchase (original receipt or photocopy). Send all information to DiRōNA Fine Dining Guarantee Registration, 355 Lexington Avenue, Suite 1700, New York, NY 10017-6603, or fax to (212) 370-9047. Only readers and diners who have registered their names and *Guide* purchases with DiRōNA by the above date are eligible for the guarantee reimbursement.

2. The DiRōNA Fine Dining Guarantee is eligible for parties up to four dining at a DiRōNA restaurant.

3. Before applying for a reimbursement from DiRōNA, diners must express in writing their reason for dissatisfaction to the responsible restaurant owner and/or manager. Diners must provide the restaurant with every opportunity to remedy their complaint in a timely manner.

4. If still unsatisfied, diners must provide a copy of the complaint, a copy of the dining receipt, and the restaurant's reply in writing to DiRōNA Award Headquarters at 355 Lexington Avenue, Suite 1700, New York, NY 10017-6603. Upon submission of these materials, which must include the correspondence between the diner and restaurant, DiRōNA will respond within 90 days with either a reimbursement check or an equivalent-value offer of dining at another DiRōNA Award restaurant.

THE AWARD
OF EXCELLENCE
FROM
DISTINGUISHED
RESTAURANTS OF
NORTH AMERICA

Distinguished Restaurants of North America
Dining Guarantee Registration

Name _____

Address _____

_____

Telephone Number _____

Where did you purchase the Guide?

_____

Please mail this page along with your proof of purchase
(original receipt or photocopy) to:

DiRōNA Fine Dining Guarantee Registration
355 Lexington Avenue
Suite 1700
New York, NY 10017
or fax to (212) 370-9047

Registration Deadline: December 31, 2004

THE AWARD
OF EXCELLENCE
FROM
DISTINGUISHED
RESTAURANTS OF
NORTH AMERICA

DiRōNA SPONSORS

PLATINUM SPONSORS

Serving Customers in the
Restaurant and Hospitality Industry

GOLD SPONSORS

GUEST INFORMANT

ROBERT MONDAVI WINERY

Cards

SILVER SPONSORS

ECOLAB®

ONEIDA®

Options
——— PHILIP MORRIS USA ———

BRONZE SPONSORS

National Restaurant Association
EDUCATIONAL FOUNDATION

artex®

NATIONAL
RESTAURANT
ASSOCIATION ®

U.S. FOODSERVICE™

SPONSORS

BECK'S

JOHNSON & WALES
UNIVERSITY

About the Publisher

Lebhar-Friedman Books is one of America's newest and most dynamic publishers of quality hardcover and paperback books. Its growing list of publishing partners includes the American Academy of Chefs, the Culinary Institute of America, *The New York Times* and the History Channel. A sister company of *Nation's Restaurant News,* Lebhar-Friedman Books is also the publisher of luminaries in the food world including John Mariani, Fred Ferretti, and Jane and Michael Stern.

Since 1967, *Nation's Restaurant News* has been the leading voice for the country's restaurant and foodservice industries. The weekly trade magazine is the ultimate resource that provides readers with the news, trends, and information they need to stay ahead of the competition. *Nation's Restaurant News* has evolved significantly over the years, adding new sections and specialists to serve the informational needs of its widely varied readership. To subscribe to *Nation's Restaurant News,* call 800-944-4676.

DiRōNA Award Scholarship Fund

The DiRōNA Award Scholarship Fund, initiated in 1989, has helped many young students achieve their goals in the culinary world. Ted Balestreri, Scholarship Committee Chairman and past DiRōNA Chairman, states that "education is the best gift we can give to our youth." Distinguished Restaurants of North America is proud to help promote distinguished dining through the education of tomorrow's leaders.

DiRōNA Award scholarships are presented to deserving individuals pursuing careers in the restaurant and foodservice industry. Recipients are selected through a review of applications from students throughout North America who exhibit a genuine interest in seeking education in preparation for a professional foodservice career.

At minimum, 10 $2,000 DiRōNA scholarships are given each year through the National Restaurant Association Educational Foundation. Three scholarships are given in the name of *Wine Spectator* magazine, one in the name of *Foodservice and Hospitality* magazine, and the remainder in the name of a past DiRōNA Chairman, in recognition for his or her contributions and commitment to the fine dining industry.

The DiRōNA Award Scholarship Fund is managed and administered by the National Restaurant Association Educational Foundation. Applicants interested in this scholarship opportunity should visit the NRAEF website, www.nraef.org, or contact the NRAEF at:

National Restaurant Association
Educational Foundation
Scholarship and Mentoring Initiative
175 West Jackson Boulevard
Suite 1500
Chicago, IL 60604-2702
Telephone: (312) 715-5385 or (800) 765-2122 ext.733
www.nraef.org

The Crow's Nest

Hotel Captain Cook

An evening at the Crow's Nest is more than dining—it is an experience. Offering stunning views of Cook Inlet and the Alaska Range from atop the Hotel Captain Cook, The Crow's Nest has been a landmark in the Great North for more than 20 years. Chef de Cuisine Loren Gahala's innovative cuisine uses only the freshest, seasonally available ingredients, including Alaskan seafood. The award-winning wine list offers more than 1,200 selections.

Seared Alaskan scallops

Intimate dining

Stunning views from lounge

Directions

In downtown, 10 min. from Anchorage International Airport

Hotel Captain Cook
4th and K Streets
Anchorage, AK 99501
PH: (907) 276-6000
FAX: (907) 343-2211
www.captaincook.com

Owners
Walter Hickel Jr.

Cuisine
New American
with French influence

Days Open
Open Mon.-Sat. for dinner

Pricing
Dinner for one,
without tax, tip, or drinks:
$40-$60

Dress Code
Casual

Reservations
Recommended

Parking
Valet, garage nearby

Features
Private room

Credit Cards
AE, VC, MC, CB, DC, DS

AWARD WINNER
SINCE 1992

The Pump House

Patio dining overlooking Chena River

Directions

Off Parks Highway, 7 min. from University of Alaska-Fairbanks and 5 min. from Fairbanks International Airport

796 Chena Pump Road
Fairbanks, AK 99709
PH: (907) 479-8452
FAX: (907) 479-8432
www.pumphouse.com

Owners
Vivian Bubbel

Cuisine
American, emphasizing Alaskan seafood

Days Open
Open daily for lunch May through September, and dinner year-round; Sunday brunch year-round

Pricing
Dinner for one, without tax, tip, or drinks: $20-$40

Dress Code
Casual

Reservations
Recommended

Parking
Free on site

Features
Private room/parties, outdoor dining, entertainment, cigar/cognac events

Credit Cards
AE, VC, MC, DS

T his unique restaurant in Alaska has been serving up Fairbanks hospitality since 1977. Relics from the town's Gold Rush past fill this National Historic Site on the banks of the Chena River. The menu features fresh Alaskan seafood —salmon is delivered to the restaurant's dock by float plane — as well as wild game and alder-smoked specialties. The Senator's Saloon is home to "The World's Most Northern Oyster Bar," and the wine list features the best of the Pacific Northwest.

Senator's saloon

Alaskan hospitality

AWARD WINNER
SINCE 1997

Highlands Bar & Grill

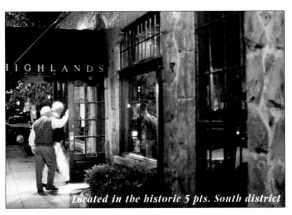

Located in the historic 5 pts. South district

The October 2001 issue of *Gourmet* magazine described this fifth best restaurant in the U.S. like this: "When we dream about an American restaurant, it looks and smells a lot like Highlands Bar & Grill...with the buttery glow of our favorite Parisian bistros..." Highlands offers a daily changing menu framed by the season with "enticing, Southern-accented [French] cooking" (R.W. Apple, *New York Times* March 2002) – fresh seafood, natural game and organic produce are standards not exceptions. The award-winning wine list is "obviously put together by someone who likes to drink wine more than he likes to show it off."

Proprietors Frank and Pardis Stitt

The marble oyster bar

AWARD WINNER
SINCE 2003

On 11th Avenue South, 15 min. from Birmingham International Airport

2011 11th Avenue South
Birmingham, AL 35205
PH: (205) 939-1400
FAX: (205) 939-1405
www.highlandsbarandgrill.com

Owners
Frank and Pardis Stitt

Cuisine
Modern American

Days Open
Open Tues.-Sat. for dinner

Pricing
Dinner for one,
without tax, tip, or drinks:
$40-$50

Dress Code
Jacket preferred

Reservations
Recommended

Parking
Valet

Features
Near theater

Credit Cards
AE, VC, MC, DC

Winston's

Winston's...a new level of epicurean pleasure.

Attached to the Riverchase Galleria, Winston's is 15 min. south of downtown, and 20 min. from the Birmingham International Airport

W inston's, the signature restaurant at The Wynfrey Hotel, offers casual elegance in a warm, cozy dining environment. Executive Chef Eric Morin brings his award-winning culinary influences from the northeast to this gracious southern setting. Chef Morin's culinary talents and passion for food are evident in the featured premium cuts of certified angus choice beef, New Zealand lamb, Chilean sea bass, North Atlantic lobster, and a carefully selected wine list. AAA Four Diamond award winner.

Executive Chef Eric Morin

Enter a truly unique and gratifying experirnce

1000 Riverchase Galleria
Birmingham, AL 35244
PH: (205) 987-1600
FAX: (205) 988-4597
www.wynfrey.com

Owners
Jim Wilson & Associates

Cuisine
Continental American

Days Open
Open Tues.-Sat. for dinner

Pricing
Dinner for one,
without tax, tip, or drinks:
$20-$40

Dress Code
Business casual

Reservations
Recommended

Parking
Valet

Features
Private parties

Credit Cards
AE, VC, MC, DC, DS

Gracious service to match this gracious Southern setting

AWARD WINNER
SINCE 2003

Ashley's At The Capital

Sumptuous surroundings

Across Markham St. from Statehouse Convention Center, 15 min. from Little Rock Nat'l Airport

111 West Markham Street
Little Rock, AR 72201
PH: (501) 374-7474
FAX: (501) 370-7092
www.thecapitalhotel.com

Owners
The Capital Hotel

Cuisine
American/Continental

Days Open
Open Mon.-Fri. for breakfast and lunch, daily for dinner, Sunday for brunch

Pricing
Dinner for one, without tax, tip, or drinks: $20-$40

Dress Code
Business casual

Reservations
Recommended

Parking
Complimentary valet, free on site, garage nearby

Features
Private room/parties, near theater

Credit Cards
AE, VC, MC, CB, DC, JCB, DS

A rkansas' finest, small luxury hotel boasts a most superlative dining experience at Ashley's At The Capital. Providing guests with award-winning American/Continental dishes, and impeccable service, Ashley's meals are attentively prepared by the hotel's executive chef, and served by a specially trained waitstaff. Wine specialists are available to assist in selecting from the hotel's 2,400-bottle wine collection, which was recognized with the Award of Excellence by *Wine Spectator* magazine.

Catering available

Historic landmark

Extensive wine collection

DiRoNA
AWARD WINNER
SINCE 1992

The Latilla

The Boulders Resort & Golden Door Spa

At The Boulders Resort and Golden Door Spa, 30 min. from Phoenix Sky Harbor Int'l Airport

34631 North
Tom Darlington Drive
Carefree, AZ 85377
PH: (480) 488-9009
FAX: (480) 488-4118
www.wyndham.com

Owners
Wyndham Hotels & Resorts

Cuisine
Regional American

Days Open
Open daily for dinner

Pricing
Dinner for one,
without tax, tip, or drinks:
$40-$60

Dress Code
Jacket suggested

Reservations
Recommended

Parking
Valet, free on site

Features
Entertainment

Credit Cards
AE, VC, MC, DS

The Latilla cuisine features American classics prepared in a contemporary style, served in a rustic, yet elegant dining room with Native American weavings, rich in history. Dramatic lighting provides spectacular views of the boulder pile, cascading waterfall, and adobe fireplace, creating the ultimate romantic atmosphere. The Latilla has received numerous accolades, including *Wine Spectator's* Award of Excellence, the Ivy Award – Top Five Professional Food Service Operators in the US, by Restaurants and Institutions, and the AAA Four Diamond Award.

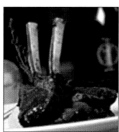

Classic, regional
American cuisine

Executive Chef
Michael Hoobler

AWARD OF EXCELLENCE

AWARD WINNER
SINCE 1993

Rustic, yet elegant dining

Wright's

Arizona Biltmore resort and Spa

Directions

At the Arizona Biltmore Resort & Spa, 20 min. from Phoenix Sky Harbor International Airport

2400 E. Missouri
Phoenix, AZ 85016
PH: (602) 954-2507
FAX: (602) 381-7600
www.arizonabiltmore.com

Owners
KSL Biltmore Resort, Inc.

Cuisine
New American

Days Open
Open daily for dinner,
Sunday for brunch

Pricing
Dinner for one,
without tax, tip, or drinks:
$40-$60

Dress Code
Business casual

Reservations
Recommended

Parking
Complimentary valet

Features
Private rooms/parties, outdoor dining, entertainment, Winemaker dinners and special events

Credit Cards
AE, VC, MC, CB, DC, DS

Wright's, the Arizona Biltmore's premiere restaurant, serves New American cuisine complemented by one of the southwest's most extensive wine lists. The striking Frank Lloyd Wright-inspired architecture and the romantic patio is elegant and grand, yet relaxed. Diverse menu selections include sautéed Maine lobster with caponata ravioli and lobster-tarragon essence; and charbroiled beef tenderloin with artichoke-potato cake and watercress, and bacon salad with blue cheese. Wright's boasts a private dining room, wine cellar and seasonal monthly Winemaker dinners.

Roasted Sonoma lamb

Wine cellar dining

Tempting desserts

AWARD WINNER
SINCE 1992

Marquesa

Mediterranean-style dining at Marquesa

Located east of Scottsdale Rd. on Princess Drive, 25 min. from Phoenix Sky Harbor Airport

7575 E. Princess Drive
Scottsdale, AZ 85255
PH: (480) 585-4848
FAX: (480) 585-2742
www.fairmont.com

Owners
Fairmont Hotels & Resorts

Cuisine
Foods of the Mediterranean Rivieras

Days Open
Open Wed.-Sat. for dinner, Sunday for brunch

Pricing
Dinner for one, without tax, tip, or drinks: $60-$80

Dress Code
Resort casual

Reservations
Recommended

Parking
Valet

Features
Private room/parties, outdoor dining, entertainment

Credit Cards
AE, VC, MC, DC, JCB, DS

There is a golden arc of culinary richness that stretches from the sun drenched coastline of Spain, through the tony seaside resort town of the Côte d'Azure, to the curve of the Italian coastline known as the region of Liguria. These Spanish, French, and Italian "Rivieras" have characteristic cuisines culled from the Mediterranean Sea, and their own diverse landscapes…creating a marvelous trail of culinary treasures in a postcard perfect setting. Marquesa, AAA Five Diamond Award winning Mediterranean restaurant at The Fairmont Scottsdale Princess, maintains its international reputation by continuously discovering new ways to prepare, and present food of the Mediterranean Rivieras such as delicate shrimp "ravioli", herb essence and braised lamb gravy.

Delicate shrimp "ravioli", herb essence, braised lamb gravy

AWARD WINNER
SINCE 1993

L'Auberge de Sedona

Terrace on the creek

Directions

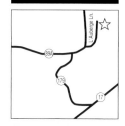

Off Highway 89A in Sedona,
2 hr. north of Phoenix Sky
Harbor International Airport

301 L'Auberge Lane
Sedona, AZ 86336
PH: (928) 282-1661
FAX: (928) 282-1064
www.lauberge.com

Overlooking the quiet beauty of Oak Creek, the charming L'Auberge de Sedona has an enchanting air. The glow of candlelight and fragrance of flowers enhances the mood while considerate service attends to every need. A sumptuous lunch and dinner menu, presenting a superb and varied repertoire of French delights, is created weekly from only the freshest of ingredients. Specialties include foie gras with Parma ham and caramelized melon, and lobster with squash, spinach, and mussel-saffron vinaigrette.

Cuisine extraordinaire

Owners
Sweeney Hotels

Cuisine
Contemporary French

Days Open
Open daily for breakfast,
lunch, and dinner

Pricing
Dinner for one,
without tax, tip, or drinks:
$60-$80

Dress Code
Jacket recommended,
tie optional

Reservations
Recommended

Parking
Free on site

Features
Private room/parties,
outdoor dining

Credit Cards
AE, VC, MC, DC, DS

French country dining

Exquisite Sunday brunch

AWARD WINNER
SINCE 1993

Anthony's in the Catalinas

A beautiful Southwestern setting

Directions

At the foot of the Catalina Mountains, a half-block north of Sunrise Road, 30 min. from Tucson International Airport

With breathtaking views of the Santa Catalina Mountains, Anthony's offers a unique dining experience. Elegant tables, set with light pink linens, fresh flowers, and Villeroy and Boch china, combine to provide an intimate setting to foster romances or friendships. The impeccable service and outstanding food is sure to impress friends as well as business associates. The award-winning wine list ensures a great selection of vintages, housed in an underground cellar.

Wine cellar

Sumptuous dining

6440 North Campbell Avenue
Tucson, AZ 85718
PH: (520) 299-1771
FAX: (520) 299-6635

Owners
Anthony and Brooke Martino

Cuisine
Continental

Days Open
Open Mon.-Fri. for lunch, daily for dinner

Pricing
Dinner for one, without tax, tip, or drinks: $30-$50

Dress Code
Business casual

Reservations
Recommended

Parking
Free on site, valet

Features
Prviate rooms, parties, entertainment, cigar/cognac events

Credit Cards
AE, VC, MC, CB, DC

Elegant dining in the main room

AWARD WINNER
SINCE 1994

The Covey

Outdoor dining

Directions

At the Quail Lodge Resort, 20 min. from Monterey Peninsula Airport

The Covey at Quail Lodge Resort and Golf Club offers inventive, contempory cuisine with a classic touch. The freshest ingredients from local farmers and fishermen are complemented by an extensive list of fine regional wines. Enjoy attentive tableside service overlooking a sparkling lake, flourishing gardens, and the rolling hills of Carmel.

Chef de cuisine
John Scherber

Pan-roasted filet mignon Rossni with foie gras, wild mushrooms and black truffle

8205 Valley Greens Drive
Carmel, CA 93923
PH: (831) 624-2888
FAX: (831) 624-3726
www.quaillodge.com

Owners
Hong Kong Shanghai Hotels Ltd.

Cuisine
Classic contemporary

Days Open
Open Mon.-Sat. for breakfast, Tues.-Sat. for dinner

Pricing
Dinner for one, without tax, tip, or drinks: $30-$40

Dress Code
Resort casual

Reservations
Recommended

Parking
Valet

Features
Private room/parties, outdoor dining

Credit Cards
AE, VC, MC, CB, DC, JCB

DiRoNA
AWARD WINNER
SINCE 1992

The French Poodle Restaurant

The dining room

The French Poodle in Carmel has established itself as a citadel of classical French cuisine on the Monterey peninsula. The original Escoffier inspired menu, as conceived by Richard Zoellin, has achieved legendary consistency that gives real comfort to those who seek culinary perfection.

Classic French cuisine

At the northwest corner of Junipero St. and Fifth, 10 min. from Monterey Airport

Junipero and Fifth
Carmel, CA 93921
PH: (831) 624-8643
FAX: (831) 375-8643

Owners
Richard and Ana Maria Zoellin

Cuisine
Classic French

Days Open
Open Mon.-Sat. for dinner

Pricing
Dinner for one,
without tax, tip, or drinks:
$40-$60

Dress Code
Business casual

Reservations
Recommended

Parking
Free on site

Features
Private room/parties

Credit Cards
AE, VC, MC, CB, DC

DiRōNA
AWARD WINNER
SINCE 1994

Pacific's Edge

Pacific's Edge-Sunset view

The most famous restaurant on the California coast announces the completion of a stunning $750,000 renovation of the award-winning Pacific's Edge, featuring the addition of a new private dining room and a temperature controlled wine cellar to house many of the 33,000 bottles from its grand award-winning wine list. Nature's beauty is complimented with the addition of beautiful earth tones, natural woods, and Highlands granite. A romantic ambience, and incredible view to be surpassed only by the spectacular cuisine.

Entrance foyer

Marinated tuna and hamachi yuzu, mustard oil, opal basil

Directions

At the Highlands Inn, Park Hyatt Carmel, 15 min. from Monterey Peninsula Airport

120 Highlands Drive
Carmel, CA 93923
PH: (831) 622-5445
FAX: (831) 626-1574
www.mfandw.com

Owners
Highlands Inn, Park Hyatt Carmel

Cuisine
French American

Days Open
Open daily for dinner, Sun. for brunch

Pricing
Dinner for one,
without tax, tip, or drinks:
$48-$75, brunch
price fix:$39

Dress Code
Jacket and tie suggested

Reservations
Recommended

Parking
Complimentary valet

Features
Private room/parties, wine events, entertainment

Credit Cards
AE, VC, MC, CB, DC, DS

Wine room

GRAND AWARD

DiRōNA
AWARD WINNER
SINCE 1993

13

Trader Vic's

The flavor of the islands

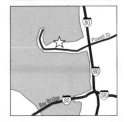

Off Interstate 80's Powell
Street exit, 20 min. from
Oakland International Airport

9 Anchor Drive
Emeryville, CA 94608
PH: (510) 653-3400
FAX: (510) 653-9384

Owners
The Bergeron family

Cuisine
Island

Days Open
Open Mon.-Sat. for lunch,
daily for dinner

Pricing
Dinner for one,
without tax, tip, or drinks:
$20-$40

Dress Code
Business casual

Reservations
Recommended

Parking
Complimentary valet

Features
Private room/parties, outdoor dining, entertainment

Credit Cards
VC, MC

Overlooking the Emeryville Marina on San Francisco Bay, Trader Vic's has been a Bay Area institution since 1934, famous for its tropical decor and island-style cuisine. Home of the original Mai Tai, Trader Vic's offers prime meats, fowl, and seasonal seafood specials cooked to preference — steamed, grilled, or barbecued in wood-fired ovens. Just 15 minutes across the Bay Bridge from downtown San Francisco. Visit Trader Vic's other locations in Palo Alto and around the world.

Mai-Tai Roa Aé

Private dining, inside or outside

DiRōNA
AWARD WINNER
SINCE 1996

The Lark Creek Inn

Entrance to the Lark Creek Inn

A short distance off Highway 101's Tamalpais Drive/ Paradise Drive exit, 1 hr. from San Francisco International Airport

234 Magnolia Avenue
Larkspur, CA 94939
PH: (415) 924-7766
FAX: (415) 924-7117
www.larkcreek.com

Owners
Bradley Ogden and Michael Dellar

Cuisine
American

E nsconced in the redwoods with a creek-side dining patio, the Lark Creek Inn is only 15 minutes north of the Golden Gate Bridge. Chef/Co-owner Bradley Ogden's daily changing menu offers farm-fresh American fare using local bounty, delivered daily. The updated, lightened conceptions are served with pride and skill. Among the specialties are applewood-smoked pork loin chop with plum compote, and grilled wild king salmon filet with corn and Maui onions. The carefully composed wine list has more than 200 selections.

Crab and onion pancake

Sun room

Days Open
Open daily for lunch and dinner, Sun. for brunch, and Sat. lunch for weddings and large parties only

Pricing
Dinner for one, without tax, tip, or drinks: $40-$60

Dress Code
Any style of dress – casual, business casual, jacket and tie – is appropriate

Reservations
Recommended

Parking
Complimentary valet, and on site lot

Features
Private room/parties, outdoor dining

Credit Cards
AE, VC, MC, DC, DS

Dining patio

AWARD OF EXCELLENCE

DiRoNA

AWARD WINNER
SINCE 1993

Wente Vineyards Restaurant

Wente Vineyards Visitors Center

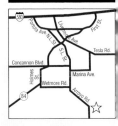

Off Highway 580 in Livermore,
30 min. from Oakland
International Airport

Wente Vineyards is a truly unique dining destination. Where else can a discriminating diner savor superlative wines and food, play on a Greg Norman-designed championship golf course, and enjoy a summer night's concert by world-renowned performers? Chef Elisabeth Schwarz's menu, which changes daily, features wine-country dishes prepared with fresh seasonal ingredients. Full-service catering is available.

Braised lamb shanks with winter vegetables

5050 Arroyo Road
Livermore, CA 94550
PH: (925) 456-2450
FAX: (925) 456-2401
www.wentevineyards.com

Owners
The Wente family

Cuisine
Wine Country

Days Open
Open daily for lunch and dinner

Pricing
Dinner for one,
without tax, tip, or drinks:
$20-$40

Dress Code
Business casual

Reservations
Recommended

Parking
Free on site

Features
Private room/parties, outdoor dining, summer concerts

Credit Cards
AE, VC, MC, DC, DS

Alfresco dining on the terrace

AWARD WINNER
SINCE 1993

Wine country dining

Dal Baffo

Main dining room

D al Baffo offers a culinary experience characterized by sophistication, elegance, and charm. The establishment features a relaxed lounge, a refined dining area, and a private banquet room. Boasting over 1,200 selections, the wine list has made *Wine Spectator's* Top 100 wine list since 1986. Chef/Owner Vincenzo Lo Grasso with the assistance of guest Chef Patrizio Sacchetto frequently creates new dishes and design concepts to ensure that Dal Baffo always offers a fresh approach, staying ahead of food and restaurant trends.

**Chef/Owner
Vincenzo Lo Grasso**

Innovative cuisine

The Siena Room

AWARD WINNER
SINCE 1992

Directions

Near Stanford Shopping Center, 30 min. from both San Francisco International and San Jose International Airports

878 Santa Cruz Avenue
Menlo Park, CA 94025
PH: (650) 325-1588
FAX: (650) 326-2780
www.dalbaffo.com

Owners
Vincenzo Lo Grasso

Cuisine
Continental/Italian

Days Open
Open Mon.-Sat.
for dinner, lunch
for private parties

Pricing
Dinner for one,
without tax, tip or drinks:
$40-$60

Dress Code
Business casual

Reservations
Recommended

Parking
Free on site

Features
Private room/parties

Credit Cards
AE, VC, MC, CB, DC, JCB, DS

17

Fresh Cream Restaurant

Monterey sunset

On Pacific Street near Fisherman's Wharf, 15 min. from Monterey Peninsula Airport and 2 hrs. from San Francisco International

Fresh Cream has been receiving critical praise for award-winning cuisine for more than 20 years. Stunning views, elegant decor, and impeccable service set the mood for imaginatively conceived and artfully presented dishes. Among the celebrated house specialties are rack of lamb Dijonnaise, roast boned duck in black currants, Holland dover sole, and delectable vegetarian creations. A diversified wine list and full bar service enhance the dining experience.

Grilled prawn appetizer

Julie and Steven R. Chesney

99 Pacific Street
Monterey, CA 93940
PH: (831) 375-9798
FAX: (831) 375-2283
www.freshcream.com

Owners
Steven R. Chesney

Cuisine
French nouvelle

Days Open
Open daily for dinner

Pricing
Dinner for one,
without tax, tip, or drinks:
$40-$60

Dress Code
Business casual

Reservations
Recommended

Parking
Garage nearby

Features
Private room/parties

Credit Cards
AE, VC, MC, CB, DC, DS

Harbor View Room

AWARD WINNER
SINCE 1994

The Sardine Factory

The Conservatory

Entering the Sardine Factory, you are transported to a bustling atmosphere that is unique, fun, and nostalgic. The combination of the freshest seafood and prime meats, award-winning wine list, and gracious service have contributed to this Monterey icon's success for over 30 years. Discover why it is a haven for those who truly love great food and wine, and has become a magnet for the rich and famous, as well as industry leaders and politicians. Recipient of numerous awards, including *Wine Spectator's* Grand Award since 1982.

Culinary creations

The Wine Cellar

Standing (l-r): Ted Balestreri, II, Ed Molin, Robert Mancuso, Bart Cutino

Seated (l-r): Ted Balestreri, Marc Cutino, Bert Cutino

AWARD WINNER
SINCE 1993

Directions

Corner of Wave and Prescott, 15 min. from Monterey Airport, 2 hrs. from San Francisco Int'l Airport

701 Wave Street
Monterey, CA 93940
PH: (831) 373-3775
FAX: (831) 373-4241
www.sardinefactory.com

Owners
Ted Balestreri and Bert Cutino

Cuisine
Seafood and prime meat

Days Open
Open daily for dinner

Pricing
Dinner for one, without tax, tip, or drinks: $20-$40

Dress Code
Upscale casual

Reservations
Recommended

Parking
Free on site, valet

Features
Private room/parties

Credit Cards
AE, VC, MC, CB, DC, DS

Fandango

Front room

Directions

South of Lighthouse on 17th Street, 20 min. from Montery Airport, and 2 hrs. from San Francisco International Airport

---

223 17th Street
Pacific Grove, CA 93950
PH: (831) 372-3456
FAX: (831) 372-2673
www.fandangorestaurant.com

Owners
Pierre and Marietta Bain

Cuisine
French bistro and seafood

Days Open
Open daily for lunch and dinner

Pricing
Dinner for one,
without tax, tip, or drinks:
$20-$40

Dress Code
Casual

Reservations
Recommended

Parking
Free on site

Features
Private room/parties

Credit Cards
AE, VC, MC, CB, DC, JCB, DS

Enjoy Fandango's freshest seafood or a variety of specialties from the grill in the warmth of a casual Mediterranean setting. Choose from salmon, swordfish, scallops, black angus beef, or Fandango's famous rack of lamb. Or, pick from a bountiful array of healthy pastas or paella, with an abundant mixture of seafood, chicken, sausages, and the valley's best vegetables touched with the finest imported seasonings. An extensive wine list complements the varied menu.

Proprietors Pierre and Marietta Bain

Rack of lamb

Upstairs dining room

AWARD WINNER
SINCE 2002

20

Club XIX

Club XIX at The Lodge at Pebble Beach

"Reproduced by permission of Pebble Beach Company."

With breathtaking views of the world-famous 18th hole at Pebble Beach Golf Links, and Carmel Bay beyond, Club XIX offers a world class dining experience at The Lodge at Pebble Beach. Under the direction of Chef Philip Baker, whose background includes some of the finest restaurants in New York, Europe, and California, Club XIX specializes in a cuisine that boasts a passionate composition of harmonious flavors from the plentiful bounty of California produce.

Outdoor dining on the patio

"Reproduced by permission of Pebble Beach Company."

Directions

On 17 Mile Drive at Pebble Beach, 15 min. from Monterey Peninsula Airport

1700 17-Mile Drive
Pebble Beach, CA 93953
PH: (831) 625-8519
www.pebblebeach.com

Owners
Pebble Beach Company

Cuisine
French

Days Open
Open daily for dinner

Pricing
Dinner for one,
without tax, tip, or drinks:
$40-$60

Dress Code
Jacket requested

Reservations
Recommended

Parking
Valet

Features
Private room/parties,
outdoor dining

Credit Cards
AE, VC, MC, CB, DC, JCB, DS

Wine Spectator
BEST OF
AWARD OF
EXCELLENCE

DiRōNA
AWARD WINNER
SINCE 1993

Auberge du Soleil

Auberge du Soleil...
an atmosphere of peace and pampering

Located in Napa Valley on Rutherford Hill Road, 1 hr. 30 min. from San Francisco International Airport

180 Rutherford Hill Road
Rutherford, CA 94573
PH: (707) 967-3111
FAX: (707) 967-3181
www.aubergedusoleil.com

Owners
Claude Rouas and
Bob Harmon

Cuisine
French Mediterranean

Days Open
Open daily for breakfast, lunch, and dinner

Pricing
Dinner for one,
without tax, tip, or drinks:
$60-$80

Dress Code
Casual

Reservations
Required

Parking
Free on site, valet

Features
Private room/parties, outdoor dining

Credit Cards
AE, VC, MC, CB, DC, DS

For over 20 years, Auberge du Soleil has been one of Napa Valley's most celebrated restaurants, and small luxury hotels. From its perch nestled in the hillside, Auberge du Soleil has been infused with a $2 million re-design of the restaurant, and the fire and passion of Chef Richard Reddington's culinary pleasures. A tasting menu is offered for lunch and dinner that can be paired with any of the over 1,500 wine selections, the largest restaurant list in the Valley.

Chef Richard Reddington

Feast of the senses

Avignon

AWARD WINNER
SINCE 1992

Biba

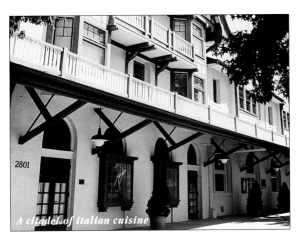

2801

A citadel of Italian cuisine

Corner of Capitol Avenue and 28th Street, 20 min. from Sacramento International Airport

2801 Capitol Avenue
Sacramento, CA 95816
PH: (916) 455-2422
FAX: (916) 455-0542
www.biba-restaurant.com

Owners
Biba Caggiano

Cuisine
Italian

Days Open
Open Mon.-Fri. for lunch,
Mon.-Sat. for dinner

Pricing
Dinner for one,
without tax, tip, or drinks:
$30-$40

Dress Code
Business casual

Reservations
Recommended

Parking
Garage nearby

Features
Parties, entertainment

Credit Cards
AE, VC, MC, DC

Owned and operated by Biba Caggiano, the acclaimed cookbook author and host of *Biba's Italian Kitchen* on The Learning Channel, Biba serves exceptional classic Italian cuisine. Pastas, gnocchi, risotto, braised rabbit, and duck are just a few of the marvelous specialties. The service is refined but friendly, ensuring a smooth and pleasurable dining experience.

Owner Biba Caggiano

Creative entrées

Dining room

AWARD WINNER
SINCE 1994

The Restaurant at Meadowood

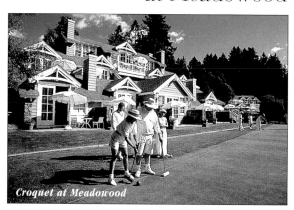

Croquet at Meadowood

At Meadowood Napa Valley Hotel, 90 min. from San Francisco International Airport

L ocated at the beautiful Meado-wood Napa Valley, a Relais & Chateaux hotel, private club, and home of the annual Napa Valley Wine Auction, this establishment overlooks the fairways, croquet lawns, and surrounding wooded hillsides. The restaurant offers a menu that reflects local bounty and the changing of the seasons. The ever-changing, prix-fixe Vintners Menu, featuring dishes paired with local wines, celebrates the restaurant's close association with the local wine-making community.

Chef Steven Tevere

900 Meadowood Lane
St. Helena, CA 94574
PH: (707) 963-3646
FAX: (707) 963-3532
www.meadowood.com

Owners
H. William Harlan

Cuisine
California wine country

Days Open
Open daily for dinner

Pricing
Dinner for one,
without tax, tip, or drinks:
$40-$60

Dress Code
Country elegant

Reservations
Recommended

Parking
Free on site

Features
Outdoor dining

Credit Cards
AE, VC, MC, CB, DC, DS

Elegant dining

Wine country chic

AWARD WINNER
SINCE 1992

Acquerello

A cquerello means watercolor in Italian, and entering the restaurant's dining room is like stepping into a painting. Pale yellow walls and original watercolors of Venetian scenes and Palladian villas are softly illuminated with Murano lamps. Suzette Gresham creatively reinvents traditional dishes from all of Italy in a contemporary style, while co-owner Giancarlo Paterlini, a leading Italian wine expert, brings an impeccable European standard to the seamless and elegant dining service.

Dining room

*Owners
Giancarlo Paterlini
and Suzette Gresham*

AWARD WINNER
SINCE 1997

Directions

In downtown San Francisco, 30 min. from San Franciso International Airport

1722 Sacramento Street
San Francisco, CA 94109
PH: (415) 567-5432
FAX: (415) 567-6432
www.acquerello.com

Owners
Giancarlo Paterlini and Suzette Gresham

Cuisine
Contemporary Italian

Days Open
Open Tues.-Sat. for dinner

Pricing
Dinner for one, without tax, tip, or drinks: $40-$60

Dress Code
Business casual

Reservations
Recommended

Parking
Garage nearby

Features
Private room/parties, near theater

Credit Cards
AE, VC, MC, DC, DS

Carnelian Room

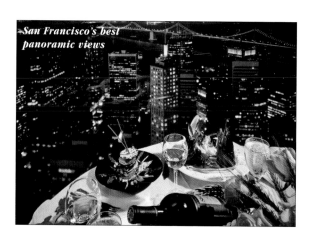
San Francisco's best panoramic views

Directions

On the top floor of the Bank of America Center, 25 min. from San Francisco Int'l Airport

555 California Street
52nd Floor
San Francisco, CA 94104
PH: (415) 433-7500
FAX: (415) 291-0815
www.carnelianroom.com

Owners
Aramark Corp.

Cuisine
American continental

Days Open
Open daily for dinner,
Sunday for brunch

Pricing
Dinner for one,
without tax, tip, or drinks:
$40-$60 (or)
Price fix: $39

Dress Code
Jacket and tie required

Reservations
Required

Parking
Available in building

Features
Private room/parties

Credit Cards
AE, VC, MC, DC, DS

The Carnelian Room, located on the top floor of the Bank of America Center, offers San Francisco's best panoramic view. Enjoy dinner or Sunday brunch in the dining room, an intimate dinner in the Tamalpais Room, or take in the view over a drink in the lounge. The best and freshest ingredients available highlight the American continental cuisine. The 40,000-bottle wine cellar has been honored with the prestigious *Wine Spectator's* Grand Award. The Carnelian Room can also host business meetings or conferences day or night, seven days a week.

World class wine cellar

General Manager
Michael Hoepke

Executive Chef David Lawrence

AWARD WINNER
SINCE 1992

Farallon Restaurant

The Pool Room

On Post Street between
Mason and Powell streets,
20 min. from San Francisco
International Airport

450 Post Street
San Francisco, CA 94102
PH: (415) 959-6969
FAX: (415) 834-1234
www.farallonrestaurant.com

Owners
Pat Kuleto and Mark Franz

Cuisine
Coastal

Days Open
Open Tues.-Sat. for lunch,
daily for dinner

Named for the windswept islands off the coast of San Francisco, Farallon is a collaboration between the renowned restaurateur/designer Pat Kuleto and acclaimed Chef Mark Franz. The unique undersea fantasy design of the restaurant's interior is the perfect setting to enjoy Chef Franz' award-winning "coastal cuisine." Menu highlights include lavender crusted tuna with local sea urchin, and black truffle capellini. For dessert, diners enjoy the creations of world-class pastry chef Emily Luchetti.

Jellyfish Bar

The wine bold

Pricing
Dinner for one,
without tax, tip, or drinks:
$40-$60

Dress Code
Business casual

Reservations
Recommended

Parking
Valet

Features
Private dining rooms
accomodating parties of
20, 50, 100, private
kitchen, near theater

Credit Cards
AE, VC, MC, DC, JCB, DS

AWARD WINNER
SINCE 2003

Fior d'Italia

Beloved by its loyal clientele

Directions

In the heart of North Beach, 30 min. from San Francisco International Airport

601 Union Street
San Francisco, CA 94133
PH: (415) 986-1886
FAX: (415) 986-7031
www.fior.com

Owners
Bob Larive

Cuisine
Italian

Days Open
Open daily for lunch and dinner

Pricing
Dinner for one, without tax, tip, or drinks: $20-$40

Dress Code
Business casual

Reservations
Recommended

Parking
Valet

Features
Private room/parties, outdoor dining

Credit Cards
AE, MC, CB, DC, JCB, DS

An important part of San Francisco's grand and glorious history for 116 years, this venerable Italian restaurant has been a leader in building the great tradition of excellent cuisine for which the city is so famous. The extensive menu boasts almost 90 items, and the Fior's loyal clientele highly rate its calamari, gnocchi, osso buco, and Caesar salad, as well as its veal and pasta dishes, all freshly prepared.

Chef Gianni Audieri and owner Bob Larive

Trattoria looks out on Washington Square

A North Beach landmark since 1886

AWARD WINNER
SINCE 2001

Fournou's Ovens

European roasting ovens

Fournou's Ovens, one of San Francisco's finest restaurants, is located in the Stanford Court Hotel atop historic Nob Hill. Enjoy a Mediterranean-themed setting and a menu that emphasizes seasonal specialties. Fournou's Ovens is named for its visual focal point, the massive, 54-square-foot European-style roasting ovens. For ten consecutive years, our wine list has been chosen as an award winner by Wine Spectator magazine. Champagne brunch is served on Saturday and Sunday.

Award-winning wine cellar

Private dining room

BEST OF
AWARD OF
EXCELLENCE

DiRōNA

AWARD WINNER
SINCE 1993

Directions

Corner of California and Powell streets, near Union Square and 25 min. from San Francisco International Airport

905 California Street
San Francisco, CA 94108
PH: (415) 989-1910
FAX: (415) 732-4017
www.renaissancehotels.com

Owners
The Stanford Court Hotel, a Renaissance Hotel

Cuisine
American, with a Mediterranean flair

Days Open
Open daily for breakfast, lunch, and dinner

Pricing
Dinner for one, without tax, tip, or drinks: $40-$60

Dress Code
Business casual

Reservations
Recommended

Parking
Valet

Features
Private room/parties, near theater

Credit Cards
AE, VC, MC, CB, DC, JCB, DS

Harris' Restaurant

Harris' Restaurant

Directions

At Van Ness and Pacific
avenues, 30 min. from San
Francisco International
Airport

Ask any San Franciscan about the City by the Bay's best steak, and they're certain to tell you about Harris', which uses a 21-day dry-aging process for its beef. The result is tender and succulent steaks that are sliced on the premises. The richly appointed dining rooms feature over-stuffed leather booths, mahogany-paneled walls, and warm murals painted by local artists. Choose a vintage from the extensive wine list, or try a famous Harris' martini.

Main dining room

2100 Van Ness Avenue
San Francisco, CA 94109
PH: (415) 673-1888
FAX: (415) 673-8817
www.harrisrestaurant.com

Owners
Ann Lee Harris, Goetz Boje

Cuisine
Steak and seafood

Days Open
Open daily for dinner

Pricing
Dinner for one,
without tax, tip, or drinks:
$40-$60

Dress Code
Business casual

Reservations
Recommended

Parking
Valet

Features
Private room/parties, entertainment

Credit Cards
AE, VC, MC, CB, DC, JCB, DS

Board room

Pacific room

AWARD WINNER
SINCE 1996

La Folie

Russian Hill Jewel

On Polk Street between Union and Green streets in Russian Hill, 40 min. from San Francisco International Airport

Since 1988, La Folie has been consistently rated as one of the top restaurants in San Francisco due to Chef/Owner Roland Passot's immense talent and undying passion for his work. The dining room offers an elegant, theatrically inspired setting with dark burgundy curtains and authentic Guignols (French puppers).The cuisine is French with northern California influences, and features such signature dishes as roasted quail and foie gras, and Maine lobster salad. Prix fixe menus are offered, and an extensive, diverse wine list complements the dinner menus.

Egg surprise

Roti of quail and squab

Main dining room

2316 Polk Street
San Francisco, CA 94109
PH: (415) 776-5577
FAX: (415) 776-3431
www.lafolie.com

Owners
Roland and Jamie Passot

Cuisine
French

Days Open
Open Mon.-Sat. for dinner

Pricing
Dinner for one,
without tax, tip, or drinks:
$60-$80

Dress Code
Elegant casual

Reservations
Recommended

Parking
Valet

Features
Private room/parties, near theater

Credit Cards
AE, VC, MC, CB, DC

AWARD WINNER
SINCE 1992

Le Central Bistro

Le Central Bistro

Since opening in 1974, this lively yet intimate establishment has become a classic San Francisco dining spot. Le Central offers French bistro cuisine expertly prepared by John and Paul Tanphanich, in an authentic French brasserie setting. Specialties of the house include the cassoulet, choucroute a l'Alsacienne, boudin noir aux pommes, steak tartare, and roasted chicken. To finish, choose from a carefully selected wine list of French and California vintages and tempting desserts.

The cassoulet

Owner Michel Bonnet

Owner Paul Tanphanich

AWARD WINNER
SINCE 1993

Directions

On Bush Street at Grant, 30 min. from San Francisco International Airport

453 Bush Street
San Francisco, CA 94108
PH: (415) 391-2233
FAX: (415) 391-3615
www.citysearch.com

Owners
Paul Tanphanich, Johnny Tanphanich, Michel Bonnet

Cuisine
French

Days Open
Open Mon.-Sat. for lunch and dinner

Pricing
Dinner for one, without tax, tip, or drinks: $40-$60

Dress Code
Business casual

Reservations
Recommended

Parking
Garage nearby

Features
Private parties, near theater

Credit Cards
AE, VC, MC, CB, JCB

L'Olivier

A French restaurant since 1978

On Davis Court between Jackson and Washington streets, 45 min. from San Francisco International Airport

465 Davis Court
San Francisco, CA 94111
PH: (415) 981-7824
FAX: (415) 981-2904
www.lolivierrestaurant.com

Owners
Guy and Christian Francoz

Cuisine
French

Days Open
Open Mon.-Fri. for lunch, Mon.-Sat. for dinner

Pricing
Dinner for one, without tax, tip, or drinks: $20-$40
(or)
Price fix: $28

Dress Code
Business casual

Reservations
Recommended

Parking
Valet

Features
Private room/parties

Credit Cards
AE, VC, MC, CB, DC, JCB, DS

Celebrating its 25th anniversary, L'Olivier is as popular as ever for anyone seeking an exceptional lunch or a very romantic dinner. The main dining room, decorated with French antiques, exudes a quiet, inviting grace and opens on to a large greenhouse filled with plants and fresh flowers. Member of "La Charte de la Bouillabaisse" de Marseille (France), this specialty is served on Friday and Saturday.

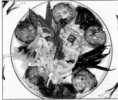

Owners Guy (left) and Christian Francoz

Sautéed scallops Provençale with fettuccini

The Green House

DiRōNA
AWARD WINNER
SINCE 2003

Postrio

Main dining-room

Directions

Located in the heart of Union Square, 30 min. from San Francisco or Oakland International Airports, 45 min. from San Jose Int'l

Postrio is celebrity Chef Wolfgang Puck's northern California jewel. Executive Chefs Mitchell and Steven Rosenthal developed a contemporary American cuisine accenting the cultural diversity of San Francisco. The glamorous dining room boasts an incredible art collection, including a private dining area designed by Dale Chihuly. The dramatic three-tiered entrance leads you into the main dining room, where a buzzing crowd of celebrities, socialites, and restaurateurs can be found.

The famous entrance

Chibuly Room

545 Post Street
San Francisco, CA 94102
PH: (415) 776-7825
FAX: (415) 776-6702
www.postrio.com

Owners
Wolfgang Puck

Cuisine
Contemporary American

Days Open
Open Mon.-Sat. for lunch, daily for dinner, Sun. for brunch, café dining 11:30am - 11:30pm

Pricing
Dinner for one, without tax, tip, or drinks: $40-$60

Dress Code
Business casual

Reservations
Recommended

Parking
Valet

Features
Private room/parties, near theater

Credit Cards
AE, VC, MC, DC, DS

The café

AWARD WINNER
SINCE 1993

Tommy Toy's Cuisine Chinoise

Main dining room

Directions

Across from the Transamerica Pyramid in the Financial District, 45 min. from San Francisco International Airport

This elegant and refined restaurant is renowned for its combination of Chinese cuisine and French service. Specialties include whole Maine lobster in peppercorn sauce and Peking duck carved tableside. Tommy Toy's has received many accolades, including Mobil's Four Star Award for Excellence and induction into *Nation's Restaurant News*' Hall of Fame.

Tommy Toy, right, with chef

655 Montgomery Street
San Francisco, CA 94111
PH: (415) 397-4888
FAX: (415) 397-0469
www.tommytoys.com

Owners
Tommy Toy, Alon Yu

Cuisine
Chinese-French

Days Open
Open Mon.-Fri. for lunch, daily for dinner

Pricing
Dinner for one, without tax, tip, or drinks: $40-$60

Dress Code
Jacket and tie requested

Reservations
Recommended

Parking
Valet, garage nearby

Features
Private room/parties

Credit Cards
AE, VC, MC, CB, DC, JCB, DS

Romantic dining

Lobster in peppercorn sauce

AWARD WINNER
SINCE 1992

Emile's Restaurant and Cooking School

Exquisite dining atmosphere

Between Williams and Reed streets, on South 2nd St., 10 min. from San Jose International airport

Emile's Restaurant enjoys the reputation as the best restaurant in San Jose and was declared "the best traditional French Restaurant in the San Francisco Bay Area" by *Zagat*. The dining room is comfortable and elegant. Fresh flowers and contemporary, hand-sculpted brass enhance the exquisite atmosphere. Emile's menu reflects the best use of peak, seasonal items. The cuisine is contemporary European, serving French, Swiss, and Italian daily specialties of fresh fish and game. The extensive, award-winning wine list includes California wines and European varieties.

Chef/Proprietor
Emile Mooser

545 South 2nd Street
San Jose, CA 95112
PH: (408) 289-1960
FAX: (408) 998-1245
www.emiles.com

Owners
Emile Mooser

Cuisine
French continental

Days Open
Open Tues.-Sat. for dinner

Pricing
Dinner for one,
without tax, tip, or drinks:
$40-$60

Dress Code
Business casual

Reservations
Recommended

Parking
Valet

Features
Private room/parties, near theater

Credit Cards
AE, VC, MC, DC, DS

AWARD WINNER
SINCE 1992

Le Papillon

Main dining room

On the corner of Saratoga Ave. and Kiely Blvd., near San Jose International Airport and 45 min. from San Francisco International Airport

410 Saratoga Avenue
San Jose, CA 95129
PH: (408) 296-3730
FAX: (408) 247-7812
www.lepapillon.com

For nearly a quarter of a century, Le Papillon has set the standard for innovative French cuisine in San Jose. Chef Scott Cooper's extensive menu showcases many unique contemporary French specialties as well as updated versions of classics. Sautéed John Dory with a shellfish vinaigrette, pan-seared Ahi tuna topped with foie gras in black currant glaze, and noisettes of red deer are a few of the highlights that keep Le Papillon a favorite destination in Silicon Valley.

Grilled rack of lamb with mild curry sauce

Chef Scott Cooper

Herb crusted halibut with dill and cherry tomatoes

Owners
Mike Mashayekh

Cuisine
Contemporary French

Days Open
Open Mon.-Fri. for lunch, daily for dinner

Pricing
Dinner for one, without tax, tip, or drinks: $40-$60 or Price Fix: $65

Dress Code
Business attire /semi-formal

Reservations
Recommended

Parking
Free on site

Features
Private rooms/catering

Credit Cards
AE, VC, MC, CB, DC, JCB, DS

AWARD WINNER
SINCE 2001

37

Paolo's Restaurant

The dining room

Paolo's has long been a favorite of Silicon Valley locals and visitors alike. Second-generation owner Carolyn Allen maintains her family's commitment to their heritage through the unique art and traditions of regional Italian cuisine, acquiring the finest local and imported ingredients. Maitre d', Jalil Samavarchian, directs a knowledgeable and professional staff in a dramatic setting overlooking Guadalupe River Park, maintains a wine list of exceptional breadth and depth, and develops uniquely personal rapport with Paolo's clientele. Paolo's style is as fashionable and contemporary today as it was when it opened more than 45 years ago.

Unmistakably Italian entrées

Private dining

AWARD WINNER
SINCE 1993

Directions

One block from the convention center in downtown San Jose, 10 min. from San Jose International Airport

333 West San Carlos Street
#150
San Jose, CA 95110
PH: (408) 294-2558
FAX: (408) 294-2595
www.paolosrestaurant.com

Owners
Carolyn Allen

Cuisine
Modern regional Italian

Days Open
Open Mon.-Fri. for lunch,
Mon.-Sat. for dinner

Pricing
Dinner for one,
without tax, tip, or drinks:
$20-$40

Dress Code
Business casual

Reservations
Recommended

Parking
Free on site

Features
Private room/parties, outdoor dining, entertainment, near theater, cigar/cognac events

Credit Cards
AE, VC, MC, CB, DC, DS

The Plumed Horse

The Green Room

Situated in the quiet village of Saratoga, The Plumed Horse offers guests a welcome retreat and panoramic views of redwoods and the Santa Cruz Mountains. Proximity to Silicon Valley, the San Jose Convention Center, and San Jose International Airport makes The Plumed Horse a convenient meeting place for those on tight schedules. The seasonal menu changes daily, and the wine list is a winner of *Wine Spectator*'s Grand Award.

The Pache family

Rack of lamb, the house specialty

GRAND AWARD

DiRōNA

AWARD WINNER
SINCE 1992

The inviting Crazy Horse Lounge

Directions

In Saratoga, 20 min. from San Jose International Airport and 45 min. from San Francisco International Airport

14555 Big Basin Way
Saratoga, CA 95070
PH: (408) 867-4711
FAX: (408) 867-6919
www.plumedhorse.com

Owners
The Pache family

Cuisine
Seasonal French country

Days Open
Open Mon.-Sat. for dinner

Pricing
Dinner for one,
without tax, tip, or drinks:
$20-$40

Dress Code
Business casual

Reservations
Recommended

Parking
Valet

Features
Private room/parties, entertainment

Credit Cards
AE, VC, MC, CB, DC

Domaine Chandon

*The Restaurant at
Domaine Chandon*

Since 1977, the Restaurant at Domaine Chandon has been a leading innovator in culinary excellence, and one of Napa Valley's most well loved destination eateries. Chef Eric Torralba creates his special version of California cuisine with a French inspiration. Chef Torralba draws his culinary inspiration from regionally grown, seasonal produce, and local farm raised poultry, and meats. The menu changes daily to reflect the best meat and produce available. Torralba's seven-course tasting menu, which pairs a different Chandon wine with each dish is fast becoming one of Domaine Chandon's signature experiences.

*Opaka-Paka
with chestnut*

*Pair a glass of sparkling
wine with your meal*

Chef Eric Torralba

Wine Spectator
AWARD
OF
EXCELLENCE

DiRōNA
AWARD WINNER
SINCE 1993

Directions

Off Highway 29 on California Drive, 90 min. from San Francisco International Airport

One California Drive
Yountville, CA 94599
PH: (707) 944-2892 (or)
800-736-2892
FAX: (707) 944-1622
www.chandon.com

Owners
Louis Vuitton Moët Hennessy

Cuisine
California with a French Mediterranean influence

Days Open
Open Thursday-Monday
for Lunch 11:30am-2pm
Dinner 6pm-9pm
Closed January

Pricing
Dinner for one,
without tax, tip, or drinks:
$80+ (or) Prix Fixe: $125
tasting menu with
Chandon wines

Dress Code
Smart casual

Reservations
Recommended

Parking
Free on site

Features
Outdoor dining

Credit Cards
AE, VC, MC, DC, DS

The French Laundry Restaurant

"The most exciting place to eat in America"

On Washington Street, 1 hr. from San Francisco Int'l Airport

6640 Washington Street
Yountville, CA 94599
PH: (707) 944-2380
FAX: (707) 944-1974

Owners
Thomas A. Keller

Cuisine
American with classic French influence

Days Open
Open Fri.-Sun. for lunch, daily for dinner

Pricing
Dinner for one, without tax, tip, or drinks: Chef's tasting menu and vegetarian price fix menus, ranging from: $115 to $135

Dress Code
Jacket required

Reservations
Required

Parking
Free on site

Features
Private parties

Credit Cards
AE, VC, MC

Nestled in the heart of one of California's top culinary destinations you will find Owner/Chef Thomas Keller's restaurant, The French Laundry. In this 19th century stone building, with views reminiscent of old world France, Chef Keller presents a variety of price fix menus offering diners progressive courses based on classical French techniques and California cuisine. The wine program offers 600-700 bottles from vintners and wineries throughout the world.

Chef/Owner
Thomas Keller

Alsatian rhubarb "Tarte" with mascarpone sorbet

Dining in a country garden

Wine Spectator
BEST OF
AWARD OF
EXCELLENCE

DiRōNA
AWARD WINNER
SINCE 1997

Anaheim White House

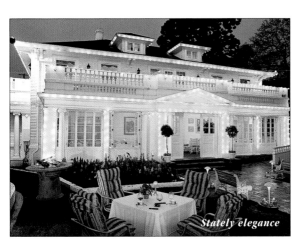

Stately elegance

2 miles northeast of
Anaheim Convention Center,
20 min. from Orange County's
John Wayne Airport

887 South Anaheim Boulevard
Anaheim, CA 92805
PH: (714) 772-1381
FAX: (714) 772-7062
www.anaheimwhitehouse.com

Occupying a lovely home built in 1909, Anaheim White House serves award-winning Northern Italian fare – homemade ravioli filled with fresh lobster and basil on a sauce of ginger and citrus is one specialty – in eight romantic dining areas. The wine list offers 250 selections from around the world. Anaheim White House is ideal for groups of all sizes, and is convenient to the Anaheim Convention Center, Arrowhead Pond, Edison Field, and area hotels.

Assortimento di Dolce

Intimate dining

Owners
Bruno Serato

Cuisine
Northern Italian

Days Open
Open Mon.-Fri. for lunch,
daily for dinner

Pricing
Dinner for one,
without tax, tip, or drinks:
$20-$40

Dress Code
Business casual

Reservations
Recommended

Parking
Valet

Features
Private room/parties, outdoor dining, entertainment

Credit Cards
AE, VC, MC

AWARD WINNER
SINCE 1998

JW's Steakhouse

Directions

Next to the Anaheim Convention Center, 20 min. from Orange County's John Wayne Airport

700 West Convention Way
Anaheim, CA 92802
PH: (714) 703-3187
FAX: (714) 750-9100

Owners
Marriott International

Cuisine
Traditional steakhouse

Days Open
Open Tues.-Sat. for dinner

Pricing
Dinner for one,
without tax, tip, or drinks:
$20-$40

Dress Code
Business casual

Reservations
Recommended

Parking
Valet

Features
Private room

Credit Cards
AE, VC, MC, CB, DC, ER, JCB, DS

Even in these health-conscious times, the lure of the perfectly done steak proves irresistible and there's no better place to indulge your passion for this most simple and glorious of foods than at JW's Steakhouse, located in the Anaheim Marriott. JW's specializes in fine Angus beef, grilled to perfection. The freshest seafood is imaginatively prepared, the salads and side dishes are robust, and the wine list is first-rate. All this, in an intimate, Old World setting.

AWARD WINNER
SINCE 1992

Mr. Stox

At East Katella Avenue and State College Boulevard, near Anaheim Convention Center and 20 min. from Orange County's John Wayne Airport

1105 East Katella Avenue
Anaheim, CA 92805
PH: (714) 634-2994
FAX: (714) 634-0561
www.mrstox.com

Owners
Chick Marshall and Ron and Debbie Marshall

Convenient to the Anaheim Convention Center, Mr. Stox has been operated by the Marshall family since 1977. The early Mission-style exterior belies the elegant dining rooms and cozy fireplace inside. The menu features Colorado lamb, veal, prime steaks, and a wide variety of fresh fish. Mr. Stox is noted for its home-baked breads and pastries, fresh pastas, and exquisite desserts. The award-winning wine cellar has a staggering 24,000 bottles.

Cuisine
Contemporary continental

Days Open
Open Mon.-Fri. for lunch, daily for dinner

Pricing
Dinner for one, without tax, tip, or drinks: $40-$60

Brothers Ron (left) and Chick Marshall, and Ron's wife, Debbie

Dress Code
Business casual

Reservations
Recommended

Elegant, fireside dining

Parking
Valet

Features
Private room/parties, entertainment

Credit Cards
AE, VC, MC, CB, DC, DS

GRAND
AWARD

DiRoNA
AWARD WINNER
SINCE 1998

The Grill on the Alley

The place for power lunches

Directions

At Dayton Way and Wilshire
Boulevard in the heart of
Beverly Hills, 20 min. from Los
Angeles International Airport

When Angelenos are in search of exceptionally fresh grill fare in a truly American setting, they head for this popular Beverly Hills restaurant, a power-lunch spot where talent agents and stars frequently talk business over steaks and martinis. The Grill's founders, Dick Shapiro, Bob Spivak, and Mike Weinstock, along with Executive Chef John Sola, have continued the legend of the great grill restaurants found in New York and San Francisco, and built a comfortable, inviting restaurant with a sophisticated big-city spirit.

The bar

9560 Dayton Way
Beverly Hills, CA 90212
PH: (310) 276-0615
FAX: (310) 276-0284
www.thegrill.com

Owners
Grill Concepts Inc.

Cuisine
American

Days Open
Open Mon.-Sat. for lunch,
daily for dinner

Pricing
Dinner for one,
without tax, tip, or drinks:
$40-$60

Dress Code
Business casual

Reservations
Recommended

Parking
Valet

Features
Private parties

Credit Cards
AE, VC, MC, DC

AWARD WINNER
SINCE 1997

Lawry's The Prime Rib

A Southern California dining legend since 1938

On North La Cienega, 30 min. from Los Angeles International Airport

100 North La Cienega Blvd.
Beverly Hills, CA 90211
PH: (310) 652-2827
FAX: (310) 657-5463
www.lawrysonline.com

Owners
Lawry's Restaurants, Inc.

Cuisine
Continental featuring
Roasted Prime Ribs of Beef

Days Open
Open daily for dinner

Pricing
Dinner for one,
without tax, tip, or drinks:
$20-$40

Dress Code
Business casual

Reservations
Recommended

Parking
Valet

Features
Private rooms/parties,
special events, entertainment
(during holidays),
wine/scotch events

Credit Cards
AE, VC, MC, DC, JCB, DS

Specializing in Roasted Prime Ribs of Beef, Lawry's The Prime Rib serves exclusively USDA certified prime quality. Aged 21 days and rock salt-roasted to perfection, the prime rib is carved to order tableside from gleaming silver carts. Fresh fish and Atlantic lobster tails are also available. Plush banquettes, classic antiques, and rich woods add to the comfortable elegance that has made Lawry's a dining legend since 1938.

Comfortable elegance

*Signature Roasted
Prime Ribs of Beef*

Tableside silver cart service

AWARD WINNER
SINCE 2004

La Vie en Rose

Main dining room

On South State College Boulevard, 15 min. from John Wayne/Orange County Airport

240 South State College Boulevard
Brea, CA 92821
PH: (714) 529-8333
FAX: (714) 529-2751
www.lavnrose.com

L a Vie en Rose is a charming reproduction of a Normandy farmhouse in the heart of Orange County. Proprietor Louis Laulhere came to America with family recipes from Gascony and Provence. La Vie en Rose means "life is rosy," and that is how an evening here will make you feel. An extensive wine list complements such specialties as roasted rack of lamb and sautéed duck breast.

Lavender Room

Summer Room

Wine Room

AWARD WINNER
SINCE 1993

Owners
Louis Laulhere

Cuisine
French Country

Days Open
Open Mon.-Fri. for lunch,
Mon.-Sat. for dinner

Pricing
Dinner for one,
without tax, tip, or drinks:
$37-$49

Dress Code
Casual elegant

Reservations
Recommended

Parking
Free on site

Features
Private rooms/parties,
outdoor dining, cognac
events and other special
events, near theater

Credit Cards
AE, VC, MC

Saddle Peak Lodge

Saddle Peak Lodge dining room

On Cold Canyon Road, 40 min. from Los Angeles International Airport, and 30 min. from Burbank Airport

419 Cold Canyon Road
Calabasas, CA 91302
PH: (818) 222-3888
FAX: (818) 222-1054
www.saddlepeaklodge.com

Owners
Dr. Ann Ehringer

Cuisine
New American

Days Open
Open Wed.-Sun. for dinner.
Sunday for brunch

Pricing
Dinner for one,
without tax, tip, or drinks:
$40-$60
(or)
Prix Fixe: $65

Dress Code
Business casual

Reservations
Required

Parking
Valet

Features
Private room/parties, outdoor dining, catering

Credit Cards
AE, VC, MC, CB, DC, JCB

Tucked into the Santa Monica Mountains, high above Malibu, the elegant Saddle Peak Lodge is regarded as the culinary showcase of the California coast. Chef Warren Schwartz' appealing New American menu features the largest selection of game in southern California, complemented by Managing Partner Gerhard Tratter's award-winning, all American wine list. Seasonal tasting menus combine the best of both. Saddle Peak's menu highlights include buffalo tartar with whole grain mustard aioli, mixed wild mushrooms in puff pastry with haricot verts, and smoked duck simmered in sweet cream, roasted elk tenderloin, and wild boar served three ways. Saddle Peak's Sunday brunch is SRO.

Fresh, seasonal ingredients, wild game and inspired cooking create a memorable dining experience

Scenic view from Saddle Peak Lodge

AWARD OF EXCELLENCE

DiRōNA

AWARD WINNER
SINCE 1997

Five Crowns

A proud member of the Lawry's fine dining family since 1965

A mile south of MacArthur Boulevard, 15 min. from Orange County's John Wayne Airport

A replica of one of England's oldest country inns, Five Crowns' charm emanates through distinctive rooms, a sunlit Greenhouse and an enchanting English garden. The menu includes USDA Certified Prime quality beef, seasonal poultry and fresh seafood selections. Five Crowns features Lawry's signature Roasted Prime Ribs of Beef, an award-winning wine list, and warm hospitality that have made the restaurant a dining legend since 1965.

The warmth of an Olde English Inn

Patio dining in the Greenhouse

3801 East Coast Highway
Corona del Mar, CA 92625
PH: (949) 760-0331
FAX: (949) 760-3987
www.lawrysonline.com

Owners
Lawry's Restaurants, Inc.

Cuisine
Continental

Days Open
Open daily for dinner,
Sun. for brunch

Pricing
Dinner for one,
without tax, tip, or drinks:
$20-$40

Dress Code
Business casual

Reservations
Recommended

Parking
Valet

Features
Private rooms/parties, special events, outdoor dining, wine dinners, weddings

Credit Cards
AE, VC, MC, DC, DS, JCB

Signature hospitality

AWARD WINNER
SINCE 1999

The Dining Room at The Ritz-Carlton, Laguna Niguel

The Dining Room

Orange County's only AAA Five-Diamond restaurant, The Dining Room is perfect for any special occasion, featuring the finest in cuisine, wine, and service. An elegant dining experience, introducing contemporary French cuisine, and culture in a sophisticated, yet relaxed atmosphere. With personal service, and attention to detail, Chef de Cuisine, Yvon Goetz, presents an exquisite à la carte or indulgent five-course food and wine paired menu.

The Wine Room

Chef de Cuisine
Yvon Goetz

Lobster Verbena

AWARD WINNER
SINCE 1992

Directions

Off the Pacific Coast Hwy. on Ritz-Carlton Drive, 25 min. from Orange County's John Wayne Airport

1 Ritz-Carlton Drive
Dana Point, CA 92629
PH: (949) 240-2000
FAX: (949) 240-0829
www.ritzcarlton.com

Owners
The Ritz-Carlton

Cuisine
Contemporary French

Days Open
Open Tues.-Sat. for dinner

Pricing
Dinner for one,
without tax, tip, or drinks:
$40-$80

Dress Code
Jackets requested

Reservations
Required

Parking
Valet

Features
Private room/parties,
wine/cognac events

Credit Cards
AE, VC, MC, CB, DC,
JCB, DS

The Cellar

Main dining room

Directions

On North Harbor Boulevard, 20 min. from Orange County's John Wayne Airport and 35 min. from Los Angeles International

Discriminating diners expect nothing less than the best — divine cuisine, impeccable service, award-winning wine selection, and a beautiful setting — and The Cellar delivers. Chef de Cuisine David Kesler has created a menu full of such memorable dishes as grilled veal chop with apples, walnuts, Calvados, and saffron parsleyed risotto, not to mention roasted breast of Muscovy duck with poached sour cherries, cherry brandy, and The Cellar's own duck stock reduction. Year after year, The Cellar maintains a tradition of gracious European cuisine and service.

Rack of lamb

Trudy and Ernest Zingg

305 North Harbor Boulevard
Fullerton, CA 92832
PH: (714) 525-5682
FAX: (714) 525-3853
www.imenu.com/thecellar

Owners
Ernest and Trudy Zingg

Cuisine
Classic French

Days Open
Open Tues.-Sat. for dinner

Pricing
Dinner for one, without tax, tip, or drinks: $20-$40

Dress Code
Business casual

Reservations
Recommended

Parking
Free on site, complimentary valet, garage nearby

Features
Private room/parties, near theater

Credit Cards
AE, VC, MC, CB, DC, JCB, DS

GRAND AWARD

DiRoNA
AWARD WINNER
SINCE 1995

Convivial bar

Gennaro's Ristorante

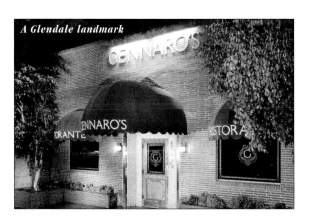

A Glendale landmark

Directions

2 blocks North of the 134 Freeway, 15 min. from Burbank-Glendale-Pasadena Airport

---

1109 North Brand Boulevard
Glendale, CA 91202
PH: (818) 243-6231
FAX: (818) 243-8628

Owners
Gennaro Rosato

Cuisine
Italian

Days Open
Open Mon.-Fri. for lunch,
Mon.-Sat. for dinner

Pricing
Dinner for one,
without tax, tip, or drinks:
$20-$40

Dress Code
Business casual

Reservations
Recommended

Parking
Valet

Features
Private parties

Credit Cards
AE, VC, MC, CB, DC

This intimate, elegant restaurant delights both loyal patrons and newcomers, who often come to celebrate special occasions. Service is warm and attentive, and the Northern Italian fare is delicious and inviting. Feast on roast pheasant with pearl onions and Marsala wine sauce, or Muscovy duck breast sautéed in port and garnished with fresh melon. "A restaurant for wine lovers," according to *Wine Spectator*; the wine list features over 150 Italian, French, and California selections.

Cozy fireplace

The bar

AWARD WINNER
SINCE 1995

The dining room

Le Saint Germain

Main dining room

L e St. Germain, described by many as the "French oasis in the desert," features exquisite, French Mediterranean cuisine. Le St. Germain has recreated the cherished Parisian traditions, and charms of a friendly French bistro. Signature dishes include, marinated baby rack of lamb, and roasted veal chop with wild mushrooms, and truffle oil. The restaurant features a spectacular main dining room, adjacent is the popular garden patio, surrounded by the sparkle of twinkling lights, and the glow of a warm fireplace.

Private Melrose Room

Climate-controlled Garden Patio

Creative entrees

AWARD WINNER SINCE 2003

Directions

On Highway 111 in Indian Wells, 20 min. from Palm Springs Regional Airport

74-985 Highway 111
Indian Wells, CA 92210
PH: (760) 773-6511
FAX: (760) 773-6510
www.lestgermain.com

Owners
Michel Despras, and
Paul Bruggmans

Cuisine
French continental

Days Open
Open daily for lunch and dinner, Sunday for brunch

Pricing
Dinner for one,
without tax, tip, or drinks:
$20-$40

Dress Code
Resort casual

Reservations
Recommended

Parking
Valet, free on site

Features
Private rooms/parties, outdoor dining, entertainment, near theater, wine dinners

Credit Cards
AE, VC, MC, CB, DC, DS

The Marine Room

Elegant dining on the surf

Off Torrey Pines Road in La Jolla Shores, 25 min. from San Diego International Airport

The Marine Room, at the La Jolla Beach & Tennis Club, has been a citadel of sophisticated dining for more than half a century. Graceful service and soft music complement an award wining wine list and the continental cuisine created by award-winning Executive Chef Bernard Guillas. The atmosphere is warm and inviting, with exhilarating ocean vistas from the beach front location. Frequently voted "Most Romantic" restaurant in the region, the Marine Room is known for its views, its service and style and its delightful cuisine.

Ruby red Ahi tuna

Executive Chef Bernard Guillas

AWARD WINNER
SINCE 1996

Marbled chocolate swan

2000 Spindrift Drive
La Jolla, CA 92037
PH: (858) 459-7222
FAX: (858) 551-4673
www.marineroom.com

Owners
La Jolla Beach & Tennis Club, Inc.

Cuisine
Continental

Days Open
Open daily for dinner, Tues.-Sat. for lunch, Sundays for brunch

Pricing
Dinner for one, without tax, tip, or drinks: $40-$60

Dress Code
Business casual

Reservations
Recommended

Parking
Free on site, valet

Features
Private parties, entertainment

Credit Cards
AE, VC, MC, CB, DC, ER, JCB, DS

Top of the Cove

Crispy shrimp, chayote and celery remoulade drizzled with Sambol chili dressing

On Prospect Street, 20 min. from San Diego International Airport

1216 Prospect Street
La Jolla, CA 92037
PH: (858) 454-7779
FAX: (858) 454-3783
www.topofthecove.com

Owners
Ronald R. Zappardino

Cuisine
American Cuisine Extraordinaire

Days Open
Open daily for lunch and dinner

Pricing
Dinner for one, without tax, tip, or drinks: $40-$60

Dress Code
Business casual

Reservations
Recommended

Parking
Valet, garage nearby

Features
Outdoor dining, cigar/cognac events

Credit Cards
AE, VC, MC, DC

Celebrating its 50th anniversary this year, the award-winning Top of the Cove has annually been named the most romantic dining experience by *San Diego Magazine* readers and has been recognized as the winner of the prestigious *Wine Spectator* Grand Award. Executive Chef Paul McCabe's fluency in Mediterranean, Southwestern, Thai, and Pacific Rim cuisine are blended into an exciting, and innovative menu classified as "American Cuisine Extraordinaire" by owner Ron Zappardino.

Grilled filet mignon

French toast, torched layers of white bread filled with Crème Brulee

Wine Spectator
GRAND AWARD

DiRōNA
AWARD WINNER
SINCE 1992

La Cachette Restaurant

Dining room at la Cachette

"One of the most important French chefs working in America today" (Angeleno, May 2003), Chef/Owner Jean Francois Meteigner continues to take the mystery and the fat out of French cooking. Highlights include Maine lobster salad served warm with classic white truffle oil dressing, seared farm raised squab with juniper berry and dry sak jus, and tenderloin of Black Angus beef with garlic shallot sauce, as well as an award-winning wine list and the divine chocolate cake.

Chef Jean Francois Meteigner

Directions

On Santa Monica Boulevard, just west of Century City, 25 min. from Los Angeles International Airport

10506 Santa Monica Blvd.
Los Angeles, CA 90025
Phone: (310) 470-4992
Fax: (310) 470-7451
www.lacachetterestaurant.com

Owners
Jean Francois Meteigner

Cuisine
French

Days Open
Open Mon.-Fri. for lunch, daily for dinner

Pricing
Dinner for one, without tax, tip, or drinks: $40-$60

Dress Code
Business casual

Reservations
Recommended

Parking
Valet

Features
Private parties, near theater

Credit Cards
AE, VC, MC, DC

Art adorns the walls

AWARD WINNER
SINCE 2004

56

Patina

Patina..."a jewel", located in the heart of Hollywood's studio district

Chef Joachim Splichal's award-winning Relais & Château restaurant features inspired cuisine with three exquisite seasonal tasting menus including wild game, seafood, and garden dishes. Patina's distinctive Chef's Table offers guests a singular dining experience with a special seven-course menu created daily from the freshest ingredients available. The acclaimed wine list offers more than 2,000 selections from around the world with expertise offered by James Beard Outstanding Wine Service nominee, sommelier Chris Meeske.

The distinctive Chef's Table

Opulent and intimate dining atmosphere

Comfortable bar/lounge

Directions

At the northwest corner of Melrose and Cole, 30 min. from Los Angeles International Airport

5955 Melrose Avenue
Los Angeles, CA 90038
PH: (323) 467-1108
FAX: (323) 467-0215
www.patinagroup.com

Owners
Joachim and
Christine Splichal

Cuisine
California French

Days Open
Open for dinner daily

Pricing
Dinner for one,
without tax, tip, or drinks:
$80+

Dress Code
Business casual

Reservations
Recommended

Parking
Valet

Features
Private room/parties,

Credit Cards
AE, VC, MC, DS

AWARD WINNER
SINCE 1993

57

The Restaurant at Hotel Bel-Air

Swan Lake: Hotel Bel-Air

Hotel Bel-Air is on Stone Canyon Rd., 30 min. from Los Angeles Int'l Airport

701 Stone Canyon Road
Los Angeles, CA 90077
PH: (310) 472-1211
FAX: (310) 476-5890
www.hotelbelair.com

Owners
Kava Holdings

Cuisine
French/California

Days Open
Open daily for breakfast, lunch, afternoon tea, and dinner, Sunday for brunch

A beloved setting for breakfast, lunch, afternoon tea, dinner, or Sunday brunch, The Restaurant at Hotel Bel-Air provides the ideal setting for a romantic meal, a social celebration, or client entertainment. The bougainvillea-draped Terrace, with heated tiles for year-round comfort, overlooks the gardens and Swan Lake. The delightful French-California menu is available both indoors, and on the Terrace, including lobster soup, a Hotel Bel-Air signature item.

The Terrace

Private dining at Table One

Pricing
Dinner for one, without tax, tip, or drinks: $40-$60

Dress Code
Jacket required for dining room after 6 p.m.

Reservations
Recommended

Parking
Valet

Features
Private room/parties, outdoor dining

Credit Cards
AE, VC, MC, DC, JCB

AWARD WINNER
SINCE 1992

Pavilion

An elegant dining experience

On Newport Center Drive,
15 min. from Orange County's
John Wayne Airport

690 Newport Center Drive
Newport Beach, CA 92660
PH: (949) 760-4920
FAX: (949) 760-8073
www.fourseasons.com/
newportbeach

E legant and understated, Pavilion at Four Seasons Hotel Newport Beach celebrates a passion for dining. With menus that change with the seasons, the finest qualities of contemporary American and classic Mediterranean cuisine are brought together to create selections that have garnered awards for outstanding and innovative dining. Recognized as the #1 restaurant in Orange County by the *2002 Zagat Survey.*

Gardens Lounge

Owners
Four Seasons Hotel
Newport Beach

Cuisine
California, with
Mediterranean influences

Days Open
Open daily for breakfast,
lunch, and dinner

Pricing
Dinner for one,
without tax, tip, or drinks:
$40-$60

Dress Code
Business casual

Reservations
Recommended

Parking
Complimentary valet

Features
Private room,
outdoor dining

Credit Cards
AE, VC, MC, CB, DC, JCB, DS

Pool

Petit Pavilion

AWARD WINNER
SINCE 1992

Le Petit Chateau

San Fernando Valley landmark

Directions

On Lankershim Boulevard
just north of Riverside Drive
in the San Fernando Valley,
10 min. from Burbank
Airport and 30 min. from
Los Angeles International

Trendy restaurants come and go, but few stand the test of time. Le Petit Chateau, a true San Fernando Valley landmark, is one of those few. It has been serving classic French country cooking for 40 years. From tender veal specialties to steaks and seafood, the menu has all your favorites (don't miss the roast duck). Le Petit Chateau is easily reached by all major freeways and is a mile from Universal Studios.

Owners Christiane and Andrew Higgs

Dining room

4615 Lankershim Boulevard
North Hollywood, CA 91602
PH: (818) 769-1812
FAX: (818) 769-3431

Owners
Andrew and Christiane Higgs

Cuisine
French

Days Open
Open Mon.-Fri. for lunch,
Mon.-Sat. for dinner

Pricing
Dinner for one,
without tax, tip, or drinks:
$20-$40

Dress Code
Business casual

Reservations
Recommended

Parking
Valet

Features
Private parties, near theater

Credit Cards
AE, VC, MC, CB, DC, DS

Le petit Château

DiRoNA
AWARD WINNER
SINCE 1996

The Hobbit

An Orange landmark since 1972

The Hobbit has offered a truly elegant dining experience since 1972, winning numerous awards in the process. The menu changes weekly. A seven-course prix fixe meal begins with champagne and hors d'ouevres in the award-winning wine cellar, which boasts more than 1,000 selections. Once seated, diners enjoy an appetizer, a fish or fowl course, and salad. Then comes a brief intermission to meet the chef-proprietor, Michael Philippi, or linger on the patio before settling in for the main course and dessert.

Owners Debra and Michael Philippi

Michael Philippi in the wine cellar

Directions

Less than a mile from Costa Mesa Freeway, 15 min. from Orange County's John Wayne Airport

2932 East Chapman Avenue
Orange, CA 92869
PH: (714) 997-1972
FAX: (714) 997-3181
www.hobbitrestaurant.com

Owners
Michael and Debra Philippi

Cuisine
Contemporary continental

Days Open
Open Tues.-Sun. for dinner

Pricing
Dinner for one,
without tax, tip, or drinks:
price Fix:$65

Dress Code
Business casual

Reservations
Required

Parking
Free on site

Features
Private room/parties

Credit Cards
VC, MC

AWARD WINNER
SINCE 1999

61

LG's Prime Steakhouse

The place for great steaks

Housed in a historic adobe building, award-winning LG's features nine different USDA Prime sizzling steaks and has an "on-premises" dry-age facility for its "Jewel in the Crown," a 20-ounce porterhouse for one, and the even bigger 30-ounce porterhouse dubbed "The Gold Strike 49er." The menu also features rack of lamb, prime rib, and fresh fish and seafood. The LG's in Palm Springs features a climate-controlled patio and bar. Our newest location in La Quinta features a retractable roof and an underground wine cellar which is available for private parties. All restaurants serve the same great menu.

Owners Gail and Leon Greenberg

Service by the armful

AWARD WINNER
SINCE 1998

Directions

On Highway 111 near the Hyatt Regency Grand Champions, 30 min. from Palm Springs Regional Airport

74-225 Highway 111
Palm Desert, CA 92260
PH: (760) 779-9799
FAX: (760) 779-1979
www.lgsprimesteakhouse.com

Owners
Leon and Gail Greenberg

Cuisine
USDA Prime steak

Days Open
Open daily for dinner

Pricing
Dinner for one,
without tax, tip, or drinks:
$40-$60

Dress Code
Casual

Reservations
Recommended

Parking
Free on site, valet

Features
Private parties

Credit Cards
AE, VC, MC, DC, DS

Wally's Desert Turtle

Semi-private dining room

On Highway 111, 25 min. from Palm Springs Regional Airport

71-775 Highway 111
Rancho Mirage, CA 92270
PH: (760) 568-9321
FAX: (760) 568-9713
www.wallysdesertturtle.com

A culinary oasis in the desert, Wally's Desert Turtle serves unforgettable continental cuisine amid the elegance of beveled, mirrored ceilings, Peruvian artifacts, and hand-painted murals. Don't miss the fresh foie gras with apricot, pistachio, organic greens, and sweet Marsala or the imported Dover sole almandine. More than 200 selections of imported and California wines complement the menu. Catering is available, and large groups can "buy out" the entire restaurant.

Rack of lamb and other delicacies

Exquisite cuisine

Garden patio

Owners
Michael Botello

Cuisine
French Continental

Days Open
Open daily for dinner
(closed July through Sept.)

Pricing
Dinner for one,
without tax, tip, or drinks:
$40-$60

Dress Code
Business casual

Reservations
Required

Parking
Valet

Features
Private room/parties, entertainment

Credit Cards
AE, VC, MC, DC

AWARD WINNER
SINCE 1994

Duane's Prime Steaks & Seafood Restaurant

Duane's Prime Steaks & Seafood Restaurant

Dining at Duane's, located at the historic Mission Inn, is a perfect way to celebrate life's successes! Our distinct style and impeccable service provide the perfect setting for your special occasion. Duane's is the only recipient of the AAA Four Diamond Award in the Inland Empire and boasts of its fourth consecutive "Golden Sceptre Award" granted by the Southern California Restaurant Writers Association.

Spanish patio

Mission Inn

AWARD WINNER
SINCE 1999

Directions

At the Mission Inn on Mission Inn Ave., 20 min. from Ontario International Airport

3649 Mission Inn Ave.
Riverside, CA 92501
PH: (909) 784-0300
FAX: 909-782-7197
www.missioninn.com

Owners
Duane Roberts

Cuisine
Prime steaks and seafood

Days Open
Open Mon.-Fri. for lunch, Mon.-Sat. for dinner, and Sun. for brunch

Pricing
Dinner for one, without tax, tip, or drinks: $40-$60

Dress Code
Business casual

Reservations
Recommended

Parking
Valet, garage nearby

Features
Private room

Credit Cards
AE, VC, MC, CB, DC, DS

Cafe Pacifica

Owner Frank Busic and Chef Eddie Zamarripa

In San Diego's historic Old Town on San Diego Ave., 10 min. from San Diego International Airport

Located in the heart of San Diego's historic Old Town, Cafe Pacifica features only the freshest seafood cuisine with a distinct California dash of the day's locally grown herbs and produce. Cafe Pacifica also serves a variety of delicious pasta dishes, Colorado rack of lamb, and steaks. There is an extensive wine list, which features the best wineries of California and Oregon, and has won the Award of Excellence from *Wine Spectator* for many years.

Soy Peanut Swordfish

World-Famous "Pomerita" Pomegrante Margarita

2414 San Diego Ave.
San Diego, CA 92110
PH: (619) 291-6666
FAX: (619) 291-0122
www.cafepacifica.com

Owner
Frank Busic

Cuisine
Seafood

Days Open
Open daily for dinner

Pricing
Dinner for one,
without tax, tip, or drinks:
$20-$40

Dress Code
Business casual

Reservations
Recommended

Parking
Valet

Features
Private room/parties, out-door dining, near theater

Credit Cards
AE, VC, MC, CB, DC, DS

AWARD WINNER
SINCE 2002

El Bizcocho

Main dining room

E l Bizcocho, the top-rated San Diego restaurant in the *Zagat Survey*, serves classical French cuisine and seasonal specialties with unparalleled service and style. Located at the Rancho Bernardo Inn, El Bizcocho seamlessly combines elegance with warmth and comfort in its newly redesigned dining room. The eloquence of the cuisine, service, and atmosphere is complemented by one of California's most extensive wine lists.

Fine French cuisine

Directions

At Rancho Bernardo Inn off Interstate 15, 25 min. from San Diego International Airport

17550 Bernardo Oaks Drive
San Diego, CA 92128
PH: (858) 675-8550
FAX: (858) 675-8443
www.jcresorts.com

Owners
JC Resorts

Cuisine
Gourmet French

Days Open
Open Mon.-Sat. for dinner, Sunday for brunch

Pricing
Dinner for one, without tax, tip, or drinks: $40-$60

Dress Code
Jacket required

Reservations
Recommended

Parking
Free on site, valet

Credit Cards
AE, VC, MC, DC, DS

AWARD WINNER
SINCE 1992

Grant Grill

The warmth and ambience of the Grant Grill

Directions

On Broadway between Third and Fourth Avenues, 10 min. from San Diego International Airport

326 Broadway
San Diego, CA 92101
PH: (619) 232-3121
EXT: 1528
FAX: (619) 239-9517

Owners
U.S. Grant
A Wyndham Historic Hotel

Cuisine
California French

Days Open
Open daily for breakfast, lunch, and dinner

Pricing
Dinner for one, without tax, tip, or drinks: $40-$60

Dress Code
Business casual

Reservations
Recommended

Parking
Valet, on site parking

Credit Cards
AE, VC, MC, DC, DS

The Grant Grill, a historical, 52-year old landmark is located in the beautiful, 91-year old historic U.S. Grant Hotel. The renowned restaurant downtown now features not only the traditional favorites of its famous Mock Turtle Soup and Beef Wellington, but the dynamic chef duo is catering to new clientele with the latest in California-French cuisine. Chef Chatten describes the new menus as entrancing with dishes that are "artistic to look at–and absolutely amazing to eat". Chatten goes on to say "At the Grant Grill, we set the highest standards. Our loyal patrons expect no less and our new clientele are thrilled to find such a hidden jewel and reintroduce local San Diegans to the rich, elegant club atmosphere of yesteryear".

Foie gras

AWARD WINNER
SINCE 1992

Mille Fleurs

Directions

In Rancho Santa Fe, 35 min. from San Diego International Airport

6009 Paseo Delicias
P.O. Box 2548
Rancho Santa Fe, CA 92067
PH: (858) 756-3085
FAX: (858) 756-9945
www.millefleurs.com

Owners
Bertrand

Cuisine
French

Days Open
Open Mon.-Fri. for lunch, daily for dinner

Pricing
Dinner for one, without tax, tip, or drinks: $60-$80

Dress Code
Business casual

Reservations
Recommended

Parking
Free on site

Features
Private room/parties, outdoor dining, entertainment

Credit Cards
AE, VC, MC, DC

Nestled in the heart of a historic village, this nationally acclaimed restaurant offers elegant cuisine in gracious surroundings. Chef Martin Woesle creates new menus daily, featuring world-renowned "Chino Farm" seasonal produce. Dining options include cozy, refined dining areas with two fireplaces, as well as a casual bar and outdoor courtyard patio. An award winning wine list complements this extraordinary culinary experience.

Refined French cuisine

Chef Martin Woesle

Patio dining

AWARD WINNER
SINCE 1992

Rainwater's on Kettner

Elegant dining

On Kettner Boulevard downtown, 5 min. from San Diego International Airport

1202 Kettner Boulevard
San Diego, CA 92101
PH: (619) 233-5757
FAX: (619) 233-6722
www.rainwaters.com

Owners
Laurel and Paddy Rainwater

Cuisine
American

Days Open
Open Mon.-Fri. for lunch, daily for dinner

Pricing
Dinner for one, without tax, tip, or drinks: $40-$60

Dress Code
Business casual

Reservations
Recommended

Parking
Free on site, valet

Features
Private room/parties, near theater and convention center

Credit Cards
AE, VC, MC, CB, DC

Since 1985, San Diego's only Eastern-style chophouse has exuded warmth and subdued elegance with rich wood paneling, intimate leather booths, and crisp white linen. Rainwater's on Kettner features prime, Midwestern, corn-fed aged beef, the finest and freshest seafood from around the world, veal, lamb, and pork chops. *Wine Spectator* has honored Rainwater's with its Best of Excellence Award since 1986, and the restaurant was chosen as one of the top steakhouses in America by *Gourmet* magazine.

Prime beef

Creative fish entrées

BEST OF
AWARD OF
EXCELLENCE

DiRōNA
AWARD WINNER
SINCE 1999

Star of the Sea

Main dining room

Directions

On Harbor Drive just north of Broadway in downtown, 5 min. from San Diego International Airport

The Star of the Sea, on San Diego's bustling bay front, creates magical moments with innovative, uncompromising coastal cuisine and caring, stylish service. The beautiful water views provide fresh sunsets, served nightly. By using only the day's freshest seafood and ingredients, Chef Brian Johnston creates coastal cuisine, unique to San Diego.

On the bay

Chef Brian Johnston

Star of the Sea
1360 Harbor Drive
San Diego, CA 92101
PH: (619) 232-7408
FAX: (619) 232-1877
www.starofthesea.com

Owners
Ghio and Mascari families

Cuisine
Seafood fine dining

Days Open
Open daily for dinner

Pricing
Dinner for one,
without tax, tip, or drinks:
$40-$60

Dress Code
Business casual

Reservations
Recommended

Parking
Valet

Credit Cards
AE, VC, MC, CB, DC, DS

AWARD WINNER
SINCE 1993

Michael's

Elegant, casual dining

Directions

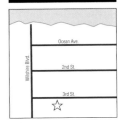

North of the intersection of Wilshire Blvd. and Third St., 30 min. from Los Angeles International Airport

Established in 1979, Michael's is renowned for providing a consistently excellent, fine dining experience. The eclectic menu is inspired by the best ingredients, cooked simply, prepared beautifully, and served impeccably in lush, art-filled indoor and outdoor settings. Michael's is the quintessential venue for elegantly casual meals, paired with handcrafted wines from around the world, served in a definitively Southern California environment.

Owner Michael McCarty

On the terrace

1147 Third Street
Santa Monica, CA 90403
PH: (310) 451-0843
FAX: (310) 394-1830
www.michaelssantamonica.com

Owners
Michael McCarty

Cuisine
New American Regional - California

Days Open
Open Mon.-Fri. for lunch, Mon.-Sat. for dinner

Pricing
Dinner for one, without tax, tip, or drinks: $40-$60

Dress Code
Casual/business casual

Reservations
Recommended

Parking
Valet

Features
Private rooms/parties, outdoor dining

Credit Cards
AE, VC, MC, DC, DS

Southern California dining

AWARD WINNER
SINCE 1992

Valentino Restaurant

Main dining room

Sicilian-born Piero Selvaggio delivers the very best of Italian food and culture to Los Angeles, in a masterpiece called Valentino Restaurant. Serving superb pastas and risottos, and entrées such as pepper-seared Ahi tuna and ossobuco braised in veal stock, this *non plus ultra* Italian restaurant continues to be rated one of the top restaurants in the country. Valentino offers a tasting menu as well, and boasts a comprehensive wine list of more than 150,000 bottles, representing more than 2,500 different varietals.

Involtini di Pesce Spada

Owner Piero Selvaggio

Wine cellar

AWARD WINNER
SINCE 1993

West of Centinela on Pico Blvd., 15 min. from Los Angeles International Airport

3115 Pico Boulevard
Santa Monica, CA 90405
PH: (310) 829-4313
FAX: (310) 315-2791
www.welovewine.com

Owners
Piero Selvaggio

Cuisine
Italian contemporary

Days Open
Open Fri. for lunch, Mon.-Sat. for dinner

Pricing
Dinner for one,
without tax, tip, or drinks:
$60-$80 (or) Price fix: $75

Dress Code
Business casual

Reservations
Recommended

Parking
Valet

Features
Private room/parties

Credit Cards
AE, VC, MC, CB, DC

Doug Arango's

*After 13 years in Palm Desert...
now on melrose in West Hollywood*

Located in the center of the design district, between Robertson and Doheny. Five min. from the heart of Beverly Hills, and 30 min. from Los Angeles International Airport

D oug Arango's opened in 1990 in Palm Desert, California…and moved its entire operation, including staff, to Los Angeles during the summer of 2003. This lively, chic restaurant is internationally known for its delicious and innovative menu, and has won the Wine Spectator Award of Excellence since 1995. House specialties include smoked salmon, veal Milanese, grilled rack of lamb with a pomegrante molasses, Pasta Vanda, award-winning pizzas, and now, world-famous lemon meringue pie.

Owner Robert Evans in his wine cellar

Bistro Salad

8826 Melrose Avenue
West Hollywood, CA 90069
www.dougarangos.com

Owners
Chris and Julia Bennett, and Robert Evans and Paula Evans

Cuisine
California

Days Open
Open Mon.-Fri. for lunch, Mon.-Sat. for dinner

Pricing
Dinner for one, without tax, tip, or drinks: $40-$60

Dress Code
Informal

Reservations
Recommended

Parking
Valet, and local street parking

Features
Outdoor dining, dining at the bar, near shopping, in design district

Credit Cards
AE, VC, MC, DC, DS

Front patio dining

AWARD WINNER
SINCE 2002

Fenix

Fenix of West Hollywood

Located in the Argyle Hotel on Sunset Blvd. in West Hollywood, minutes from Beverly Hills and Hollywood, and 26 min. from Los Angeles International Airport

8358 Sunset Blvd.
West Hollywood, CA 90069
PH: (323) 848-6677
FAX: (323) 654-9287
www.argylehotel.com

Cuisine
French Asian

Days Open
Open daily for breakfast and lunch, Mon.-Sat. for dinner, Sunday for brunch

Pricing
Dinner for one,
without tax, tip, or drinks:
$30-$50

Dress Code
Business casual

Reservations
Recommended

Parking
Valet

Features
Private parties, outdoor dining, entertainment

Credit Cards
AE, MC, DC, DS

F enix Restaurant- on the "hippest" strip in L.A.- Sunset Strip. Perenial, fabu restaurant of the Hollywood in-crowd. French Asian cuisine will delight your taste buds.

Overlooks Sunset Blvd.

Lounge with the "in" crowd

AWARD WINNER
SINCE 1998

Renaissance

Main dining room

Celebrating its 12th anniversary, Renaissance has gained international renown for its innovative cuisine, casually elegant service, and extensive wine program — all in a relaxed and cozy room. Chef/Owner Charles Dale delights diners with such specialties as Hot Date rack of lamb, crispy Chilean sea bass with artichokes, shiitakes, and foie gras, and two tasting menus that change nightly. Don't miss the fabulous desserts!

Honey and apple-glazed medallions of free range veal

Chef/Owner Charles Dale

AWARD WINNER
SINCE 1999

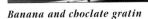

Banana and choclate gratin

Directions

At East Hopkins and S. Monarch in Aspen, 10 min. from Aspen Airport

304 East Hopkins
Aspen, CO 81611
PH: (970) 925-2402
FAX: (970) 925-6634
www.renaissancerestaurant.com

Owners
Charles Dale and Rob Ittner

Cuisine
Modern French, Spa Menu

Days Open
Open daily for dinner
(closed May and October)

Pricing
Dinner for one,
without tax, tip, or drinks:
$60-$80

Dress Code
Casual elegant

Reservations
Recommended

Parking
Valet nearby

Features
Private room/parties, outdoor dining, near theater

Credit Cards
AE, VC, MC, DC

Syzygy

Famous Aspen dining and entertainment

On East Hyman Avenue, 10 min. from Aspen Airport

520 East Hyman Avenue
Aspen, CO 81611
PH: (970) 925-3700
FAX: (970) 925-5593

Owners
Walt Harris

Cuisine
Creative

Days Open
Open daily for dinner
(Closed mid-April to early June, and mid-Oct. to mid-Nov.)

Pricing
Dinner for one,
without tax, tip, or drinks:
$40-$60

Dress Code
Casual

Reservations
Recommended

Parking
Valet

Features
Private parties, entertainment

Credit Cards
AE, VC, MC, DC, DS

Upstairs and unmarked, this restaurant is for those who like sleek, modern design, and sophisticated food that blends international flavors. Syzygy's menu combines elements of French, Southwestern, Italian, and Asian cuisines. Specialties include elk tenderloin with ancho chile, country potatoes, warm sun-dried fig chutney, and Madeira glaze. The atmosphere is intimate yet casual, and there is an extensive wine list including over 700 French, Italian, and American wines. Enjoy late-night jazz in one of eight cozy booths.

Exective Chef Martin Oswald

Sophisticated, international cuisine

AWARD WINNER
SINCE 1993

Mirabelle Restaurant at Beaver Creek

Dining room

Directions

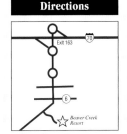

Across from Welcome Center at the Beaver Creek Resort, 20 min. from Eagle County Airport and 2 hrs. from Denver International

55 Village Road
Avon, CO 81620
PH: (970) 949-7728
FAX: (970) 845-9578

Owners
Daniel and Nathalie Joly

Cuisine
Contemporary European/Belgian

Days Open
Open Mon.-Sat. for dinner (closed late April through late May and November)

Pricing
Dinner for one, without tax, tip, or drinks: $40-$60

Dress Code
Casual

Reservations
Recommended

Parking
Parking lot around the ranch house

Features
Private room/parties, outdoor dining

Credit Cards
AE, VC, MC, DS

Old world charm meets great new world food at this new French little Ranch house, a romantic hideaway tucked into the woods of Beaver Creek Valley. In this intimate and lovely setting; Daniel Joly, Master Chef of Belgium, has created a menu using only the freshest ingredients. Signature dishes include Colorado rack of lamb with rosemary and garlic, hot foie gras with Mirabelle plums accented with a reduction of sweet Alsatain wine. Exacting service and an award-winning wine list makes Mirabelle Restaurant the perfect setting for a romantic evening.

Master Chef Daniel Joly

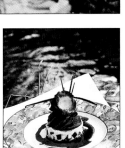

Roasted elk with black truffle mashed potatoes

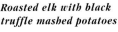

AWARD WINNER
SINCE 1994

Beano's Cabin

Beano's Cabin

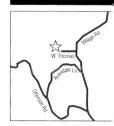

On Beaver Creek Mountain, 30 min. from Eagle County Airport

Post Office Box 915
Avon, CO 81620
PH: (970) 845-5770
Reservations: (970) 949-909
FAX: (970) 845-5769
www.beavercreek.com
www.mountainevents.com

Owners
Vail Resorts

Cuisine
Colorado cuisine

Days Open
Open daily for dinner Dec.-mid-April, Wed.-Sun. for dinner June-Sept.

Pricing
Dinner for one, without tax, tip, or drinks: $60-$80

Dress Code
Casual

Reservations
Required

Parking
Garage nearby

Features
Semi-private room/parties, live entertainment

Credit Cards
AE, VC, MC, DC, DS

B eano's Cabin is a destination restaurant high in the Rocky Mountains. This AAA Four-Diamond eatery combines spectacular views with a memorable dining adventure in the Larkspur Bowl of Beaver Creek, Colorado. In the winter months your experience begins with a snowcat-drawn sleigh ride up Beaver Creek Mountain. In the summertime, guests may arrive on horseback or take a wagon ride pulled by antique tractors. Once there, diners delight in the five-course menu offering unique choices paired with award-winning wine selections and excellent service.

Beano's dining room

AWARD WINNER
SINCE 1993

Charles Court

Charles Court patio

At The Broadmoor resort, 25 min. from Colorado Springs Municipal Airport

One Lake Avenue
Colorado Springs, CO 80906
PH: (719) 577-5774
FAX: (719) 577-5709
www.broadmoor.com

Owners
Broadmoor Hotel

Cuisine
American regional

Days Open
Open daily for dinner

Pricing
Dinner for one,
without tax, tip, or drinks:
$40-$60

Dress Code
Business casual

Reservations
Recommended

Parking
Free on site, valet

Features
Private parties, outdoor dining, cigar/cognac events, chef's table

Credit Cards
AE, VC, MC, CB, DC, DS

I deal for intimate dinners and entertaining clients, Charles Court at Broadmoor West offers fine dining without the formality. Impeccable service complements exceptional American regional cuisine, a seasonal tasting menu of Colorado game and fresh seafood. For parties of 10, the private Chef's table is a culinary world unto itself, with a specially created menu and complementing wines.

Roast loin of Colorado elk

AWARD WINNER
SINCE 1999

Chef's table

Broker Restaurant

Dining in an original bank vault

Directions

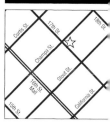

Located in the old Denver Nat'l Bank Building, 40 min from Denver Int'l Airport

821-17th Street at Champa
Denver, CO 80202
PH: (303) 292-5065
FAX: (303) 292-2652
www.brokerrestaurant.com

Owners
Ed Novak and Jerry Fritzler

Cuisine
American

Days Open
Open Mon.-Fri. for lunch, daily for dinner

Pricing
Dinner for one,
without tax, tip, or drinks:
$40-$60

Dress Code
Business casual

Reservations
Recommended

Parking
Valet

Features
Private room/parties, cigar/cognac events

Credit Cards
AE, VC, MC, CB, DC, JCB, DS

The Broker Restaurant is celebrating its 30th year in business. It is located in the old Denver National Bank Building, built in 1903, situated in the original bank vault. The Broker has one of the largest wine cellars in the region, and serves its famous complimentary shrimp bowl with every dinner. Specialties include filet Wellington, prime rib, Alaskan salmon, and Colorado rack of lamb. The Broker is a living Denver landmark.

Complimentary shrimp bowl served at every table

Manager/Co-Owner Jerry Fritzer, and Executive Chef Jeff French

Private dining in the wine cellar

AWARD WINNER
SINCE 1998

Palace Arms at The Brown Palace Hotel

Four-star dining

In the heart of downtown, 25 min. from Denver International Airport

321 17th Street
Denver, CO 80202
PH: (303) 297-3111
FAX: (303) 312-5900
www.brownpalace.com

Owners
Quorum Hotels and Resorts

Cuisine
Continental

Days Open
Open Mon.-Fri. for lunch, daily for dinner

Pricing
Dinner for one, without tax, tip, or drinks: $40-$60

Dress Code
Jacket required for dinner

Reservations
Recommended

Parking
Valet

Features
Private room

Credit Cards
AE, VC, MC, CB, DC, DS

One of downtown's only four-star restaurants, the Palace Arms, located in the Brown Palace Hotel, consistently earns accolades from *Gourmet, Bon Appetit,* and *Zagat.* The Napoleonic setting of this exquisite room with its 17th-century antiques provides the perfect complement to impeccable service and culinary artistry. Contemporary classics are blended with old world favorites, creating an unparalleled dining experience. The wine list boasts more than 900 selections and consistently earns the *Wine Spectator's* Best of Award of Excellence.

The atrium

AWARD WINNER
SINCE 1992

Strings

The Atrium

11 blocks from downtown, 25 min. from Denver International Airport

1700 Humboldt Street
Denver, CO 80218
PH: (303) 831-7310
FAX: (303) 860-8812
www.stringsrestaurant.com

Owners
Noel Cunningham

Cuisine
Casual contemporary

Days Open
Open Mon.-Fri. for lunch, daily for dinner

Pricing
Dinner for one, without tax, tip, or drinks: $20-$40

Dress Code
Casual

Reservations
Recommended

Parking
Complimentary valet

Features
Private room/parties, outdoor dining, near theater

Credit Cards
AE, VC, MC, DC, DS

Noel Cunningham and Executive Chef Amy Vitale feature a creative and diverse menu with signature favorites such as cashew crusted seabass, Dungeness crab cakes and penne bagutta. Strings boasts a diversified high quality wine list at very affordable prices. The restaurant has an upbeat cozy feeling and the contemporary menu and décor add a buzz of energy. Guest attire ranges from jeans and khakis, to jackets and ties, and all feel welcome. Customized parties from 10-100 people are served in four private rooms upon request, and catering services are available as well. Strings has been known for its great service, where the management and staff make sure your visit is a memorable one. We invite you to come and enjoy a long time Denver favorite.

... a long time Denver favorite

Chef/Owner Noel Cunningham

AWARD WINNER
SINCE 1993

Tante Louise

Romantic atmosphere

E. Colfax Ave.

Colorado Blvd

Eudora St

Monaco Parkway

On East Colfax, 25 min. from Denver International Airport

4900 East Colfax
Denver, CO 80220
PH: (303) 355-4488
FAX: (303) 321-6312
www.TanteLouise.com

Owners
Corbin "Corky" Douglass III

Cuisine
Contemporary French and New American

Days Open
Open Mon.-Sat. for dinner

Pricing
Dinner for one, without tax, tip, or drinks: $40-$60

Dress Code
Business casual

Reservations
Recommended

Parking
Valet

Features
Private room/parties, outdoor dining

Credit Cards
AE, VC, MC, CB, DC, DS

A one-of-a-kind restaurant reminiscent of an elegant French country inn, Tante Louise features intimate dining areas accented by glowing fireplaces, stained glass, gracious service, and warm hospitality. Executive Chef Duy Van Pham's contemporary and seasonal French and New American menu features presentations such as Colorado lamb loin, pan-roasted duck breast, fresh Alaskan halibut, sweetbreads, and degustation des legumes. An award-winning wine list features more than 600 selections.

Salmon vermouth crème

Charcuterie pate

Seasonal patio dining

Wine Spectator
AWARD OF EXCELLENCE

DiRōNA

AWARD WINNER
SINCE 1998

Restaurant Picasso

Table with a mountain view

Directions

At Lodge and Spa at Cordillera, 25 min. from Eagle County Airport

Serving up light interpretations of European fare, Restaurant Picasso, at the Lodge and Spa at Cordillera, allows guests to enjoy world-class cuisine and breathtaking views of New York Mountain and the Sawatch Range. The ultimate touch before dining is a tour of the wine cellar, completely renovated with customized racks and wine memorabilia. Come dine with Executive Chef Fabrice Beaudoin and allow him to create true "works of art for the palate."

Executive Chef Fabrice Beaudoin

Sliced elk tenderloin

2205 Cordillera Way
Edwards, CO 81632
PH: (970) 926-2200
FAX: (970) 926-2486
www.cordillera-vail.com

Owners
Felix Posen

Cuisine
European/Continental

Days Open
Open daily for breakfast, lunch, and dinner

Pricing
Dinner for one, without tax, tip, or drinks: $20-$38

Dress Code
Jacket and tie suggested

Reservations
Recommended

Parking
Free on site, valet

Features
Private room/parties, entertainment, wine cellar dining

Credit Cards
AE, VC, MC, DC, DS

AWARD WINNER
SINCE 1993

84

The Cliff House Dining Room

The Cliff House at Pikes Peak

On Cañon Avenue, 20 min. from Colorado Springs Airport

306 Cañon Avenue
Manitou Springs, CO 80829
PH: (888) 212-7000, ext. 615
FAX: (719) 685-3913
www.thecliffhouse.com

Owners
Jim S. Morley

Cuisine
Continental nouveau

Days Open
Open daily for breakfast, lunch, and dinner

Pricing
Dinner for one, without tax, tip, or drinks: $40-$60

Dress Code
Business casual

Reservations
Recommended

Parking
Valet

Features
Private room/parties, outdoor dining

Credit Cards
AE, VC, MC, DC

The AAA four-diamond Cliff House Dining Room is one of the premier dining experiences in Colorado. Two-time performer at The James Beard House, The Cliff House team of culinarians uses a wealth of local ingredients and cross-cultural techniques to provide a unique Colorado culinary experience. The service is prompt, informative, and discreet. The wine list focuses on "new world" selections, and has recently exceeded 670 selections.

Fruits de mer

The Cliff House dining room

General Manager Paul York in the wine cellar

AWARD WINNER SINCE 2004

Larkspur Restaurant

Private dining room at Lakespur

"The most dynamic restaurant in the area. Each Meal is a dining adventure."
Wine Spectator Magazine

Located at the base of Vail Mountain in the Golden Peak Lodge, Larkspur Restaurant & Bar offers ski-in/ski-out lunch daily and fine dining nightly with valet parking. Larkspur's elegant interior combines high style and intimacy in a warm and inviting atmosphere. The award-winning wine list offers many excellent selections to pair with Chef Thomas Salamunovich's innovative contemporary American cuisine. Visit Larkspur's Market in the winter for take-out gourmet coffees, pastries, sandwiches and rotisserie chickens.

Liberty Duck

Chef/Owner Thomas Salamunovich, Managing Director Adam Baker

AWARD WINNER
SINCE 2004

Apple pie for dessert

Directions

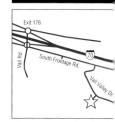

In the Golden Peak Lodge, 2 hrs. from Denver International Airport, and 1 hr. from Eagle-Vail Airport

458 Vail Valley Drive
Vail, CO 81657
PH: (970) 479-8050
FAX: (970) 479-8052
www.larkspurvail.com

Owners
Thomas Salamunovich

Cuisine
Contemporary American

Days Open
Open Mon.-Fri. for lunch, daily for dinner

Pricing
Dinner for one, without tax, tip, or drinks: $40-$60

Dress Code
Business casual

Reservations
Recommended

Parking
On site

Features
Private room/parties, outdoor dining

Credit Cards
AE, VC, MC

Vail • CO

Left Bank Restaurant

The dining room

Owned and operated since 1970 by Chef Luc Meyer and his wife Liz, this landmark restaurant presents consistently fine French/Mediterranean cuisine in surroundings warmed by family antiques and paintings. Specialties include bouillabaisse, Colorado lamb, trout, salmon, elk, and soufflés. The service is prompt and courteous, and the award-winning wine list features vintages from France and California.

Owners Luc and Liz Meyer

Fine art, fine dining

Directions

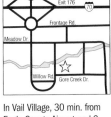

In Vail Village, 30 min. from Eagle County Airport and 2 hrs. from Denver International

183 Gore Creek Drive
Vail, CO 81657
PH: (970) 476-3696
FAX: (970) 476-3723

Owners
Liz and Luc Meyer

Cuisine
French

Days Open
Open daily except Wed.
(closed mid-April through mid-June and Oct. through mid-Nov.)

Pricing
Dinner for one,
without tax, tip, or drinks:
$20-$40

Dress Code
Casual

Reservations
Recommended

Parking
Garage nearby

Features
Private parties, near theater

Credit Cards
None accepted

AWARD WINNER
SINCE 1992

87

Ludwig's

The Sonnenalp Resort of Vail

In Vail Village, 30 min. from Eagle County Airport and 2 hr from Denver International

20 Vail Road
Vail, CO 81657
PH: (970) 476-5656
FAX: (970) 476-1639
www.sonnenalp.com

Owners
Johannes Faessler

Cuisine
International

Days Open
Open daily for dinner

Pricing
Dinner for one,
without tax, tip, or drinks:
$20-$40

Dress Code
Jacket and tie optional

Reservations
Recommended

Parking
Valet

Features
Private room/parties, outdoor dining on terrace

Credit Cards
AE, VC, MC, DC

Located at the Sonnenalp Resort of Vail in the heart of Vail Village, Ludwig's is a gourmet dining experience. The cozy decor, hand-painted ceilings, and terrace overlooking Gore Creek make for truly inviting surroundings. The chef's innovative international cuisine is accompanied by an award-winning wine list. Come dine in a candlelit setting complemented by impeccable Sonnenalp service. Member of The Leading Small Hotels of the World.

Ludwig's Restaurant

Blue Spruce Suite

Terrace dining at Ludwig's

AWARD WINNER
SINCE 1993

Terra Bistro

At the Vail Mountain Lodge & Spa on East Meadow Drive, 1 hr. 45 min. from Denver International Airport

352 East Meadow Drive
Vail, CO 81657
PH: (970) 476-6836
FAX: (970) 476-6451
www.vailmountainlodge.com

Owners
VML, LLC

Cuisine
Contemporary American/fusion

Days Open
Open daily for dinner

Pricing
Dinner for one,
without tax, tip, or drinks:
$20-$40

Dress Code
Casual

Reservations
Recommended

Parking
Garage nearby, valet

Features
Private room/parties, near theater, outdoor dining

Credit Cards
AE, VC, MC, DC, DS

Terra Bistro, located at the Vail Mountain Lodge and Spa, continues to win accolades for its creative and healthy contemporary American cuisine. Executive Chef Kevin Nelson uses organic produce, poultry, and meats in fashioning his diverse menu. Vibrant flavors and innovative combinations from the Far East, Mediterranean, and South American cultures are a few of the trademarks of Terra Bistro that have been incorporated into their health-conscious cuisine. Terra Bistro is a winner of *Wine Spectator's* Award of Excellence.

Main dining room at Terra Bistro

Creative and healthy cuisine

AWARD WINNER
SINCE 1999

Wildflower

The Lodge at Vail

In Vail Village, 30 min. from Eagle County Airport and 2 hrs. from Denver International

174 East Gore Creek Drive
Vail, CO 81657
PH: (970) 476-5011
FAX: (970) 476-7425
www.lodgeatvail.com

Owners
The Lodge at Vail a
Rockresorts Vail Resorts, Inc

Cuisine
Creative American

Days Open
Open daily for dinner

Pricing
Dinner for one,
without tax, tip, or drinks:
$40-$60

Dress Code
Casual

Reservations
Highly recommended

Parking
Valet

Features
Outdoor dining,
entertainment

Credit Cards
AE, VC, MC, DC, DS

Vail's No. 1 restaurant in the *Zagat Survey* and only recipient of Mobil's Four Star Award, Wildflower —at The Lodge at Vail — is an eternal celebration of spring with giant flower arrangements in bloom year round. Executive Chef Brian Kay along with Chef de cuisine Thomas Newstead and Maître d' Bernie McManus serve creative interpretations of contemporary American cuisine, ranging from cornmeal crusted turbot with roasted baby fennel with shaved black truffle in a grain mustard broth, to cream of parsnip and salsify soup with cinnamon oil and toasted almonds.

Gardenlike ambience

Wildflower-filled patio

**AWARD WINNER
SINCE 1993**

Rebeccas

Proprietors Rebecca Kirhoffer and Reza Khorshidi

On Glenville Road, across from the firehouse, 10 min. from Westchester County Airport

265 Glenville Road
Greenwich, CT 06831
PH: (203) 532-9270
FAX: (203) 532-9271

Owners
Rebecca Kirhoffer and Reza Khorshidi

Cuisine
Modern American

Days Open
Open Tues.-Fri. for lunch, Tues.-Sat. for dinner

Pricing
Dinner for one,
without tax, tip, or drinks:
$60-$80

Dress Code
Business casual

Reservations
Recommended

Parking
Free on site

Credit Cards
AE, VC, MC, DC

Tucked away in the backcountry of Greenwich, CT, Rebeccas serves an elegant, modern American menu behind a glass-walled kitchen. "…pay attention to the delectable cooking done by Reza Khorshidi at Rebeccas in Greenwich…whose mix of sharp flavors and brittle textures makes him exemplary of modern American cuisine." – John Mariani. "…the fare from Chef Reza Khorshidi is marked by French technique and simplicity…" – *Food and Wine*. Signature dishes include two soups in one bowl, foie gras dumpling in a black truffle broth, lobster with lemon risotto, and Kobe beef with a red Bordeaux reduction.

The kitchen counter dining seats

The Restaurant

Wine Spectator
AWARD
OF
EXCELLENCE

DiRōNA
AWARD WINNER
SINCE 2003

Cavey's Restaurant

The bar

On East Center Street just off Main Street, 20 min. from Bradley International Airport

Cavey's is actually two restaurants in one building — an elegant French restaurant on the lower level, and a more casual Northern Italian restaurant upstairs, offering jazz piano on weekends. Both are furnished with art and antiques, and in the French restaurant, fabric wall coverings and a profusion of fresh flowers. Both restaurants have earned critical acclaim, including *Wine Spectator*'s Best of Award of Excellence.

Private dining room

Dining room

45 East Center Street
Manchester, CT 06040
PH: (860) 643-2751
FAX: (860) 647-9368

Owners
Steve Cavagnaro

Cuisine
Modern French and Northern Italian

Days Open
Open Mon.-Sat. for dinner

Pricing
Dinner for one, without tax, tip, or drinks: $40-$60

Dress Code
Business casual

Reservations
Recommended

Parking
Free on site

Features
Private rooms/parties, entertainment

Credit Cards
AE, VC, MC

AWARD WINNER
SINCE 1993

Bernard's Inn at Ridgefield

Incomparable French cuisine in an elegant, country inn setting

Talented husband and wife Chef team, Bernard and Sarah Bouissou, have taken this 125-year-old Connecticut landmark and breathed new life into it. The atmosphere is charming and warm, made more so by fireplaces in several of the rooms. The New York Times food critic praised Bernard's food as "excellent and beguiling." Signature dishes include foie gras three ways, and scallops baked in the shell with truffle and leek fondue.

Exquisite food and charming ambience

Bernard and Sarah Bouissou, Chef/Owners

Sea scallops baked in shell with truffle and leek fondue

AWARD WINNER
SINCE 1993

Directions

On West Lane off Main St., 1 hr. from LaGuardia International Airport

20 West Lane
Ridgefield, CT 06877
PH: (203) 438-8282
FAX: (203) 431-3614
www.bernardsridgefield.com

Owners
Bernard and Sarah Bouissou

Cuisine
Contemporary French

Days Open
Open Tues.-Sun. for lunch and dinner, Special Price Fix brunch on Sunday

Pricing
Dinner for one, without tax, tip, or drinks: $40-$60

Dress Code
Business casual

Reservations
Recommended

Parking
Free on site, valet (weekends)

Features
Private room/parties, outdoor dining/wedding gardens

Credit Cards
AE, VC, MC, CB, DC, DS

701 Restaurant

On Pennsylvania Ave. near the U.S. Naval Memorial, 15 min. from Reagan National Airport

7̄01 Restaurant overlooks the cascading fountains of the US Naval Memorial, and features international cuisine in a supper club setting. Tuna tartare is one specialty served by Chef Trent Conry. The interior is divided by a series of fluid curves in materials as rich and eclectic as etched glass held within chrome panels, polished walnut, granite, and layered torn silk paper. Well-spaced tables and comfortable chairs create an atmosphere of intimacy. There is nightly entertainment and a vodka, caviar and champagne lounge tucked behind the piano.

Supper club dining

Live jazz

International Bar

701 Pennsylvania Ave. NW
Washington, DC 20004
PH: (202) 393-0701
FAX: (202) 393-6439
www.701Restaurant.com

Owners
Ashok Bajaj

Cuisine
Modern American

Days Open
Open Mon.-Fri. for lunch and daily for dinner

Pricing
Dinner for one,
without tax, tip, or drinks:
$30-$40

Dress Code
Business casual

Reservations
Recommended

Parking
Complimentary valet

Features
Private room/parties, outdoor dining, live jazz, near theater

Credit Cards
AE, VC, MC, DC

Vodka and caviar bar
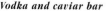

AWARD WINNER
SINCE 1997

1789 Restaurant

Georgetown elegance

Tucked away on one of Georgetown's quiet residential streets, 1789 feels like an elegant country inn. Beyond the curbside valet of the two-story Federal townhouse, the setting is refined yet cozy, with Limoges and crystal-clad tables before a blazing fire. Chef Ris Lacoste's seasonal American menu has charmed critics and connoisseurs alike. Every bit as tempting are the fresh breads and desserts by Pastry Chef Joslyn Bergmann. Dinner specialties include salmon and caviar cocktail, roasted rack of lamb with feta potatoes and merlot sauce, and Nantucket bay scallops.

Fireside dining

Middleburg Room

Chef Ris Lacoste

AWARD WINNER
SINCE 1992

Directions

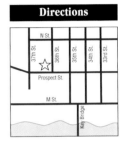

At 36th and Prospect streets in Georgetown, 10 min. from Reagan National Airport

1226 36th Street NW
Washington, DC 20007
PH: (202) 965-1789
FAX: (202) 337-1541
www.1789restaurant.com

Owners
Sally F. Davidson
John G. Laytham

Cuisine
Seasonal American

Days Open
Open daily for dinner

Pricing
Dinner for one,
without tax, tip, or drinks:
$40-$60 (or) Price fix: $30
(pre-theater)

Dress Code
Jacket required

Reservations
Recommended

Parking
Complimentary valet

Features
Private room/parties, near theater

Credit Cards
AE, VC, MC, CB, DC, DS

Bombay Club

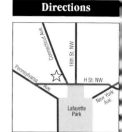

Located on Connecticut Ave. near Farragut Square, across from the White House, 15 min. from Reagan National Airport

Elegant dining

The Bombay Club emulates characteristics of the old clubs of India. The elegant environment with pale pastels, ceiling fans, and a profusion of greenery is designed to create a warm and inviting gathering place for relaxation and regeneration. The cuisine is the finest of India, utilizing only the best quality ingredients to create a harmony of subtle flavors. Specialties, prepared by Executive Chef Ramesh Kaundal, include tandoori salmon and green chili chicken. The sophisticated cuisine is enhanced by refined service and live piano music.

815 Connecticut Ave. NW
Washington, DC 20006
PH: (202) 659-3727
FAX: (202) 659-5012
www.BombayclubDC.com

Owners
Ashok Bajaj

Cuisine
Indian

Days Open
Open Mon.-Fri. for lunch, daily for dinner, Sunday for brunch

Pricing
Dinner for one, without tax, tip or drinks: $30-$40

Dress Code
Business casual

Reservations
Recommended

Parking
Complimentary valet

Features
Outdoor dining, pianist, near theater

Credit Cards
AE, VC, MC, DC

AWARD WINNER
SINCE 1993

1789 Restaurant

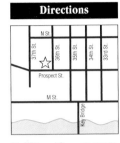

At 36th and Prospect streets in Georgetown, 10 min. from Reagan National Airport

1226 36th Street NW
Washington, DC 20007
PH: (202) 965-1789
FAX: (202) 337-1541
www.1789restaurant.com

Georgetown elegance

Owners
Sally F. Davidson
John G. Laytham

Cuisine
Seasonal American

Days Open
Open daily for dinner

Tucked away on one of Georgetown's quiet residential streets, 1789 feels like an elegant country inn. Beyond the curbside valet of the two-story Federal townhouse, the setting is refined yet cozy, with Limoges and crystal-clad tables before a blazing fire. Chef Ris Lacoste's seasonal American menu has charmed critics and connoisseurs alike. Every bit as tempting are the fresh breads and desserts by Pastry Chef Joslyn Bergmann. Dinner specialties include salmon and caviar cocktail, roasted rack of lamb with feta potatoes and merlot sauce, and Nantucket bay scallops.

Fireside dining

Middleburg Room

Pricing
Dinner for one, without tax, tip, or drinks: $40-$60 (or) Price fix: $30 (pre-theater)

Dress Code
Jacket required

Reservations
Recommended

Parking
Complimentary valet

Features
Private room/parties, near theater

Credit Cards
AE, VC, MC, CB, DC, DS

Chef Ris Lacoste

AWARD WINNER
SINCE 1992

Bombay Club

Elegant dining

The Bombay Club emulates characteristics of the old clubs of India. The elegant environment with pale pastels, ceiling fans, and a profusion of greenery is designed to create a warm and inviting gathering place for relaxation and regeneration. The cuisine is the finest of India, utilizing only the best quality ingredients to create a harmony of subtle flavors. Specialties, prepared by Executive Chef Ramesh Kaundal, include tandoori salmon and green chili chicken. The sophisticated cuisine is enhanced by refined service and live piano music.

Directions

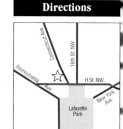

Located on Connecticut Ave. near Farragut Square, across from the White House, 15 min. from Reagan National Airport

815 Connecticut Ave. NW
Washington, DC 20006
PH: (202) 659-3727
FAX: (202) 659-5012
www.BombayclubDC.com

Owners
Ashok Bajaj

Cuisine
Indian

Days Open
Open Mon.-Fri. for lunch, daily for dinner, Sunday for brunch

Pricing
Dinner for one, without tax, tip or drinks: $30-$40

Dress Code
Business casual

Reservations
Recommended

Parking
Complimentary valet

Features
Outdoor dining, pianist, near theater

Credit Cards
AE, VC, MC, DC

AWARD WINNER
SINCE 1993

The Caucus Room

Welcome to The Caucus Room

On 9th Street NW, 15 min.
from Reagan National Airport

401 9th Street NW
Washington, DC
PH: (202) 393-1300
FAX: (202) 393-6066
www.thecaucusroom.com

Owners
Michael Sternberg

Cuisine
American steak and seafood

Days Open
Open Mon.-Fri. for lunch,
Mon.-Sat. for dinner

Pricing
Dinner for one,
without tax, tip, or drinks:
$20-$40

Dress Code
Business casual

Reservations
Recommended

Parking
Valet

Features
Private room/parties

Credit Cards
AE, VC, MC, CB, DC, DS

Enter a place where ambience is defined by cherry wood paneling, gleaming marble, and plush carpeting…where celebrated cuisine delights the senses…where discerning service is teamed with warm hospitality…where democrats and republicans come together after the day's work is done. A stone's throw from the White House and Capitol Hill is The Caucus Room…what critics call "a monument to fine dining" and "a veritable 'who's who' of politics, business, and dining in DC."

The wine cellar

The Lincoln Room

Dine where discerning service is teamed with warm hospitality

AWARD WINNER
SINCE 2004

Galileo

Dining room

Chef Roberto Donna's four-star restaurant, Galileo, features award-winning contemporary and traditional cuisine of his native Piedmont region of northern Italy. In addition to an elegant dining room, Galileo offers guests private dining options in its wine room and private party room. There is also a "chef's table" for up to eight guests in the kitchen and a covered outdoor terrace. Chef Donna's "Laboratorio del Galileo" offers a unique dining experience with its open kitchen and spectacular 10-12 course tasting menu. An award winning wine list complements Galileo's daily changing menu and a selection of over 75 cheeses from around the world is a delicious finale to any meal.

"Laboratorio del Galileo"

**Chef/Owner
Roberto Donna**

AWARD WINNER
SINCE 1992

Private dining in the Wine Room

Directions

On 21st Street NW off
Washington Circle, 20 min.
from Reagan National Airport

1110 21st Street NW
Washington, D.C. 20036
PH: (202) 293-7191
FAX: (202) 331-9364
www.robertodonna.com

Owners
Roberto Donna

Cuisine
Northern Italian

Days Open
Open Mon.-Fri. for lunch and
daily for dinner

Pricing
Dinner for one,
Without tax, tip, or drinks:
$40-$60

Dress Code
Business casual

Reservations
Recommended

Parking
Valet: Mon.-Sat.

Features
Private room/parties, outdoor dining, near theater,
wine events, cooking classes

Credit Cards
AE, VC, MC, DC

Kinkead's, An American Brasserie

Signature seafood entrees

On I Street between 20th and 21st streets, near George Washington Univ., 15 min. from Ronald Reagan International Airport

2000 Pennsylvania Avenue NW
Washington, DC 20006
PH: (202) 296-7700
FAX: (202) 296-7688
www.kinkead.com

Owners
Robert Kinkead

Cuisine
American cuisine, specializing in seafood

Days Open
Open daily for lunch and dinner

Pricing
Dinner for one, without tax, tip, or drinks: $40-$60

Dress Code
Business casual

Reservations
Recommended

Parking
Valet

Features
Private room/parties, entertainment

Credit Cards
AE, VC, MC, DC, DS

This four-star restaurant is led by one of the brightest stars in American cuisine, Chef Bob Kinkead. Its setting is elegance spiced with jazz. Its food is a world of fresh tastes brought together in imaginative creations. The dazzling menu changes daily, with an emphasis always on seafood. Dishes range from spectacular grilled fish selections to unique specialties, such as rare pepper-crusted tuna with grilled portabellas and pepita-crusted salmon with crab, chilies, and a corn relish.

Catalan grilled whole fish

Chef/Owner Bob Kinkead

Downstairs café features live jazz

AWARD WINNER
SINCE 1996

Marcel's

French atmosphere

Directions

On Pennsylvania Avenue, NW, 10 min. from Reagan National Airport

2401 Pennsylvania
Avenue NW
Washington, DC 20037
PH: (202) 296-1166
FAX: (202) 296-6466
www.marcelsdc.com

Owners
Robert Wiedmaier

Cuisine
French Belgian

Days Open
Open daily for dinner

Pricing
Dinner for one,
without tax, tip, or drinks:
$60-$80

Dress Code
Business casual

Reservations
Recommended

Parking
Valet

Features
Private parties, outdoor dining, entertainment, limo service to Kennedy Center

Credit Cards
AE, VC, MC, DC

Acclaimed Chef Robert Wiedmaier opened Marcel's in 1999 to rave reviews of his French cuisine with a Flemish flair, derived from his Belgian heritage. Signature dishes that have Washingtonians, and critics talking are his seared foie gras, flemish osso bucco, and light-as-air Boudin Blanc complemented by his outstanding wine list. Marcel's also offers a pre-theater menu that includes complimentary roundtrip limousine service to the nearby Kennedy Center.

Chef/Owner
Robert Wiedmaier

Boudin Blanc

AWARD WINNER
SINCE 2003

Melrose

Melrose at Park Hyatt Washington

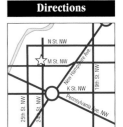

At the Park Hyatt Washington at 24th and M streets, 20 min. from Reagan National Airport

1201 24th Street NW
Washington, DC 20037
PH: (202) 419-6755
FAX: (202) 419-6699
www.parkhyatt.com

Owners
Park Hyatt Washington

Cuisine
New American

Days Open
Open daily for breakfast, lunch, and dinner

Pricing
Dinner for one, without tax, tip, or drinks: $40-$60

Dress Code
Business casual

Reservations
Recommended

Parking
Complimentary valet

Features
Private room/parties, near theater, dinner and dancing on Sat. night

Credit Cards
AE, VC, MC, DS

A culinary destination for over 15 years, Executive Chef Brian McBride continues to astonish guests with his worldwide cuisine. Guests will dine amidst the elegantly understated dining room and sunlit patio, paired with the refined hospitality of his seasoned waitstaff. Museum quality works of notable artists such as Pablo Picasso, Fernand Leger, Joan Miro, and Henri Matisse grace the entrance and walls of Melrose, providing the framework for Chef McBride's own culinary creations. Melrose is a recipient of the AAA Four-Diamond Award.

Elegantly understated dining

Wine Spectator
AWARD OF EXCELLENCE

DiRōNA
AWARD WINNER
SINCE 2001

Michel Richard Citronelle

Dining room and wine cellar

L ocated in the heart of Georgetown, Citronelle features an open, state-of-the-art kitchen, with a wonderful by-the-stove Chef's table. Experience Michel's unique style of French cuisine in an atmosphere that can best be described as magical. Menu selections include eggs Beluga, and Michel's osso bucco, as well as his whimsical signature desserts. A variety of prix fixe menus are offered. The showcase wine cellar is the city's largest and features over 8,000 bottles. See why *Conde Nast* (May 1999) listed Michel Richard Citronelle as "one of the world's 50 most exciting restaurants!"

State-of-the-art kitchen

Owner Michel Richard by the Mood Wall

Beautiful view of Chef's table

AWARD WINNER
SINCE 2001

Directions

At The Latham Hotel on M Street, NW, 20 min. from Reagan National Airport

3000 M Street, NW
Washington, DC 20007
PH: (202) 625-2150
FAX: (202) 339-6326
www.citronelledc.com

Owners
Michel Richard

Cuisine
French

Days Open
Open Mon.-Fri. for lunch, daily for breakfast and dinner

Pricing
Dinner for one, without tax, tip, or drinks: $80+

Dress Code
Jacket required

Reservations
Recommended

Parking
Valet

Features
Private room/parties, Chef's Table, near theater

Credit Cards
AE, VC, MC, DC

Morrison-Clark Historic Inn

Directions

Two blocks from the convention center downtown, 15 min. from Reagan National Airport

1015 L Street NW
Washington, DC 20001
PH: (202) 898-1200
FAX: (202) 289-8576
www.morrisonclark.com

Owners
Classic Hospitality

Cuisine
Global/American

Days Open
Open Mon.-Sat. for dinner

Pricing
Dinner for one,
without tax, tip, or drinks:
$20-$40

Dress Code
Business casual

Reservations
Recommended

Parking
Complimentary valet

Features
Private room/parties,
outdoor dining

Credit Cards
AE, VC, MC, CB, DC, DS

Historic charm

A Victorian mansion dating to Abraham Lincoln's administration, Morrison-Clark is the only Inn in the nation's capital listed on the National Register of Historic Places, and its restaurant is consistently rated among Washington's finest. The main dining room is highlighted by gilded mirrors, Italian marble fireplaces, and lace curtains. The chef's global American cuisine has regional influences, and changes seasonally. During pleasant weather, guests can dine in the lovely courtyard.

AWARD WINNER
SINCE 1994

Nora

Elegant, romantic dining

Photo credit: Koji Hayashi

Restaurant Nora – the country's first certified organic restaurant – combines elegant dining with the finest organic ingredients. Originally a 19th-century carriage house, the main dining room has been artistically transformed to create a warm, romantic atmosphere enjoyed by politicians, celebrities, and diners alike. Nora's eclectic menu, which changes daily, offers healthful dishes that make the most of local seasonal produce, and is accompanied by an extraordinary wine list.

Grilled rosemary marinated New York strip steak with eggplant-red pepper ragout

19th-century carriage house

Chef/Owner Nora Pouillon

AWARD WINNER
SINCE 1994

Directions

Just north of Dupont Circle or the corner of Florida Ave. and R Street, 15 min. from Reaga National Airport

2132 Florida Avenue NW
Washington, DC 20008
PH: (202) 462-5143
FAX: (202) 234-6232
www.noras.com

Owners
Nora Pouillon

Cuisine
New American/Organic

Days Open
Open Mon.-Sat. for dinner

Pricing
Dinner for one,
without tax, tip, or drinks:
$40-$60

Dress Code
Elegant casual

Reservations
Recommended

Parking
Valet

Features
Private room/parties,

Credit Cards
AE, VC, MC,

The Oceanaire Seafood Room

"Vintage supper club dining" at The Oceanaire Seafood Room

Ranked one of the most popular seafood restaurants in Washington, DC, this "cosmopolitan" send-up of a vintage supper club that's styled after a '40's-era luxury ocean liner is appointed with cherry wood and red-leather booths, and infused with a "clubby, old-money" atmosphere. The daily changing menu showcases "intelligently" prepared fish dishes that "recall an earlier time of elegant" dining; what's more, "nothing" is "snobbish here, and the oyster bar is fantastic."

Fresh...at the oyster bar

Chef Rob Klink

Steak-cut Alaskan halibut

AWARD WINNER
SINCE 2004

On F Street NW, 10 min. from Reagan National Airport

1201 F Street NW
Washington, DC 20004
PH: (202) 347-2277
FAX: (202) 347-9858
www.theoceanaire.com

Owners
Hal Hecht and Rob Klink

Cuisine
Seafood

Days Open
Open Mon.-Fri. for lunch, daily for dinner

Pricing
Dinner for one, without tax, tip, or drinks: $20-$40

Dress Code
Business casual

Reservations
Recommended

Parking
Valet

Features
Private room/parties, cigar/cognac events

Credit Cards
AE, VC, MC, CB, DC, DS

The Oval Room

Main dining room

The Oval Room is an elegant and sophisticated restaurant, near Farragut Square across from the White House, which accounts for its popularity among politicians, journalists, lobbyists, lawyers and former Presidents. The setting is contemporary and chic. It offers private dining. Chef Frank Morales' seasonal contemporary American cuisine has charmed critics and connoisseurs alike. Among the favorites are the golden cod cakes and hand harvested sea scallops, with caramelized cauliflower and baby bok choy. *USA Today* said The Oval Room's flower-bedecked patio is one of the best outdoor dining experiences in the United States.

Private dining

Directions

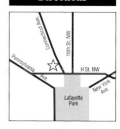

Located on Connecticut Ave. near Farragut Square, across from the White House, 15 min. from Reagan National Airport

800 Connecticut Ave. NW
Washington, DC 20006
PH: (202) 463-8700
FAX: (202) 785-9863
www.ovalroom.com

Owners
Ashok Bajaj

Cuisine
Contempory American

Days Open
Open Mon.-Fri. for lunch,
Mon.-Sat. for dinner

Pricing
Dinner for one,
without tax, tip, or drinks:
$30-$40

Dress Code
Business casual

Reservations
Recommended

Parking
Complimentary valet

Features
Private room/parties, outdoor dining, entertainment, near theater

Credit Cards
AE, VC, MC, DC

AWARD WINNER
SINCE 1999

The Prime Rib

A dramatic setting

In the heart of the Nation's Capital on K Street, between 20th and 21st streets, 15 min. form Reagan National Airport

2020 K Street, NW
Washington, DC 20006
PH: (202) 466-8811
FAX: (202) 466-2010
www.theprimerib.com

Owners
C. Peter Beler

Cuisine
American/Steakhouse

Days Open
Open Mon.-Fri. for lunch, Mon.-Sat. for dinner

Pricing
Dinner for one, without tax, tip, or drinks: $60-$75

Dress Code
Jacket and tie required

Reservations
Recommended

Parking
Valet

Features
Entertainment

Credit Cards
AE, VC, MC, CB, DC

The Prime Rib makes every occasion a special one. Our dramatic setting evokes a 1940's Manhattan supper club, taking you back to a time when dining out was romantic, and civilized. Everything about The Prime Rib– our tuxedoed waitstaff, dress code, our black lacquered walls with Louis Icart lithographs, and live music nightly, is designed to create this feeling of timeless elegance. We feature prime-aged beef, the freshest seafood, and an award-winning wine list.

Timeless elegance

Live music nightly

AWARD WINNER
SINCE 1992

Ristorante i Ricchi

Tuscan dining room

Directions

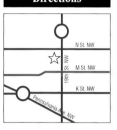

One block south of Dupont Circle on 19th Street, 10 min. from Reagan National Airport

1220 19th Street NW
Washington, DC 20036
PH: (202) 835-0459
FAX: (202) 872-1220
iricchi@aol.com
www.iricchi.net

Owners
Christianne Ricchi

Cuisine
Italian, Tuscan, and regional

Days Open
Open Mon.-Fri. for lunch and Mon.-Sat. for dinner

Pricing
Dinner for one, without tax, tip, or drinks: $40-$60

Dress Code
Business casual

Reservations
Recommended

Parking
Valet

Features
Private room/parties

Credit Cards
AE, VC, MC, CB, DC

Ristorante i Ricchi is designed to resemble a Florentine country villa, with its open kitchen and roaring wood-burning oven as the focal point. Owner and Executive Chef Christianne Ricchi invites you to savor the authentic flavors of Tuscany, from hearty pastas and risottos to succulent Florentine-style steaks and chops, savory grilled fish and fowl, and freshly baked Tuscan-style bread. All this and an award-winning wine list make this restaurant a must-go.

Chef/Owner Christianne Ricchi

Tortelloni

Intimate dining

AWARD WINNER
SINCE 1992

Sam & Harry's

Main dining room

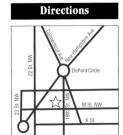

Near Dupont Circle, 15 min. from Reagan National Airport

A classic American steakhouse and a longtime favorite among Washingtonians, Sam & Harry's offers exceptional food, fine wines, great cigars, and personalized service. The menu features prime aged steaks, a veal T-bone, pristinely grilled fish, and fresh Maine lobster, all in generous portions. Colorful jazz paintings, animated jazz sculptures, a visible wine cellar, and intimate private dining rooms create a romantic and clubby atmosphere.

Owners Larry Work and Michael Sternberg

Club-like atmosphere

1200 19th Street NW
Washington, DC 20036
PH: (202) 296-4333
FAX: (202) 785-1070
www.samandharrys.com

Owners
Larry Work and
Michael Sternberg

Cuisine
Classic American
steakhouse

Days Open
Open Mon.-Fri. for lunch,
Mon.-Sat. for dinner

Pricing
Dinner for one,
without tax, tip, or drinks:
$40-$60

Dress Code
Business casual

Reservations
Recommended

Parking
Valet after 5:30 pm

Features
Private rooms/parties

Credit Cards
AE, VC, MC, CB, DC, DS

Classic entrées and an award-winning wine selection

AWARD WINNER
SINCE 1995

Taberna del Alabardero

Rio Frio Room

Located four blocks from the White House on I Street (entrance on 18th Street), 10 min. from Reagan National Airport

1776 I Street, NW
Washington, DC 20006
PH: (202) 429-2200
FAX: (202) 775-3713
www.alabardero.com

Owners
Luis de Lezama

Cuisine
Traditional and contemporary cuisines of Spain

Days Open
Open Mon.-Fri. for lunch and Mon.-Sat. for dinner

Pricing
Dinner for one, without tax, tip, or drinks: $50-$70

Dress Code
Business casual

Reservations
Recommended

Parking
Complimentary garage parking validated next door

Features
Private room/parties, entertainment, near theater

Credit Cards
AE, VC, MC, DC, JCB, DS

Bringing a sophisticated Spanish kitchen to the nation's capital, Taberna del Alabardero offers an abundance of regional specialties. Under Chef Enrique sanchez "Quike", the menu features authentic dishes such as tapas, fried squid, and salted codfish, as well as surprises like a leek terrine with wild mushrooms or hake with roasted peppers. The restaurant regularly plays host to diplomats and dignitaries.

Elegant dining

La Granja Room

AWARD WINNER
SINCE 1999

110

The Willard Room

The Willard InterContinental Hotel

The *Willard Room* is nestled in one of D.C.'s most historic hotels, the Willard InterContinental Washington. Surrounded by rich oak panels, marbled columns, and chandeliers, guests enjoy a wide selection of seasonal dishes designed by the restaurant's chef de cuisine, Denis Soriano, who combines local products with flavors from around the world. The *Willard Room's* star maître d', Francisco Nieto, orchestrates a sublime dining experience for guests. The *Willard Room* is the recipient of the prestigious AAA Four Diamond Award, the Exxon Mobil Four Star Award, and the DiRōNA Award, as well as *Wine Spectator's* Award of Excellence. According to the *Zagat Survey 2003*, "...amid 'stunning' surroundings with 'ornate' appointments, an 'impeccable' service team brings to the table 'marvelous' New American-New French fare, leading legions to avow that it's '*the*' place to 'celebrate' an occasion..."

Chef De Cuisine
Denis Soriano

The Willard Room

Maître d' Francisco Nieto

AWARD WINNER
SINCE 1992

Directions

Located in the historic Willard InterContinental Hotel, 15 min. from Reagan National Airport

Willard InterContinental Hotel
1401 Pennsylvania Avenue NW
Washington, DC 20004
PH: (202) 628-9100
FAX: (202) 637-7326
www.washington.interconti.com

Owners
Willard InterContinental Hotel

Cuisine
French-American

Days Open
Open Mon.-Fri. for breakfast, and lunch, Mon.-Sat. for dinner

Pricing
Dinner for one,
without tax, tip, or drinks:
$40-$60
(or) Price fix: $55 – 3-course,
$85 – 5-course

Dress Code
Business elegant,
jacket preferred

Reservations
Recommended

Parking
Valet, free on site (dinner only)

Features
Pianist on Fri. and Sat. nights, private parties available

Credit Cards
AE, VC, MC, CB, DC, DS

Columbus Inn

Patio dining

Off Interstate 95 in Wilmington
20 min. from Philadelphia
International Airport

The flagship of the 1492 Hospitality Group, the Columbus Inn, housed in a beautiful and historic stone building, serves up a memorable dining experience in Delaware's largest city. Attentive service and a wine list cited for excellence by *Wine Spectator* complement the kitchen's innovative creations, such as calypso spiced grilled free range chicken breast and sautéed jumbo lump crab cake. Cigars, single malt scotches, and fireplaces in each dining room add to the ambience.

Davis Sezna

Gracious hospitality

Private dining room

2216 Pennsylvania Avenue
Wilmington, DE 19806
PH: (302) 571-1492
FAX: (302) 571-1111
www.columbusinn.com

Owners
Davis Sezna, David Peterson
and Joe Van Horn

Cuisine
American regional

Days Open
Open Mon.-Fri. for lunch,
daily for dinner (Sun. for
brunch)

Pricing
Dinner for one,
without tax, tip, or drinks:
$20-$40

Dress Code
Upscale casual

Reservations
Suggested

Parking
Free on site, valet

Features
Private room/parties, outdoor dining, entertainment, near theater, cigar/cognac events

Credit Cards
AE, VC, MC, DC, DS

AWARD WINNER
SINCE 1997

Maison & Jardin

A central Florida favorite since 1958

Oriental rugs, Austrian crystal, and antique, Venetian framed mirrors help create the exquisite atmosphere that is the hallmark of Maison & Jardin. The cuisine is of classical European style but with a distinct American touch. Selections include prime veal, lamb, and aged beef, as well as exotic fresh game and fowl and local seafood, all prepared by Executive Chef Hans Spirig. Maison & Jardin's impressive wine cellar contains over 1,300 different selections from around the world.

Main dining room

Owner William R. Beuret and Executive Chef Hans Spirig

Creative entrées

AWARD WINNER
SINCE 1993

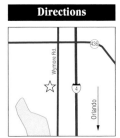
430 South Wymore Road
Altamonte Springs, FL 32714
PH: (407) 862-4410
FAX: (407) 862-5507
www.maison-jardin.com

Owners
William R. Beuret

Cuisine
Contemporary continental

Days Open
Open Tues.-Sat. for dinner

Pricing
Dinner for one, without tax, tip, or drinks: $35-$50

Dress Code
Business casual

Reservations
Preferred

Parking
Free on site

Features
Private room/parties, near theater

Credit Cards
AE, VC, MC, CB, DC

The Grill

The Ritz-Carlton, Amelia Island

With the warmth and charm that typifies Southern hospitality, The Grill welcomes guests with breathtaking panoramic views of the Atlantic Ocean. One of only six AAA Five Diamond restaurants in the state, the staff is renowned for their impeccable and pampering service. Only the freshest seafood, grilled meats and wild game are flown to the island from all over the world. Guests will delight in the international cuisine infused with Southern ingredients along with a selection of over 500 fine wines.

The Grill

*Chef de Cuisine
Scott Crawford*

AWARD WINNER
SINCE 1999

Directions

Located in The Ritz-Carlton, Amelia Island, 25 min. from the Jacksonville International Airport

4750 Amelia Island Parkway
Amelia Island, FL 32034
PH: (904) 277-1100
FAX: (904) 491-6703
www.ritzcarlton.com

Owners
The Ritz-Carlton
Amelia Island

Cuisine
International cuisine with Southern influences

Days Open
Open Tues.-Sat. for dinner,
Sunday for brunch

Pricing
Dinner for one,
without tax, tip, or drinks:
$65+

Dress Code
Jacket required for gentlemen

Reservations
Required

Parking
Valet

Features
Lounge entertainment

Credit Cards
AE, VC, MC, DC, DS

Chef Allen's

Front view of restaurant

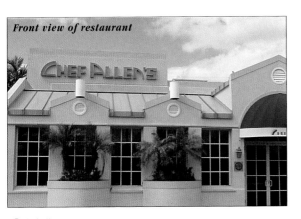

At N.E. 191st Street, 1 block east of Biscayne Blvd., 15 min. from Ft. Lauderdale Hollywood International Airport

19088 N.E. 29th Avenue
Aventura, FL 33180
PH: (305) 935-2900
FAX: (305) 935-9062
www.chefallen.com

Chef Allen's is *Gourmet* magazine's top table in South Florida and *Zagat* reviewers voted Chef Allen's cuisine best in Miami in 2003. Chef Allen's signature tropical Palm tree cuisine blends the flavors of the Caribbean, Latin America, South East Asia and the exotic mediterranean. The most gifted Chef in the region, he specializes in fresh local seafood. Don't miss his mango-macadamia nut and rum soufflé.

Chef Allen Susser

Owners
Allen Susser

Cuisine
Palm tree

Days Open
Open daily for dinner

Pricing
Dinner for one,
without tax, tip or drinks:
$60-$80

Dress Code
Business casual

Reservations
Recommended

Parking
Valet

Features
Private room/parties

Credit Cards
AE, VC, MC, DC

Reception at the bar

Rack of shrimp

AWARD WINNER
SINCE 1992

Arturo's Ristorante Italiano

Celebrating 20 years in
Boca Raton (1983-2003)

Directions

On North Federal Highway,
30 min. from Palm Beach
International Airport and
30 min. north of Fort
Lauderdale International
Airport

A rturo's Ristorante is one of South Florida's most acclaimed dining establishments. The cuisine is authentic Italian, and the display window allows guests to view pastas, breads, and desserts being prepared on the premises. Executive Chef Elisa Gismondi's repertoire ranges from osso buco to lobster Fradiavolo. In addition to the bar and elegantly furnished main dining room, Arturo's has the beautiful Garden Room and the intimate Wine Cellar for small parties.

The Garden Room

The Wine Cellar

AWARD WINNER
SINCE 1999

6750 North Federal Highway
Boca Raton, FL 33487
PH: (561) 997-7373
FAX: (561) 988-7259
www.arturosrestaurant.com

Owners
Vincent and Rosaria
Gismondi

Cuisine
Italian Continental

Days Open
Open Mon.-Fri. for lunch,
daily for dinner

Pricing
Dinner for one,
without tax, tip, or drinks:
$20-$40

Dress Code
Jacket required

Reservations
Recommended

Parking
Valet

Features
Private room/parties,
entertainment, cigar/
cognac events

Credit Cards
AE, VC, MC, CB, DC, DS

116

La Vieille Maison

A romantic table for two

On East Palmetto Park Road, 25 min. from Ft. Lauderdale International Airport

Built in 1928 in Addison Mizner's architectural style, La Vieille Maison features an outdoor courtyard with fountains, and lush tropical foliage set amidst gnarled, live oak trees. A gallery of paintings, art objects, and antiques highlights the French country dining rooms. Voted most romantic in all Palm Beach County publications, and listed #1 for décor, wine, romantic ambience, and service in *Zagat's* survey 2003, while the contemporary Provençal cuisine is rated #2 with 27 points.

Owner/Manager
Leonce Picot

770 East Palmetto Park Road
Boca Raton, FL 33432
PH: (561) 391-6701
FAX: (561) 368-4507

Owners
Leonce and Carolyn Picot

Cuisine
Contemporary French
Provençal

Days Open
Open daily for dinner
(closed Sunday during
summer months)

Pricing
Dinner for one,
without tax, tip or drinks:
$40-$50

Dress Code
Business casual

Reservations
Recommended

Parking
Valet

Features
Private rooms/parties,
outdoor dining

Credit Cards
AE, VC, MC, DC

*Outdoor courtyard
with fountains*

AWARD WINNER
SINCE 1992

Maxwell's Chophouse

Grill Room

Directions

On Palmetto Park Road, 3 min. from Ft. Lauderdale, and West Palm Beach International airports

501 East Palmetto Park Roa Boca Raton, FL 33432
PH: (561) 347-7077
FAX: (561) 347-7079

Owners
Babette Haddad and Melissa Haddad Malaga

Cuisine
American/steakhouse

Days Open
Open Mon.-Fri. for lunch, daily for dinner

Pricing
Dinner for one, without tax, tip or drinks: $40-$60

Dress Code
Business casual

Reservations
Recommended

Parking
Valet

Features
Private room/parties, entertainment, cigar/ cognac events

Credit Cards
AE, VC, MC, DC

Celebrating 10 years as Boca Raton's classic steakhouse, this award winning chophouse continues to be recognized by experts for its extraordinary food and distinguished elegance. Housed in a beautiful landmark building, Maxwell's is filled with old world charm creating a club-type ambience. Chophouse steaks are aged on premises, and grilled to perfection. Patrons enjoy fresh seafood including giant lobster and stone crabs, sinful side dishes like garlic mashed potatoes and creamed spinach, as well as daily specials. A select wine list and homemade desserts make for a memorable meal. The Grill Room with its lively piano bar and lite menu is a favorite late-night spot.

Boca Raton landmark

Co-proprietors
Babette Haddad and
Melissa Haddad Malaga

AWARD WINNER
SINCE 2003

Classic steakhouse fare

118

Christy's Restaurant

Miami's landmark restaurant

For more than 20 years, Christy's has provided South Florida with a consistent base of impeccable food and service. Romantically lit red dining rooms offer a comfortable and intimate atmosphere where guests can enjoy choice selections from the varied menu including enormous aged Chicago steaks, prime rib, duck, and seafood. The restaurant serves its cold and crisp award-winning Caesar salad with every entrée. At Christy's, you will find, time after time, the dining experience is always excellent.

Filet mignon

The Oak Room

AWARD WINNER
SINCE 1996

Directions

Off Miricle Mile on Ponce de Leon Blvd., 15 min. from Miami International Airport

3101 Ponce de Leon Blvd.
Coral Gables, FL 33134
PH: (305) 446-1400
FAX: (305) 446-3257

Owners
Michael Namour

Cuisine
American Steakhouse

Days Open
Open Mon.-Fri. for lunch, daily for dinner

Pricing
Dinner for one, without tax, tip, or drinks: $20-$40

Dress Code
Business casual

Reservations
Recommended

Parking
Free on site

Features
Private room/parties,

Credit Cards
AE, VC, MC, CB, DC, DS

Norman's

Theater Kitchen-Dining Room

Since 1995, Norman's continues to receive numerous awards and accolades for its innovative and distinct menu featuring new-world cuisine. Three beautifully appointed dining rooms, furnished by local artisans, help create an extraordinary dining experience. A dramatic theater kitchen showcases Chef Van Aken and his staff. Signature dishes include pecan crusted Louisiana catfish with a fried green tomato and the Rhum & pepper painted grouper on a mango-habanero mojo. An award-winning wine list and impeccable service contribute to a memorable evening.

Rhum & pepper painted grouper on a mango-habanero mojo

Chef Van Aken

Main dining room

AWARD WINNER
SINCE 1997

Directions

On Almeria Ave. three blocks south of Miracle Mile, 10 min. from Miami International Airport

21 Almeria Avenue
Coral Gables, FL 33134
PH: (305) 446-6767
FAX: (305) 446-7909
www.normans.com

Owners
Norman Van Aken and
Carl Bruggemeier

Cuisine
New World cuisine

Days Open
Open Mon.-Sat. for dinner

Pricing
Dinner for one,
without tax, tip, or drinks:
$55

Dress Code
Business casual

Reservations
Recommended

Parking
Valet, garage nearby

Features
Private room/parties, near theater

Credit Cards
AE, VC, MC, DC

Brooks Restaurant

Your wine is served

On South Federal Highway, 30 min. from Fort Lauderdale-Hollywood International Airport

I n the capable hands of the second generation managing this South Florida landmark, Brooks Restaurant makes either an intimate dinner for two or a lavish party an experience to remember. The dining rooms are adorned with Queen Anne chairs, crisp linens, and soft candlelight, the perfect backdrop for inspired continental American cuisine featuring such standards as individual rack of lamb and sweet soufflés. The imaginative wine list has more than 300 selections.

Main dining room

500 South Federal Highway
Deerfield Beach, FL 33441
PH: (954) 427-9302
FAX: (954) 427-9811
www.brooks-restaurant.com

Owners
Perron, Howe, and Gaudree families

Cuisine
Continental, American

Days Open
Open Tues.-Sun. for dinner

Pricing
Dinner for one,
without tax, tip, or drinks:
$20-$40

Dress Code
Business casual

Reservations
Recommended

Parking
Free on site, valet

Features
Private room/parties

Credit Cards
AE, VC, MC, DC, DS

Intimate dining

AWARD WINNER
SINCE 2001

Dakotah 624

A new American bistro

Dakotah 624, a New American bistro which opened in 1996, is still garnering accolades and drawing record crowds. Under the supervision of Chef/Owner Ron Radabaugh and General Manager Michelle Waterhouse, Dakotah 624 has brought to South Palm Beach County its unique blend of culinary influences from areas as diverse as New Orleans, San Francisco, New England, Florida, and the Caribbean. The result – Gold Coast cuisine, a sensual feast of delicious flavors, and eye-popping presentations. Equally sensational is the award-winning martini bar featuring over 100 martinis and infusions.

Chef/Owner Ron Radabaugh

Gold Coast cuisine

Owners Ron and Renee Radabaugh

AWARD WINNER
SINCE 2002

Directions

On East Atlantic Avenue, 20 min. from West Palm Beach International Airport

270 East Atlantic Avenue
Delray Beach, FL 33444
PH: (561) 274-6244
FAX: (561) 274-8189
www.dakotah624.com

Owners
Ron and Renee Radabaugh

Cuisine
New American bistro

Days Open
Open Mon.-Sat. for dinner, Sun. for dinner Nov.-May

Pricing
Dinner for one, without tax, tip, or drinks: $20-$40

Dress Code
Business casual

Reservations
Recommended

Parking
Valet, parking available

Features
Private room/parties, outdoor dining, entertainment, near theater, cigar/cognac events, off premise catrering

Credit Cards
AE, VC, MC, CB, DC, DS

Beach Walk Café

Beach Walk Café dining room

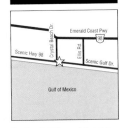

On the 1st floor of the Inn at Crystal Beach, 20 min. Fort Walton Beach Airport

2996 Scenic Highway 98 East
Destin, FL 32541
PH: (850) 650-7100
FAX: (850) 650-7051
www.beachwalkcafe.com

Owners
Tim Creehan

Cuisine
Gulf Coast, with French, Italian and Asian flavors

Days Open
Open daily for lunch and dinner

Pricing
Dinner for one, without tax, tip, or drinks: $35-$45

Dress Code
Casual/Business casual

Reservations
Recommended

Parking
Free on site, valet

Features
Private room/parties, outdoor dining

Credit Cards
AE, VC, MC, DS

Destin's only fine-dining restaurant on the Gulf of Mexico…Beach Walk Café, a *Florida Trend* "Top 25 Restaurant", is ideal for intimate beachfront dining or power lunches. Amy Grant, Vince Gill, Timothy Hutton, and Cybill Sheperd, to name a few, have enjoyed Chef Creehan's exceptional cuisine. "We're not just another place to eat; we're a family business, totally committed to the wishes of our guests," explains Chef/Owner Tim Creehan. Simply put…Creehan is "one of Florida's emerging culinary talent." – Robert Tolf for *Bon Appétit*.

Chef/Owner Tim Creehan
Credit: Cooking Light

Thai Chicken salad

Beachfront dining

DiRoNA
AWARD WINNER
SINCE 2004

Elephant Walk

At the Sandestin Golf and Beach Resort, 20 min. from Ft. Walton Beach Airport

9300 Highway 98 West
Destin, FL 32550
PH: (850) 267-4800
FAX: (850) 267-6121
www.sandestin.com

Owners
Sandestin/IntraWest

Cuisine
Florida influenced continental cuisine

Days Open
Open daily for dinner, seasonally for lunch

Pricing
Dinner for one, without tax, tip, or drinks: $20-$40

Dress Code
Resort casual

Reservations
Recommended

Parking
Free on site

Features
Entertainment, outdoor dining

Credit Cards
AE, VC, MC, DC

Elephant Walk Restaurant, Sandestin's award-winning dining experience overlooking the sugar-white sand and emerald waters of the Gulf of Mexico, features fresh local seafood and creative coastal contemporary cuisine. Guests can choose to enjoy their meal al fresco, from the Elephant Walk patio, overlooking the dunes with intoxicating views of the Gulf of Mexico. In the evening, cocktails are served in the upstairs lounge, which features breathtaking sunsets.Elephant Walk Restaurant has earned four consecutive DiRōNA Awards.

Elephant Walk Restaurant

AWARD WINNER
SINCE 1998

Seagar's

The Dining Room at Seagar's

Directions

In the Hilton at the Sandestin Golf and Beach Resort, 20 min. from Ft. Walton Beach Airport

4000 Sandestin Blvd. South
Destin, FL 32550
PH: (850) 622-1500
FAX: (850) 267-2935
www.sandestinbeachhilton.com

Owners
Sandcastles, Inc.

Cuisine
Steakhouse and seafood

Days Open
Open daily for dinner

Pricing
Dinner for one,
without tax, tip, or drinks:
$40-$60

Dress Code
Slacks and collared shirts

Reservations
Recommended

Parking
Free on site

Features
Private rooms/parties, entertainment, cigar/cognac events, extensive wine list & captian service

Credit Cards
AE, VC, MC, CB, DC, DS

For an extraordinary dining experience, indulge at Seagar's Prime Steaks & Seafood. Seagar's, located at the Hilton Sandestin Beach offers the finest of aged beef, fresh seafood, and tableside preparations found anywhere as well as over 500 wines to choose from. In the style of fine New York steakhouses, Seagar's is classically furnished in mahogany and brass, with rich carpeting accenting the hard wood floors and lighted sconces along the walls that add finish to the ambience.

Executive Chef Bruce McAdoo

The Lounge

The Wine Room

AWARD WINNER
SINCE 2004

The Black Pearl

Best celebration restaurant

On Main Street, two blocks east of the dunedin marina, 35 min. from Tampa International Airport

The Black Pearl offers a total dining experience: intimate setting, professional service, and the finest New American cuisine. This combination has led to numerous accolades, including: Top 20 New Florida Restaurants, *Florida Trend magazine*, 1998; one of Tampa Bay's Top Ten Restaurants 1998, *Tampa Tribune*; Best Upscale Restaurant/1998, Best Chef/1999, and Best Restaurant to Celebrate a Special Occasion/1999, 2000, *Tampa Bay* magazine. Oven-steamed Prince Edward Island mussels with coconut milk, red Thai curry and lime, and veal paillards with vanilla bean and mushroom sauce are house specialties.

A twist on our Cedar Planked Salmon

Award-winning entrées

315 Main Street
Dunedin, FL 34698
PH: (727) 734-3463 (DINE)
FAX: (727) 771-8086

Owners
Kathleen La Roche

Cuisine
New American

Days Open
Open daily for dinner

Pricing
Dinner for one,
without tax, tip, or drinks:
$20-$40

Dress Code
Business casual

Reservations
Recommended

Parking
Free on site

Features
Private parties

Credit Cards
AE, VC, MC, CB, DC, DS

Art deco dining intimacy

AWARD WINNER
SINCE 2001

Eduardo de San Angel

Eduardo de San Angel–Ft. Lauderdale

On Commercial Blvd. near Bayview Drive, 15 min. from Ft. Lauderdale International Airport

2822 East Commercial Blvd.
Ft. Lauderdale, FL 33308
PH: (954) 772-4731
FAX: (954) 772-0794

Owners
Eduardo Pria

Cuisine
Mexican infused international cuisine

Days Open
Open Mon.-Sat. for dinner

Pricing
Dinner for one, without tax, tip or drinks:
$40-$60

Dress Code
Business casual

Reservations
Recommended

Parking
Free on site

Features
Private room

Credit Cards
AE, VC, MC, CB, DC, DS

In some schools of thought, conventional wisdom will lend itself to Mexican food being tacos and burritos, with chips and salsa on the tables. Eduardo de San Angel defies conventional wisdom and brings Mexican food to a higher and more refined level. Chef/Owner Eduardo Pria and his unique blend of true-to-form traditional Mexican sauces and meticulous preparation of the freshest foods available have won many awards. Eduardo de San Angel is a destination restaurant for sophisticated diners from all over the globe.

Chef/Owner Eduardo Pria

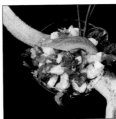

Chef Pria's Margarita De Camarones

Cozy dining rooms fashioned after a small hacienda

AWARD WINNER
SINCE 1998

127

Jackson's Steakhouse

Upscale dining at its finest

On East Las Olas Blvd., 12 min. from Ft. Lauderdale International Airport

Succulent USDA Prime steaks and chops, fresh seafood, including live Maine lobster, and made-to-order dessert soufflés help to make Jackson's Steakhouse a premier South Florida restaurant. Located on exciting Las Olas Boulevard, Jackson's has earned a reputation for warm, caring, professional service... "professionals serving professionals." The ambience is understated elegance, exquisite mahogany millwork, dramatic lighting, rich fabrics and warm live jazz. World class cigar area's to enjoy a great cigar and stunning non-smoking dining rooms for those not inclined. The food, the ambience, and the location make the Jackson's Steakhouse experience... "upscale dining at its best".

Main dining room

Understated elegance

450 East Las Olas Boulevard
Ft. Lauderdale, FL 33301
PH: (954) 522-4450
FAX: (954) 522-1911

Owner
Jack Jackson

Cuisine
Sophisticated American

Days Open
Open daily for dinner

Pricing
Dinner for one, without tax, tip, or drinks: $20-$40

Dress Code
Business casual

Reservations
Recommended

Parking
Valet

Features
Private room/parties, entertainment, near theater, cigar/cognac events

Credit Cards
AE, VC, MC, CB, DC, DS

AWARD WINNER
SINCE 2002

Atlantic's Edge at Cheeca Lodge & Spa

Beautiful views of the ocean at Atlantic's Edge

"Florida Keys" cuisine at its finest is served in Atlantic's Edge, Cheeca's newly renovated gourmet restaurant. Sweeping views of the Atlantic Ocean inspire your appetite for the best, fresh, local seafood in South Florida. Regionally inspired soups, fresh salads, and tantalizing, award-winning desserts complete the menu. Dine in relaxed, elegant privacy in the newly-opened, eight-seat "Redbone Room." Specialties include hearts of palm salad, Florida lobster, and crispy snapper.

Excutive Chef Andy Niedenthal

Chilled fresh hearts of palm salad with yellow tomato sorbet

Cheeca Lodge & Spa

AWARD WINNER SINCE 1993

Directions

Located on Matecumbe Key, on the Atlantic Ocean side at mile marker 82, 1 hr. 30 min. from Miami International Airport

Mile Marker 82 US Highway 1
Islamadora, FL 33026
PH: (305) 664-4651 (or)
(800) 327-2888
FAX: (305) 664-2083
www.cheeca.com

Owners
Vail Resorts

Cuisine
Contemporary American

Days Open
Open daily for dinner.
Sunday for brunch (seasonal)

Pricing
Dinner for one,
without tax, tip or drinks:
$20-$40

Dress Code
Casual

Reservations
Recommended

Parking
Complimentary valet

Features
Private room/parties, out-door dining, entertainment

Credit Cards
AE, VC, MC, CB, DC

Bistro AIX

On San Marco Blvd. near Phillips, 20 min. from Jacksonville International Airport

At Bistro AIX the food world comes together, combining the down-to-earth culinary styles of France, Italy, Spain, and Greece, sprinkled with a fascinating California seasoning. One of Jacksonville's top 25 restaurants, the menu features house-smoked salmon, steak frites, wood-fired pizzas, seafood, and risotto. The award-winning interior includes an open kitchen and a chef's bar, bringing warmth and aromas into the dining room. Bistro AIX features an extensive list of wines by the glass.

Grilled salmon over french green lentils, pancetta, portobello, and sweet corn "succotash"

Bistro AIX partners Scott and Ann Riley, Chef Tom Gray, Terry and Mike Schneider

1440 San Marco Boulevard
Jacksonville, FL 32207
PH: (904) 398-1949
FAX: (904) 398-9386
www.bistroX.com

Owners
AIX Restaurants Inc.

Cuisine
Seasonal Mediterranean and French

Days Open
Open Mon.-Fri. for lunch, daily for dinner

Pricing
Dinner for one, without tax, tip or drinks: $20-$40

Dress Code
Business casual

Reservations
None accepted

Parking
Free on site

Features
Private room/parties, catering, outdoor dining, near theater

Credit Cards
AE, VC, MC, CB, DC, DS

AWARD WINNER
SINCE 2004

Sterling's of Avondale

Florida's award-winning, Sterling's of Avondale

Located in historic Avondale on St. Johns Ave., 20 min. from Jacksonville Int'l Airport

3551 St. Johns Ave.
Jacksonville, FL 32205
PH: (904) 387-0700
www.sterlingsofavondale.com

Owners
Frank Gallo Jr.

Cuisine
Continental

Days Open
Open Mon.-Sat. for lunch,
Mon.-Sun. for dinner,
Sunday for brunch

Pricing
Dinner for one,
without tax, tip, or drinks:
$20-$40

Dress Code
Business casual

Reservations
Recommended

Parking
Free on site

Features
Private room/parties,
outdoor dining

Credit Cards
AE, VC, MC, DS

Sterling's of Avondale has been selected as one of Florida's 20 best restaurants for the past three years, winning *Florida Trend's*, Golden Spoon Award for 2000, 2001, 2002 and 2003. Featuring the finest steaks, fresh seafood, lamb, and veal specials, a bar that offers top shelf labels, and an extensive wine list. Located in historic Avondale, just minutes from downtown. Two private dining rooms are available for private events.

STERLINGS
of Avondale

AWARD WINNER
SINCE 2001

Giovanni's

Private Chef's Tasting Table in Wine Room

On Beach Blvd., 30 min. from Jacksonville International Airport

Opened in 1972 by husband and wife team, Giovanni and Nella Acireale, Giovanni's has maintained a reputation for consistent, personalized service, and fine food. Giovanni's serves innovative, multi-continental cuisine with an Italian flair, complemented by an extensive wine list that received the *Wine Spectator* Award of Excellence. The restaurant features a private room with a Chef's Tasting Table for fabulous gourmet fare created by Executive Chef Toni Acireale. The atmosphere is further enhanced by nightly piano tunes trickling down from the upstairs piano bar.

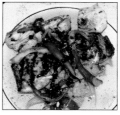

Grilled Mahi over mashed sweet potatoes

Artwork by Mora adorns the interior

1161 Beach Blvd.
Jacksonville Beach, FL 32250
PH: (904) 249-7787
FAX: (904) 249-1334
www.giovannirestaruant.com

Owners
Giovanni, Nella and Toni Acireale

Cuisine
Innovative multi-continental with an Italian flair

Days Open
Open Mon.-Sat. for dinner

Pricing
Dinner for one,
without tax, tip, or drinks:
$40-$60

Dress Code
Business casual

Reservations
Recommended

Parking
Valet

Features
Private room/parties, entertainment

Credit Cards
AE, VC, MC

Ostrich with buffalo mozzarella salad

AWARD WINNER
SINCE 2004

Alice's at La te da

Chef Alice Weingarten visiting with guests

In La te da Guest House on famous Duval Street, 8 min. from Key West International Airport

James Beard, Fodor, and *Zagat* recognized Chef Alice Weingarten's philosophy that food should be, among other things, comforting. Her cuisine bespeaks her other beliefs: food should be delicious, beautiful, and composed of a variety of flavors and textures. *Bon Appetit* described a "New World Fusion Confusion" of whimsical Asian, Mediterranean, and Caribbean creations, with her aunt's meatloaf thrown in for good measure. Alice's at La te da offers relaxed, tropical, poolside dining on two outdoor levels.

Chef Alice's award-winning pure passion salad

Chef Alice Weingarten

1125 Duval Street
Key West, FL 33040
PH: (305) 296-6706, ext. 39
FAX: (305) 292-2692
www.Aliceskeywest.com

Owners
Chef Alice Weingarten and Bart Hofford

Cuisine
New World Fusion Confusion

Days Open
Open Tues.–Sat. for breakfast and lunch, daily for dinner. Sunday for brunch

Pricing
Dinner for one, without tax, tip or drinks: $20-$40

Dress Code
Casual

Reservations
Recommended

Parking
Local street parking

Features
Private parties, outdoor dining, entertainment

Credit Cards
AE, VC, MC, DS

Chef Alice's tuna tempura roll- a Key West addiction!

AWARD WINNER
SINCE 2004

Square One Restaurant

Main dining room

Square One Restaurant is a Key West favorite that features a classic baby grand piano by the door and candlelit tables set with stemware on white linens. The cuisine, created by Executive Chef Matthew Cox, is New American classic with Caribbean influences. The menu changes with the chef's creativity and the availability of fresh products. Entrées include Long Island duck, grilled New Zealand rack of lamb, and Angus filet of beef.

Sea scallops

Courtyard dining

AWARD WINNER
SINCE 1996

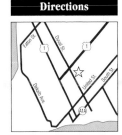

At Duval Square, 10 min. from Key West Airport

1075 Duval Street, C12
Duval Square
Key West, FL 33040
PH: (305) 296-4300
FAX: (305) 292-5039
www.squareonerestaurant.com

Owners
Michael Stewart

Cuisine
New American

Days Open
Open daily for dinner

Pricing
Dinner for one,
without tax, tip, or drinks:
$20-$40

Dress Code
Casual

Reservations
Recommended

Parking
Free on site

Features
Private parties, outdoor dining, entertainment

Credit Cards
AE, VC, MC, CB, DC, DS

Ristorante Paradiso

"La Citta Ideale"...Ristorante Paradiso

On Lucerne Avenue in Lake Worth, 10 min. from West Palm Beach International Airport

Paradiso serves regional Italian cuisine that is reminiscent of the Amalfi Coast. Enter through a classic Italian café with an array of homemade desserts, and gelato by pastry chef Leonardo Cuomo. Calamari alla griglia con insalate di carciofi, risotto Veneziana con balsamico al tartufo, dentice con scarola, are featured on the 2003 menu by Chef/Owner Angelo Romano. An impressive mural of "La Citta Ideale" adds to the undeniable charm of Paradiso's main dining room.

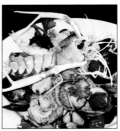

Risotto Frutti Di Mare

625 Lucerne Avenue
Lake Worth, FL 33460
PH: (561) 547-2500
FAX: (561) 547-9235
www.paradisolakeworth.com

Owners
Angelo Romano and Antonio Tasca

Cuisine
Regional Italian

Days Open
Open daily for lunch and dinner

Pricing
Dinner for one, without tax, tip or drinks: $40-$60

Dress Code
Business casual

Reservations
Recommended

Parking
Valet, free on site

Features
Private room/parties, outdoor dining

Credit Cards
AE, VC, MC, DC, DS

Chef/Owner
Angelo Romano

AWARD WINNER
SINCE 2004

The Colony Dining Room

Colony Dining Room

Nestled on a pristine Gulf of Mexico beach, The Colony Dining Room is the centerpiece of the world famous Colony Beach & Tennis Resort. For over 30 years, The Colony has set the standard for fine dining in Sarasota, and continues to delight guests with superb contemporary Continental cuisine, fabulous water views and one of this nation's most famous wine lists. An international staff provides impeccable service including traditional tableside presentations.

Maine lobster, vanilla-roasted vegetables with ginger lemongrass cream

Seared tuna with tomato-coconut salsa

Chairman Dr. Murray "Murf" Klauber and President & GM Katherine Klauber Moulton

AWARD WINNER
SINCE 1992

Directions

At The Colony Beach & Tennis Resort, 15 min. from Sarasota-Bradenton International Airport

1620 Gulf of Mexico Drive
Longboat Key, FL 34228
PH: (941) 383-5558
FAX: (941) 387-0250
www.colonybeachresort.com

Owners
Dr. Murf Klauber

Cuisine
Regional continental

Days Open
Open daily for breakfast, lunch, and dinner

Pricing
Dinner for one,
without tax, tip, or drinks:
$40-$60

Dress Code
Business casual

Reservations
Recommended

Parking
Valet

Features
Private room/parties, outdoor dining, entertainment, cigar/cognac events

Credit Cards
AE, VC, MC, CB, DC, DS

136

Euphemia Haye

The Hayeloft Lounge

On the northern end of Longboat Key, 30 min. from Sarasota-Bradenton International Airport

Euphemia Haye's menu is as inspired and eclectic as the art, antiques, and music that adorn this award-winning restaurant. Since 1980, Executive Chef/Owner Raymond Arpke has turned out consistently extraordinary cuisine—roast duck, flambéed prime peppered steak, fresh seafood, and classic Caesar salad. A comprehensive wine list complements this varied menu. Complete your dining in the Hayeloft, an upstairs lounge and dessert room serving top shelf sprits, dessert wines and vintage ports, with live music nightly.

Main dining room

The owners, Chef Raymond and D'Arcy Arpke

Dessert selection

5540 Gulf of Mexico Drive
Longboat Key, FL 34228
PH: (941) 383-3633
FAX: (941) 387-8336
www.euphemiahaye.com

Owners
Raymond and D'Arcy Arpke

Cuisine
Global eclectic

Days Open
Open daily for dinner

Pricing
Dinner for one,
without tax, tip, or drinks:
$40-$60

Dress Code
Sporty-chic

Reservations
Recommended

Parking
Free on site

Features
Lounge and dessert room,
lesson luncheons, live music

Credit Cards
VC, MC, CB, DC, DS

AWARD WINNER
SINCE 1994

blue door at Delano

Delano's Blue Door

On Collins Avenue, 30 min. from Miami International Airport

1685 Collins Avenue
Miami Beach, FL 33139
PH: (305) 674-6400
FAX: (305) 674-5649
www.opentable.com

Owners
Ian Schrager and Jeffrey Chodorow

Cuisine
French with a tropical accent

Days Open
Open daily for breakfast, lunch, and dinner

Pricing
Dinner for one, without tax, tip, or drinks: $60-$80
(or)
Claude Troisgros' tasting menu at $79.00

Dress Code
Elegant, business casual

Reservations
Required

Parking
Valet, garage nearby

Features
Private parties, outdoor dining, near theater, wine dinners

Credit Cards
AE, VC, MC, DC, DS

Blue Door is Miami's finest dining destination featuring a chic, all-white theme designed by Philippe Starck. World-renowned Chef Claude Troisgros' French technique and tropical ingredients are evident in his signature dishes including Loup Cajou, a sea bass in brown sauce with cashew nuts. For dessert, enjoy Crêpe Passion, a passionfruit soufflé. Blue Door has been awarded an "Exceptional Rating" by the *Miami Herald,* "Best New Restaurant of the Year" by *Esquire Magazine,* and many "Top…." accolades from *Zagat's.*

Big Ravioli

*Blue Door
Brasserie area*

Crabavocat

AWARD WINNER
SINCE 2003

The Forge Restaurant

The Forge Restaurant

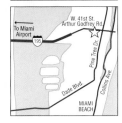

On Arthur Godfrey Road off 195 east, 20 min. from Miami International Airport

The Forge Restaurant is home to the #1 steak in America, and one of the world's finest wine cellars as recognized by Wine Spectator. In addition to the five dramatically elegant dining rooms, the famed Wine Cellar contains more than 300,000 vintages in an eight-room cellar beneath the restaurant, and the Forge Bar is the epicenter of activity, a natural destination for people-watching. Classics that comprise American steak-house cuisine – slow-grilled, dry-aged steaks, the freshest seafood, and the definitive Caesar salad – star next to creative pasta dishes and inspired Mediterranean specials.

432 Arthur Godfrey Road
Miami Beach, FL 33140
PH: (305) 538-8533
FAX: (305) 538-7733
www.theforge.com

Owners
Shareef Malnik

Cuisine
French Steakhouse

Days Open
Open daily for dinner

Pricing
Dinner for one,
without tax, tip or drinks:
$60-$80

Dress Code
Business casual

Reservations
Recommended

Parking
Valet

Features
Private room/parties, out-door dining, entertainment, cigar/cognac events

Credit Cards
AE, VC, MC

Owner
Shareef Malnik

Super steak

Wine Cellar

AWARD WINNER
SINCE 1992

Smith & Wollensky

Smith & Wollensky, Miami Beach

This magnificent waterfront location in South Beach offers unparalleled vistas of the Atlantic Ocean, and the downtown Miami skyline. An endless parade of ships pass through the Government Cut shipping channel just outside the restaurant's huge picture windows. The restaurant seats up to 600; 450 on two floors, plus 100 in the Grill, and 70 in Mrs. Wollensky's Cigar Bar. Private dining rooms are available for groups of 20 to 130, and the outdoor waterfront Raw Bar can be used for cocktail parties and dinner for up to 60.

Magnificent waterfront dining

The Raw Bar

AWARD WINNER
SINCE 2003

Directions

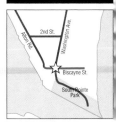

On Washington Avenue at South Pointe Park, 30 min. from Miami Int'l Airport

One Washington Avenue
Miami Beach, FL 33139
PH: (305) 673-2800
FAX: (305) 673-5943
www.smithandwollensky.com

Owners
Smith & Wollensky
Restaurant Group

Cuisine
American, steakhouse

Days Open
Open daily for lunch, and dinner, Sunday for brunch

Pricing
Dinner for one,
without tax, tip or drinks:
$40-$60

Dress Code
Business casual

Reservations
Recommended

Parking
Valet

Features
Private room/parties,
outdoor dining

Credit Cards
AE, VC, MC

Tantra Restaurant and Lounge

Tantra—experience the senses

Everything from the softly-lit marble water wall, to the fresh-cut grass beneath your feet, the sleek ultra-suede banquettes, the frolic-friendly cargo net in the infamous VIP room, the pressed copper and mahogany bars, the steamy DJ booth where sensual tunes spin till dawn, the Egyptian hookah pipes with flavored tobacco, and the authentic tantric sculptures, has been designed to awaken each of your five senses. The food also dazzles, reflecting both owner Tim Hogle's dedication to aphrodisiac cuisine and Chef Michael Bloise's own signature culinary style, featuring a creative blend of flavors from the Orient, Europe, and the Caribbean.

Grilled filet mignon with Cuban coffee sauce

The Tantra Love Apple

AWARD WINNER SINCE 2003

Directions

On Pennsylvania Avenue, near Espanola Way, 15 min. from Miami International Airport

1445 Pennsylvania Avenue
Miami Beach, FL 33139
PH: (305) 672-4765
FAX: (305) 672-2084
www.tantrarestaurant.com

Owners
Tim Hogle and
Irina Korneeva

Cuisine
Aphrodesiac/Mediterranean and Caribbean influences

Days Open
Open daily for dinner

Pricing
Dinner for one,
without tax, tip or drinks:
$60-$80

Dress Code
Business casual

Reservations
Recommended

Parking
Valet, garage nearby

Features
Private room/parties, out-door dining, entertainment, near theater, cigar/cognac events

Credit Cards
AE, VC, MC

Chardonnay Restaurant

Located on Tamiami Trail North, 30 min. from Ft. Myers International Airport

2331 Tamiami Trail North
Naples, FL 34103
PH: (239) 261-1744
FAX: (239) 261-4587
www.chardonnayrestaurant.com

Owners
Rene Nicolas and Jean Claude Martin

Cuisine
French

Days Open
Open Mon.-Sat. for dinner (daily for dinner in season; closed in August)

Pricing
Dinner for one, without tax, tip or drinks: $20-$40

Dress Code
Business casual

Reservations
Recommended

Parking
Valet, free on site

Features
Private room/parties

Credit Cards
AE, VC, MC, DC

The Chardonnay Restaurant proudly serves the finest French cuisine set in a Victorian setting overlooking a pond with lovely waterfalls. Exquisite European service, an award-winning wine list, and casual elegance make Chardonnay the one and only choice in Naples for a unique dining experience. Our award-winning chefs prepare a variety of dishes including Dover sole, Florida pompano, veal sweetbreads, and such simple items as the finest filet mignon, and sirloin steaks.

Chardonnay Restaurant
...Champagne Room

Wine Spectator
AWARD OF EXCELLENCE

DiRoNA
AWARD WINNER
SINCE 2004

The Dining Room

Grand Floridan design

Located in The Ritz-Carlton on Vanderbilt Beach Rd., 10 min. from Naples Airport, and 35 min. from Ft. Myers Int'l Airport.

280 Vanderbilt Beach Road
Naples, FL 34108
PH: (239) 598-3300
FAX: (239) 598-6690
www.ritzcarlton.com

The only AAA Five Diamond restaurant in southwest Florida, our signature restaurant, and the centerpiece of our culinary offerings, The Dining Room serves French cuisine with a regional accent. Artfully prepared delicacies are complemented by the finest vintages from our wine cellar, and served in surroundings overlooking our tropical gardens. For a more exclusive dinner for up to 20 guests, our separate Private Dining Room allows guests to create, with our chef, a customized menu reflective of their personal tastes.

Carpaccio of scallop

Chef Arnaud Berthelier

Owners
The Ritz-Carlton, Naples

Cuisine
French cuisine with regional accent

Days Open
Open Tues.-Sat. for dinner, Sunday for brunch

Pricing
Dinner for one, without tax, tip, or drinks: $60-$80

Dress Code
Jacket required, tie optional

Reservations
Required

Parking
Valet

Features
Private parties, entertainment

Credit Cards
AE, VC, MC

AWARD WINNER
SINCE 1997

Lafite

Main dining room

L afite, at the Registry Resort in Naples, is southwest Florida's most exclusive restaurant and is rapidly gaining national acclaim for its superb continental cuisine and outstanding international wines. Savor the special creations of Chef de Cuisine Virgile Brandel amid the delicious aromas and elegant decor of the intimate dining areas. Entrées include pomegranate laquered pouisson, and burgundy marinated loin of venison.

Duet of turbot and John Dory with kumquat butter

Chef de Cuisine Virgile Brandel

AWARD WINNER
SINCE 1992

An experience to remember

Directions

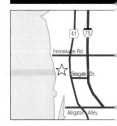

At the Registry Resort, 10 min. from Naples Airport

475 Seagate Drive
Naples, FL 34103
PH: (239) 597-3232
FAX: (239) 597-7168
www.registryresort.com

Owners
Boca Resorts Inc.

Cuisine
French-American

Days Open
Open daily for dinner

Pricing
Dinner for one,
without tax, tip, or drinks:
$60-$80

Dress Code
Jacket required

Reservations
Required

Parking
Valet

Features
Private room/parties,
harpist, near theater

Credit Cards
AE, VC, MC, CB, DC, ER, JCB, DS

144

Marie-Michelle's Restaurant On The Bay

Owner Marie-Michelle Rey

Directions

On Gulf Shore Boulevard North, in Venetian Village, 10 min. from Naples and 30 min. from Ft. Myers Airports

4236 Gulf Shore Boulevard N.
Naples, FL 34103
PH: (239) 263-0900
FAX: (239) 263-0850
www.mariemichelle.com

Owners
MarieMichelle Rey

Cuisine
French

Days Open
Open daily for lunch and dinner (closed Sundays in the off season)

Pricing
Dinner for one, without tax, tip, or drinks: $20-$40

Dress Code
Business casual

Reservations
Recommended

Parking
Valet

Features
Outdoor dining, entertainment, near theater

Credit Cards
AE, VC, MC

With her spectacular open terrace on the water of Venetian Bay Marie-Michelle brings a little corner of the French Riviera to the heart of Naples. The restaurant offers a rare combination of stunning views and superb cuisine. During lunch you may see playful dolphins jumping for joy. At dinner you will be surrounded by the twinkling stars. Executive Chef Kyle creates a cuisine that will delight your eyes as much as your palette. There's nothing quite like it! What a wonderful surprise! Please visit our website at www.mariemichelle.com

AWARD WINNER
SINCE 1999

Le Mistral

Main dining room

On US Highway One, 15 min. from West Palm Beach and 1 hr. and 30 min. from Miami international airport

L e Mistral Restaurant is a jewel of French culinary delights. The dining room, dressed in white and blue Provençal fabric, is reminiscent of dining in Provence. The friendly and knowledgeable staff makes you feel right at home. Chef/Owner Christian Depond serves classic French Provençal cuisine including his award-winning Bouillabaisse and fish soup, Dover sole meuniere, lamb filet, and veal medallions with morel mushroom sauce. Enjoy the homemade desserts as a prefect ending to a "slice of life" in southern France.

Chef/Owner Christian Depond

Veal filet with Morel mushroom sauce

12189 US Highway One
North Palm Beach, FL 3340
PH: (561) 622-3009
FAX: (561) 626-9911
www.lemistralrestaurant.ne

Owners
Christian & Nicole Depond and James & Nathalie Bethea

Cuisine
French Provençal

Days Open
Open daily for dinner
(Tuesday.-Sunday in summe

Pricing
Dinner for one,
without tax, tip, or drinks:
$20-$40

Dress Code
Business casual

Reservations
Recommended

Parking
Free on site

Features
Near Kravis arts center

Credit Cards
AE, VC, MC, DC

French Piece Montee

AWARD WINNER
SINCE 2001

146

Ruth's Chris Steak House

Filet mignon

T his is the steak that steak lovers rave about! Ruth's Chris Steak House specializes in USDA Prime beef. Strips, filets, ribeyes, T-bones, and porterhouses are aged to exacting standards, broiled to perfection, and served sizzling. An award-winning wine list features premium vintages by the glass. The service is attentive, knowledgeable, and friendly.

The place for great steaks

Directions

On U.S. 1, 25 min. from Palm Beach International Airport

661 U.S. 1
North Palm Beach, FL
33408
PH: (561) 863-0660
FAX: (561) 863-3670
www.ruthschris.com

Owners
Ruth's Chris Steak House

Cuisine
Steaks, seafood

Days Open
Open daily for dinner

Pricing
Dinner for one,
without tax, tip, or drinks:
$40-$60

Dress Code
Business casual

Reservations
Recommended

Parking
Valet

Features
Private rooms/parties,
cigar/cognac events

Credit Cards
AE, VC, MC, CB, DC, DS

AWARD WINNER
SINCE 2001

Arthur's 27

Arthur's Aviary

Located at the Walt Disney World Resort 25 min. from Orlando International Airport

Arthur's 27 at the Wyndham Palace Resort & Spa in the Walt Disney World Resort has consistently been considered one of the most romantic restaurants in Central Florida. Dine on five-star, award-winning continental cuisine while you enjoy panoramic views of fireworks displays and downtown Disney. Winner of every major culinary award, Arthur's 27 offers unparalleled service and an unforgettable dining experience.

Pan Seared Chiliean Sea Bass

1900 Buena Vista Drive
Orlando, FL 32830
PH: (407) 827-3450
FAX: (407) 827-3103
www.wyndham.com

Owners
Wyndham Hotels & Resorts

Cuisine
Continental

Days Open
Open daily for dinner

Pricing
Dinner for one,
without tax, tip, or drinks:
$60-$80

Dress Code
Business casual

Reservations
Recommended

Parking
Valet

Features
Private room/parties,
entertainment, cigar/
cognac events

Credit Cards
AE, VC, MC, CB, DC, ER,
JCB, DS

Casually elegant

Theresa Conners,
Chef de Cuisine

AWARD WINNER
SINCE 1999

Atlantis

At the Renaissance Orlando Resort, 17 min. from Orlando International Airport

---

6677 Sea Harbor Drive
Orlando, FL 32821
PH: (407) 351-5555
FAX: (407) 363-9247
www.atlantisorlando.com

Owners
The Renaissance Orlando Resort

Cuisine
Seafood

Days Open
Open Tues.-Sat. for dinner

Pricing
Dinner for one,
without tax, tip, or drinks:
$20-$40

Dress Code
Casual

Reservations
Recommended

Parking
Free on site, valet

Features
Private room/parties, entertainment, cigar/cognac events

Credit Cards
AE, VC, MC, CB, DC, JCB, DS

Intimate dining

Atlantis, located at the Renaissance Orlando Resort, offers an elegant, intimate atmosphere where you can enjoy the finest fresh seafood entrées prepared by Executive Chef Mitsuo Miyashita. The menu is complemented by an extensive wine list, and dinner is served by a gracious and accommodating staff. The restaurant has won the AAA Four Diamond award annually since 1988.

DiRōNA
AWARD WINNER
SINCE 1992

Charley's Steak House

Managing partner Bill Dan Beaver and his Executive Chef

Charley's Steak House, family owned and operated since 1974, offers a most memorable dining experience, featuring USDA prime and choice aged steaks, and fresh seafood. Steaks, chicken, chops, and market fresh fish are cooked over a combination of oak and citrus wood. Charley's offers an impressive and extensive list of over 800 wines to complement signature steaks, making them one of the top ten steakhouses of America since 1995.

Private rooms available

32 oz. Porterhouse

Steaks hand-cut daily

AWARD WINNER
SINCE 2003

Directions

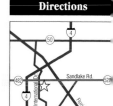

On International Drive, 20 min. from Orlando International Airport

8255 International Drive
Suite 100
Orlando, FL 32819
PH: (407) 363-0228
FAX: (407) 354-4617
www.charleyssteakhouse.com

Owners
Ron Woodsby

Cuisine
Steak and seafood

Days Open
Open daily for dinner

Pricing
Dinner for one,
without tax, tip or drinks:
$20-$40

Dress Code
Business casual

Reservations
Recommended

Parking
Free on site

Features
Private room/parties,
outdoor dining,
cigar/cognac events

Credit Cards
AE, VC, MC

Christini's Ristorante Italiano

The art of exceptional dining

C hris Christini has set the standard for service, quality, and professionalism with over 35 years of distinctive culinary experience as a restaurateur. Christini's impeccable reputation has drawn celebrities and dignitaries from around the world. To enter Christini's is to enter Italy. The music, the aromas, and a rose for each lady typify the Christini's charm.

Mr. Chris Christini

Directions

On Dr. Phillips Blvd. near The Marketplace, 20 min. from Orlando International Airport

7600 Dr. Phillips Blvd.
Orlando, FL 32819
PH: (407) 345-8770
FAX: (407) 345-8700
www.christinis.com

Owners
Chris Christini

Cuisine
Italian

Days Open
Open daily for dinner

Pricing
Dinner for one,
without tax, tip or drinks:
$40-$60

Dress Code
Business casual

Reservations
Recommended

Parking
Free on site

Features
Private room/parties, entertainment

Credit Cards
AE VC, MC, CB, DC, DS

DiRōNA
AWARD WINNER
SINCE 1995

DUX

DUX dining room

The Peabody Orlando, 15 min. from Orlando International Airport

The Peabody Orlando's signature restaurant, DUX, offers cuisine at its very finest. The room's décor and furnishings provide the perfect combination of ambience and luxurious comfort. Service is impeccable and unobtrusive. Menus change weekly allowing Chef K. David Clawson to prepare true culinary and artistic masterpieces that will delight even the most jaded palates. The wine room, a *Wine Spectator* Award of Excellence recipient, features over 2,000 selections to complement any meal.

Chef David Clawson

9801 International Drive
Orlando, FL 32819
PH: (407) 345-4550
FAX: (407) 345-4501
www.peabodyorlando.com

Owners
The Peabody Hotel Group

Cuisine
American haute cuisine

Days Open
Open Mon.-Sat. for dinner only

Pricing
Dinner for one, without tax, tip, or drinks: $40-$60

Dress Code
Elegant casual

Reservations
Recommended

Parking
Complimentary parking, valet

Features
Private parties

Credit Cards
AE, VC, MC, CB, DC, DS

Wine Cellar

The Peabody Orlando

AWARD WINNER
SINCE 1994

La Coquina

At the Hyatt Regency Grand Cypress, 20 min. from Orlando International Airport

1 Grand Cypress Boulevard
Orlando, FL 32836
PH: (407) 239-1234
FAX: (407) 239-3800
www.hyattgrandcypress.com

Hyatt Regency Grand Cypress

Orlando's premier luxury resort, minutes from area attractions, located on the magnificent 1,500-acre Grand Cypress Resort. This 750-room hotel offers five restaurants, four lounges, 45 holes of Jack Nicklaus designed award-winning golf and The Academy of Golf, a world renowned Equestrian Center, a unique lagoon shaped pool with water-slides and whirlpools, 21-acre Lake Windsong with beach area. Boutique spa services and a complete health & fitness center available.

Main dining room

Poolside elegance

Owners
Grand Cypress Florida Inc.

Cuisine
New World

Days Open
Sunday for brunch

Pricing
For one,
Price Fix: $49.95 (adult)
$27.95 (children under 12)
excluding holiday pricing

Dress Code
Resort upscale

Reservations
Required

Parking
Free on site, valet

Features
Contact hotel for information on private and specialty events

Credit Cards
AE, VC, MC, CB, DC, JCB, DS

AWARD WINNER
SINCE 1992

Manuel's on the 28th

Main dining room

Corner of Livingston and Orange, 25 min. from Orlando International Airport

390 North Orange Avenue
Bank of America Building
Suite 2800
Orlando, FL 32801
PH: (407) 246-0633
FAX: (407) 246-6575
www.culinaryconceptsinc.com

L ocated atop the Bank of America Building, Manuel's on the 28th offers a breathtaking view of Orlando through floor-to-ceiling windows. The contemporary world menu has nightly specialties of exotic game and seafood. Complementing the cuisine is world-class service and a wine list with the finest California and international selections. Celebrate a special occasion, close a business deal, or simply enjoy an elegant evening 28 stories up, where all the elements come together for a majestic dining experience.

Exotic game

Intimate dining

Owners
Hal Valdes, Chef Tony Pace, and Manny Garcia

Cuisine
Contemporary world

Days Open
Open Tues.-Sat. for dinner

Pricing
Dinner for one, without tax, tip, or drinks: $40-$60

Dress Code
Business casual, jacket and tie preferred

Reservations
Recommended

Parking
Garage nearby

Features
Private parties, near theater, cognac events

Credit Cards
AE, VC, MC, CB, DC, DS

From left, Chef Tony Pace, Manny Garcia, and Hal Valdes

AWARD WINNER
SINCE 1997

154

Cafe Cellini

Cafe Cellini dining room

Nestled between the Atlantic Ocean and the Intracoastal Waterway, 25 min. from Palm Beach International Airport

Palm Beach President
2505 South Ocean Blvd.
Palm Beach, FL 33480
PH: (561) 588-1871
FAX: (561) 582-0335

Owners
Gregory Gavakis

Cuisine
Continental

Days Open
Open daily for dinner

Pricing
Dinner for one,
without tax, tip or drinks:
$20-$40

Dress Code
Business casual

Reservations
Recommended

Parking
Valet

Features
Private parties, near theater

Credit Cards
AE, VC, MC, DC

Cafe Cellini is known for its excellent service and its exquisite Continental cuisine. The dining room is accented by fine works of art depicting Mediterranean vistas, where Owner Gregory Gavakis is always on hand meeting and greeting guests. Chef Steyn Van Wyk's menu offers such dishes as Florida pompano papillote, Dover sole, succulent roast duck, and flavorful and tender prime beef dishes. Diners are sure to find an appropriate accompaniment from the noteworthy wine list.

Broiled Chilean sea bass with leek sauce and tomato relish

*Chef Steyn Van Wyk,
Owner Gregory Gavakis*

Pecan-brandy tart with fresh berries and vanilla bean ice cream

DiRoNA
AWARD WINNER
SINCE 2003

Café L'Europe

Bistro dining

Directions

S. Ocean Blvd.

S. County Rd.

Royal Palm Way | Brazilian Ave. | Australian Ave.

Cocoanut Row

Corner of Brazilian Avenue and South County Road, 20 min. from Palm Beach International Airport

331 South County Road
Palm Beach, Florida 33480
PH: (561) 655-4020
FAX: (561) 659-6619
www.cafeleurope.com

C afé L'Europe continues a tradition of excellence, superior service, unique ambience, and quality international cuisine with a dash of contemporary American flavor. This romantic, flower-filled restaurant is one of the most beautiful and elegant in Palm Beach and has three distinct dining rooms for a great dining experience: the formal dining room, the bistro, and the wine room. The award-winning wine list boasts over 1,200 selections. Piano music is played nightly, with jazz on Fridays and Saturdays in the bistro.

Dining room

Private room

Owners
Norbert and Lidia Goldner

Cuisine
French, with contemporary American influence

Days Open
Open Tues.-Fri. for lunch, daily for dinner

Pricing
Dinner for one, without tax, tip, or drinks: $40-$60

Dress Code
Business casual

Reservations
Recommended

Parking
Valet

Features
Private room/parties

Credit Cards
AE, VC, MC, DC

Escabe of red snapper

BEST OF
AWARD OF
EXCELLENCE

DiRōNA
AWARD WINNER
SINCE 1993

The Flagler Steakhouse

The Breakers Ocean Clubhouse featuring The Flagler Steakhouse

The Flagler Steakhouse provides exceptional quality and service in the comfortable atmosphere of a traditional steakhouse. Located at The Breakers Ocean Golf & Tennis Clubhouse, The Flagler Steakhouse features rich interiors and magnificent panoramic views of the Ocean Golf Course from outdoor terrace seating. The focus of the menu is on the finest USDA prime grade meats available. Signature dishes include the colossal prime rib chop, steak au poivre, and Chateaubriand for two. Specialties from the "surf" are equally mouth-watering, and include daily seafood specials, and classics such a Maine lobster and shrimp scampi.

Expansive views of the Ocean Golf Course from the terrace

Prime steaks and chops are served in the comfort of a traditional steakhouse

Directions

At The Breakers off South County Road, 10 min. from Palm Beach International Airport

Two South County Road
Palm Beach, FL 33480
PH: (561) 659-8488
FAX: (561) 659-8485
www.thebreakers.com

Owners
Flagler System, Inc.

Cuisine
American/USDA Prime Steaks & Chops

Days Open
Open daily for lunch and dinner

Pricing
Dinner for one, without tax, tip, or drinks:
$60-$80

Dress Code
Business casual

Reservations
Recommended

Parking
Valet

Features
Private parties, outdoor dining

Credit Cards
AE, VC, MC, DC, DS

AWARD WINNER
SINCE 2004

157

L'Escalier

L'Escalier

At The Breakers off South County Road, 15 min. from Palm Beach International Airport

L'Escalier, recipient of the AAA Five Diamond Award, offers one of the country's most unforgettable dining experiences. Reminiscent of the dining rooms of France's most elegant chateaus, the room is accented by antique mirror panels, lush fabrics, and exquisite tapestries. Two new exhibition kitchens are infused with innovation and vitality. Passionately committed master chefs introduce a new benchmark in modern French cuisine with specialties such as pan roasted Palmetto Farms squab, timbale of jumbo lump crab, roast rack and grilled saddle of lamb, and a daily presentation of foie gras. The masterful servers have flawless tableside knowledge, and the 6,500-bottle wine cellar is one of the world's most acclaimed collections.

Wine cellar

Open display kitchen

One South County Road
Palm Beach, FL 33480
PH: (561) 659-8480
FAX: (561) 655-3740
www.thebreakers.com

Owners
The Breakers Palm Beach

Cuisine
Modern French

Days Open
Open Tues.-Sat. for dinner

Pricing
Dinner for one,
without tax, tip, or drinks:
$60-$80, tasting menus
starting at $70

Dress Code
Jacket for men

Reservations
Recommended

Parking
Complimentary preferred valet

Features
Private room/parties, near theater, nightly tasting menu

Credit Cards
AE, VC, MC, CB, DC, DS

Pan seared foie gras

GRAND AWARD

DiRoNA
AWARD WINNER
SINCE 2001

Café Chardonnay

Award-winning dining

A DiRōNA award winner since 1994, Café Chardonnay has been recognized as one of Palm Beach County's finest dining establishments. Chef Luis Ceballos prepares a creative, eclectic American cuisine which patrons can enjoy in a colorful, elegant, and romantic setting. Menu options include Macadamia nut crusted yellowtail snapper and roasted full rack of Australian lamb. The staff consists of highly trained, knowledge-able professionals, and the award-winning wine list features over 600 wines. A visit to Café Chardonnay is guaranteed to be an exquisite experience for the senses.

Eclectic cuisine

Elegant, romantic dining

The Wine Bar

Directions

On PGA Blvd. west of North Military Trail, 20 min. from West Palm Beach International Airport

4533 PGA Blvd.
Palm Beach Gardens, FL 33418
PH: (561) 627-2662
FAX: (561) 627-3413
www.CafeChardonnay.com

Owners
Frank Eucalitto

Cuisine
Eclectic American

Days Open
Open Mon.-Fri. for lunch, daily for dinner

Pricing
Dinner for one, without tax, tip, or drinks: $25-$45

Dress Code
Upscale casual

Reservations
Recommended

Parking
Free on site

Features
Private parties, outdoor dining

Credit Cards
AE, VC, MC, DC, DS

AWARD WINNER
SINCE 1994

Darrel & Oliver's Cafe Maxx

A landmark in Pompano Beach

On East Atlantic Boulevard, 25 min. from Fort Lauderdale/Hollywood International Airport

2601 East Atlantic Boulevard
Pompano Beach, FL 33062
PH: (954) 782-0606
FAX: (954) 782-0648
www.cafemaxx.com

Owners
Darrel Broek, Oliver Saucy

Cuisine
Regional Floridian

Days Open
Open daily for dinner

Pricing
Dinner for one,
without tax, tip, or drinks:
$40-$60

Dress Code
Tastefully casual

Reservations
Recommended

Parking
Valet

Features
Private room/parties

Credit Cards
AE, VC, MC, DC, DS

Cafe Maxx has a 17-year history of presenting consistently fresh, innovative regional Floridian cuisine. The menu may change daily, allowing Executive Chef Oliver Saucy to prepare only the freshest entrees, which might include lobster from Maine, Key West dolphin, salmon from Norway, Midwestern beef, or free-range chicken from Colorado. Mediterranean, Asian, tropical, or Southwestern are among the seasonal choices. A cozy award-winning wine bar is a popular pre-dinner gathering spot.

Salmon with Champagne Beurre Blanc

Darrel Broek and Oliver Saucy

AWARD WINNER
SINCE 1993

160

95 Cordova Restaurant and Cobalt Lounge

Sultan's Room at 95 Cordova

In the heart of the historic district, 1 hour from Jacksonville International Airport

L ocated in the historic, AAA Four-Diamond Casa Monica Hotel, the award-winning 95 Cordova Restaurant and Cobalt Lounge offers new world electric cuisine in a plush, romantic ambience. Led by Executive Chef Rene Nyfeler, the menu is a combination of Asian, Mediterranean, Caribbean, and Moroccan influences. Dine in the relaxed elegance in the main dining room or one of three private wine rooms. As seen on the Travel Channel and the Food Network.

Chef Rene Nyfeler

New world, electric cuisine

95 Cordova Street
St. Augustine, FL 32084
PH: (904) 819-6018
FAX: (904) 810-6811
www.95cordova.com
www.casamonica.com

Owners
Richard C. Kessler

Cuisine
Progressive world

Days Open
Open daily for breakfast, lunch, and dinner

Pricing
Dinner for one, without tax, tip or drinks: $40-$60

Dress Code
Casual

Reservations
Recommended

Parking
Valet

Features
Private room/parties, outdoor dining, entertainment, near theater

Credit Cards
AE, VC, MC, CB, DC, En Route, JCB, DS

Dining in exotic ambience

AWARD WINNER
SINCE 2004

La Parisienne

Nestled in the heart of the nation's oldest city

At Hypolita and Spanish streets downtown, 1 hr. 15 min. from Orlando International Airport and less than 1 hr. from Daytona and Jacksonville airports

Nestled in the heart of the nation's oldest city, amid the art galleries, B&B's and shop's, La Parisienne's Executive Chef Bruce Lawrence offers cuisine influenced from around the globe. Brunch offers the traditional favorites and some surprises; outstanding dinners are accompanied by the Chef's house-made amuses, breads, and sorbets. Maître d' Ernest John Ziembroski has created a *Wine Spectator* Award of Excellence wine list, featuring special ports and dessert wines, to bring your meal to a memorable conclusion.

Exquisite interior design

Pistachio-encrusted rack of lamb

60 Hypolita Street
St. Augustine, FL 32084
PH: (904) 829-0055
FAX: (904) 829-1816
www.laparisienne.net

Owners
Len and Kristy Weeks

Cuisine
Contemporary French

Days Open
Open daily for dinner, and Sat.-Sun. for lunch and brunch

Pricing
Dinner for one, without tax, tip, or drinks: $20-$40

Dress Code
Dressy casual to formal

Reservations
Recommended

Parking
Parking lot nearby

Features
Private parties, special events, wine dinners

Credit Cards
AE, VC, MC, DS, DC

Pastry chef's sweet sensations

Wine Spectator
AWARD OF EXCELLENCE

DiRōNA
AWARD WINNER
SINCE 2001

Café L'Europe

Directions

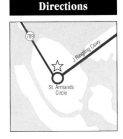

On St. Armands Circle, 20 min. from Sarasota-Bradenton International Airport

St. Armands Circle

On January 23, 1973 Café L'Europe (Sarasota) opened its doors to the dining public. 30 years later, with its rich history of colorful patrons and successful alumni, few restaurants in the state of Florida can match its impact on a community's dining heritage. Café L'Europe is located in the fashionable Saint Armands Circle shopping centre, in circus magnate John Ringling's original real estate office built in 1926. Now long considered the "grand dame" of Sarasota restaurants, today's Café L'Europe strikes the perfect balance between tradition and innovation, featuring creative menu choices that endure time and trend. Generations have relied upon Café L'Europe for gracious and attentive service, award-winning cuisine and world class wine and spirits!

Gracious service, award-winning cuisine

Chef Keith Daum

AWARD OF EXCELLENCE

DiRōNA

AWARD WINNER SINCE 1992

431 St. Armands Circle
Sarasota, FL 34236
PH: (941) 388-4415
FAX: (941) 388-2362
www.cafeleurope.net

Owners
Titus Letschert

Cuisine
Traditional European

Days Open
Open nightly for dinner and seasonally for lunch

Pricing
Dinner for one,
without tax, tip, or drinks:
$20-$40

Dress Code
Resort casual

Reservations
Recommended

Parking
Valet

Features
Private room/parties, outdoor dining, entertainment, near theater, full service catering

Credit Cards
AE, VC, MC, CB, DC, DS

Michael's on East

Dining room

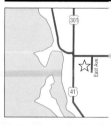

On East Avenue South in Midtown Plaza, 15 min. from Sarasota-Bradenton International Airport

Sarasota's most celebrated restaurant is dazzling guests with its vibrant decor, reminiscent of a 1930s private dining club. The look is matched by the restaurant's inspired contemporary American cuisine, impeccable service, and distinguished wine list—just what you would expect from this recipient of eleven consecutive Golden Spoon Awards, as one of Florida's top 20 restaurants.

Sarasota's most inspired cuisine

Co-proprietors Michael Klauber and Philip Mancini

1212 East Avenue South
Midtown Plaza
Sarasota, FL 34239
PH: (941) 366-0007
FAX: (941) 955-1945
www.bestfood.com

Owners
Michael Klauber and Philip Mancini

Cuisine
Contemporary American

Days Open
Open Mon.-Fri. for lunch, daily for dinner

Pricing
Dinner for one, without tax, tip, or drinks: $40-$60

Dress Code
Business casual

Reservations
Recommended

Parking
Valet

Features
Private room/parties, near theater

Credit Cards
AE, VC, MC, DC

AWARD WINNER
SINCE 1993

Armani's

Main dining room

Located on top of the Hyatt Regency Westshore, Armani's is the classic embodiment of a beautiful, tranquil place to dine, enjoyed by both visitors and Tampa residents alike. A rich harvest of northern Italian selections and an extravagant antipasto bar awaits diners' contemplation. The chef and his staff prepare a variety of traditional entrées with tantalizing poultry, beef, and seafood. Succulent veal is the house specialty. Other distinguished awards include Mobil's Four-Star Award, AAA Four Diamond Award, and *Wine Spectator.*

Antipasto Misto

Antipasto bar

AWARD WINNER
SINCE 1992

Directions

At the Hyatt Regency Westshore on Tampa Bay, 5 min. from Tampa International Airport

Hyatt Regency Westshore
6200 Courtney Campbell Causeway
Tampa, FL 33607
PH: (813) 207-6800
FAX: (813) 207-6804
www.armanisrestaurant.com

Owners
Hyatt Hotels Corporation

Cuisine
Northern Italian

Days Open
Open Mon.-Sat. for dinner

Pricing
Dinner for one,
without tax, tip, or drinks:
$40-$60

Dress Code
Business casual

Reservations
Requested

Parking
Free on site, valet

Features
Live entertainment, wine tasting, wine dinners

Credit Cards
AE, VC, MC, CB, DC, ER, JCB, DS

Bern's Steak House

On South Howard Avenue, 20 min. from Tampa International Airport

1208 South Howard Avenue
Tampa, FL 33606
PH: (813) 251-2421
FAX: (813) 251-5001
www.bernssteakhouse.com

Owners
David and Christina Laxer

Cuisine
Steak house

Days Open
Open daily for dinner

Pricing
Dinner for one,
without tax, tip, or drinks:
$40-$60

Dress Code
Business casual

Reservations
Recommended

Parking
Free on site, valet

Features
Entertainment, wine cellar
and kitchen tours

Credit Cards
AE, VC, MC, CB, DC, DS

Classical elegance in lobby

Internationally known for its vast wine collection, perfectly aged steaks, and famous dessert room, Bern's Steak House offers a world-class, incomparable dining experience. When Bern Laxer opened in 1956, he envisioned Bern's as Art in Steaks. Today, son David continues this tradition of excellence with a gastronomic adventure that includes prime steaks cut-to-order, 24 choices of caviar, and organic vegetables grown on Bern's farm. Plus, Laxer and Executive Chef Pierola unveiled the first new menu in 30 years, complete with 95 excellent new choices. For oenophiles, the 6,500 label wine collection, a perennial Grand Award winner, provides ample opportunity for exploration and, after dinner, guests can relax upstairs in a private booth with a signature dessert or one of the 1,000+ after-dinner spirits, wines and cordials.

Owner David Laxer

Executive Chef/Culinary Director Jeannie Pierola

GRAND AWARD

DiRōNA

AWARD WINNER
SINCE 1992

Charley's Steak House and Market Fresh Fish

"We've got steaks"...and then some

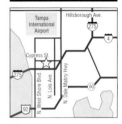

On West Cypress, between the Doubletree and the Sheraton Suites Tampa Airport Hotels, 5 min. from Tampa Int'l Airport

4444 West Cypress Street
Tampa, FL 33607
PH: (813) 353-9706
FAX: (813) 353-9510
www.charleyssteakhouse.com

Owners
Ronald E. Woodsby

Cuisine
Steak and fresh seafood

Days Open
Open daily for dinner

Pricing
Dinner for one,
without tax, tip, or drinks:
$20-$40

Dress Code
Business casual

Reservations
Highly recommended

Parking
Valet, free on site

Features
Private room/parties,
wine events

Credit Cards
AE, VC, MC

Charley's Steak House and Market Fresh Fish, Tampa, is the "talk of the town." The rich, warm, antique ambience, combined with the "best of the best" staffing assures a pleasurable experience for all. Signature dishes such as USDA prime and choice beef, daily fresh fish, seafood, veal, pork, chicken and more are cooked over citrus and oak woods. Charley's offers an extensive, award-winning wine list of over 1,000 wines to pair with your dinner.

Michael Opalenik, G.M. and operating partner

AWARD WINNER
SINCE 2004

Donatello

Main dining room

One block north of Kennedy Blvd., 5 min. from Tampa International Airport

232 North Dale Mabry Highway
Tampa, FL 33609
PH: (813) 875-6660
FAX: (813) 876-3644
www.donatellorestaurant.com

Owners
Guido Tiozzo

Cuisine
Northern Italian

Days Open
Open Mon.-Fri. for lunch, daily for dinner

Pricing
Dinner for one, without tax, tip or drinks: $40-$60

Dress Code
Business casual

Reservations Policy
Recommended

Parking
Free on site, valet

Features
Private rooms, live music nightly, cigar lounge

Credit Cards
AE, VC, MC, CB, DC, JCB, D

Donatello, named after the famous Florentine sculptor, has been a Tampa tradition since 1984, serving the finest Northern Italian cuisine. Immediately as guests step inside, they are welcomed and catered to from the first sip of wine to the roses that are given at the end of every meal. Exquisite culinary creations include fresh oysters cooked in the shell with spinach and cream and fresh hand-rolled pasta, and osso bucco. Recipient of Wine Spectator Award since 2000.

Owner Guido Tiozzo

Dessert table

AWARD OF EXCELLENCE

AWARD WINNER
SINCE 2001

SideBern's

SideBern's Modern Main Dining Room

W hen Bern's Steak House owner, David Laxer enlisted Chef Partner Jeannie Pierola, to create a sibling restaurant to the venerable Bern's Steak House, a star was born. SideBern's, a hip, fine dining haven in the Soho district of Tampa features a sophisticated menu with cutting edge cuisine served in a stylish, relaxed atmosphere. SideBern's philosophy – One World Under Food – offers guests a global array of flavors, ingredients and culinary traditions to choose from daily. The interior is washed in aqua, accented with high ceilings, wood beams, and brushed steel. For the ultimate gastronomic exposition, the glassed-in Chef's Suite offers a birds-eye view of the kitchen, and multi-course tasting menus complemented by SideBern's globally-focused wine list that is a *Wine Spectator* Award of Excellence winner.

Private Dining in the Chef's Suite

SideBern's Signature Dim Sim

AWARD OF EXCELLENCE

AWARD WINNER
SINCE 1994

Directions

In the Soho district of Tampa, on W. Morrison Ave., 20 min. from Tampa International Airport

2208 S. Morrison Avenue
Tampa, FL 33606
PH: (813) 258-2233
FAX: (813) 259-9463
www.bernssteakhouse.com

Owners
David Laxer and
Jeannie Pierola

Cuisine
Global

Days Open
Open Mon.-Sat. for dinner

Pricing
Dinner for one,
without tax, tip, or drinks:
$20-$40

Dress Code
Elegant casual

Reservations
Recommended

Parking
Valet

Features
Private room/parties,
outdoor dining

Credit Cards
AE, VC, MC, DC, DS

Café du Soir

Dining room

Recognized as one of Vero Beach's best restaurants, Valerie and Yannick Martin's Café du Soir offers an elegant country French setting paired with the skillfully prepared cuisine of French-born Yannick. A distinctive air of authenticity and a true European feel entices diners to relax and enjoy a wide array of dishes, such as sautéed Dover sole with white butter sauce, onion-encrusted grouper with a caramelized onion-bacon confit, and delicious roasted rack of lamb with herb-garlic sauce. Café du Soir is a well-established restaurant with a solid reputation for quality cuisine and service — a true destination.

Chef and Proprietors
Yannick and Valerie
Martin

One of three
dining rooms

AWARD WINNER
SINCE 1997

Directions

At the end of Royal Palm Pointe, east of Indian River Boulevard, 1 hr. 45 min. from both Orlando International and Palm Beach International airports

21 Royal Palm Pointe
Vero Beach, FL 32960
PH: (561) 569-4607
FAX: (561) 569-4607

Owners
Yannick and Valerie Martin

Cuisine
French

Days Open
Open daily for dinner (closed Sun. and Mon. during summer)

Pricing
Dinner for one, without tax, tip, or drinks: $22-$40

Dress Code
Business casual

Reservations
Recommended

Parking
Free on site

Features
Private room/parties, outdoor dining

Credit Cards
AE, VC, MC, DC

Ruth's Chris Steak House

Filet mignon

This is the steak that steak lovers rave about! Ruth's Chris Steak House specializes in USDA Prime beef. Strips, filets, ribeyes, T-bones, and porterhouses are aged to exacting standards, broiled to perfection, and served sizzling. An award-winning wine list features premium vintages by the glass. The service is attentive, knowledgeable, and friendly.

Directions

In the Winter Park Mall, 25 min. from Orlando International Airport

610 N. Orlando Avenue
Winter Park, FL 32789
PH: (407) 622-2444
FAX: (407) 622-4455
www.ruthschris.com

Owners
Ruth's Chris Steak House

Cuisine
Steaks, seafood

Days Open
Open daily for dinner

Pricing
Dinner for one,
without tax, tip, or drinks:
$40-$60

Dress Code
Business casual

Reservations
Recommended

Parking
Valet

Features
Private rooms/parties

Credit Cards
AE, VC, MC, DC, DS

AWARD OF EXCELLENCE

AWARD WINNER
SINCE 1998

The Abbey

Stained glass, vaulted ceilings

On Ponce de Leon Avenue in midtown, 15 min. from Hartsfield Atlanta International Airport

163 Ponce de Leon Avenue
Atlanta, GA 30308
PH: (404) 876-8532
FAX: (404) 876-8832
www.theabbeyrestaurant.com

Owners
Bill Swearingen

Cuisine
Contemporary classic

Days Open
Open daily for dinner

Pricing
Dinner for one,
without tax, tip, or drinks:
$30-$50

Dress Code
Business casual

Reservations
Recommended

Parking
Free on site

Features
Entertainment/pianist

Credit Cards
AE, VC, MC, CB, DC, JCB, DS

E stablished in 1968, The Abbey is a gothic church converted into Atlanta's most-honored restaurant. Vaulted ceilings, massive stained-glass windows, and waiters in monk robes create a medieval atmosphere. Executive Chef Philippe Haddad prepares a varied, contemporary classic continental cuisine, which includes seared Maine sea scallops with rock shrimp, portabella vegetarian Napoleon, and grilled elk chops. Their wine list, cited for excellence by *Wine Spectator,* complements the dinner menu.

Fine cuisine

Romantic setting

AWARD WINNER
SINCE 1999

Atlanta Grill

Stylish, comfortable décor at Atlanta Grill

Located in The Ritz-Carlton, in the heart of downtown Atlanta, at the corner of Peachtree and Ellis streets, 15 min. from Atlanta Hartsfield Int'l Airport

181 Peachtree Street
Atlanta, GA 30303
PH: (404) 221-6550
FAX: (404) 688-0400
www.atlantagrill.com

Owners
The Ritz-Carlton, Atlanta

Cuisine
Southern regional

Days Open
Open daily for breakfast, lunch, and dinner, and Sunday brunch

Pricing
Dinner for one, without tax, tip, or drinks: $40-$60

Dress Code
Business casual

Reservations
Recommended

Parking
Free on site, valet

Features
Private room/parties, outdoor dining, entertainment, near theater

Credit Cards
AE, VC, MC, CB, DC, En Route, DS

Atlanta Grill offers award-winning southern regional cuisine, and superb grilled steaks, chops, and seafood in a warm, club-like atmosphere. Specialties include grilled breast of duck, white and black truffle grits, braised collard greens and grilled Virginia farms pork tenderloin, smoked bacon baked beans, caramelized Georgia peaches, plus an outstanding wine list. The popular "Cheater's Booth" accommodates up to six in an intimate table setting with privacy drapes. The veranda overlooks famous Peachtree Street.

Veranda overlooking Peachtree Street

Premium spirits and wines offered at downtown's popular gathering place

DiRōNA
AWARD WINNER
SINCE 1992

Bone's Restaurant

Main dining room

On Piedmont Road in Buckhead, 30 min. from Hartsfield Atlanta International Airport

3130 Piedmont Road
Atlanta, GA 30305
PH: (404) 237-2663
FAX: (404) 233-5704

Owners
Susan DeRose and Richard Lewis

Cuisine
Steakhouse

Days Open
Open Mon.-Fri. for lunch, daily for dinner

Pricing
Dinner for one, without tax, tip, or drinks: $40-$60

Dress Code
Casual upscale

Reservations
Recommended

Parking
Valet

Features
Private room/parties

Credit Cards
AE, VC, MC, CB, DC, DS

B one's has long been a "must visit" in Buckhead. Its clubby atmosphere, award-winning food, and 10,000-bottle wine cellar have made it a favorite choice for local dinners. The walls are covered with photographs of Atlanta landmarks and caricatures of local personalities. Executive Chef Gregory Gammage prepares such specialties as prime beef, live Maine lobster, and lamb chops.

The Back Room

Restaurant

Menu specialties

AWARD WINNER
SINCE 1996

Chopstix

Chopstix delivers a memorable dining experience

Located on Roswell Road in the heart of Atlanta, 30 min. from Hartsfield International Airport

4279 Roswell Road
Atlanta, GA 30342
PH: (404) 255-4868
FAX: (404) 255-4803
www.chopstixatlanta.com

From the heart of Atlanta to the beaches of the Mississippi Gulf Coast, Chopstix carries a reputation for greatness. Renowned Chef Philip Chan perfected his Asian specialties to include flavors unmatched by even the most world-class chefs. His award-winning cuisine includes an original red snapper delicacy, spicy pine nut chicken, and thick, full-flavored steaks. Located in both Atlanta, and Biloxi, Mississippi, Chopstix offers an experience that rewards even the most discriminating dining enthusiasts.

Upscale Chinese cuisine

Owners
Philip Chan and Alvin Yin

Cuisine
Chinese (upscale)

Days Open
Open Mon.-Fri. for lunch, daily for dinner

Pricing
Dinner for one, without tax, tip, or drinks: $20-$40

Dress Code
Business casual

Reservations
Recommended

Parking
Free on site

Features
Private room/parties, entertainment

Credit Cards
AE, VC, MC, DC, DS

Superior service

Asian specialties

AWARD WINNER
SINCE 1995

Atlanta • GA

City Grill

Dining at the City Grill

Situated in the historic Hurt Building, City Grill has one of the most beautiful and dramatic dining rooms in Atlanta. Owner Karen Bremer describes her style of food as "American cuisine, straight up with a twist." Features fresh fish, steak, pork entrées, and many creative appetizers. The dinner menu changes daily to take advantage of the freshest ingredients of the season. City Grill has won numerous awards, including the *AAA* Four-Diamond Award, *Zagat's* Top Five in Atlanta, and *Wine Spectator's* Award of Excellence for the past ten years.

"American cuisine, straight up with a twist"

Owner Karen Bremer

AWARD OF EXCELLENCE

DiRōNA

AWARD WINNER
SINCE 1992

Directions

In the historic Hurt Building
10 min. from Hartsfield
Atlanta International Airport

50 Hurt Plaza
Suite 200
Atlanta, GA 30303
PH: (404) 524-2489
FAX: (404) 529-9474
www.citygrillatlanta.com

Owners
Karen Bremer

Cuisine
New American

Days Open
Open Mon.-Fri. for lunch,
Mon.-Sat. for dinner

Pricing
Dinner for one,
without tax,
tip, or drinks:
Price fix: $45-$65

Dress Code
Business casual

Reservations
Recommended

Parking
Valet (dinner only), garage
nearby (validated at lunch)

Features
Private rooms/parties,
cigar/cognac & wine events

Credit Cards
AE, VC, MC, CB, DC, DS

La Grotta Ristorante Italiano

Delightful dining atmosphere

In Buckhead on Peachtree Road NE, 25 min. from Hartsfield Atlanta International Airport

2637 Peachtree Road NE
Atlanta, GA 30305
PH: (404) 231-1368
FAX: (404) 231-1274
www.la-grotta.com

For over two decades, La Grotta Ristorante Italiano has been known for its classic Northern and regional Italian cuisine. The atmosphere is private and elegant yet relaxed. Co-owner and Executive Chef Antonio Abizanda prepares grilled specialties and vegetarian dishes, as well as homemade pastas, fresh seafood, veal, and beef. Complementing the varied menu is an extensive wine list. There is also a private terrace overlooking a beautiful garden for outside dining.

Hearty Italian cuisine

Imaginative creations

Owners
Sergio Favalli and
Antonio Abizanda

Cuisine
Northern and regional
Italian

Days Open
Open Mon.-Sat. for dinner

Pricing
Dinner for one,
without tax, tip, or drinks:
$20-$40

Dress Code
Jacket suggested

Reservations
Recommended

Parking
Valet

Features
Private parties, outdoor
dining, near theaters

Credit Cards
AE, VC, MC, CB, DC, JCB, DS

*Owners Antonio Abizanda
and Sergio Favalli*

AWARD WINNER
SINCE 1997

177

Nikolai's Roof

Main dining room

Directions

Atop the Hilton Atlanta
downtown, 20 min.
from Hartsfield Atlanta
International Airport

Hilton Atlanta
255 Courtland Street NE
Atlanta, GA 30303
PH: (404) 221-6362
FAX: (404) 221-6811
www.atlanta.hilton.com

Nikolai's Roof, gracing the top floor of the downtown Hilton, offers guests a spectacular view, striking interior, and delectable French continental cuisine. Executive Chef Johannes Klapdohr's meticulously executed menu also features Russian specialties. Special marinated Russian vodkas and caviar from the Caspian Sea are popular items. The cuisine, the wine list, and the outstanding service orchestrated by maitre d' Henk Jeurink have proven to be an unparalleled combination, earning Nikolai's Roof four stars from Mobil.

Take the outside elevator to Nikolai's Roof

Owners
Hilton Hotel Corp.

Cuisine
French continental

Days Open
Open Mon.-Sat. for dinner

Pricing
Dinner for one,
without tax, tip, and drinks
4-course menu: $63
Chef's menu: $84

Dress Code
Neat casual

Reservations
Required

Parking
Free on site, valet, garage
nearby

Features
Private room/parties, near
theater, cigar/cognac event

Credit Cards
AE, VC, MC, CB, DC, DS

AWARD WINNER
SINCE 1992

South City Kitchen

South City kitchen with the midtown Atlanta skyline

Located on Crescent Avenue in midtown, 20 min. from Hartsfield Atlanta International Airport

1144 Crescent Avenue
Atlanta, GA 30309
PH: (404) 873-7358
FAX: (404) 873-0317
www.southcitykitchen.com

Owners
Fifth Group Restaurants

Cuisine
Contemporary southern

Days Open
Open daily for lunch and dinner, Sunday for brunch

Pricing
Dinner for one, without tax, tip, or drinks: $15-$25

Dress Code
Business casual

Reservations
Recommended

Parking
Ample public parking nearby

Features
Private parties, outdoor dining, near theater and museum

Credit Cards
AE, VC, MC, DC

The new southern cuisine of midtown's South City Kitchen, featuring the charm of the old south, the energy of a big city grill, and the warmth of a neighborhood soul food kitchen, have earned both popular and critical acclaim. Specialties of the house include She-crab soup, fried green tomatoes, shrimp, scallops, and grits, and jerk pork tenderloin. South City Kitchen is open daily for lunch and dinner, plus Sunday brunch.

Maryland crabcake with whole grain mustard sauce and chow-chow

Bar and Exhibition Kitchen

Wine Spectator
AWARD OF EXCELLENCE

DiRōNA
AWARD WINNER
SINCE 2003

Hi Life kitchen & Cocktails

A dining experience, sure to impress

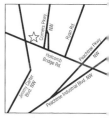

Corner of Holcomb Bridge
Road and Jimmy Carter
Blvd., in the Corners Court,
25 min. from Hartsfield
Atlanta International Airport

3380 Holcomb Bridge Road
Norcross, GA 30092
PH: (770) 409-0101
FAX: (770) 409-1160
www.atlantahilife.com

Owners
Christopher Pyun, John
Metz, and Thomas DiGiorgio

Cuisine
Eclectic American

Days Open
Open Mon.-Fri. for lunch,
daily for dinner

Pricing
Dinner for one,
without tax, tip, or drinks:
$20-$40

Dress Code
Business casual

Reservations
Recommended

Parking
Free on site

Features
Private room, outdoor dining

Credit Cards
AE, VC, MC, DC

With the finest in food, beverage, and service, Hi Life Kitchen & Cocktails has come to be one of Atlanta's best restaurants. The innovative menu delights with American classics and is complemented by an all-American wine list. Using only the freshest, seasonal ingredients, specialties include a decadent four-course lobster tasting menu, beef tenderloin medallions, and grilled veal rib chop. With the guarantee of an inimitable dining experience, Hi Life will continue to impress for many years to come.

Classic American cuisine

The bar

Owners John Metz, Thomas DiGiorgio, and Christopher Pyun

AWARD WINNER
SINCE 2002

Elizabeth on 37th

Enjoy Savannah cuisine at its best

On east 37th and Drayton Street, in the Victorian District, 25min. from Savannah International Airport

105 East 37th Street
Savannah, GA 31401
PH: (912) 236-5547
FAX: (912) 232-1095
www.elizabethon37th.com

Owners
Greg and Karen Butch,
Deanne and Gary Butch

Cuisine
Southern regional

Days Open
Open daily for dinner

Pricing
Dinner for one,
without tax, tip, or drinks:
$40-$60

Dress Code
Business casual

Reservations
Required

Parking
Free on site

Features
Private parties

Credit Cards
AE, VC, MC, DC, DS

Elizabeth on 37th, the creation of Chef Elizabeth Terry, is a fine dining restaurant located in a historic, turn-of-the-century mansion, in the Victorian District of Savannah. The menu is inspired by southern tradition, making extensive use of the freshest local seafood, garden produce, and herbs, fresh grown, on the premises. The dining experience combines New Southern cuisine, carefully chosen wine and spirits, and gracious hospitality in comfortable, attractive surroundings.

high praise for food, service, and surroundings

AWARD WINNER
SINCE 1992

The Olde Pink House Restaurant & Planters Tavern

Elegant southern dining

The Olde Pink House Restaurant and Planters Tavern is a national historic landmark and an internationally acclaimed destination for elegant southern dining located in the historic district overlooking Reynolds Square. Shrimp and grits cake and crispy flounder are specialties served in Savannah's only 18th-century mansion. Flanking floor to ceiling brick hearths, velvet sofas and gleaming brass provide a dramatic setting for Gail Thurmond at her Steinway baby grand.

Overlooking Reynolds Square

The cozy clubrooms

AWARD WINNER
SINCE 2001

Directions

In the historic district overlooking Reynolds Square, 2 min. from Savannah International Airport

23 Abercorn
Savannah, GA 31401
PH: (912) 232-4286
FAX: (912) 231-1934

Owners
Donna, Kiara, and Jeff Balish

Cuisine
Southern seafood

Days Open
Open daily for dinner

Pricing
Dinner for one,
without tax, tip, or drinks:
$20-$40

Dress Code
Casual

Reservations
Recommended

Parking
Garage nearby, local street parking

Features
Private room/parties, entertainment, near theater

Credit Cards
AE, VC, MC

Alan Wong's Restaurant

Chef/Owner Alan Wong

Directions

On South King Street, 20 min. from Honolulu International Airport

1857 S. King Street
Honolulu, HI 96826
PH: (808) 949-2526
FAX: (808) 951-9520
www.alanwongs.com

Owners
Alan Wong

Cuisine
Hawaii regional cuisine

Days Open
Open daily for dinner

Pricing
Dinner for one,
without tax, tip, or drinks:
$40-$60 (or) Price Fix:
$65/$85

Dress Code
Business casual

Reservations
Recommended

Parking
Valet

Features
Outdoor dining on enclosed lanai

Credit Cards
AE, VC, MC, DC, JCB

At Alan Wong's Restaurant, award-winning Chef/Owner Alan Wong and his staff offer guests a unique taste of Hawaii regional cuisine. Utilizing the freshest of locally grown produce and the bounties of the Pacific Ocean results in Chef Wong's personal adaptation of contemporary style cooking as seen in dishes like Ginger-crusted Onaga with Miso sesame vinaigrette, and grilled lamb chops with Macadamia-coconut crust —taking fresh Island ingredients and giving them an extraordinary twist. The outcome is dishes that stretch the palate and exercise the senses.

Enjoy the unique taste of Hawaii regional cuisine

AWARD WINNER
SINCE 1999

Bali by the Sea

Ahi Trio

At the Hilton Hawaiian Village Beach Resort & Spa in Waikiki, 30 min. from Honolulu International Airport

Hilton Hawaiian Village Beach Resort & Spa
2005 Kalia Road
Honolulu, HI 96815
PH: (808) 949-4321
FAX: (808) 947-7926
www.hawaiianvillage.hilton.com

Owners
Hilton Hotels Corporation

Cuisine
Pacific Rim

Days Open
Open Mon.-Sat. for dinner

Pricing
Dinner for one,
without tax, tip, or drinks:
$40-$60

Dress Code
Evening resort attire

Reservations
Recommended

Parking
Complimentary valet,
validated self-parking

Features
Semi-private rooms

Credit Cards
AE, VC, MC, CB, DC, JCB, DS

Overlooking Waikiki Beach, Bali by the Sea offers a memorable dining experience under the watchful eye of Maitre d' Alicia Antonio, with delicious island-inspired cuisine, and elegant surroundings on the mezzanine level of the famous Hilton Hawaiian Village Rainbow Tower. Our Restaurant Chef Roberto Los Baños applies Pacific Rim techniques to the signature dishes including Sautéed Opakapaka crusted with Macadamia Nuts and Cilantro with Kaffir Lime Sauce and Roast Rack of Sonoma Lamb with Orange Hoisin Glaze. Complement your dinner with a wine selection from our list featuring celebrated European, Australian and American vineyards.

Chef Roberto Los Baños

Fine dining

Opakapaka

AWARD OF EXCELLENCE

DiRōNA
AWARD WINNER
SINCE 1993

184

La Mer

Halekulani, on the beach at Waikiki

Directions

Located on Kalia Road overlooking Waikiki Beach, 25 min. from Honolulu International Airport

2199 Kalia Road
Honolulu, HI 96815
PH: (808) 923-2311
FAX: (808) 931-5039
www.halekulani.com

Owners
Halekulani Corporation

Cuisine
French

Days Open
Open daily for dinner

Pricing
Dinner for one,
without tax, tip, or drinks:
$40-$60

Dress Code
Long-sleeved collared
dress shirt or jacket
required for gentlemen

Reservations
Recommended

Parking
Free on site, valet

Features
Private room/parties,
cigar/cognac events

Credit Cards
AE, VC, MC, CB, JCB

A rich sensory experience of superb taste, impeccable service, and exquisite neoclassic French cuisine is enhanced by the ever-present sound of "la mer", the sea. Yves Garnier, Chef de Cuisine creates seasonal menus reflecting the freshest local ingredients and perfecting what he calls his "cuisine de soleil" or "cuisine of the sun." La Mer, the only AAA Five Diamond restaurant in Hawaii, has received numerous accolades including Best Business Restaurant by Gourmet; America's 50 Best Hotel Restaurants by Food & Wine; Top Ten Food Ranking, Honolulu by Zagat Survey.

Elegant ocean front dining

Michelin-starred,
Yves Garnier

Bouillabaisse showcasing
local fish

AWARD WINNER
SINCE 1992

Michel's on the Beach at the Colony Surf

Michel's by night with views of Waikiki

At the end of Kalakaua Ave in Waikiki's "Gold Coast", 25 min. from Honolulu Int'l Airport

For forty-three years the sound of gentle waves, spectacular sunsets and Waikiki city lights have beckoned diners to Michel's on the Beach, at the Colony Surf. Guests enjoy the Renaissance of French Classic Cuisine, and can choose from an extensive selection of wines, while enjoying Michel's breathtaking ocean views. Executive chef Eberhard "Hardy" Kintscher prepares delectable culinary masterpieces incorporating fresh-island fare, as Michel's tuxedo-clad waitstaff provides world-class service. Visit Michel's for classically inspired French Cuisine, with a touch of "aloha".

Executive Chef Eberhard Kintscher, and General Manager Philip Shaw

The Renaissance of classic French cuisine

2895 Kalakaua Avenue
Honolulu, HI 96815
PH: (808) 923-6552
FAX: (808) 526-3758
www.michelshawaii.com

Owners
D.G. Andy Anderson

Cuisine
New French Renaissance, a blend of classic French and Island flavors

Days Open
Open daily for dinner

Pricing
Dinner for one,
without tax, tip, or drinks:
$40-$60

Dress Code
Business casual

Reservations
Recommended

Parking
Valet

Features
Private/semi-private/parties entertainment, near theater beachfront dining

Credit Cards
AE, VC, MC, DC, JCB, DS

AWARD WINNER
SINCE 2001

Cafe Portofino

Harp music nightly with Giovanni

Directions

In New Harbor Mall across from the Kauai Marriott, 5 minutes from Lihue Airport

3501 Rice Street #208
Lihue, HI 96766
PH: (808) 245-2121
FAX: (808) 246-0553
www.cafeportofino.com

Owners
Giuseppe Avocadi

Cuisine
Classic Northern Italian

Days Open
Open daily for dinner

Pricing
Dinner for one,
without tax, tip, or drinks:
$20-$40

Dress Code
Business casual

Reservations
Recommended

Parking
Free on site

Features
Private parties, outdoor dining, entertainment, near theater, cigar/cognac events

Credit Cards
AE, VC, MC, CB, DC, JCB

Come and enjoy true authentic Italian cuisine at the award-winning Cafe Portofino. Its hardworking owners, settlers from Italy, are committed to high food quality and professional service. The bright, spacious, and cheerful restaurant offers a variety of tasty and generous entrées, including fine pastas, fresh seafood, great osso buco, sensational ahi carpaccio and many other specialties. The restaurant also features heavenly homemade gelati that is prepared daily.

Owner Giuseppe Avocadi and Chef receiving the DiRōNA award

Elegant selections

AWARD WINNER
SINCE 1999

Main dining room

801 Steak & Chop House

The 801 Bar

On Grand Ave. between 8th & 9th streets, 15 min. from Des Moines International Airport

At 801 Steak & Chop House the finest aged USDA prime steaks and chops, jumbo live Maine lobsters, and an international wine list (*Wine Spectator* Award of Excellence) are matched with extraordinary service. Located in the Principal Financial Tower, 801 recalls the elegance and abundance of the 1920s. 801 offers private boardroom dining, receptions, and cocktail parties. President George Bush, Arnold Palmer, Elton John, Dan Rather, Tom Brokaw, Peter Jennings, and Larry King can be counted among the many distinguished guests.

General Manager James Foreman

Fine wine and fresh seafood

801 Grand Avenue
Des Moines, IA 50309
PH: (515) 288-6000
FAX: (515) 288-4083
www.801steakandchop.com

Owners
James P. Lynch, Jr.

Cuisine
Prime Steakhouse

Days Open
Open Mon.-Fri. for lunch,
Mon.-Sat. for dinner

Pricing
Dinner for one,
without tax, tip, or drinks:
$40-$60

Dress Code
Business casual

Reservations
Recommended

Parking
Garage nearby

Features
Private room/parties,
cigar/cognac events

Credit Cards
AE, VC, MC, DC, DS

Wine & cigar room

AWARD WINNER
SINCE 2003

Beverly's Restaurant

O verlooking Lake Coeur d'Alene, Beverly's Restaurant features distinctive entrées ranging from Midwestern Prime Grade beef and fresh seafood flown in twice weekly to such exotic fare as Priest River buffalo and Idaho ostrich. Guests dine amid casual elegance in comfortable surroundings and are pampered by an attentive staff. The wine cellar has been consistently cited for excellence by *Wine Spectator*.

Rick Powers, Director of Food and Beverage, with Executive Chefs Rod Jessick (left) and Jim Barrett

Beverly's dining room

The Coeur d'Alene Resort

AWARD WINNER
SINCE 1992

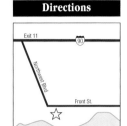

At the Coeur d'Alene Resort, off Exit 11 of Interstate 90, 40 min. from Spokane (WA) International Airport

The Coeur d'Alene Resort
P.O. Box 7200
115 Front Street
Coeur d'Alene, ID 83814
PH: (208) 765-4000, ext. 23
or (800) 688-4142
FAX: (208) 676-7292
www.cdaresort.com

Owners
Duane B. Hagadone and Jerald J. Jaeger

Cuisine
Seafood and beef with a Northwest flair

Days Open
Open daily for lunch and dinner

Pricing
Dinner for one, without tax, tip, or drinks: $20-$40

Dress Code
Resort casual

Reservations
Recommended

Parking
Free on site, valet

Features
Private room/parties, entertainment in lounge

Credit Cards
AE, VC, MC, CB, DC, DS

189

Le Titi de Paris

Main dining room

Proprietor and Executive Chef Pierre Pollin and Chef de Cuisine Michael Maddox serve innovative French cuisine — sautéed salmon with cider sauce is a signature dish — in a comfortably elegant setting. The main dining room is tailored somewhat formally with upholstered seating and hues of plum and gold. The wine list offers more than 1,100 selections, and a degustation dinner with wine flight is available.

*Michael Maddox
and Pierre Pollin*

Creative entrées

Sophisticated elegance

AWARD WINNER
SINCE 1992

Directions

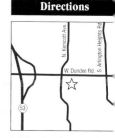

At West Dundee Road (Route 68) and Kennicott Avenue, two blocks east of Route 53 and 30 min. from O'Hare International Airport

1015 West Dundee Road
Arlington Heights, IL 60004
PH: (847) 506-0222
FAX: (847) 506-0474
www.letitideparis.com

Owners
Pierre and Judith Pollin

Cuisine
Innovative French

Days Open
Open Thurs.-Fri. for lunch,
Tues.-Sat. for dinner

Pricing
Dinner for one,
without tax, tip, or drinks:
$40-$60

Dress Code
Business casual

Reservations
Required

Parking
Free on site

Features
Private room/parties

Credit Cards
AE, VC, MC, CB, DC, JCB, DS

190

Ambria

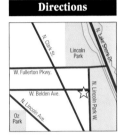

On North Lincoln Park West,
45 min. from O'Hare
International and Midway
airports

2300 N. Lincoln Park West
Chicago, IL 60614
PH: (773) 472-5959
FAX: (773) 472-9077
www.leye.com

Owners
Gabino Sotelino

Cuisine
Modern classic French

Days Open
Open Mon.-Sat. for dinner

Pricing
Dinner for one,
without tax, tip, or drinks:
$60-$80

Dress Code
Jacket and tie required

Reservations
Required

Parking
Valet

Features
Private room/parties

Credit Cards
AE, VC, MC, DC, DS

Extraordinary French dining experience

Ambria affords an extraordinary dining experience featuring the seasonal cuisine, Legere, of Chef/Owner Gabino Sotelino. It is an innovative culinary approach that relies on the use of the freshest ingredients and cooking techniques while enhancing the food's natural flavors. This award-winning restaurant specializes in game, seafood, and extraordinary desserts. Tiny shaded lamps on each table, and massive urns filled with fresh flowers, combined with art nouveau architectural touches create an elegant, romantic setting. Awards include a four-star rating from *Chicago Magazine, Chicago Tribune,* and *Mobil Travel Guide,* the AAA Five Diamond Award, *Wine Spectator's* Award of Excellence, Gault Millau (17 or 20/3 Toques) and Best of Chicago from *Zagat's*

AWARD WINNER
SINCE 1992

Arun's Restaurant

Main dining room

Directions

			Montrose Ave.
			Berteau Ave.
			Belle Plaine Ave.
			☆ Irving Park

At North Kedzie Avenue
and West Irving Park Road
in northwest Chicago,
20 min. from O'Hare
International Airport

4156 North Kedzie Avenue
Chicago, IL 60618
PH: (773) 539-1909
FAX: (773) 539-2125
www.arunsthai.com

Owners
Arun Sampanthavivat

Cuisine
Thai

Days Open
Open Tues.-Sun. for dinner

Pricing
Dinner for one,
without tax, tip, or drinks:
Price Fix:$85

Dress Code
Business casual

Reservations
Required

Parking
Valet

Features
Private room

Credit Cards
AE, VC, MC, CB, DC, DS

A run's exclusive "chef's design menu" is a fixed-price, 12-course dinner that gives customers the chance to explore the many tantalizing flavors (including the various degrees of spiciness) and exciting textures of refined Thai cuisine. In addition to the most prominent award, (James Beard Foundation's Best Chef, Midwest), *The New York Times* called Arun's "America's best Thai restaurant" and the *Chicago Tribune* pronounced it "a civic treasure." Arun's interior reflects the harmonious balance of contemporary simplicity and classical elegance, with cut and patterned panels of deep mahogany as well as lustrous Thai silks and exquisite paintings. A variety of fine wines, a full-service bar, and the popular Thai Singha lager add to the unforgettable dining experience.

Exquisite presentation, tantalizing flavors

Chef/Owner Arun Sampanthavivat

AWARD WINNER
SINCE 1998

Chicago Chop House

Chicago Chop House...main dining room

On West Ontario between Clark and Dearborn streets in the River North area, 45 min. from O'Hare International Airport

60 West Ontario
Chicago, IL 60610
PH: (312) 787-7100
FAX: (312) 787-3219
www.chicagochophouse.com

I f you are looking for a taste of Chicago you will find it here at Chicago Chop House – chosen as one of the top ten steakhouses in the country since 1991. Only prime-aged steaks that are hand-cut on the premises are featured on the menu, and *Chicago Magazine* awarded the New York boneless strip steak the "Best" in Chicago. The wine list has received the prestigious *Wine Spectator* Award of Excellence. The clubby atmosphere includes over 1,400 photographs of old Chicago.

Prime New York strip

Owners
Bill Farrahi, Susan Gayford, and John Pontarelli

Cuisine
Steak

Days Open
Open Mon.-Fri. for lunch, daily for dinner

Pricing
Dinner for one, without tax, tip, or drinks: $20-$40

Dress Code
Business casual

Reservations
Recommended

Parking
Valet

Features
Private parties, entertainment

Credit Cards
AE, VC, MC, CB, DC, JCB, DS

Partners: Chef Bill Farrrahi, John Pontarelli, and Susan Gayford

AWARD WINNER
SINCE 2004

Cité Elegant Dining

Breathtaking views atop Lake Point Tower

This 70th floor showplace boasts new menu selections from Executive Chef Oscar Ornelas, impeccable service, elegant décor, and breathtaking 360-degree panoramic views making Cité the most romantic setting in Chicago. Also perfect for dazzling parties.

Grilled swordfish with cilantro lime sauce

Nightly views

Oven-roasted quail with port wine and fig reduction

**AWARD WINNER
SINCE 2004**

Directions

On the 70th floor of the Lake Point Tower, 30 min. from Midway and O'Hare International airports

505 North Lake Shore Drive
Chicago, IL 60611
PH: (312) 644-4050
FAX: (312) 644-4066
www.citechicago.com

Owners
Ms. Evangeline Gouletas

Cuisine
Contemporary American
with French influence

Days Open
Open daily for dinner

Pricing
Dinner for one,
without tax, tip, or drinks:
$40-$60
(or)
Prix fixe: $79.00

Dress Code
Business casual

Reservations
Recommended

Parking
Valet

Features
Private room/parties, entertainment, near theater,
cigar/cognac events

Credit Cards
AE, VC, MC, CB, DC, DS

Coco Pazzo

Exciting decor

Near the Merchandise Mart in the River North area, 30 min. from O'Hare International and Midway airports

300 West Hubbard Street
Chicago, IL 60610
PH: (312) 836-0900
FAX: (312) 836-0257
www.tribads.com/cocopazzo

Owners
Pino Luongo

Cuisine
Italian

Days Open
Open Mon.-Fri. for lunch, daily for dinner

Pricing
Dinner for one,
without tax, tip, or drinks:
$40-$60

Dress Code
Business casual

Reservations
Recommended

Parking
Valet

Features
Private parties, near theater, cigar/cognac events

Credit Cards
AE, VC, MC, CB, DC

Coco Pazzo serves authentic regional Italian cuisine with an emphasis on Tuscan specialties. Among the entrées are Florentine steak and ossobuco. The casually elegant restaurant is housed in a converted loft building with beamed ceilings, Australian cypress floors, brick walls, and large bay windows. Blue velvet drapes and theatrical lighting enhance the setting, and customers can see beyond the 80-foot antique bar into the open kitchen, which is dominated by a ceramic-tiled wood-burning oven.

Spaghetti aglio

Jack Weiss, vice president, operations and Pino Luongo, owner

AWARD WINNER
SINCE 1998

The Dining Room at The Ritz-Carlton Chicago

The Ritz-Carlton's lobby fountain

On East Pearson at Water Tower Place, 45 min. from O'Hare and 30 min. from Midway airports

160 East Pearson Street
Chicago, IL 60611
PH: (312) 573-5223
FAX: (312) 266-9623
www.fourseasons.com/chicagorc

The Dining Room presents an atmosphere of quiet luxury, elegant service, and the finest French contemporary cuisine. Chef Sarah Stegner offers a personalized eight-course tasting menu, a five-course degustation menu, and a five-course vegetarian degustation menu. The award-winning wine list offers a large selection with particular emphasis on Bordeaux, Burgundy, and California boutique wines. The Dining Room also offers an elegant alternative for hosting private breakfasts and lunches.

The Dining Room

Chef Sarah Stegner

Owners
Four Seasons Hotels and Resorts

Cuisine
Contemporary French

Days Open
Open Tues.-Sun. for dinner, Sunday for brunch

Pricing
Dinner for one, without tax, tip, or drinks: $60-$80

Dress Code
Jacket required

Reservations
Recommended

Parking
Valet

Features
Entertainment

Credit Cards
AE, VC, MC, DC, DS

GRAND
AWARD

DiRōNA
AWARD WINNER
SINCE 1992

Everest

Alsatian heart and palate brought to the USA

Directions

Located in the Chicago Stock Exchange Bldg., 30 min. from O'Hare International Airport

440 South LaSalle Street
Chicago, IL 60605
PH: (312) 663-8920
FAX: (312) 663-8802
www.everestrestaurant.com

Owners
Jean Joho

Cuisine
Personalized French

Days Open
Open Tues.-Sat. for dinner

Pricing
Dinner for one,
without tax, tip, or drinks:
$80+

Dress Code
Jacket and tie required

Reservations
Required

Parking
Free on site, valet

Features
Private room/parties,
near theater

Credit Cards
AE, VC, MC, C, DC, En
Route, JCB, DS

Soaring above the skyline on the 40th floor of the Chicago Stock Exchange building, Chef/Proprietor J. Joho's Mobil Award-winning, AAA Five-Diamond Everest restaurant serves Chicago's finest personalized cuisine. Joho's distinctive cuisine is a blend of European influences and widely available American ingredients. Everest offers a multi-course degustation dinner, as well as a pre-theater, three-course menu; all served by a formal, knowledgeable wait staff. Chef Joho developed expertise not only in the business of restaurants and hotels, but in pastries, cheese, and wine.

AWARD WINNER
SINCE 1993

Gene & Georgetti

The original bar and dining room

Corner of Illinois & Franklin, 30 min. from O'Hare International Airport and 20 min. from Midway Airport

Gene & Georgetti continues to be the classic Chicago steakhouse for over sixty years, serving only the best prime, aged steaks and chops, as well as a host of Italian specialties and seafood prepared by Executive Chef Mario Navarro. Signature dishes include Chicken Vesuvio and our famous "Garbage Salad." The clubby steakhouse atmosphere, superior service, and unequalled food quality make for a truly extraordinary dining experience. Gene & Georgetti ... a real Chicago institution!

Signature dishes

Owners Marion and Tony Durpetti

The new Fireside Room

500 North Franklin Street
Chicago, IL 60610
PH: (312) 527-3718
FAX: (312) 527-2039

Owners
Tony and Marion Durpetti

Cuisine
Steakhouse

Days Open
Open Mon.-Sat. for lunch and dinner, Sundays for major conventions

Pricing
Dinner for one, without tax, tip, or drinks:
$40-$60

Dress Code
Business casual

Reservations
Recommended

Parking
Free on site, valet

Features
Private room/parties. near theater

Credit Cards
AE, VC, MC, DC

AWARD WINNER
SINCE 2001

La Strada Ristorante

Owner Michael Mormando

Since 1981, La Strada has been serving a worldwide clientele of discriminating diners. Guests are served by a formal, knowledgeable wait staff in a comfortable dining atmosphere created by warm woods, polished marble, and wine displays. The cuisine is classic Italian, featuring fresh fish and shellfish, prime steaks, and veal. Specialty pastas include fettuccini alfredo with scallops, lobster fra diavolo, and bucatini amatriciana. The wine list includes international selections, and grappas and cognacs accommodate you after dinner at the piano bar.

Prime veal chops

Discriminating dining

Classic Italian cuisine

AWARD WINNER
SINCE 1997

Directions

On North Michigan Ave. and Randolph St., 30 min. from O'Hare International and 20 min. from Midway airports

155 North Michigan Avenue
Chicago, IL 60601
PH: (312) 565-2200
FAX: (312) 565-2216
www.lastradaristorante.com

Owners
Nicholas and Michael Mormando

Cuisine
Classic Italian

Days Open
Open Mon.-Fri. for lunch, Mon.-Sat. for dinner, occasional Sundays

Pricing
Dinner for one, without tax, tip, or drinks: $20-$40 (or) Prix Fixe: $30

Dress Code
Business casual

Reservations
Accepted

Parking
Valet

Features
Private room/parties, entertainment, near theater

Credit Cards
AE, VC, MC, CB, DC, DS

Lawry's The Prime Rib

The former McCormick Mansion

Just off the Magnificent Mile, located in the 1890s McCormick Mansion, 30 min. from O'Hare International Airport

Specializing in Roasted Prime Ribs of Beef, Lawry's The Prime Rib serves exclusively USDA certified prime quality. Aged 21 days and rock salt-roasted to perfection, the prime rib is carved to order tableside from gleaming silver carts. Fresh fish and Atlantic lobster tails are also available. Just off the Magnificent Mile, Lawry's occupies the 1890s McCormick Mansion whose opulent history resonates in the sweeping spiral staircase, rich woods and warm hospitality.

Elegant spiral staircase

Signature Roasted Prime Ribs of Beef

100 East Ontario Street
Chicago, IL 60611
PH: (312) 787-5000
FAX: (312) 787-1264
www.lawrysonline.com

Owners
Lawry's Restaurants, Inc.

Cuisine
Continental featuring Roasted Prime Ribs of Beef

Days Open
Open Mon.-Fri. for lunch, daily for dinner

Pricing
Dinner for one, without tax, tip, or drinks: $20-$40

Dress Code
Business casual

Reservations
Recommended

Parking
Valet

Features
Private rooms/parties, special events, entertainment (holidays only), wine events

Credit Cards
AE, VC, MC, DC, JCB, DS

Tableside silver cart service

AWARD WINNER
SINCE 2004

Smith & Wollensky, Chicago

Smith & Wollensky, Chicago...helping to revive the North River area

Smith & Wollensky may be a New York steakhouse, but it has taken on its own personality in Chicago. Here you'll find the signature USDA Prime dry-aged beef that made the steak house famous 25 years ago in New York City. There are seven dining areas, including Mrs. Wollensky's Cigar Bar, and a Wine Cellar for private parties. The location offers intimate views of the Chicago River and is adjacent to the Chicago landmark twin towers of Marina City. The restaurant is a major player in the revival of the City's River North area.

Mrs. Wollensky's Cigar Bar

Dining at the bar

AWARD WINNER
SINCE 2004

Directions

On North State Street, 30 min. from O'Hare International Airport

318 North State Street
Chicago, IL 60610
PH: (312) 670-9900
FAX: (312) 670-0997
www.smithandwollensky.com

Owners
Smith & Wollensky Restaurant Group, Inc.

Cuisine
Steakhouse

Days Open
Open daily for lunch and dinner

Pricing
Dinner for one, without tax, tip, or drinks: $40-$60

Dress Code
Business casual

Reservations
Recommended

Parking
Valet

Features
Private room/parties, outdoor dining, cigar/cognac events

Credit Cards
AE, VC, MC, CB, DC, JCB, DS

Vivere

Main dining room

On West Monroe between Clark and Dearborn in the Loop, 30 min. from O'Hare International Airport

 One of a trio of restaurants in the Italian Village complex, Vivere is both a feast for the eyes and palate. Conical light fixtures, gilded scrolls, wrought-iron stair rails, and a stained-glass ceiling are hallmarks of the classy, recently redesigned dining room. The eclectic surroundings perfectly complement the innovative cuisine, which runs along the lines of pheasant-filled pasta with butter, sage, and parmesan cheese, and salmon with tomato gazpacho sauce, zucchini rosettes, and infused sweet herb oil. The wine list is a *Wine Spectator* Grand Award winner.

Al, Gina, and Frank Capitanini

Duck breast with fruit and balsamic reduction

71 West Monroe
Chicago, IL 60603
PH: (312) 332-4040
FAX: (312) 332-2656
www.italianvillage-chicago.com

Owners
Capitanini family

Cuisine
Regional contemporary Italian

Days Open
Open Mon.-Fri. for lunch, Mon.-Sat. for dinner

Pricing
Dinner for one,
without tax, tip, or drinks:
$20-$40

Dress Code
Business casual

Reservations
Recommended

Parking
Valet, garage nearby

Features
Private room/parties, near theater

Credit Cards
AE, VC, MC, CB, DC, JCB, DS

AWARD WINNER
SINCE 1998

Va Pensiero

Refined Solera Room

Directions

On Oak Ave. between Davis and Grove streets, 25 min. from O'Hare International Airport

1566 Oak Avenue
Evanston, IL 60201
PH: (847) 475-7779
FAX: (847) 475-7825
www.va-p.com

Owners
Jeffrey S. Muldrow

Cuisine
Italian

Days Open
Open daily for dinner

Pricing
Dinner for one, without tax, tip, or drinks: $20-$40

Dress Code
Evening casual

Reservations
Recommended

Parking
Valet

Features
Private room/parties, outdoor dining

Credit Cards
AE, VC, MC, CB, DC, JCB, DS

Executive Chef Jeff Muldrow creates award-winning authentic, rustic Italian cuisine, lovingly prepared and artfully presented. Va Pensiero specializes in homemade pastas and breads, seafood, veal and lamb dishes, the freshest vegetables, and exquisite desserts. The setting for this popular restaurant is as charming as it is romantic. Three dining rooms, including a sun-kissed patio, create a relaxed and intimate setting for memorable evenings. Classic columns and Italianate tile floors complement the singular and creative cuisine.

Elegant Verdi Room

Managing Partner Brett Callis, guest Chef Deborah Madison, Chef/Owner Jeffrey Muldrow

Rustic, authentic preparations

AWARD WINNER
SINCE 2002

Carlos' Restaurant

Dining room

For more than a decade and a half, residents of Chicago's North Shore have been coming to Carlos' for those significant celebrations that call for a memorable meal. They come for the comfortable, understated elegance of the intimate dining room, accented by mirrors and flowers, and for the stylish, satisfying, beautifully presented fare, such as tournedos of coriander dusted cervena venison and sautéed Chilean sea bass. The wine list is a winner of *Wine Spectator's* Grand Award.

Strawberry almond tart

Pinenut-crusted rack of Australian baby lamb

AWARD WINNER
SINCE 1992

Stately elegance

Directions

North of Chicago in Highland Park, 40 min. from O'Hare International Airport

429 Temple Avenue
Highland Park, IL 60035
PH: (847) 432-0770
FAX: (847) 432-2047
www.carlos-restaurant.com

Owners
Carlos and Debbie Nieto

Cuisine
Contemporary French

Days Open
Open Wed.-Mon. for dinner

Pricing
Dinner for one,
without tax, tip, or drinks:
$60-$80

Dress Code
Jacket required

Reservations
Required

Parking
Valet

Features
Private room/parties

Credit Cards
AE, VC, MC, CB, DC, JCB, DS

Café 36

Dining room

R einhard Barthel Sr. and his son, Reinhard Jr., impress customers and critics alike with exceptional cuisine and outstanding service in their charming French-style restaurant. Acclaimed by the *Chicago Tribune* and *Chicago Sun-Times*, Café 36 maintains high standards to ensure a memorable experience with each visit. Expect such tempting specialties as braised stuffed leg and tenderloin of rabbit in lingonberry cabernet jus, and sautéed ostrich medallions with pink peppercorns, wild mushrooms, and brandy demi glace. The wine list is extensive.

Owners Reinhard Barthel Sr. and Reinhard Barthel Jr.

Venison ragout in puff pastry

Chef Reinhard Barthel Jr.

DiRōNA
AWARD WINNER
SINCE 1997

Directions

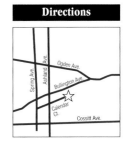

Seven miles north of the Stevenson Expressway in the southeast suburb of LaGrange, 20 min. from O'Hare International Airport

22 Calendar Court
LaGrange, IL 60525
PH: (708) 354-5722
FAX: (708) 354-5042

Owners
Reinhard Barthel Sr. and
Reinhard Barthel Jr.

Cuisine
French bistro

Days Open
Open Mon.-Fri. for lunch,
daily for dinner

Pricing
Dinner for one,
without tax, tip, or drinks:
$20-$40

Dress Code
Business casual

Reservations
Recommended

Parking
Free on site

Features
Private room/parties

Credit Cards
AE, VC, MC, DC, DS

The English Room at the Deer Path Inn

The dining room

In the North Shore community of Lake Forest, 30 min. from O'Hare International Airport

255 East Illinois Road
Lake Forest, IL 60045
PH: (847) 234-2280
FAX: (847) 234-3352
www.dpihotel.com

Owners
Michel T. Lama,
General Manager

Cuisine
Continental

Days Open
Open daily for breakfast, lunch, and dinner

Pricing
Dinner for one,
without tax, tip, or drinks:
$20-$40

Dress Code
Business casual

Reservations
Recommended

Parking
Free on site

Features
Private room/parties,
outdoor dining

Credit Cards
AE, VC, MC, DC, DC, DS

F or patrons accustomed to elegance, The English Room at the Deer Path Inn has been a dining destination since 1929. International culinary experience is paired with the finest seasonal foods to suit discriminating tastes. Move from starters, such as Maine lobster roll or foie gras, to seared sea bass with "forbidden" black rice, prime New York strip steak, or grilled veal chop. Complement these with a selection from the award-winning wine cellar.

Roasted venison with raspberry sauce

General Manager Michel T. Lama
Executive Chef Khellil Abderezak

Seared filet of Dover sole with beurre blanc sauce

Wine Spectator
AWARD OF EXCELLENCE

DiRōNA
AWARD WINNER
SINCE 2001

Le Vichyssois

A popular Lakemoor destination

Enjoy a day in the country and then relax with a delicious dinner prepared by Chef Bernard Cretier at his French country inn, now in its 25th year. Fresh fish, steak, veal, and duck are the bill of fare at Le Vichyssois, where the specialties of the house include mushroom cigar, salmon en croute, and, of course, the namesake soup, served hot or cold. Le Vichyssois is equidistant from Chicago and Milwaukee.

The main dining room

The bar

Understated elegance

Directions

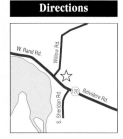

On Route 120, 2 miles west of Route 12, 45 min. from O'Hare International Airport

220 West Route 120
Lakemoor, IL 60050
PH: (815) 385-8221
Fax: (815) 385-8223
www.levichyssois.com

Owners
Bernard and Priscilla Cretier

Cuisine
French

Days Open
Open Wed.-Sun. for dinner

Pricing
Dinner for one,
without tax, tip, or drinks:
$40-$60

Dress Code
Business casual

Reservations
Recommended

Parking
Free on site

Features
Private room/parties

Credit Cards
VC, MC, CB, DC, JCB

AWARD WINNER
SINCE 1992

Tallgrass

Tallgrass...elegant, intimate dining

On State Street, 30 min.
from Midway Airport

1006 South State Street
Lockport, IL 60411
PH: (815) 838-5566
FAX: (815) 588-0397

Tallgrass is one of those restaurants — small, elegant, intimate — that you cherish, and come back to again, and again. Not only for the superb cuisine of master chef Robert Burcenski, co-owner, but also for the warm welcome extended by co-owner, J. Thomas Alves, who acts as both maître d' and erudite sommelier. Highly acclaimed chef Robert Burcenski "prepares elegantly garnished contemporary cuisine reflecting a world of influences...Tallgrass also boasts an intelligent, reasonably priced wine list featuring small West Coast producers."

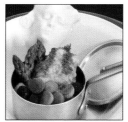

*Modern French cuisine,
elegantly garnished*

*Master Chef
Robert Burcenski*

Owners
Robert Burcenski and
J. Thomas Alves

Cuisine
Modern French

Days Open
Open Wed.-Sun. for dinner

Pricing
Dinner for one,
without tax, tip, or drinks:
$45-$65

Dress Code
Jacket required

Reservations
Required

Parking
Free on site

Features
Private room/parties

Credit Cards
MC, CB

Sweet temptations

AWARD WINNER
SINCE 1992

Carlucci Rosemont

Entrance to Carlucci Rosemont

Directions

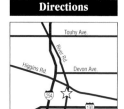

In the Riverway complex, on North River Rd., 5 min. from O'Hare Int'l Airport

Carlucci in Rosemont, imports a breath of Tuscany for a dining experience that reflects the spirit and flavors of Italy. Robust, and simple are features of the menu, taking Tuscan cuisine to a new level. Vaulted ceilings with Renaissance Italian style murals, and honey-toned walls create rustic warmth in the dining room. Open seven days for lunch, and dinner. Private dining rooms for groups from 10-200.

Main dining room

Bar

6111 N. River Road
Rosemont, IL 60018
PH: (847) 518-0990
FAX: (847) 518-0999
www.carluccirestaurant.com

Owners
Joe Carlucci

Cuisine
Tuscan Italian

Days Open
Open Mon.-Fri. for lunch, daily for dinner

Pricing
Dinner for one, without tax, tip, or drinks: $20-$40

Dress Code
Business casual

Reservations
Recommended

Parking
Valet, free on site

Features
Private rooms and theater style seating for meetings, parties, near theater, outdoor dining

Credit Cards
AE, VC, MC, DC, DS

...alio Room

AWARD WINNER
SINCE 1996

Restaurant at the Canterbury

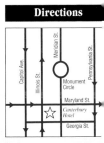

Atrium

On South Illinois Street, one block from the Indian Convention Center and RC Dome and 10 min. from Indianapolis International Airport

The Restaurant at the Canterbury is just off the lobby of the historic Canterbury Hotel in the heart of downtown Indianapolis. The intimate ambience and unobtrusive, professional service are sure to exceed the expectations of the most discriminating guests. Expect American and Continental cuisine expertly prepared by Executive Chef Scott DeSalvo.

Dining room

123 South Illinois Street
Indianapolis, IN 46225
PH: (317) 634-3000
FAX: (317) 262-8111
www.canterburyhotel.com

Owners
DND

Cuisine
American and Continental

Days Open
Open daily for breakfast, lunch, and dinner

Pricing
Dinner for one, without tax, tip, or drinks: $40-$60

Dress Code
Jacket requested

Reservations
Recommended

Parking
Complimentary valet

Features
Private room/parties, near theater

Credit Cards
AE, VC, MC, CB, DC, JCB,

Lounge

AWARD WINNER
SINCE 1995

210

The Oakroom at the Seelbach Hilton

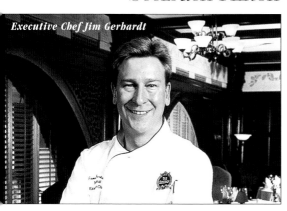

Executive Chef Jim Gerhardt

Kentucky's first and only AAA Five-Diamond restaurant is located in the historic Seelbach Hilton. Come savor the best of Bluegrass Country. French rib chop of pork with green tomato pawpaw relish and country ham jus is just one of the many irresistible creations that emerge from the kitchen of award-winning Executive Chef Jim Gerhardt. The wine cellar has more than 1,000 selections, and the bar, cited by *The Independent* of London as one of the top 50 bars in the world, is stocked with more than 40 varieties of bourbon.

Bourbon French rib of pork

Chef de Cusine Michael Cunha

BEST OF AWARD OF EXCELLENCE

DiRoNA
AWARD WINNER
SINCE 1999

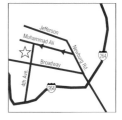

In downtown Louisville, 10 min. from Standiford Field Airport

The Seelbach Hilton
500 4th Avenue
Louisville, KY 40202
PH: (502) 807-3463
FAX: (502) 585-9240
www.seelbachhilton.com

Owners
Interstate Hotels and Resorts

Cuisine
Kentucky fine dining

Days Open
Open Fri. for lunch,
daily for dinner,
Sunday for brunch

Pricing
Dinner for one,
without tax, tip, or drinks
$40-$60

Dress Code
Business casual

Reservations
Recommended

Parking
Complimentary valet

Features
Private rooms/parties, near theater, cigar/cognac events

Credit Cards
AE, VC, MC, DC, JCB, DS

Vincenzo's

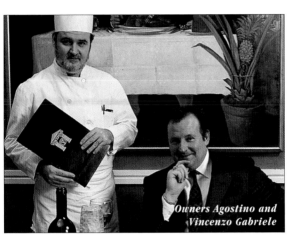

At South 5th and Market streets in downtown Louisville, 15 min. from Louisville International Airport

150 South 5th Street
Louisville, KY 40202
PH: (502) 580-1350
FAX: (502) 580-1355
www.vincenzosdining.com

Owners
Vincenzo Gabriele and Agostino Gabriele

Cuisine
Continental, Italian

Days Open
Open Mon.-Fri. for lunch, Mon.-Sat. for dinner

Pricing
Dinner for one,
without tax, tip, or drinks:
$20-$40

Dress Code
Business casual

Reservations
Recommended

Parking
Valet

Features
Private room/parties, outdoor dining, near theater, cigar/cognac events

Credit Cards
AE, VC, MC, CB, DC

V incenzo's represents brothers Agostino and Vincenzo Gabriele's personal dreams for a place of hospitality where friends old and new can come for a truly special evening, whether a simple meal or a multicourse tour de force. The menu reflects the owners' European heritage and training. In addition to continental classics, Vincenzo's offers "Eurospa" heart-healthy cuisine to meet a growing preference among guests for lighter fare.

Owners Agostino and Vincenzo Gabriele

Your host

Your chef

AWARD WINNER
SINCE 1993

Le Parvenu Restaurant

Charming house with porch dining

On Williams Blvd., near Airline Highway, 3 min. from Louis Armstrong International Airport

A charming 55-year-old house, seating 70 with a small bar, fronted with a large covered porch, and surrounded by a spacious yard and flower gardens, the cuisine at Le Parvenu Restaurant is "Innovative American Creole." Chef Dennis uses his European training, knowledge of American products, and love for New Orleans flavors to formulate elegance in Creole dining. The menu features local seafood, veal, beef, duck, and lamb dishes all prepared and presented with American elegance.

Chef Dennis and Kelly Hutley

House specialty-Lobster Le Parvenu

509 Williams Blvd.
Kenner, LA 70062
PH: (504) 471-0534
FAX: (504) 471-0537

Owners
Dennis and Kelly Hutley

Cuisine
Innovative American Creole

Days Open
Open Tues.-Sat. for lunch and dinner, Sunday for Brunch

Pricing
Dinner for one, without tax, tip, or drinks: $40-$60

Dress Code
Business casual

Reservations
Recommended

Parking
Free on site

Features
Semi-private rooms/parties, near theater, outdoor dining

Credit Cards
AE, VC, MC, DC, DS

Elegant, Creole dining

AWARD WINNER
SINCE 2003

La Provence

La Provence

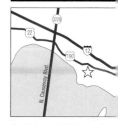

Directions

On Highway 190 East, 45 min. from Louis Armstrong International Airport

25020 Highway 190 East
Lacombe, LA 70445
PH: (985) 626-7662
FAX: (985) 626-9598

Owners
Chris Kerageorgiou

Cuisine
French Provencale

Days Open
Open Wed.-Sat. for dinner,
Sunday for brunch

Pricing
Dinner for one,
without tax, tip, or drinks:
$20-$40

Dress Code
Business casual

Reservations
Recommended

Parking
Free on site

Features
Private room/parties,
entertainment

Credit Cards
AE, VC, MC, DC

If a sense of harmony pervades the rooms at La Provence, it's no accident. Everything here reflects Chef/Owner Chris Kerageorgiou's talent for hospitality. In the piney woods near Lacombe, across Lake Pontchartrain from New Orleans, Chef Kerageorgiou has created a corner of southern France, complete with welcoming hearths, quaint memorabilia, and a menu reflecting the soul-warming flavors of Provence. The wine cellar features regional French wines that complement the award-winning dinner menu.

Chef/Owner Chris Kerageorgiou

A corner of southern France

Patio dining

AWARD WINNER
SINCE 1993

214

Arnaud's Restaurant

Sunday brunch and jazz

Arnaud's Creole cuisine excites today just as it has since 1918, with world-famous originals prepared by Executive Chef Tommy DiGiovanni. Shrimp Arnaud, oysters Bienville, trout meuniere, and grilled Louisiana quail are among the specialties. Savor lunch or dinner in quiet elegance, or dine less formally in the Jazz Bistro with live jazz nightly. Superb wines complement your meal. Sunday brunch is a lively occasion set to the rhythm of a traditional Dixieland band.

Mardi Gras Museum

Pompano duarte

Owners Jane and Archie Casbarian

AWARD WINNER
SINCE 1992

Directions

In the heart of the French Quarter at Bourbon Street, 30 min. from Louis Armstrong International Airport

813 Rue Bienville
New Orleans, LA 70112
PH: (504) 523-5433
FAX: (504) 581-7908
www.arnauds.com

Owners
Archie and Jane Casbarian

Cuisine
Classic Creole and French

Days Open
Open Sun.-Fri. for lunch, daily for dinner, Sun. for brunch

Pricing
Dinner for one, without tax, tip or drinks: $20-$40

Dress Code
Business casual at lunch, jacket and tie preferred at dinner

Reservations
Recommended

Parking
Validated at garage nearby

Features
Private room/parties, entertainment, near theater

Credit Cards
AE, VC, MC, CB, DC, DS

Bayona

In the French Quarter

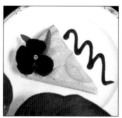

On Dauphine Street in the French Quarter, 30 min. from Louis Armstrong International Airport

Housed in a 200-year old cottage in the heart of the French Quarter, Bayona offers a casually elegant dining atmosphere and consistently outstanding service. Co-owner and Executive Chef Susan Spicer emphasizes the flavors of the Mediterranean but also incorporates Alsace, Asia, India, and the American Southwest. Specialties include grilled shrimp with coriander sauce and black bean cakes, and grilled duck breast with pepper jelly glaze. Select the perfect bottle of wine from Bayona's extensive wine list.

Dinner in the courtyard

Lemon-buttermilk tart

Co-owner and Executive Chef, Susan Spicer

430 Dauphine Street
New Orleans, LA 70112
PH: (504) 525-4455
FAX: (504) 522-0589
www.bayona.com

Owners
Regina Keever and Susan Spicer

Cuisine
French/Mediterranean

Days Open
Open Mon.-Fri. for lunch, Mon.-Sat. for dinner

Pricing
Dinner for one, without tax, tip, or drinks: $20-$40

Dress Code
Casual

Reservations
Required

Parking
Garage nearby

Features
Private room/parties, outdoor dining, near theater

Credit Cards
AE, VC, MC, CB, DC, JCB, DS

AWARD WINNER
SINCE 1993

Bistro at Maison de Ville

Courtyard fountain

L ocated in the luxurious Hotel Maison de Ville, this bistro has a justly deserved reputation for introducing bright young culinary talent to an enthusiastic and appreciative public. Most recently recognized as "Top Haute Restaurant" by the *Zagat Guide* and "America's Top Tables" by *Gourmet* magazine, the eatery has a loyal following among local and national gourmands. Diners order from an innovative seasonal menu of traditional French bistro selections and New Orleans culinary favorites.

Bistro dining

Chef Greg Picolo

Exquisite entrées

AWARD WINNER
SINCE 2001

Directions

In the heart of the French Quarter, 30 min. from Louis Armstrong International Airport

727 Toulouse St.
New Orleans, LA 70130
PH: (504) 528-9206
FAX: (504) 589-9939
www.maisondeville.com

Owners
Meristar

Cuisine
Nouvelle Creole

Days Open
Open daily for lunch and dinner

Pricing
Dinner for one, without tax, tip, or drinks: $20-$40

Dress Code
Business casual

Reservations
Recommended

Parking
Garage nearby

Features
Outdoor dining

Credit Cards
AE, VC, MC, DC, DS

Broussard's Restaurant

In the French Quarter, 30 min. from Louis Armstrong International Airport

French Quarter landmark since 1920

In a city that joyously celebrates fine dining as an art form, Broussard's has been a fixture for nearly a century and was presented with the prestigious Ivy Award for 2002. Located in the heart of the French Quarter, Broussard's blends old architecture, classic food, and tradition to achieve a dining experience one is not likely to forget. Chef/Proprietor Gunter Preuss is a master of traditional Creole cooking. Try the veal Broussard or the seafood bouillabaisse.

819 Conti Street
New Orleans, LA 70112
PH: (504) 581-3866
FAX: (504) 581-3873
www.broussards.com

Owners
The Preuss Family

Cuisine
French Creole

Days Open
Open daily for dinner

Pricing
Dinner for one,
without tax, tip or drinks:
$40-$60

Dress Code
Business casual

Reservations
Recommended

Features
Private room/parties, outdoor dining, entertainment, near theater, cigar/cognac events

Credit Cards
AE, VC, MC

Louisiana Bouillabaisse

Chef Gunter Preuss

Delice

AWARD WINNER
SINCE 1998

Christian's Restaurant

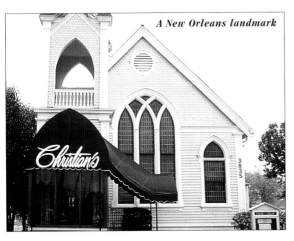

A New Orleans landmark

At Iberville and Scott streets one block from Canal Street, 25 min. from Louis Armstrong International Airport

3835 Iberville Street
New Orleans, LA 70119
PH: (504) 482-4924
FAX: (504) 482-6852
www.
neworleansrestaurants.
com

C hristian's Restaurant is located in an old church, one of the most unusual restaurant settings in this historic city. The dining room has beautiful stained-glass windows, cathedral ceilings, and greenery, which offers a charming atmosphere for dining. Christian's specializes in delicately blending New Orleans Creole and classic French cuisine, creating such entrées as filet au poivre, bouillabaisse Marseillaise, stuffed eggplant, or roasted half duckling with sweet peppercorn sauce. Complement lunch or dinner with a bottle of wine from our extensive award-winning wine list.

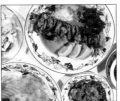

An extensive wine selection complements the culinary excellence

A unique setting for elegant dining

Owners
Hank Bergeron

Cuisine
New Orleans Creole and classic French

Days Open
Open Tues.-Fri. for lunch, Tues.-Sat. for dinner

Pricing
Dinner for one, wthout tax, tip, or drinks: $20-$40

Dress Code
Business casual

Reservations
Recommended

Parking
Free on site

Credit Cards
AE, VC, MC, DC

Welcome to Christian's

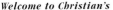

AWARD WINNER
SINCE 1992

Commander's Palace

A New Orleans landmark

In the middle of the Garden District on Washington Avenue, 30 min. from Louis Armstrong International Airport

1403 Washington Avenue
New Orleans, LA 70001
PH: (504) 899-8221
FAX: (504) 891-3242
www.commanderspalace.com

Since 1880, Commander's Palace has been a beloved New Orleans landmark known for the award-winning quality of its food, service, and charming dining rooms. Commander's cuisine reflects the best of the city, and both Creole and American heritages, as well as dishes of Commander's own creation. Try exciting menu additions such as shrimp cognac and andouille grits or stick to the classics with pecan crusted Gulf fish. With outstanding food, wine and the warm, spirited personalities of the staff, Commander's Palace promises to be a wonderful experience.

The Garden Room

Owners
Ella, Dottie, Lally Brennan and Ti Martin

Cuisine
Haute Creole

Days Open
Open Mon.-Fri. for lunch, daily for dinner, Saturday and Sunday for brunch

Pricing
Dinner for one, without tax, tip, or drinks: $40-$60

Dress Code
Jacket and tie preferred

Reservations
Recommended

Parking
Valet

Features
Private room/parties

Credit Cards
AE, VC, MC, CB, DC, DS

AWARD WINNER
SINCE 1993

220

Galatoire's Restaurant

Downstairs dining room

Since 1905 Galatoire's has served traditional French Creole cuisine in a historic, elegant, and euphoric atmosphere in the French Quarter. The extensive menu reads like a catalogue of ageless New Orleans favorites: shrimp rémoulade, creole gumbo, Crabmeat Maison, shrimp Clemenceau, lamb chops béarnaise, pompano with sautéed crabmeat Meunière, and banana bread pudding. Considered the grande dame of New Orleans' old-line restaurants, tradition has been maintained for nearly a century with little change through the decades. Galatoire's — indulge in the tradition.

Crabmeat Maison

Shrimp rémoulade

Grilled redfish, shrimp, and crabmeat meunière

AWARD WINNER
SINCE 2001

Directions

In the French Quarter, 25 min. from Louis Armstrong International Airport

209 Bourbon Street
New Orleans, LA 70130
PH: (504) 525-2021
FAX: (504) 525-5900
www.galatoires.com

Owners
The Galatoire family

Cuisine
French Creole

Days Open
Open Tues.-Sun. for lunch and dinner

Pricing
Dinner for one, without tax, tip or drinks: $20-$40

Dress Code
Jacket required at dinner and on Sunday

Reservations
Taken for second floor only

Parking
Garage nearby

Features
Private room/parties

Credit Cards
AE, VC, MC, DC, DS

The Grill Room

The Grill Room, located on the second floor of the Windsor Court Hotel, has gained awards for fine dining since it opened in 1984. From its inception, dining at The Grill Room has been a tradition for New Orleanians and guests. The restaurant specializes in contemporary American cuisine. Under the direction of Executive Chef Jonathan Wright, his culinary team has created a diverse style that couples century-old methods and techniques with nontraditional ingredients. The cross-cultural menu is complemented by one of the finest wine cellars in the region.

Chef Jonathan Wright

Le Salon Lounge & Bar

AWARD WINNER
SINCE 1992

Directions

Located on the second floor of the Windsor Court Hotel, 25 min. from Louis Armstrong International Airport

300 Gravier Street
New Orleans, LA 70130
PH: (504) 522-1992
FAX: (504) 596-4513
www.windsorcourthotel.com

Owners
Orient-Express Hotels

Cuisine
Contemporary American

Days Open
Open daily for breakfast, lunch, and for dinner

Pricing
Dinner for one,
without tax, tip, or drinks:
$40-$60

Dress Code
Jacket required, tie optional
(for dinner only)

Reservations
Recommended

Parking
Valet, free on site

Features
Entertainment

Credit Cards
AE, VC, MC, CB, DC, ER, JCB, DS

Lafitte's Landing Restaurant at Bittersweet Plantation

Directions

At Claiborne and Railroad avenues, 1 hr. from Louis Armstrong International Airport and 1 hr. from Baton Rouge Regional Airport

The Gingry Board Room

Celebrating 25 years in the heart of plantation country, Lafitte's Landing Restaurant at Bittersweet Plantation is one of the most renowned eateries in South Louisiana. The restaurant, which also has bed-and-breakfast accommodations, is housed in the former home of Chef John Folse, Bittersweet Plantation. Lafitte's Landing has won numerous national and international awards, including induction into the Fine Dining Hall of Fame in 1989.

Venison Carencro

Chef John Folse

404 Claiborne Avenue
Donaldsonville, LA 70346
PH: (225) 473-1232
FAX: (225) 473-1161
www.jfolse.com

Owner
Chef John D. Folse, CEC, AAC

Cuisine
Louisiana Indigenous

Days Open
Open Sun. for lunch, Wed.-Sat. for dinner

Pricing
Dinner for one,
without tax, tip, or drinks:
$20-$40

Dress Code
Upscale casual

Reservations
Recommended

Parking
Free on site, valet

Features
Outdoor dining,
wine events

Credit Cards
AE, VC, MC, DS

Bed-and-breakfast accommodations

AWARD WINNER
SINCE 1996

Ruth's Chris Steak House

Filet mignon

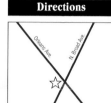

At N. Broad and Orleans avenues, convenient to the French Quarter and convention center and 20 min. from Louis Armstrong International Airport

711 N. Broad Street
New Orleans, LA 70119
PH: (504) 486-0810
FAX: (504) 486-1324
www.ruthschris.com

Owners
Ruth's Chris Steak House

Cuisine
Steaks, seafood

Days Open
Open Sun.-Fri. for lunch, daily for dinner

Pricing
Dinner for one, without tax, tip, or drinks: $40-$60

Dress Code
Business casual

Reservations
Recommended

Parking
Valet

Features
Private rooms/parties

Credit Cards
AE, VC, MC, DC, DS

This is the steak that steak lovers rave about! Ruth's Chris Steak House specializes in USDA Prime beef. Strips, filets, ribeyes, T-bones, and porterhouses are aged to exacting standards, broiled to perfection, and served sizzling. An award-winning wine list features premium vintages by the glass. The service is attentive, knowledgeable, and friendly.

Elegant dining

Wine Spectator
AWARD OF EXCELLENCE

DiRōNA
AWARD WINNER
SINCE 1999

Smith's Louis XVI Restaurant Français

Courtyard at Christmas

In a city famous for food, Louis XVI has maintained its commitment to style, refinement, and quality for more than a quarter century. Executive Chef Agnes Bellet applies today's techniques to the French classics, creating beautiful dishes immersed in natural flavors. A romantic evening spent overlooking the Mediterranean courtyard, complete with tropical foliage and a picturesque fountain, has become an integral part of the New Orleans experience.

Exquisite French cuisine

Clients enjoy fine dining

Executive Chef Agnes Bellet

AWARD WINNER
SINCE 1993

Directions

In the St. Louis Hotel in the French Quarter, 20 min. from Louis Armstrong International Airport

730 Bienville Street
New Orleans, LA 70130
PH: (504) 581-7000
FAX: (504) 524-8925
www.louisxvi.com

Owners
Mark C. Smith III

Cuisine
French

Days Open
Open daily for breakfast and dinner

Pricing
Dinner for one, without tax, tip, or drinks:
$40-$60

Dress Code
Business casual

Reservations
Recommended

Parking
Free on site

Credit Card
AE, VC, MC, CB, DC

75 Chestnut

Dining room

In the heart of the Beacon Hill neighborhood, 15 min. from Logan Airport

Nestled in the historic Beacon Hill neighborhood of downtown Boston, Zagat describes 75 Chestnut as "sultry, sexy, and all around fabulous." Known as "the most romantic" restaurant in Boston, 75 Chestnut provides an intimate setting for its creatively prepared classic dishes with a contemporary flair. Combining exceptional food, wine, and service, 75 Chestnut, with its cozy bar, offers a truly memorable dining experience in an elegant atmosphere.

(l to r) Corp. Chef Markus Ripperger, Owner Thomas Kershaw, Exec. Chef Michael Heath

75 Chestnut Street
Boston, MA 02108
PH: (617) 227-2175
FAX: (617) 227-3675
www.75chestnut.com

Owners
Thomas A. Kershaw

Cuisine
American contemporary

Days Open
Open daily for dinner,
Sunday for brunch
(Sept.- June)

Pricing
Dinner for one,
without tax, tip, or drinks:
$20-$40

Dress Code
Business casual

Reservations
Recommended

Parking
Valet nightly, garage nearby

Features
Seasonal changing menu
with Special wine tastings

Credit Cards
AE, VC, MC, DC, DS

Cozy bar

AWARD WINNER
SINCE 2003

Anthony's Pier 4

Spectacular city and harbor views

On Northern Ave., 5 min. from Logan International Airport

---

140 Northern Avenue
Boston, MA 02110
PH: (617) 482-6262
FAX: (617) 426-2324
www.pier4.com

Anthony's Pier 4 is one of Boston's most prestigious culinary landmarks. This world-renowned restaurant has catered to a local, national, and international clientele for 40 years with its incomparable selections and innovative preparations, such as lobster from its own lobster company in Maine, fresh New England seafood, imported Dover sole, prime steaks, and an award-winning wine list of more than 500 selections. The lobby is lined with photographs of the heads of state, famous athletes, and Hollywood stars who have dined there.

**Anthony's Pier 4
Clambake Special**

Founder Anthony Athanas

Owners
Anthony Athanas and sons:
Anthony Athanas, Jr., Michael Athanas, Robert Athanas, Paul Athanas

Cuisine
New England regional and international, with emphasis on seafood and lobster

Days Open
Open daily for lunch and dinner

Pricing
Dinner for one,
without tax, tip, or drinks:
$20-$40

Dress Code
Business casual

Reservations
Recommended

Parking
Free on-site, valet

Features
Private room/parties, outdoor dining, cigar and wine events

Credit Cards
AE, VC, MC, CB, DC, JCB, DS

**Alfresco dining overlooking
Boston Harbor**

AWARD WINNER
SINCE 1996

The Bay Tower

Main dining room

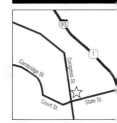

On 60 State St., adjacent to Fanueil Hall Market Place, 10 min. from Logan Airport

The Bay Tower offers an unparalleled dining experience with breathtaking views of Boston Harbor, 33 floors above Fanueil Hall Market Place. The menu features New England favorites with global accents, as well as elegant specialty dishes by Executive Chef Paul Diogenes. The Bay Tower has received numerous awards including "top 100 restaurants" by Restaurants and Institutions, Award of Excellence by *Wine Spectator,* and Mobil's Three-Star Award.

General Manager and Executive Chef Paul Diogenes

60 State Street
Boston, MA 02109
PH: (617) 723-1666
FAX: (617) 723-7887
www.baytower.com

Owners
Bay Tower, Inc.

Cuisine
New England favorites with global accents

Days Open
Open for dinner
Mon.-Sat.

Pricing
Dinner for one, without tax, tip, or drinks: $40-$60

Dress Code
Business casual

Reservations
Recommended

Parking
Garage nearby

Features
Private room/parties, entertainment, near theater

Credit Cards
AE, VC, MC, CB, DC, JCB, DS

Baked lobster with saffron seafood stuffing

AWARD WINNER
SINCE 1992

Grill 23 & Bar

Dining room

G rill 23 & Bar, located in the historic Salada Tea Building in Boston's Back Bay, opened its doors in 1983 and was conceived as the premier steak and seafood grill in Boston. Chef Jay Murray's menu boasts prime, dry-aged beef, and innovative fish presentations complemented by the freshest of New England's seasonal produce and herbs. An exhibition kitchen allows diners to enjoy front row seats for the theatre of meal preparation. The wine list received the Award of Excellence from *Wine Spectator*.

Shellfish sampler

Executive Chef Jay Murray

Boston's premier steak & seafood grill

**AWARD WINNER
SINCE 1998**

Directions

Corner of Berkeley and Stuart streets in Boston's Back Bay, 20 min. from Logan Airport

161 Berkeley Street
Boston, MA 02116
PH: (617) 542-2255
FAX: (617) 542-5114
www.grill23.com

Owners
SBH Corp

Cuisine
American/Steakhouse

Days Open
Open daily for dinner

Pricing
Dinner for one,
without tax, tip, or drinks:
$60-$80

Dress Code
Business casual

Reservations
Recommended

Parking
Valet

Features
Private room/parties, near theater, cigar/cognac events

Credit Cards
AE, VC, MC, CB, DC, DS

Hamersley's Bistro

The corner of Tremont and Clarendon in Boston's historic South End, 20 min. from Logan International Airport

Main dining room

V isit what *Gourmet Magazine* has named one of its "Personal Favorites." Experience the warm welcome of the elegant dining room, the innovation and consistency of the seasonal menus, the diverse and eclectic wine list, and the gracious hospitality that has made Hamersley's Bistro the South End dining destination for over 15 years. Enjoy a satisfyingly simple, hearty meal, prepared from seasonally fresh local ingredients. Hamersley's is an elegant Boston translation of the homey, family-run country bistros of France. Hamersley's bistro has been unanimously praised by critics, including the coveted "★★★★" rating from *The Boston Globe* and the *Boston Herald* and top ranking from *Gourmet, Food & Wine,* and *Zagat's.* During the spring and summer months, outdoor dining from the Bistro Menu is available on the Tremont Street patio.

Pan roasted lobster

Seasonal patio dining

553 Tremont Street
Boston, MA 02116
PH: (617) 423-2700
FAX: (617) 423-7710
www.hamersleysbistro.com

Owners
Gordon and Fiona Hamersle

Cuisine
Contemporary bistro inspire
by France and Italy

Days Open
Open daily for dinner

Pricing
Dinner for one,
without tax, tip, or drinks:
$40-$60

Dress Code
Business casual

Reservations
Recommended

Parking
Valet, garage nearby

Features
Private room/parties,
outdoor dining

Credit Cards
AE, VC, MC, DC, DS

AWARD WINNER
SINCE 1993

Icarus

A romantic setting for an intimate dinner

Directions

Corner of Appleton and Tremont in Boston; 20 minutes from Logan Airport

3 Appleton St.
Boston, MA 02116
PH: (617) 426-1790
FAX: (617) 426-2150
www.icarusrestaurant.com

Owners
Chris Douglass

Cuisine
American regional

Days Open
Daily for dinner

Pricing
Dinner for one,
without tax, tip, or drinks:
$40-$60

Dress Code
Business casual

Reservations
Recommended

Parking
Valet

Features
Private room/parties, live jazz on Fridays

Credit Cards
AE, VC, MC, DC

For nearly 20 years, Chef and Co-owner Chris Douglass' American regional menu has continued to set the standard for fine dining in Boston's exciting South End. Locally grown produce, the finest farm-raised meat and poultry, and the freshest New England seafood complemented by sumptuous desserts and an award-winning wine list assure a memorable dining experience. Icarus features a lovely two-level dining room appointed in rich woods and mission furniture, accented by soft lighting and spacious seating.

Icarus features the award-winning cuisine of Chef Chris Douglass.

Private dining room is the perfect spot for a business or social function.

ICARUS
RESTAURANT • BAR

DiRoNA
AWARD WINNER
SINCE 1994

L'Espalier

A beautiful setting

In the heart of Back Bay, 20 min. from Logan International Airport

30 Gloucester Street
Boston, MA 02115
PH: (617) 262-3023
FAX: (617) 375-9297
www.lespalier.com

A culinary exploration in an 1886 Back Bay townhouse, L'Espalier was the first independently owned restaurant to bring haute cuisine to Boston. Twenty years later, it remains a chic and modern restaurant featuring Chef/Proprietor Frank McClelland's innovative New England-French cooking based on local ingredients. Three beautifully appointed rooms provide the setting for your dining experience. L'Espalier is one block from the Hynes Convention Center, the Prudential Center, and Copley Place, and within walking distance of Symphony Hall.

Slow-roasted Muscovy duck breast

Owners
Frank and Catherine McClelland

Cuisine
New England French

Days Open
Open Mon.-Sat. for dinner

Pricing
Dinner for one, without tax, tip, or drinks: $60-$80

Dress Code
Business casual

Reservations
Required

Parking
Valet

Features
Private room/parties

Credit Cards
AE, VC, MC, DC

Quiet atmosphere

Chef/Proprietor Frank McClelland

AWARD WINNER
SINCE 1993

Seasons

Nationally renowned dining at Seasons

Nationally renowned Seasons, offers an outstanding atmosphere, and an exquisite seasonal menu complemented by an extensive all-American wine list. Overlooking Faneuil Hall, Seasons consistently earns praise from food and wine critics around the world. Chef Houlihan demonstrates his talents by creatively marrying local produce, hand-selected New England seafood, and the finest farm-raised meat and poultry. Specialties include Bostonian chowder, tempura battered lobster, citrus-glazed Long Island duck breast, and seared Ahi tuna.

Seared Ahi tuna

Chef Brian Houlihan

AWARD WINNER
SINCE 1992

Directions

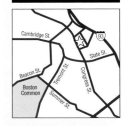

At Faneuil Hall Marketplace, overlooking city skyline, 15 min. from Logan International Airport

Millennium Bostonian Hotel
Faneuil Hall Marketplace
Boston, MA 02109
PH: (617) 523-3600
FAX: (617) 523-2593
www.millenniumhotels.com

Owners
Millennium Hotels
and Resorts

Cuisine
American Regional

Days Open
Open daily for breakfast,
Mon.-Fri. for lunch,
Tues.-Sat. for dinner

Pricing
Dinner for one,
without tax, tip, or drinks:
$35-$50

Dress Code
Business casual

Reservations
Recommended

Parking
Valet

Features
Private room

Credit Cards
AE, VC, MC, DS

Top of the Hub

Enjoy a spectacular view of Boston

In the Prudential Center, at Boylston and Ring Road, 1! minutes from Logan Airport

800 Boylston Street
Prudential Center, 52nd Fl.
Boston, MA 02119
PH: (617) 536-1775
FAX: (617) 859-8298
www.selectrestaurants.com

Owners
Select Restaurants

Cuisine
Creative American

Days Open
Open daily for lunch and dinner, Sunday brunch

Pricing
Dinner for one,
Without tax, tip, or drinks:
$20-$40

Dress Code
Business casual

Reservations
Recommended

Parking
Garage in building, validate parking

Features
Entertainment and dancing nightly, private room/parties, near theaters

Credit Cards
AE, VC, MC, CB, DC, DS

At Top of the Hub, the breathtaking panorama is matched only by the award-winning new American cuisine of Executive Chef Dean Moore. Elegantly presented and exquisitely prepared, each entrée at the Top of the Hub is a meal to remember. Located atop the landmark Prudential Center in the fashionable Back Bay, the Top of the Hub is life on a whole different level.

The finest cuisine

Live jazz nightly

Private function rooms can accommodate an intimate reception for 10, or a banquet for 500

AWARD WINNER
SINCE 1998

234

Chillingsworth

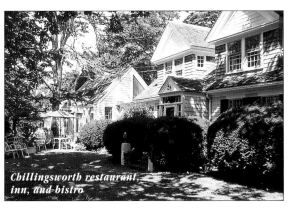

Chillingsworth restaurant, inn, and bistro

An antique Cape house surrounded by six acres of lawns and gardens is the setting for Chef/Owner Nitzi Rabin's eclectic, seasonal, tasting menus based upon the bounty of local shellfish, seafood, and boutique produce suppliers. *Zagat*, the *Robb Report*, and *The New York Times* all consider Chillingsworth a destination restaurant. The rooms are beautifully appointed with period antiques and fresh flowers. The *Bistro at Chillingsworth* offers a casual a la carte menu in the adjacent greenhouse and on the patio for both lunch and dinner, plus there is a comfortable bar and lounge. Three deluxe Guest Rooms are available.

Foie gras raviolis

The Alcove Table overlooks the Terrace Room

Chef Nitzi Rabin in front of the Gazebo

Wine Spectator
AWARD OF EXCELLENCE

DiRōNA
AWARD WINNER SINCE 1993

Directions

On Route 6A (Main St.) in Brewster, 1.1 miles east of the Route124 intersection; 20 mins. from Hyannis Airport

2449 Main Street
Brewster, MA 02631
PH: (508) 896-3640
PH: (800) 430-3640
FAX: (508) 896-7540
www.chillingsworth.com

Owners
Nitzi and Pat Rabin

Cuisine
Modern French, regional American

Days Open
Fine Dining Table d'Hote Tues.-Sun. for dinner, Bistro dinner Tues.-Sun., 7 nights in season and Bistro luncheon Tues.- Sun. (check shoulder season schedule)

Pricing
Dinner for one, without tax, tip, or drinks:
Table d'Hote: $59-$69, Bistro dinner: $15-$25

Dress Code
Business casual

Reservations
Recommended

Parking
Free on site

Features
Private rooms available, outdoor dining, monthly vintner's dinner

Credit Cards
AE, VC, MC, DC, DS

235

Wheatleigh

Wheatleigh

Directions

In the Berkshires town of Lenox, 1 hr. from Connecticut's Bradley International Airport

According to *The New York Times*, the Wheatleigh dining experience is "a table fit for a prince." The small luxury hotel with a European flavor is a replica of a 16th-century Florentine palazzo, built in the Berkshires by an American industrialist as a wedding gift for his daughter. Guests enjoy the chef's contemporary interpretation of classical French food utilizing a large network of local organic farmers.

Chef J. Bryce Whittlesey

Enter the "Wheatleigh dining experience"

Hawthorne Road,
P.O. Box 824
Lenox, MA 01240
PH: (413) 637-0610
FAX: (413) 637-4507
www.wheatleigh.com

Cuisine
Eclectic American

Days Open
Open daily for lunch and dinner, Sunday for brunch

Pricing
Dinner for one, wthout tax, tip or drinks: $80+

Dress Code
Jacket and tie preferred

Reservations
Required

Parking
Free on site, valet

Features
Private room/parties, near theater, cigar/cognac event

Credit Cards
AE, VC, MC, DC

The dining room

AWARD WINNER
SINCE 1992

21 Federal

Welcome to 21 Federal

21 Federal is housed in an 1847 Greek revival building right in the heart of downtown Nantucket. The ever-changing menu of new and traditional American cuisine is sure to please both locals, and worldly visitors. The restaurant's reputation of culinary excellence is paired with an award-winning wine list. A large main bar, and a cozy wine bar are popular before and after dinner destinations.

Downstairs dining room

A popular dinner destination

Another evening at 21 Federal

AWARD WINNER
SINCE 2002

Directions

In downtown Nantucket, 10 min. from Nantucket Airport

Federal Street
Nantucket, MA 02554
PH: (508) 228-2121
FAX: (508) 228-2962
www.21federal.net

Owners
Nelson Doubleday

Cuisine
New & Traditional American

Days Open
Open daily for dinner
(closed Dec. 10 thru April 18)

Pricing
Dinner for one,
without tax, tip, or drinks:
$40-$60

Dress Code
Business casual

Reservations
Recommended

Parking
Local street parking

Features
Private room/parties, outdoor dining

Credit Cards
AE, VC, MC

Òran Mór

Dining room

Photo credit: © Andy Ryan

Near Nantucket Yacht Club, on South Beach Street, 10 min. from Nantucket Airport

At Òran Mór, experience creative international food, based on a classically trained chef, set in a candle lit, intimate dining room. Listen to jazz greats as you consider our wine list which concentrates on domestic and French selections, worldly house pours, and over 60 half bottles. Òran Mór received the highest rating from *Zagat* amongst all the restaurants on Nantucket. Òran Mór is a small 55-seat restaurant in Nantucket town on the second floor, ten min. from Nantucket Airport and a 2 min. walk from the steamship.

Photo credit: © Andy Ryan

Evening dining

Photo credit: © Andy Ryan

The Wallace Family

2 South Beach Street
Nantucket, MA 02554
PH: (508) 228-8655
FAX: (508) 228-2498
www.nantucket.net/
Food/oranmor

Owners
Kathleen and
Peter Wallace

Cuisine
International

Days Open
Open daily for dinner

Pricing
Dinner for one,
without tax, tip, or drinks:
$40-$60

Dress Code
Business casual

Reservations
Recommended

Parking
Free on site

Credit Cards
AE, VD, MC

Photo credit: © Andy Ryan

Grilled baby octopus with roasted tomatoes

AWARD WINNER
SINCE 2003

Sonoma Restaurant

**Sonoma Restaurant...
intimate, elegant dining**

Located in Post Office
Place on Worcester Road,
90 min. from Logan
International Airport, and
15 min. from Worcester
Regional Airport

20 Worcester Road
Princeton, MA 01541
PH: (978) 464-5775
FAX: (978) 464-5003
www.sonoma-
princeton.com

Owners
Bill Brady

Cuisine
Global

Days Open
Open Wed.-Sun.
for dinner

Pricing
Dinner for one,
without tax, tip, or drinks:
$20-$40

Dress Code
Business casual

Reservations
Recommended

Parking
Free on site

Features
Private room/parties,
entertainment, wine dinners

Credit Cards
AE, VC, MC, CB, DC, DS

Chef/owner Bill Brady provides his guests with the ultimate dining experience in a relaxed and gracious setting. Described as "intimate, elegant and quite unforgettable," Sonoma offers the ultimate in global cuisine to produce a fusion of cultures and tastes. Praised for innovative combinations of the finest ingredients and imaginative presentations, the menu changes constantly to provide only the freshest and most seasonal products.

Global cuisine

AWARD WINNER
SINCE 2004

The Dan'l Webster Inn

The Dan'l Webster Inn

Directions

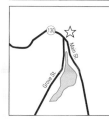

On Main St. in Sandwich;
20 min. from Hyannis
Municipal Airport, 95 min.
from Logan Airport

149 Main Street
Sandwich, MA 02563
PH: (800) 444-3566;
(508) 888-3622
FAX: (508) 888-5156
www.danlwebsterinn.com

The centerpiece of Cape Cod's oldest village, the Inn is the essence of elegance, featuring 54 individually appointed guest rooms. Dine in one of five distinctive dining rooms, each providing a unique and intimate dining experience. The Chef's fusion of unique regional ingredients creates a true contemporary American cuisine which has been inspired by Cape Cod—world famous for its magnificent bounty of fresh seafood. The menu is complemented by the expert pastry chef's decadent desserts and one of the most acclaimed wine cellars in the region.

Grilled breast of duckling over raspberry sauce

The Music Room

Owners
The Catania family

Cuisine
Contemporary/American

Days Open
Daily for lunch and dinner,
Sunday brunch

Pricing
Dinner for one,
without tax, tip, or drinks:
$20-$40

Dress Code
Casual

Reservations
Recommended

Parking
Free on site

Features
Entertainment,
private room/parties

Credit Cards
AE, VC, MC, CB, DC, DS

The Conservatory

AWARD WINNER
SINCE 1995

The Chanticleer

Main dining room

In the village of Siasconset at the eastern end of Nantucket Island, 7 min. from Nantucket Airport

Celebrating its 33rd year of excellence, The Chanticleer, under the loving direction of Chef/Proprietor Jean-Charles Berruet and his wife, Anne, is a restaurant without peer. Certainly the setting is about as perfect as anyone could wish for: multipaned windows looking out to gardens full of climbing roses and a delightful carousel horse. The cuisine is traditional French, with an emphasis on local fruits and vegetables, Nantucket seafood, game birds, and prime meats. The wine cellar is amazing: 1,200 French and California selections, more than 40,000 bottles in all.

Rose garden entrance

Chocolate soufflé

*Chef/Proprietor
Jean-Charles Berruet*

9 New Street
Box 601
Siasconset, MA 02564
PH: (508) 257-6231
FAX: (508) 257-4154
www.thechanticleerinn.com

Owners
Jean-Charles and Anne Berruet

Cuisine
French, seafood

Days Open
Open Tues.-Sun. for lunch and dinner

Pricing
Dinner for one, without tax, tip, or drinks: $60-$80

Dress Code
Jacket required

Reservations
Required

Parking
Free on site

Features
Private room/parties, outdoor dining, cigar/cognac events, catering

Credit Cards
AE, VC, MC, DC

AWARD WINNER
SINCE 1993

The Summer House Restaurant

Beautiful décor designed for romance

An evening at The Summer House has been described as "out of another place and time." According to the *2001 Zagat Guide*, "It's what a Nantucket dining experience should be." Using only the freshest ingredients, Executive Chef and owner Michael Farrell brings creative, contemporary cuisine of the highest quality to Nantucket. One of Chef Michael's signature dishes is seared Chilean sea bass with lump crab meat, apple smoked bacon, and chive potato cake with vermouth beurre blanc. Diners enjoy piano music nightly.

Executive Chef and owner Michael Farrell

Seared scallops with black bean vinaigrette

Lobster salad

AWARD WINNER
SINCE 1999

Directions

Five miles from the center of the historic district of Nantucket Town, 10 min. from Nantucket Airport

17 Ocean Avenue
Siasconset, MA 02554
PH: (508) 257-9976
FAX: (508) 257-6740

Owners
Michael Farrell

Cuisine
Contemporary American

Days Open
Open daily for dinner
(in season, May 14-Oct 12)

Pricing
Dinner for one,
without tax, tip, or drinks:
$60-$80

Dress Code
Casual elegant

Reservations
Recommended

Parking
Free on site

Features
Private room/parties, outdoor dining, entertainment

Credit Cards
AE, VC, MC

Silks at Stonehedge Inn

French cuisine in the country

Designed after a luxurious English country manor, Stonehedge Inn is nestled in 36 acres of New England horse country. Considered by *Wine Spectator Magazine*, *The Boston Globe*, *Food & Wine Magazine*, and *USA Today* as a culinary destination, Executive Chef Eric Brujan combines his classic French techniques with New England's seasonal fish, game, and produce. The wine collection includes over 90,000 bottles, many of which are cellared in the Inn's wine cave, as well as a wine list with over 2,000 selections. Luxurious overnight accommodations available for those wishing to enjoy a culinary getaway.

Impeccable cuisine and European service

Grilled lobster with summer fondue

Owner Levent Bozkurt

GRAND AWARD

DiRōNA
AWARD WINNER
SINCE 1992

Directions

On Route 113 east of Route 3; 45 min. from Logan Airport, 25 min. from Manchester, NH Airport

160 Pawtucket Blvd.
Tyngsboro, MA 01879
PH: (978) 649-4400
FAX: (978) 649-9256
www.stonehedgeinn.com

Owners
Levent and Dawn Bozkurt

Cuisine
New French

Days Open
Open daily for breakfast,
Mon.-Sat. for lunch,
Tues.-Sun. for dinner,
Sun. for brunch

Pricing
Dinner for one,
without tax, tip, or drinks:
$60-$80

Dress Code
Jacket preferred

Reservations
Recommended

Parking
Valet, free on site

Features
Outdoor dining, private parties, monthly wine dinners, wine cave (tours upon request)

Credit Cards
AE, VC, MC, CB, DC, JCB, DS

Il Capriccio Ristorante e Bar

Dining room

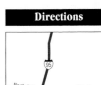

Chef/Owner Richard Barron

The *New York Times* notes that "Il Capriccio combines the friendliness of a neighborhood place with sophisticated food and an extraordinary collection of Italian wines". And in *USA Today*, "They get the freshest ingredients and don't cut corners." In business for more than 20 years, Il Capriccio maintains a commitment to quality in food, wine, and service.

Directions

On corner of Main & Prospect St., 35 min. from Logan International Airport

888 Main Street
Waltham, MA 02453
PH: (781) 894-2234
FAX: (781) 891-3227
www.bostonchefs.com

Owners
Jeannie Rogers and Richard Barron

Cuisine
Regional northern Italian

Days Open
Open Mon.-Sat. for dinner

Pricing
Dinner for one,
without tax, tip, or drinks:
$40-$60

Dress Code
Business casual

Reservations
Recommended

Parking
Free on site

Features
Private room, near theater

Credit Cards
AE, VC, MC, CB, DC, DS

AWARD WINNER
SINCE 2002

Northwoods

Dining room

Directions

At Melvin and Ridgely avenues, 30 min. from Baltimore-Washington International Airport

Located in the quaint West Annapolis shopping district, this eatery features a menu that seamlessly combines Northern Italian, French, and American culinary cultures and focuses on the abundant local seafood. Hosts Russell and Leslie Brown welcome diners into their lovely restaurant to experience Zuppa de Pesce, Tournedoes Cezanne, or one of the wonderful daily fresh fish specials. An award-winning wine list and a garden terrace for al fresco dining complete the experience.

Zuppa de pesce

Outdoor dining on the terrace

609 Melvin Avenue
Annapolis, MD 21401
PH: (410) 268-2609
FAX: (410) 268-0930
www.restaurant.com/
northwoods

Owners
Russell and Leslie Brown

Cuisine
Continental

Days Open
Open daily for dinner

Pricing
Dinner for one,
without tax, tip, or drinks:
$20-$40

Dress Code
Business casual

Reservations
Recommended

Parking
Free on site

Features
Outdoor dining

Credit Cards
AE, VC, MC, CB, DC, DS

Owners Russell and Leslie Brown

AWARD WINNER
SINCE 1992

Da Mimmo
Finest Italian Cuisine

La Dolce Vita Dining Room

For more than two decades, Chef Mimmo Cricchio has prepared gourmet Italian food cooked to order in Baltimore's Little Italy. In addition to the delectable cuisine—dishes such as tortellini Pavarotti, lobster Tetrazzini, and red snapper Adriatica—this family-run restaurant offers a casually intimate atmosphere, fine service, and a memorable wine list. While the locals love Da Mimmo, it also draws many visitors, and offers complimentary limo service to and from hotels.

Co-owners/Chefs Mimmo and Mary Ann Cricchio and staff

Best veal chop in Baltimore

The tradition lives on in Baltimore's Little Italy

AWARD WINNER
SINCE 1999

Directions

In Little Italy, a short walk from the Inner Harbor and 20 min. from Baltimore-Washington International Airport

217 South High Street
Baltimore, MD 21202
PH: (410) 727-6876
FAX: (410) 727-1927
www.damimmo.com

Owners
Mimmo and Mary Ann Cricchio

Cuisine
Gourmet Italian

Days Open
Open daily for lunch and dinner

Pricing
Dinner for one, without tax, tip, or drinks: $20-$40

Dress Code
Elegant casual

Reservations
Recommended

Parking
Free on site, valet

Features
Private room/parties, entertainment, cigar/cognac events in lounge

Credit Cards
AE, VC, MC, CB, DC

246

DELLA NOTTE Ristorante of Little Italy

The Colonnade

E njoy classic Italian cuisine as well as innovative new-world culinary creations featuring South Atlantic lobster, New Zealand langostino, Maryland rockfish, Chesapeake bay oysters, Colorado lamb, free-range veal and certified angus steaks. Choose from an extensive wine list concentrating on Tuscany, Piedmont and California with vertical selections reaching back into the seventies and eighties. Savor a vintage port, cognac, brandy or grappa while listening to piano vocalist perform nightly in the cocktail lounge.

Frutti di Mare

Semifreddo alla Limone

Gen. Mgr. Rita Lymperopoulos, Maître d' Enrico Vitucci, and Co-owner Lisa Julio

AWARD WINNER
SINCE 2003

Directions

In Little Italy, at its junction with the Inner Harbor, 20 min. from Baltimore-Washington International Airport

801 Eastern Avenue
Baltimore, MD 21202
PH: (410) 837-5500
FAX: (410) 837-2600
www.dellanotte.com

Owners
Ted and Lisa Julio

Cuisine
Innovative and traditional Italian

Days Open
Open daily for lunch and dinner

Pricing
Dinner for one, without tax, tip, or drinks: $20-$40

Dress Code
Business casual

Reservations
Recommended

Parking
Free on site

Features
Private room/parties, entertainment, cigar/cognac events, piano bar

Credit Cards
AE, VC, MC, CB, DC, DS

Hampton's

The city's only Mobil Four-Star and AAHS Five-Star-Diamond restaurant

In the Harbor Court Hotel in downtown Baltimore, 20 min. from Baltimore-Washington International Airport

550 Light Street
Baltimore, MD 21202
PH: (410) 234-0550,
ext. 3424
FAX: (410) 385-6194
www.harborcourt.com

Owners
David Murdock

Cuisine
New American

Days Open
Open Tues.-Sun. for dinner,
Sun. for brunch

Pricing
Dinner for one,
without tax, tip, or drinks:
$40-$60

Dress Code
Jacket and tie required

Reservation
Recommended

Parking
Complimentary valet

Features
Entertainment

Credit Cards
AE, VC, MC, DC

ocated at the Harbor Court Hotel in Baltimore's scenic Inner Harbor, Hampton's serves innovative American cuisine in an elegant Edwardian setting. "Dining at Hampton's is a four-star experience all the way around," *Baltimore Magazine* declared. An award-winning wine list, ample table privacy, and a breathtaking view of the harbor contribute to the elegance. The Sunday champagne brunch has become a Baltimore tradition.

Seasonal menus emphasize classic cooking techniques with interesting flavors

A feast for the eyes as well as the palate

Lightly scented gardenias are a signature part of each table setting

DiRōNA
AWARD WINNER
SINCE 1992

Tragara Ristorante

Elegant banquet room

On Cordell Avenue, 20 min. from Reagan National Airport, 30 min. from Baltimore-Washington Int'l Airport

4935 Cordell Avenue
Bethesda, MD 20814
PH: (301) 951-4935
FAX: (301) 951-0401
www.tragara.com

Owners
Claude Amsellem

Cuisine
Italian

Days Open
Open Mon.-Fri. for lunch, daily for dinner

Pricing
Dinner for one, without tax, tip, or drinks: $20-$40

Dress Code
Business casual

Reservations
Recommended

Parking
Complementary valet

Features
Private room/parties

Credit Cards
AE, VC, MC, CB, DC

With its Italian chandelier and curving marble staircase, Tragara Ristorante has been providing a lavish setting, excellent service, and exquisite food since 1987. Chef Michael Laudier offers daily specials reflecting seasonal availability including a light antipasto, home-made traditional pastas, and entrees such as lobster, jumbo shrimp, and 100% natural hormone-free Buffalo sirloin steak. For dessert try the exotic sorbets and gelati. The excellent wine list is a "Best Wine List" winner from the *Wine Spectator*, 1996-2002.

Ossobuco Milanese

Owner Claude Amsellem and Chef Michel Laudier

Dining room

AWARD WINNER
SINCE 1994

Rudys' 2900 Restaurant

Rudys' 2900 Restaurant

On Baltimore Blvd. (Rte 140), 35 min. from Baltimore-Washington International Airport

Nestled in the rolling farmland of Maryland's Carroll County, Rudys' 2900 has been astonishing and delighting diners since 1983. With its superb styling of contemporary American cuisine and global classics such as, Rudys' lobster pot pie with baby vegetables, and champagne sauce, Mediterranean seafood bouillabaisse, potato crusted grouper, and barbequed rack of lamb, Rudys' 2900 is one of the outstanding four-star eateries in the region. Rudys' 2900's success is largely due to the talents of its two owners, certified Master Chef Rudy Speckamp, and maître d' Rudy Paul.

Chalet Room

Peach Room

2900 Baltimore Blvd.
Finksburg, MD 21048
PH: (410) 833-5777
FAX: (410) 526-2201
www.rudys2900.com

Owners
Rudy Speckamp and
Rudy Paul

Cuisine
Contemporary American

Days Open
Open Tues.-Fri. for lunch,
Tues.-Sat. for dinner

Pricing
Dinner for one,
without tax, tip, or drinks:
$20-$40
(or)
Prix Fixe:$21.95

Dress Code
Business casual

Reservations
Recommended

Parking
Free on site

Features
Private room/parties

Credit Cards
AE, VC, MC, DC, DS

Downstairs banquet room

AWARD WINNER
SINCE 1992

Stone Manor

18th-century charm

Just outside Fredrick, MD conveniently located near Baltimore and Wash. D.C., 30 min. from Baltimore-Washington International Airport

Savor the exceptional cuisine, luxurious suites, and 18th-century charm of this 114-acre country estate. Chef Charles Zeran's contemporary cuisine is presented in semi prix fixe format, with suggested wine tastings. The fare changes often, with seasonal specialties such as cauliflower soup with amaretto and sautéed sea scallops, and venison chop with sweet potatoes and blackberry curry demiglace. Complete your dining experience with sweet creations such as pineapple "ravioli" with coconut pastry cream and cactus pear sorbet. The menus are complemented by Stone Manor's list of over 500 wines.

Creative entrées

Sumptuous desserts

5820 Carroll Boyer Road
Middletown, MD 21769
PH: (301) 473-5454
FAX: (301) 371-5622
www.stonemanor.com

Cuisine
Contemporary American

Days Open
Open Tues.-Sun. for lunch,
Wed.-Sun. for dinner

Pricing
Dinner for one,
without tax, tip, or drinks:
$60-$80

Dress Code
Business casual

Reservations
Required

Parking
Free on site

Features
Private room/parties

Credit Cards
AE, VC, MC, DS, DC

Extensive wine list

AWARD WINNER
SINCE 1998

251

Old Angler's Inn

A romantic winter getaway

End of McArthur Blvd., 20 min. from Reagan National Airport and 30 min. from Dulles International Airport

A most charming dining spot, the Old Angler's Inn has been immortalized in countless Washington D.C. novels as a romantic winter getaway, sitting before the fireplace and perusing the menu. It is equally glorious in the summer when the main action moves to the incomparable terrace. Chef Robert Bates uses fresh, seasonal ingredients for his menu which includes foie gras with figs, whole boneless squab, and grilled veal chops with sauerkraut and Riesling. The Chef also enjoys creating tasting menus which are available as five or seven courses.

Roasted rack of lamb

A delicious appetizer

10801 McArthur Blvd.
Potomac, MD 20854
PH: (301) 299-9097
FAX: (301) 983-0630
www.oldanglersinn.com

Owners
Mrs. O. Reges

Cuisine
American

Days Open
Open Tues.-Sun. for lunch and dinner

Pricing
Dinner for one, without tax, tip, or drinks: $40-60 (or) Price Fix: $55/$65/$75

Dress Code
Business casual

Reservations
Recommended

Parking
Free on site

Features
Private room/parties, outdoor dining

Credit Cards
AE, VC, MC, CB, DC

AWARD WINNER
SINCE 1998

208 Talbot

Historic charm

On Route 33 in St. Michaels on Maryland's Eastern Shore, 1 hr. from Baltimore-Washington International Airport

Chef-owned and operated, 208 Talbot is located in historic St. Michaels, just minutes from Chesapeake Bay. The innovative cuisine served in this charming establishment reflects the Eastern Shore's bounty of fresh seafood and produce. *Travel and Leisure* included the roasted oysters and crispy soft-shell crabs at 208 Talbot among the "Seven Wonders of the Eastern Shore." The atmosphere is casually elegant, and the excellent food, well-chosen wine list, and exceptional service guarantee a wonderful dining experience.

208 North Talbot Street
St. Michaels, MD 21663
PH: (410) 745-3838
FAX: (410) 745-6507
www.208talbot.com

Owners
Paul Milne and
Candace Chiaruttini

Cuisine
Innovative American

Days Open
Open Wed.-Sun. for dinner
(closed mid-February to
mid-March)

Pricing
Dinner for one,
without tax, tip, or drinks:
$40-$60

Dress Code
Casual

Reservations
Recommended

Parking
Free on site

Credit Cards
VC, MC, DS

AWARD WINNER
SINCE 1996

Sherwood's Landing at the Inn at Perry Cabin

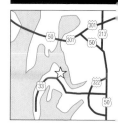

Nautically themed Sherwood Landing

The Chesapeake and its surrounding rich farmland have long been a source of romance and inspiration for artists of all disciplines. The Inn's Master Chef Mark Salter is no exception. Well acquainted with area watermen and farmers, Chef Salter adds his own gift for color, taste and texture to the freshest local seafood, fowl, and produce to create award-winning cuisine, lauded as among the finest on the eastern shore.

Chef Mark Salter

Chef Salter's Chesapeake bouillabaisse

Al fresco dining

Wine Spectator
AWARD OF EXCELLENCE

DiRōNA
AWARD WINNER
SINCE 1998

Directions

On Watkins Lane, 1 hr. and 30 min. from Baltimore-Washington International Airport

308 Watkins Lane
St. Michaels, MD 21663
PH: (410) 745-2200
FAX: (410) 745-3348
www.perrycabin.com

Owners
Orient-Express Hotels

Cuisine
Eclectic continental accented by regional ingredients

Days Open
Open daily for breakfast, lunch, tea, and dinner

Pricing
Dinner for one, without tax, tip, or drinks: $60-$80

Dress Code
Smart casual and jacket recommended for dinner

Reservations
Recommended

Parking
Free on site

Features
The Miles Room for private parties, outdoor dining, cigar/cognac, and jazz events

Credit Cards
AE, VC, MC, CB, DC, DS

The Milton Inn

On York Road, 40 min. From Baltimore-Washington International Airport

14833 York Road
Sparks, MD 21152
PH: (410) 771-4366
FAX: (410) 771-4184

Owners
Michael Stishan and
Brian Boston

Cuisine
Regional American

Days Open
Open Mon.-Fri. for lunch,
daily for dinner

Pricing
Dinner for one,
without tax, tip, or drinks:
$40-60 (or)
Price fix: $33 (Sun.-Fri.)

Dress Code
Business casual

Reservations
Recommended

Parking
Free on site

Features
Private room/parties,
outdoor dining,
off premises catering

Credit Cards
AE, VC, MC, CB, DC, DS

The Milton Inn, a 250-year-old fieldstone building, is considered among Maryland's historic treasures. Opened as a restaurant in 1947, the Milton Inn has become known for exceptional regional American fare, served elegantly in the country manor tradition. Rack of lamb, jumbo lump crab cakes, duck, and rockfish highlight the seasonal menu. The Inn has engendered a legacy of romance, as it is host to engagements, weddings, and celebrations of other personal milestones.

*The Milton Inn –
a historic treasure*

*Elegant dining in the
country manor tradition*

AWARD WINNER
SINCE 1998

Chef/Owner Brian Boston

Antrim 1844

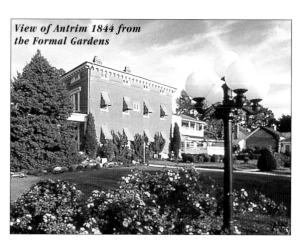

View of Antrim 1844 from the Formal Gardens

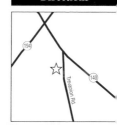

In Taneytown, 1 hr. from Baltimore-Washington International Airport and 1 hr. 15 min. from Reagan National Airport

30 Trevanion Road
Taneytown, MD 21787
PH: (800) 858-1844
FAX: (410) 756-2744
www.antrim1844.com

Owners
Richard and Dorothy Mollett

Cuisine
New American

Days Open
Open daily for dinner

Pricing
Dinner for one,
without tax, tip, or drinks:
Price fix: $62.50

Reservations
Required

Parking
On site

Features
Private room/parties, entertainment, cigar-cognac events, wine tasting, 29 guest rooms

Credit Cards
AE, VC, MC, DC, DS

Antrim 1844 Country House Hotel is a magnificently restored mid-19th century estate rich in Civil War history and only 12 miles from Gettysburg. Chef Michael Gettier creates a six course prefixe dining experience each evening in the restaurant complimented by owner Richard Mollett's award-winning wine list. Enhance your visit by staying in one of the twenty-nine romantic guest rooms, and suites. A *"must see"* if in the Baltimore-Washington area.

The McCaleb Room

Entrance hall

Chef Michael Gettier and Owner Richard Mollett

AWARD WINNER
SINCE 1999

The White Barn Inn

The White Barn Inn in full bloom

The White Barn Inn is the only restaurant in New England to be honored with the AAA Five Diamond Award for ten consecutive years. The restaurant, housed in two meticulously restored barns, seats 120 guests for dinner. Antiques, 19th-century oil paintings, and soft candlelight provide an ideal setting for celebrating life's memorable occasions. Specialties of the house include Maine seafood, farm-raised venison, and quail.

Executive Chef
Jonathan Cartwright

Romantic dining

AWARD WINNER
SINCE 1993

Directions

80 min. from Logan Airport;
25 miles from Portland, ME

P.O. Box 560 C
37 Beach Avenue
Kennebunkport, ME 04046
PH: (207) 967-2321
FAX: (207) 967-1100
www.whitebarninn.com

Owners
Laurence Bongiorno

Cuisine
Contemporary American with
New England influences

Days Open
Daily for dinner

Pricing
Dinner for one,
without tax, tip, or drinks:
$80+

Dress Code
Jacket required

Reservations
Required

Parking
Complimentary valet

Features
Private wine room

Credit Cards
AE, VC, MC

Clay Hill Farm

Wooded retreat

Two miles west of Ogunquit Square in York; 75 mins. from Boston's Logan International Airport

Clay Hill Farm's menu of New American cuisine combines traditional New England favorites with contemporary specials. Start with the award-winning lobster bisque, followed by entrée specialties like roast duckling, French-cut rack of lamb, and a wide variety of fresh local seafood preparations. Over 200 wine varietals from around the world complement any meal. For dessert, try the white chocolate crème brulée, then conclude your special evening with a stroll through the beautiful gardens and bird sanctuary.

Ambience of yesteryear

Chef Melissa Ettinger

Artistic presentations

AWARD WINNER
SINCE 1999

220 Clay Hill Road
York, ME 03907
PH: (207) 361-2272
FAX: (207) 646-0938
www.clayhillfarm.com

Owners
The Lewis Family

Cuisine
New American

Days Open
Daily for dinner, in season

Pricing
Dinner for one,
without tax, tip, or drinks:
$20-$40

Dress Code
Business casual

Reservations
Recommended

Parking
Valet

Features
Entertainment, near theater, private room/parties

Credit Cards
AE, VC, MC, DS

Giovanni's Ristorante

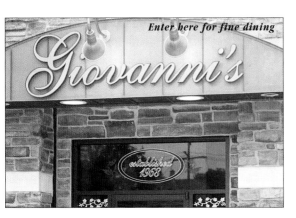

Enter here for fine dining

Near the Rouge River and Bridge, 15 min. from Detroit Metro International Airport

330 South Oakwood Boulevard
Detroit, MI 48217
PH: (313) 841-0122
FAX: (313) 841-3947
www.giovannisristorante.com

Owners
Frances C. and
Randy J. Truant

Cuisine
Italian

Days Open
Open Tues.-Fri. for lunch,
Tues.-Sat. for dinner

Pricing
Dinner for one,
without tax, tip or drinks:
$20-$40

Dress Code
Business casual

Reservations
Recommended

Parking
Free on site

Features
Private room/parties,
near theater

Credit Cards
AE, VC, MC, DC

Giovanni's has been a family-owned business for 30 years, from its humble beginnings as a pizzeria to the fine-dining establishment of today. The eatery offers the greatest level of quality and authenticity possible, from the bistecca calamari fritta and the homemade gnocchi di patate verde, to the fresh seafood flown in from Boston. Its old-world charm and elegance, combined with a comfortable, congenial atmosphere make even the most distant stranger feel at home.

Randy Truant and his mother, Frances Truant

A gracious setting

Intimate main dining room

AWARD WINNER
SINCE 2001

Opus One

Elegant dining

Directions

In downtown Detroit, two blocks from the Renaissanc Center, 35 min. from Detroi Metropolitan Airport

565 East Larned Street
Detroit, MI 48226
PH: (313) 961-7766
FAX: (313) 961-9243
www.opus-one.com

Owners
James C. Kokas and
Edward R. Mandziara

Cuisine
American with Continental fla

Days Open
Open Mon.-Fri. for lunch,
Mon.-Sat. for dinner

Pricing
Dinner for one,
without tax, tip, or drinks:
$40-$60

Dress Code
Business casual

Reservations
Recommended

Parking
Valet

Features
Private room/parties, entertainment, shuttle service to
theaters, offsite catering

Credit Cards
AE, VC, MC, CB, DC, DS

Opus One's elegant, polished interior reflects the attention to detail evident in the food and service here. Orchestrated specialties like rack of lamb a la greque and shrimp Helene are prime examples of the stylish yet classic dishes offered at lunch, dinner and a wide range of private banquets The award-winning wine list includes an assortment of current releases as well as a more challenging selection of vintages.

Front dining room

Jim Kokas and Ed Mandziara

AWARD WINNER
SINCE 1992

The Rattlesnake Club

Main dining room overlooking river front

Directions

At the foot of Jos. Campau in downtown, 2 1/2 miles east of the Renaissance Center and 20 min. from Detroit Metropolitan Airport

300 River Place
Detroit, MI 48207
PH: (313) 567-4400
FAX: (313) 567-2063

Owner
Jimmy Schmidt

Cuisine
New American

Days Open
Open Mon.-Fri. for lunch,
Mon.-Sat. for dinner

Pricing
Dinner for one:
without tax, tip, or drinks:
$40-$60

Dress Code
Business casual

Reservations
Recommended

Parking
Valet

Features
Private parties, catering services, outdoor dining, entertainment, near theater

Credit Cards
AE, VC, MC

C hef/Owner Jimmy Schmidt transformed a warehouse space into a carefully appointed, beautifully designed restaurant with breathtaking views of the Detroit skyline and the Windsor, Ontario, waterfront. Works by noted artists Jasper Johns, Jim Dine, and Frank Stella adorn the restaurant and private dining rooms. Jimmy Schmidt's food, too, is a work of art. Among his signature dishes are prime CAB steaks and chops, Lake Ontario Perch and white chocolate ravioli.

Lake Ontario perch sautéed with watercress sauce

Chef/Owner Jimmy Schmidt

AWARD WINNER
SINCE 1993

261

The Whitney

Directions

"An American restaurant in an American palace"

In the University Cultural Center of Detroit, on Woodward Ave., 30 min. from Detroit Metropolitan Airport

4421 Woodward Avenue
Detroit, MI 48201
PH: (313) 832-5700
FAX: (313) 832-2159
www.thewhitney.com

Owner
Richard P. Kughn, John McCarthy, and Ronald D. Fox

Cuisine
American

Days Open
Open daily for dinner, Sunday for brunch

Pricing
Dinner for one:
without tax, tip, or drinks:
$40-$60

Dress Code
Jacket and tie suggested

Reservations
Recommended

Parking
Valet

Features
Private room/parties, entertainment near theater

Credit Cards
AE, VC, MC

The Whitney, Detroit's most elegant dining venue, occupies an historic Romanesque-style 52-room mansion, with a grand staircase illuminated by Tiffany windows. Since opening in 1986, it has been a favorite of celebrities, dignitaries and locals. Executive Chef Keith Supian prepares a modern American cuisine including signature dishes such as mushroom-dusted North Atlantic wild sturgeon with foie gras ravioli, and a roulade of pheasant. A new steak house menu has been added, and a vegetarian prix fixe dinner is available nightly. Leave room for a changing array of elegant and creative desserts.

The Grand Hall

First floor dining room

The Music Room

AWARD WINNER
SINCE 1993

Ristorante Café Cortina

Private party room with outside European courtyard

On West 10 Mile Road east of Orchard Lake Road, 20 min. from Detroit Metropolitan Airport

R istoranté Café Cortina, which opened in 1976 has earned a reputation as the "best kept secret" in Metropolitan Detroit. It's warm atmosphere, with romantic fireside dining, and consistently excellent presentation of northern Italian regional cooking has been praised by the local and national media. This is a true "ristorante" where loyal clientele, restaurateurs, celebrities, and well-traveled diners return repeatedly to experience the exquisitely prepared food and genuine Italian hospitality.

Dolci Italiani

30715 West 10 Mile Road
Farmington Hills, MI 48336
PH: (248) 474-3033
FAX: (248) 474-9064
www.cafecortina.com

Owners
Tonon family

Cuisine
Regional Italian

Days Open
Open Mon.-Fri. for lunch,
Mon.-Sat. for dinner

Pricing
Dinner for one,
without tax, tip, or drinks:
$40-$60

Dress Code
Business casual

Reservations
Suggested

Parking
Valet

Features
Private room/parties, outdoor dining, entertainment,
cigar/cognac events

Credit Cards
AE, VC, MC, CB, DC, DS

Il giardino

La famiglia Tonon

Wine Spectator
AWARD OF EXCELLENCE

DiRōNA
AWARD WINNER
SINCE 1997

Tribute

Main dining room

Directions

On 12 Mile Road just west of Orchard Lake Road, 25 min. from Detroit Metro International Airport

This first-class destination restaurant in the lovely suburb of Farmington Hills offers top-rated Asian-fusion food in a dynamic contemporary setting. Classically trained chef Takashi Yagihashi has created a menu that features such items as wild mushroom-crusted beef tenderloin served with fingerling potatoes and beef marrow-filled tortellini, sashimi dressed in tangy yuzu (Asian citrus fruit) vinaigrette, and the locally familiar Lake Superior walleye, served on rock shrimp risotto.

Seared scallops

Chef Takashi Yagihashi

31425 West 12 Mile Road
Farmington Hills, MI 48334
PH: (248) 848-9393
FAX: (248) 848-1919
www.tribute-restaurant.com

Owners
Epoch Restaurant Group

Cuisine
Contemporary French with Asian Influences

Days Open
Open Tues.-Sat. for dinner

Pricing
Dinner for one,
without tax, tip, or drinks:
$60-$80

Dress Code
Business casual

Reservations
Required

Parking
Valet

Features
Private room/parties

Credit Cards
AE, VC, MC, CB, DC, DS

Chilled Maine lobster

AWARD WINNER
SINCE 2001

The Lark

A country inn

Consistently named Michigan's most romantic restaurant, The Lark also was first-place winner in *Gourmet's* Top Table Awards and the best restaurant in North America in *Condé Nast Traveler's* readers poll. A European-style country inn with outdoor tables in season, The Lark presents an eclectic menu, ranging from the latest French creations to Maine lobsters and steak. An award-winning wine cellar houses 1,000 selections.

Dining room

Jim and Mary Lark and Chef Marcus Haight

Walled garden

AWARD WINNER
SINCE 1992

Directions

At Farmington and Maple roads, 40 min. from Detroit Metropolitan Airport

6430 Farmington Road
West Bloomfield, MI 48322
PH: (248) 661-4466
FAX: (248) 661-8891
www.thelark.com

Owners
James D. Lark

Cuisine
French

Days Open
Open Tues.-Sat. for dinner

Pricing
Dinner for one,
without tax, tip, or drinks:
$65-$80

Dress Code
Jacket and tie required

Reservations
Required

Parking
Free on site

Features
Private parties,
outdoor dining

Credit Cards
AE, VC, MC, DC

The St. Paul Grill

Dining room at
The St. Paul Grill

Directions

At the Saint Paul Hotel near
Market and Fifth streets, 2
min. from Minneapolis-St.
Paul International
Airport

The charming views of Rice Park are surpassed only by the food and service at this popular Twin Cities restaurant. The menu reflects the best of American cuisine — the freshest fish, aged beef, fresh poultry and game — prepared simply and then finished with a cutting-edge culinary element. You'll find such classic regional favorites as beer-battered walleye and roast beef hash with fried eggs. There is an impressive wine list and a collection of single malt scotches.

Bill Morrissey and Billy Ellis

Porterhouse with fresh asparagus

350 Market Street
St. Paul, MN 55102
PH: (651) 224-7455
FAX: (651) 228-3810
www.stpaulhotel.com

Owners
350 Market St., Inc.,
managed by Morrissey
Hospitality Cos.

Cuisine
American

Days Open
Open daily for lunch and
dinner

Pricing
Dinner for one,
without tax, tip, or drinks:
$20-$40

Dress Code
Upscale casual

Reservations
Recommended

Parking
Valet, garage nearby

Features
Near theater and sports

Credit Cards
AE, VC, MC, DC, DS

The Grill Bar

AWARD WINNER
SINCE 2001

Lord Fletcher's Old Lake Lodge

A beautiful day at Lord Fletcher's

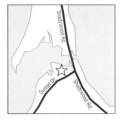

On Lake Minnetonka, 30 min. from Minneapolis-St. Paul International Airport

Warm hospitality and creative cuisine abound while dining amid the beautiful lakeside surroundings of Lord Fletcher's Old Lake Lodge on Lake Minnetonka. *Minneapolis-St.Paul* magazine says Lord Fletcher's has the best view of any restaurant in the Twin Cities. The service is second to none, and the fare is creatively and beautifully prepared: acclaimed walleye pan-fried in herb butter topped with almonds, miso glazed salmon with pineapple chutney, and grilled free range chicken breast with shrimp tarragon sauce.

Outdoor dining at its best

3746 Sunset Drive
Spring Park, MN 55384
PH: (952) 471-8513
FAX: (952) 471-8937
www.lordfletchers.com

Owners
William O. Naegele

Cuisine
American with global flair

Days Open
Open Mon.-Sat. for lunch, daily for dinner, Sun. for brunch

Pricing
Dinner for one, without tax, tip, or drinks: $20-$40

Dress Code
Business casual

Reservations
Recommended

Parking
Free on site, valet

Features
Private parties, outdoor dining, entertainment

Credit Cards
AE, VC, MC, DC, DS

AWARD WINNER
SINCE 1999

Jasper's

Jasper's

Jasper's, Kansas City's most popular Italian market and restaurant, has reopened in the Watts Mill Shopping Center, and continues its award-winning dedication to fine Italian cuisine and impeccable service. The menu features the famous shrimp Livornese, Caesar salad, peppered steak, pasta, chops, fresh seafood, and fresh baked breads and pastries. The wine list includes over 200 selections from Italy. The bar features Kansas City's largest selection of grappa and espresso drinks. Jasper's dedication to fine Italian cuisine and impeccable service resulted in Jasper's becoming the most awarded restaurant in Kansas City.

Chef/Owner Jasper Mirabile, Jr.

Host entryway and bar

Tuscany fireside dining

DiRōNA
AWARD WINNER
SINCE 2002

Directions

West 103rd Street East in the Watts Mill Shopping Center, 40 min. from Kansas City International Airport

1201 West 103rd Street
Kansas City, MO 64114
PH: (816) 941-6600
FAX: (816) 941-4346
www.jasperskc.com

Owners
Leonard and Jasper Mirabile

Cuisine
Italian

Days Open
Open Mon.-Fri. for lunch,
Mon.-Sat. for dinner

Pricing
Dinner for one,
without tax, tip, or drinks:
$20-$40

Dress Code
Business casual

Reservations
Accepted at lunch and
before 6:00 p.m.

Parking
Free on site

Features
Private room/parties,
outdoor dining

Credit Cards
AE, VC, MC, CB, DC, DS

The Peppercorn Duck Club

Mixed grill specialty

Located in the Hyatt Regency Crown Center, 20 min. from Kansas City International Airport

2345 McGee Street
Kansas City, MO 64108
PH: (816) 435-4199
FAX: (816) 435-4190
www.crowncenter.hyatt.com

Owners
Hyatt Regency Crown Center

Cuisine
American

Days Open
Open Mon.-Sat. for lunch and dinner

Pricing
Dinner for one, without tax, tip, or drinks: $20-$40

Dress Code
Casual/Business casual

Reservations
Recommended

Parking
Valet, garage nearby

Features
Private room/parties, near theater, cigar/cognac events, rotisserie duck

Credit Cards
AE, VC, MC, CB, DC, DS, JCB, En Route

The staff at The Peppercorn Duck Club will serve you with talent, business acumen, and quality. Beyond these professional qualifications is another less tangible, but equally critical, attribute: commitment. Our guests are the cornerstones of our business and our commitment to provide them with the highest quality of service is the mission of all Peppercorn Duck Club employees. Enjoy one of Kansas City's finest dining options. Let The Peppercorn Duck Club, an award-winning restaurant, orchestrate your next dining experience.

Ultra chocolate bar

AWARD WINNER
SINCE 1992

Al's

Family service for 77 years

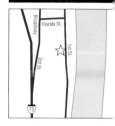

At North First and Biddle streets near the river in downtown, 20 min. from Lambert-St. Louis International Airport

A l's, after more than 77 years of family operation at the same location, is a beloved institution in the Gateway City. Instead of a printed menu, the day's available seafoods and meats are presented to you on a silver platter, while an amiable table captain describes the preparation of each entrée and suggests suitable accompaniments. Drinks in the riverboat lounge are a delightful interlude.

Riverboat Lounge

Classic Italian sculptures

1200 North First Street
St. Louis, MO 63102
PH: (314) 421-6399

Owners
Al Barroni

Cuisine
Italian American

Days Open
Open Mon.-Sat. for dinner

Pricing
Dinner for one,
without tax, tip, or drinks:
$40-$60

Dress Code
Jacket required

Reservations Policy
Recommended

Parking
Valet

Features
Private room/parties

Credit Cards
AE, VC, MC

Views of the Gateway City

AWARD WINNER
SINCE 1996

Benedetto's Ristorante

Main dining room

One of St. Louis' premier Italian gourmet restaurants, this formal and intimate establishment offers patrons the true definition of European flair. Benedetto Buzzetta's hard work and dedication is evident in every dish that is prepared. Service is refined but friendly, ensuring the ultimate Italian dining experience. Tantalizing specialties include Pappardelle Paesana and Filetto Ripieno.

Owner Benedetto Buzzetta

Indoor garden

Directions

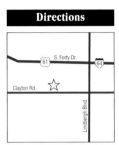

In Frontenac, 15 minutes from Lambert St. Louis International Airport

10411 Clayton Road
Frontenac, MO 63131
PH: (314) 432-8585
FAX: (314) 432-3199

Owners
Benedetto Buzzetta

Cuisine
Gourmet Italian

Days Open
Open Mon.-Fri. for lunch, daily for dinner

Pricing
Dinner for one, without tax, tip or drinks: $20-$40

Dress Code
Jacket and tie required

Reservations
Recommended

Parking
Free on site

Features
Entertainment, live music, private room/parties

Credit Cards
AE, VC, MC, DC, DS

AWARD WINNER
SINCE 1997

271

Dominic's

Welcome to Dominic's

Directions

At Wilson Avenue and Hereford Street on the Hill, 20 min. from Lambert-St. Louis International Airport

5101 Wilson Avenue
St. Louis, MO 63110
PH: (314) 771-1632
FAX: (314) 771-1695

Owners
Dominic Galati

Cuisine
Classic Northern Italian

Days Open
Open Mon.-Sat. for dinner

Pricing
Dinner for one,
without tax, tip, or drinks:
$20-$40

Dress Code
Jacket preferred

Reservations
Recommended

Parking
Free on site, valet

Features
Private room/parties,
cigar/cognac events

Credit Cards
AE, VC, MC, DC, DS

Superior food, exquisite tableside service, and meticulous attention to detail has helped build a dedicated following at Dominic's. There is an open yet cozy feel to the dining room. Owner and Executive Chef Dominic Galati prepares such Northern Italian specialties as fettuccine Verdi with shrimps and sweet peppers, and veal chops with truffles. Dominic's also boasts one of St. Louis' most generous wine cellars.

Veal scallopine alla crema

Elegant dining

Dominic and Jackie Galati

AWARD WINNER
SINCE 1992

G.P. Agostino's

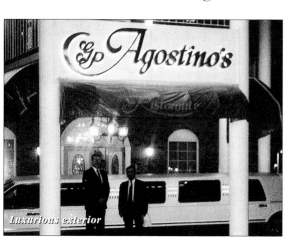

Luxurious exterior

At G.P. Agostino's, love for delicious, well-presented food, served in elegant surroundings, has been an Agostino family tradition for two generations. Executive Chef Paul Gabriele uses only the freshest ingredients, finest spices, and purest Italian cheeses when preparing the menu, which highlights Northern Italian specialties. A varied wine list and delicious desserts complete a memorable meal.

Elegant presentation

Owners Paul Gabriele and John Gabriele

AWARD WINNER
SINCE 1995

Directions

In the western suburbs of St. Louis, 20 min. from Lambert-St. Louis International Airport

15846 Manchester Road
Ellisville, MO 63011
PH: (636) 391-5480
FAX: (636) 391-3892

Owners
Rosa Gabriele Agostino and family

Cuisine
Northern Italian

Days Open
Open Tues.-Fri. for lunch, daily for dinner

Pricing
Dinner for one, without tax, tip, or drinks: $20-$40

Dress Code
Jacket and tie optional

Reservations
Recommended

Parking
Free on site

Features
Private room/parties, outdoor dining, cigar/cognac events

Credit Cards
AE, VC, MC, CB, DC, JCB, DS

Giovanni's Little Place

*Chef/Owner
Carmelo Gabriele
serves Italian cuisine*

Directions

In the western suburbs on
Manchester Road, 20 min.
from Lambert-St. Louis
International Airport

14560 Manchester Road
St. Louis, MO 63011
PH: (636) 227-7230
FAX: (636) 227-9917

Owners
Carmelo and Maria Gabriele

Cuisine
Italian

Days Open
Open Mon.-Sat. for dinner

Pricing
Dinner for one,
without tax, tip, or drinks:
$20-$40

Dress Code
Business casual

Reservations
Recommended

Parking
Free on site

Features
Private room/parties

Credit Cards
AE, VC, MC, DC, DS

Set in a little row of shops along busy Manchester Road, Giovanni's Little Place is an extraordinary Italian restaurant. The atmosphere is quiet and sophisticated. Abstract paintings line the walls, tables are set with silver and floral china, and candles flicker, warming the scene. Chef/Owner Carmelo Gabriele serves Italian cuisine. The house specialty is Involtini Di Vitello Alla Sinatra, and Vitello Saltimbocca Alla Giovanni is another favorite. Many dishes are prepared tableside, and the wait staff aims to please.

*Owners Carmelo and
Maria Gabriele*

AWARD WINNER
SINCE 1995

Giovanni's on the Hill

Standing: son Carmelo, daughter Lisa, son and Chef Frank
Seated: Owner Giovanni Gabriele and wife Fina

Critically acclaimed for being one of the most "European" of eateries in the U.S., Giovanni's on the Hill is the epitome of Italian dining in St. Louis. Many famous palates have savored Chef Gabriele's unique pasta dishes, such as Giovanni's signature dish Presidential farfalline al salmone, created for President Reagan's inauguration in 1981, and melenzana alla Conca D'oro, a pasta and eggplant dish created some years ago for Paul and Linda McCartney. Giovanni's is listed in the Millennium Issue of *America's Elite 2000*.

Special for the McCartneys

Owner Giovanni Gabriele
flanked by sons Carmelo
(left), and Francesco

Wall of awards

AWARD WINNER
SINCE 1992

Directions

On Shaw Avenue on the Hill, 20 min. from Lambert-St. Louis International Airport

5201 Shaw Avenue
St. Louis, MO 63110
PH: (314) 772-5958
FAX: (314) 772-0343

Owners
Giovanni Gabriele

Cuisine
Classic Italian

Days Open
Open Mon.-Sat. for dinner

Pricing
Dinner for one, without tax, tip, or drinks: $40-$60

Dress Code
Business casual, jacket recommended

Reservations
Recommended

Parking
Free on site, valet

Features
Private rooms/parties

Credit Cards
AE, VC, MC, DC

John Mineo's Italian Restaurant

Main dining room

On the corner of Clayton and Mason, 20 min. from Lambert St. Louis International Airport

Owned and operated by John and Anna Mineo since 1973, John Mineo's Italian Restaurant serves top-notch Italian cuisine with five-star service. Chefs and servers alike finish the preparation of many dishes tableside. The sea bass, Dover sole, and veal chop are among the most popular entrees. Don't miss John Mineo's heavenly dessert drink, made from French vanilla ice cream, creme de cacao, and Amaretto. Four main dining areas accommodate all manner of social and business gatherings.

John Mineo Sr. and John Jr.

13490 Clayton Road
St. Louis, MO 63131
PH: (314) 434-5244
FAX: (314) 434-0714

Owners
John Mineo

Cuisine
Italian

Days Open
Open daily for dinner

Pricing
Dinner for one,
without tax, tip or drinks:
$20-$40

Dress Code
Business casual

Reservations
Recommended

Parking
Free on site

Features
Private room/parties

Credit Cards
AE, VC, MC, CB, DC, DS

AWARD WINNER
SINCE 1994

The Seventh Inn

Private dining room

Experience distinguished, five-star continental dining in elegant, relaxed surroundings at The Seventh Inn, a St. Louis landmark for more than 30 years. The glow of candlelight and the fragrance of fresh flowers enhance the mood, while professional servers attend to one's every need. Under the direction of Executive Chef Else Barth, the menu is varied, featuring more than 150 entrées. Fresh fish and aged beef are specialties.

Excellent cuisine in an elegant setting

A team of outstanding chefs

A TRAVEL HOLIDAY RESTAURANT
100 SEVEN TRAILS DR.   ST. LOUIS, MO 63011
227-6686

AWARD WINNER
SINCE 1994

Directions

In Ballwin, 30 min. from Lambert-St. Louis International Airport

100 Seven Trails Drive
St. Louis, MO 63011
PH: (636) 227-6686
FAX: (636) 227-6595
www.theseventhinn.com

Owners
Else M. Barth and
Lucie T. Sinn

Cuisine
Continental

Days Open
Open daily for dinner

Pricing
Dinner for one,
without tax, tip, or drinks:
$20-$40

Dress Code
Business casual

Reservations
Recommended

Parking
Valet

Features
Private room/parties,
entertainment

Credit Cards
AE, VC, MC, DC, DS

Tony's

Wine room

In downtown St. Louis, near the base of the Gateway Arch, 20 min. from Lambert-St. Louis International Airport

Tony's, within the shadow of the mighty Gateway Arch, welcomes guests from all over to an evening of elegant dining. The restaurant has a reputation for fine service—captains and waiters indulge the most discriminating diners with tableside preparation. The Italian menu, prepared by owner and Executive Chef Vincent P. Bommarito, emphasizes prime beef and veal and fresh seafood. An extensive wine collection and an array of mouthwatering desserts complete the meal.

Bommarito family: from left, James, Vincent P., Anthony, and Vincent J.

Rack of lamb

Dining room

410 Market Street
St. Louis, MO 63102
PH: (314) 231-7007
FAX: (314) 231-4740

Owners
Vincent J. Bommarito

Cuisine
Italian

Days Open
Open Mon.-Sat. for dinner

Pricing
Dinner for one,
without tax, tip, or drinks:
$40-$60

Dress Code
Jacket required

Reservations
Recommended

Parking
Valet

Credit Cards
AE, VC, MC, CB, DC, DS

BEST OF
AWARD OF
EXCELLENCE

DiRōNA

AWARD WINNER
SINCE 1992

Port House

Serving seafood and USDA prime-aged beef; presented beautifully, served with attentive style

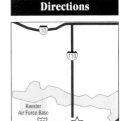

Located in the Beau Rivage Resort and Casino, 20 min. from Gulfport-Biloxi International Airport

Located inside MGM MIRAGE's AAA Four Diamond resort Beau Rivage, Port House offers the premier dining experience in the southern region of the United States. The experience includes indulging in exceptionally fresh, artfully presented seafood, lobster, 16 delectable ways, and the very best USDA prime dry-aged beef, while looking out onto four 'windows' which are actually four enormous 10,000-gallon aquariums, featuring more than 100 species of tropical and salt-water fish, sharks and coral reef.

The wine tower of art glass...a Port House exclusive design

Executive Chef Joseph Friel

VP Food & Beverage George Goldhoff

875 Beach Blvd.
Biloxi, MS 39530
PH: (228) 386-7737
FAX: (888) 750-7111
www.beaurivage.com

Owners
MGM MIRAGE

Cuisine
Contemporary steak and seafood

Days Open
Open Mon.-Sat. for dinner

Pricing
Dinner for one, without tax, tip, or drinks:
$60-$80

Dress Code
Business casual

Reservations
Required

Parking
Free on site, valet

Features
Private parties

Credit Cards
AE, VC, MC, CB, DC, JCB, DS

AWARD WINNER
SINCE 2004

279

Fairbanks Steakhouse

In Hollywood, winning has a flavor all its own

Located south of Memphis off I-61 on Hwy. 304, 30 min. from Memphis International Airport

1150 Casino Strip Resorts Boulevard
Robinsonville, MS 38664
PH: (800) 871-0711
FAX: (662) 357-7831
www.hollywoodcasinotunica.com

Owners
Penn National Gaming, Inc.

Cuisine
Steakhouse

Days Open
Open daily for dinner

Pricing
Dinner for one,
without tax, tip, or drinks:
$40-$60

Dress Code
Business casual

Reservations
Required

Parking
Free on site, valet

Features
Wine events

Credit Cards
AE, VC, MC, DS

Fairbanks Steakhouse, in Hollywood Casino, serves up a premier dining experience with mouthwatering certified Black Angus beef, lobsters, and gourmet specialty dishes. The restaurant is a delight for the eye, with motion picture memorabilia from the Douglas Fairbanks era and the amazing Fairbanks Wall of Wine, which holds 1,500 bottles. A humidor fully stocked with premium cigars will satisfy the most discriminating customers.

Hollywood Casino

Casino floor

A premier dining experience

AWARD WINNER
SINCE 1998

Jack Binion's Steak House

J ack Binion's Steak House is located inside the Horseshoe Casino and Hotel in Tunica, Mississippi and is known as Jack Binion's signature restaurant. Only the finest USDA Prime mid-western beef and sumptuous seafood are good enough for this menu. This formal dining room offers guests the opportunity to indulge their tastebuds. Lauded in reviews, and recognized with an award of excellence from *Wine Spectator* magazine, Horseshoe houses one of the largest wine cellars in the area.

Formal dining

The finest USDA prime mid-western beef served here

AWARD WINNER
SINCE 2004

Hotel lobby

Directions

Located 12 miles south of Memphis, on Highway 61, 30 min. from Memphis International Airport

1021 Casino Center Drive
Robinsonville, MS 38632
PH: (800) 303-7463
FAX: (662) 357-5530

Owners
Jack Binion

Cuisine
Steakhouse and Seafood

Days Open
Open daily for dinner

Pricing
Dinner for one,
without tax, tip, or drinks:
$40-$60

Dress Code
Business casual

Reservations
Required

Parking
Free on site, valet, covered parking garage

Features
Private room/parties, entertainment, near theater, cigar/cognac events

Credit Cards
AE, VC, MC, DS

Horizons at The Grove Park Inn Resort & Spa

Horizons - an unforgettable, epicurean delight

F or dining that lives up to The Grove Park Inn's reputation for grandeur, visit Horizons. With dazzling innovations on classic cuisine, a world-class wine list, and impeccable service, the hours you spend here add up to more than a meal; an evening here promises an unforgettable epicurean adventure. Ask about seating at our Chef's Table in the Horizons' kitchen – it's the ultimate culinary experience.

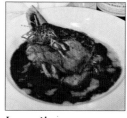

Innovative, classic cusine

Professional, impeccable service

AWARD WINNER
SINCE 1993

Directions

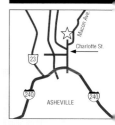

On Macon Avenue at The Grove Park Inn, 25 min. from Asheville Regional Airport

290 Macon Avenue
Asheville, NC 28804
PH: (828)-252-2711 or
(800) 438-5800 (reservations)
FAX: (828) 253-7053
www.groveparkinn.com

Owner
The Grove Park Inn
Resort & Spa

Cuisine
Innovative classic

Days Open
Open Tues.-Sat. for dinner
(Open daily for dinner
Oct.-Dec.)

Pricing
Dinner for one,
without tax, tip, or drinks:
$60-$80

Dress Code
Jacket required

Reservations
Recommended

Parking
Valet

Features
Private room/parties,
entertainment, cigar/cognac
events

Credit Cards
AE, VC, MC, DC, DS

Campania

Campania...fine dining in a friendly, neighborhood restaurant

Located on northwest corner in Harris Teeter Shopping Center, 20 min. from Charlotte Douglas International Airport

6414 Rea Road
Charlotte, NC 28270
PH: (704) 541-8505
FAX: (704) 846-2640
www.campaniacharlotte.com

Owner
Ciro and Suzanne Marino

Cuisine
Italian

Days Open
Open Mon.-Sat. for dinner

Campania, nestled in the quaint neighborhood of Piper Glen, surrounded by golden walls, rich wood, and candlelight offers you southern Italian cuisine that is contemporary, yet authentic. Ciro and Suzanne Marino bring you the tastes that make Italian food so grand and seductive. Chef Marino enjoys introducing wines from every corner of his native land, and demonstrates his undying passion for food with culinary delights of his heritage.

Owners Ciro and Suzanne Marino

Wines from the Chef's native, Campania, complement his passion for food

Pricing
Dinner for one,
without tax, tip, or drinks:
$20-$40

Dress Code
Business casual

Reservations
Recommended

Parking
Free on site

Features
Private parties, outdoor dining, near theater

Credit Cards
AE, VC, MC, CB, DC, DS

Wine Spectator
AWARD OF EXCELLENCE

DiRōNA
AWARD WINNER
SINCE 2004

The Capital Grille

The Capital Grille

Located across from the Blumenthal Performing Arts Center, The Capital Grille boasts an atmosphere of power dining, relaxed elegance, and style. Nationally acclaimed for dry aging steaks on premises, The Capital Grille serves classic steakhouse offerings such as chops, large North Atlantic lobsters, and fresh seafood. The restaurant features an award-winning wine list, and professional, gracious service. Let the masters of steak provide the perfect dining experience.

Chef Ray Bell

Classic steakhouse fare

Signature Stoli Doli

AWARD WINNER
SINCE 2003

Directions

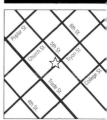

At the IJL Financial Center, on North Tryon Street, 10 min. from Charlotte Douglas International Airport

201 North Tryon Street
Charlotte, NC 28202
PH: (704) 348-1400
FAX: (704) 348-4263
www.thecapitalgrille.com

Owner
Rare Hospitality/
Sean O'Brien

Cuisine
Steakhouse

Days Open
Open Mon.-Fri. for lunch,
daily for dinner

Pricing
Dinner for one,
without tax, tip, or drinks:
$40-$50

Dress Code
Business casual

Reservations
Recommended

Parking
Complimentary valet
(after 6:00 pm)

Features
Private room/parties, near
theater, cigar/cognac event

Credit Cards
AE, VC, MC,CB, DC, DS

284

Elizabeth's Café & Winery

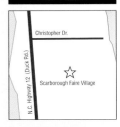

On Duck Road in
Scarborough Faire Village,
1 hr. 20 min. from Norfolk
International Airport

1177 Duck Road
Scarborough Faire
Duck, NC 27949
PH: (252) 261-6145
www.elizabethscafe.com

Owner
Leonard G. Logan, Jr.

Cuisine
Eclectic

Days Open
Open daily for dinner, May –
September. (Call for monthly
off-season dinner schedule)

Pricing
Dinner for one,
without tax, tip, or drinks:
$40-$60

Dress Code
Casual

Reservations
Recommended

Parking
Free on site

Features
Private room/parties

Credit Cards
AE, VC, MC, CB, DC, DS

This romantic hideaway nestled among the trees in Scarborough Faire Village has received international recognition for the pairing of food and wine. The menu changes nightly, reflecting the daily purchase of the freshest ingredients available offering a la carte and two different prix fixe wine dinners. With over 1650 wine selections, the wine program has garnered international awards, and a yearly Best of Award of Excellence from *The Wine Spectator* since 1993.

Chef Brad Price

Owner Leonard Logan at the Stone Grotto Wine Cellar

AWARD WINNER
SINCE 2004

Stars Waterfront Café

The view from every table

This island treasure features the creative cuisine of Executive Chef Charles Zeran, and Pastry Chef Colleen Zeran, who received DiRoNA awards for four consecutive years in the Washington, DC area before bringing their talents to the Carolina coast. Multi-ethnic influences and unexpected crossovers of sweet and savory provide constant surprises in the ever-changing menu, always including the freshest of seafood, and aged meats and game. The area's best wine list recently receiving *Wine Spectator* Magazine's 2003 Award of Excellence and exceptional service make for a truly memorable dining experience. The stunning sunset views from every table in the intimate, forty-seat dining room, the casual bar, or the lush tropical deck complete the magic that is Stars.

Colleen and Charles Zeran, pastry chef and executive chef

A rare combination of stunning views and superb food

AWARD WINNER
SINCE 2004

Directions

Just over the causeway bridge in Ocean Isle Beach, on Causeway Drive, 45 min. from Myrtle Beach Airport

14 Causeway Drive
Ocean Isle Beach, NC 28469
PH: (910) 579-7838
FAX: (910) 575-0159
www.starswaterfrontcafe.com

Owner
Tripp Sloane and Debbie Sloane Smith

Cuisine
Contemporary American

Days Open
Open daily for dinner (in summer season)
Open Wed.-Sat. for dinner (off season)

Pricing
Dinner for one,
without tax, tip, or drinks:
$20-$40

Dress Code
Casual

Reservations
Recommended

Parking
Free on site

Features
Private parties, outdoor dining, entertainment

Credit Cards
AE, VC, MC

The Fearrington House

The Fearrington House

Directions

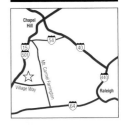

Located on US 15-501, eight miles south of Chapel Hill, 30 min. from Raleigh-Durham Airport.

The Fearrington House
2000 Fearrington Village
Pittsboro, NC 27312
PH: (919) 542-2121
FAX: (919) 542-4202
www.fearrington.com

Owner
R.B. Fitch

Cuisine
Southern, Continental

Days Open
Open Tues.-Sun. for breakfast and dinner

Pricing
Dinner for one,
without tax, tip, or drinks:
$60-$80

Dress Code
Jacket recommended

Reservations
Suggested

Parking
Free on site

Features
Private room/parties, outdoor dining, overnight accommodations

Credit Cards
AE, VC, MC

Traditional southern hospitality awaits you at this elegant country inn set amidst floral gardens in the heart of a picturesque village. Relax in the beautiful suites and guestrooms, each individually decorated with antique furniture, original artwork, and bouquets of fresh flowers. Experience the charm of regional cuisine by soft candlelight, and enjoy poetry readings, wine tastings, and garden visits throughout the year.

Southern hospitality awaits you

Guestrooms and suites

Enjoy regional cuisine

AWARD WINNER
SINCE 1992

The Angus Barn

Rustic barn atmosphere

In the Angus Barn's wine cellar dining room, you will be surrounded by 1,200 selections of wine as you savor the chef's gourmet cuisine. Or, you can feast on steaks and seafood in the rustic barn atmosphere of the original dining rooms. The Angus Barn is proud to be one of the few U.S. restaurants that ages its own beef. This strict control over the aging process ensures the highest quality Angus beef. Be sure to try their award-winning chocolate chess pie.

WIne cellar dining room

Quality aged beef

Owner Van Eure

AWARD WINNER
SINCE 1996

Directions

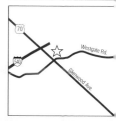

On Highway 70 between Raleigh and Durham, 7 min. from Raleigh-Durham Airport

9401 Glenwood Avenue
Raleigh, NC 27617
PH: (919) 787-3505
FAX: (919) 783-5568
www.angusbarn.com

Owner
Van Eure

Cuisine
American steakhouse

Days Open
Open daily for dinner

Pricing
Dinner for one,
without tax, tip, or drinks:
$40-$60

Dress Code
Business casual

Reservations
Recommended

Parking
Free on site, complimentary valet

Features
Private room/parties, entertainment, cigar/cognac events

Credit Cards
AE, VC, MC, DC, DS

Bedford Village Inn

The Porch Garden

Directions

Off Highway 101, 10 min. from Manchester Airport and 1 hr. 15 min. from Boston's Logan International

The Bedford Village Inn, a multi-million-dollar farm estate restoration that received the Four Diamond Award rating for dining and lodging, features its award-winning cuisine in eight intimate dining rooms—each graced with exotic orchids and fresh flower arrangements—and casual fare in The Tap Room. Executive Chef Kevin Kapalka leads a notable culinary team. Beginning with perhaps an appetizer of pan-seared Jonah crab cakes and continuing on to porcini crusted native cod, everything that emerges from the kitchen will delight even the most discriminating palate. An expanded wine cellar houses more than 8,000 bottles. The Inn's 14 luxury suites are bathed in Italian marble and have whirlpools and spacious sitting areas.

Overlook Room...rich, cherry-paneled room with fireside dining

East Room...smart, stylish, and chic

2 Village Inn Lane
Bedford, NH 03110
PH: (603) 472-2001
FAX: (603) 472-2379
www.bedfordvillageinn.com

Owners
Jack and Andrea Carnevale

Cuisine
Contemporary regional New England

Days Open
Open daily for breakfast, lunch, and dinner

Pricing
Dinner for one, without tax, tip, or drinks: $20-$40

Dress Code
Business casual

Reservations
Recommended

Parking
Free on site

Features
Private room/parties

Credit Cards
AE, VC, MC, CB, DC

The Tap Room

AWARD WINNER
SINCE 1996

The Dining Room at The Mount Washington Hotel

Mt. Washington Hotel...the touchstone of refined New England hospitality

Since 1902, the elegant Dining Room at The Mount Washington Hotel has satisfied a multiplicity of palates amid relaxed formality. Crystal chandeliers and Tiffany stained-glass windows set a romantic tone for a dance to the accompaniment of an orchestra. Always in the vanguard of culinary art and science, Executive Chef Calvin Belknap utilizes New England's freshest ingredients to offer his acclaimed "New American Regional" cuisine. This AAA Four-Diamond restaurant offers a distinctive dining experience reminiscent of a time gone by.

The Princess Lounge

Executive Chef Calvin Belknap

Tempting diners with "New American Regional" cuisine

AWARD WINNER
SINCE 2004

Directions

Set in the heart of New Hampshire's White Mountains known as Bretton Woods on Route 302, 1 hr. and 30 min. from Manchester International Airport

Route 302
Bretton Woods, NH 03575
PH: (603) 278-1000
FAX: (603) 278-8828
www.mtwashington.com

Owners
MWH Preservation Limited Partnership

Cuisine
New American Regional

Days Open
Open daily for breakfast and dinner

Pricing
Dinner for one,
without tax, tip, or drinks:
Prix fixe: $50

Dress Code
Jacket required

Reservations
Recommended

Parking
Free on site, valet

Features
Private rooms/parties, entertainment

Credit Cards
AE, VC, MC, DS

Peregrines'

Main dining room

At the Atlantic City Hilton
Casino Resort, 20 min. from
Atlantic City International
Airport

Boston Avenue at the
Boardwalk
Atlantic City, NJ 08401
PH: (609) 340-7400
FAX: (609) 340-4879
www.hiltonac.com

Owners
Park Place Entertainment

Cuisine
Regional and international
contemporary

Days Open
Open Thurs.-Sun. for dinner

Pricing
Dinner for one,
without tax, tip, or drinks:
$40-$60

Dress Code
Business casual

Reservations
Recommended

Parking
Valet, garage nearby

Credit Cards
AE, VC, MC, DC, DS, CB

This exclusive five-star culinary centerpiece is an award-winning achievement with an exquisite sense of excellence. Named for the Peregrine falcons that have made the Atlantic City Hilton's penthouse ledge their annual summer home, this establishment offers regional and international contemporary cuisine featuring gourmet seafood.

Elegance at the Hilton

AWARD WINNER
SINCE 1997

The Bernards Inn

The Great Room

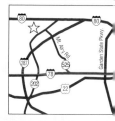

On southbound Route 202 in downtown Bernardsville, 40 min. from Newark International Airport

The Bernards Inn was created as a sumptuous retreat for discerning travelers, first welcoming guests in 1907. It is a tranquil retreat where history surrounds you, graceful architecture shelters you, privacy comforts you, and gracious hospitality envelops you. Chef and co-owner Edward Stone's fine menu of contemporary American fare reflects nature's seasonal bounty. His culinary innovations are enhanced by an award-winning wine list with over 655 selections and 11,000 bottles in inventory.

Maine lobster and prawns

Wine cellar

Executive Chef Edward Stone

27 Mine Brook Road
Bernardsville, NJ 07924
PH: (908) 766-0002
FAX: (908) 766-4604
www.bernardsinn.com

Owners
Richard and Kim Schlott, and Edward and Ann Stone

Cuisine
Progressive American

Days Open
Open Mon.-Fri. for lunch, Mon.-Sat. for dinner

Pricing
Dinner for one, without tax, tip, or drinks: $40-$60

Dress Code
Business casual; jacket required on Saturday only

Reservations
Recommended

Parking
Free on site

Features
Private room/parties, outdoor dining, wine cellar, entertainment, near theater

Credit Cards
AE, VC, MC, DC

AWARD WINNER
SINCE 1999

Ram's Head Inn

Gracious courtyard

Seven miles from the casinos of Atlantic City and 10 min. from Atlantic City International Airport

9 West White Horse Pike
Galloway, NJ 08205
PH: (609) 652-1700
FAX: (609) 748-1588
www.ramsheadinn.com

Owners
The Knowles family

Cuisine
American

Days Open
Open Tues.-Fri. for lunch, Tues.-Sun. for dinner

Pricing
Dinner for one, without tax, tip, or drinks: $20-$40

Dress Code
Jackets required, ties optional

Reservations
Recommended

Parking
Free on site, valet

Features
Private room/parties, entertainment, near theater, cigar/cognac events

Credit Cards
AE, VC, MC, CB, DC, DS

Ram's Head Inn offers quiet, distinctively American dining in an elegant country atmosphere. This delightful restaurant is filled with authentic antiques and augmented by a gracious courtyard. Set on five country acres with sprawling gardens and flower-lined fences, the property has received the AAA Four Diamond Award, "Best of the Shore" (*Atlantic City Magazine*), and "Best of the Best" (*New Jersey Monthly*).

Private dining room

Phyllo purse of portobello mushroom

Executive Chef Luigi Baretto

AWARD WINNER
SINCE 1994

Panico's

Owner Frank Panico (1939-2003)

Noted for fine wines and innovative Italian cuisine, Panico's has received raves from the *Star-Ledger* of Newark and *The New York Times*. Executive Chef Gregg Freda uses only the very best and freshest ingredients, and his creations are brought to the table by a legion of formally dressed, unobtrusive servers. Entrées include Chilean sea bass wrapped in Parma ham, pan seared, and served over lemon thyme couscous with a brown butter vinaigrette; and grilled beef tenderloin topped with a Chippolini crust and served with a garlic and shallot red wine sauce.

Porcini and black trumpet sformato

Fresh Maine lobster tail wrapped with spinach and filet of sole

Stone crab risotto

AWARD WINNER
SINCE 1994

Directions

At Church and George streets in New Brunswick, near Route 18 and 25 min. from Newark International Airport

103 Church Street
New Brunswick, NJ 08901
PH: (732) 545-6100
FAX: (732) 545-7346
www.panicosrestaurant.com

Owners
Frank Panico

Cuisine
Italian

Days Open
Open Mon.-Fri, for lunch,
Mon.-Sat. dinner

Pricing
Dinner for one,
without tax, tip, or drinks:
$80+

Dress Code
Jacket requested

Reservations
Recommended

Parking
Garage nearby

Features
Private room/parties, near theater

Credit Cards
AE, VC, MC, DC, DS

The Saddle River Inn

A tranquil setting

Directions

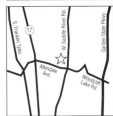

Off West Saddle River Road
on Barnstable Ct., 40 min.
from Newark International
Airport

2 Barnstable Court
Saddle River, NJ 07458
PH: (201) 825-4016
FAX: (201) 934-8910
www.saddleriverinn.com

Owners
Hans and Imelda Egg

Cuisine
French/New American

Days Open
Open Tues.-Fri. for lunch,
Tues.-Sat. for dinner

Pricing
Dinner for one,
without tax, tip, or drinks:
$40-$60

Dress Code
Jacket and tie required

Reservations
Required

Parking
Free on site

Features
Private room/parties

Credit Cards
AE, VC, MC

A rustic country location alongside a tranquil pond provides the perfect backdrop for a superb dining experience at the Saddle River Inn. Chef Hans Egg delights his guests with innovative creations and a unique approach to classic French cuisine combined with contemporary American accents. The highest quality food, expertly prepared, and superbly presented, is his hallmark. First-rate service is provided by a staff trained in the European tradition of professionalism and gracious attention to detail.

The dining room

Chef/Proprietor Hans Egg

AWARD WINNER
SINCE 2001

The Dining Room

Sophisticated charm, exquisite cuisine

Hilton Short Hills
41 John F. Kennedy Parkway
Short Hills, NJ 07078
PH: (973) 379-0100
FAX: (973) 379-6870
www.hiltonshorthills.com

The Dining Room at the Hilton Short Hills, led by Executive Chef Walter Leffler and Chef de Cuisine James Haurey, is New Jersey's only AAA Five Diamond restaurant. It offers imaginative French country cuisine, an extensive wine cellar, expert wine pairing, a refreshingly friendly staff, and soothing harp music. A private dining room is available for celebrations with up to 18 guests.

*Executive Chef
Walter Leffler*

Owners
Hilton Hotels Corporation

Cuisine
American with French country accents

Days Open
Open Tues.-Sat. for dinner

Pricing
Dinner for one, without tax, tip, or drinks:
$60-$80

Dress Code
Jacket and tie required

Reservations
Required

Parking
Free on site

Features
Private room, harpist, cigar/cognac events

Credit Cards
AE, VC, MC, CB, DC, ER, JCB, DS

The private dining room

AWARD OF EXCELLENCE

AWARD WINNER
SINCE 1999

Diamond's

Soft tones for dining

On Kent Street in the Chambersburg Restaurant District, 10 min. from Mercer County Airport, 35 min. from Philadelphia International, and 50 min. from Newark International

D iamond's, nestled on a block of immaculate, working-class homes, is the crown jewel of the historic Chambersburg Restaurant District in New Jersey's capital city. The restaurant's understated exterior yields to a plush cocktail lounge and dining room that combine Old World grace with accents of contemporary chic. Anthony J. and Thomas M. Zucchetti, the brothers who own Diamond's and were born just two doors away, specialize in authentic Italian cuisine, as well as prime dry-aged steaks and fresh seafood. The wine list is legendary, and the lounge has a fully stocked humidor.

Plenty of room for events

Tempting Italian cuisine

A friendly place to gather

AWARD WINNER
SINCE 1998

132 Kent Street
Trenton, NJ 08611
PH: (609) 393-1000
FAX: (609) 393-1672
www.diamondsrestaurant.com

Owners
Anthony J. Zucchetti and Thomas M. Zucchetti

Cuisine
Italian

Days Open
Open Mon.-Fri. for lunch, daily for dinner

Pricing
Dinner for one, without tax, tip, or drinks: $20-$40

Dress Code
Business casual

Reservations
Recommended

Parking
Free on site, valet

Features
Private room/parties, near theater, cigar/cognac events

Credit Cards
AE, VC, MC, CB, DC, DS

Highlawn Pavilion

Main dining room

On Eagle Rock Reservation's scenic overlook, 15 min. from Newark International Airport

Highlawn Pavilion offers an unmatched view of Manhattan's skyline. Distinctive American cuisine with European and Asian accents is served in a turn-of-the-century Florentine-style villa with a unique open kitchen. Voted among "America's Top Tables" by readers of *Gourmet*, it has become one of the area's most exciting restaurants. *New Jersey Monthly* awarded Highlawn Pavilion its "best atmosphere" and "most romantic dining" accolades.

Sashimi tuna sushi roll, tuna tartare & pepper seared tuna

Eagle Rock Reservation
West Orange, NJ 07052
PH: (973) 731-3463
FAX: (973) 731-0034
www.highlawn.com

Owners
The Knowles family

Cuisine
American/International

Days Open
Open Mon.-Fri. for lunch, daily for dinner

Pricing
Dinner for one, without tax, tip, or drinks: $20-$40

Dress Code
Jacket required, tie preferred

Reservations
Recommended

Parking
Free on site, valet

Features
Private room/parties, near theater, cigar/cognac events

Credit Cards
AE, VC, MC, CB, DC, DS

A view of Manhattan

Piano Bar

AWARD WINNER
SINCE 1995

The Manor

Your path to extraordinary dining

Directions

Bordering Marriott Residence Inn, Montclair Golf Club and Eagle Rock Reservation, 15 min. from Newark International Airport

111 Prospect Avenue
West Orange, NJ 07052
PH: (973) 731-2360
FAX: (973) 731-5168
www.themanorrestaurant.com

Owners
The Knowles family

Cuisine
New World contemporary haute cuisine

Days Open
Open Wed.-Fri. for lunch, Tues.-Sun. for dinner

A gracious manor house set amid acres of magnificent gardens, The Manor combines distinctive gourmet cuisine, superb service, and elegant decor. Bob Lape of *Crain's New York Business* declares its Terrace Lounge "outstanding dining — perfect for a business lunch." Voted among "America's Top Tables" by readers of *Gourmet*, the restaurant is also the recipient of the AAA Four Diamond Award as well as *Wine Spectator's* Grand Award.

Crepinette of beef on a bed of summer vegetables

Exective Chef Jochen Voss

Pricing
Dinner for one, wthout tax, tip, or drinks:
$20-$40

Dress Code
Jacket required, tie preferred

Reservations
Recommended

Parking
Free on site, valet

Features
Private room/parties, entertainment, near theater, cigar/cognac events

Credit Cards
AE, VC, MC, CB, DC, DS

The Knowles family: Doris and, from left, Harry, Kurt, and Wade K.

AWARD WINNER
SINCE 1992

The Ryland Inn

The Ryland Inn

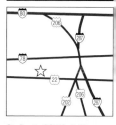

On Route 22 West, 1 hr. from New York City and Philadelphia, and 35 min. from Newark International Airport

D ining takes on new meaning at The Ryland Inn, as Craig Shelton offers guests a creative and delightful approach to culinary artistry through his award-winning contemporary American-French cuisine. This gracious 200-year-old inn set amid rolling hills provides the venue that defines the ultimate dining experience. It has also earned worldwide recognition that extends beyond food to a selection of fine wines, and an unerring attention to presentation and service. The chef maintains a 3-acre organic herb and vegetable garden.

Blanquette of steamed turbot

THE RYLAND INN

Route 22 West
Whitehouse, NJ 08888
PH: (908) 534-4011
FAX: (908) 534-6592
www.therylandinn.com

Owners
Craig Shelton

Cuisine
Contemporary American-French

Days Open
Open daily for dinner

Pricing
Dinner for one,
without tax, tip, or drinks:
$60-$80

Dress Code
Business casual

Reservations
Recommended

Parking
Valet

Features
Private room/parties, cigar/cognac events, wine events

Credit Cards
AE, VC, MC, CB, DC, DS

Chef/Owner Craig Shelton

Wine Spectator
BEST OF
AWARD OF
EXCELLENCE

DiRoNA
AWARD WINNER
SINCE 1996

Ranchers Club of New Mexico

Ranchers Club Lounge

In the Albuquerque Hilton at Menaul and University, 10 minutes from Albuquerque International Sunport

1901 University Boulevard NE
Albuquerque, NM 87102
PH: (505) 889-8071
FAX: (505) 837-1715
www.albuquerquehilton.com

Owners
Ocean Properties

Cuisine
Authentic grill/classic American

Days Open
Open Mon.-Fri. for lunch, daily for dinner

Pricing
Dinner for one, without tax, tip, or drinks: $40-$60

Dress Code
Business casual

Reservations
Required

Parking
Free on site

Features
Private room/parties, entertainment

Credit Cards
AE, VC, MC, CB, DC, DS

The Ranchers Club is a dining experience that no visitor to the Land of Enchantment should miss. It offers food prepared on an authentic gridiron grill over a variety of aromatic wood embers, such as mesquite, hickory, sassafras, and apple. The eatery specializes in ample portions of corn-fed, dry-aged USDA prime beef. House specialties also include certified American bison and roasted venison loin. An award-winning wine list complements the mouthwatering selections.

Enjoy five-star dining

Let the culinary sensations entice you.

AWARD WINNER
SINCE 1994

301

Coyote Café

Experience the unexpected and irresistible

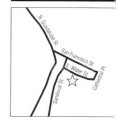

In downtown Santa Fe between Galisteo and Don Gaspar, 1 hr. 15 min. from Albuquerque International Sunport

132 West Water Street
Santa Fe, NM 87501
PH: (505) 983-1615
FAX: (505) 989-9026
www.coyote-cafe.com

Mark Miller's Coyote Café continues to be Santa Fe's most famous and celebrated restaurant, feted by critics and return visitors alike. The dazzling blend of flavors draws on the traditional cuisines of the southwest, Latin America and the Mediterranean to create the unexpected and irresistible. Must-have dishes include griddled buttermilk pancakes with chipotle prawns, and the pecan-wood grilled "Cowboy-Cut" dry aged rib chop. An extensive award-winning wine list is complemented by a full bar with the best selection of premium tequilas in the state.

Owner Mark Miller

Owner
Mark Miller

Cuisine
Modern Southwestern

Days Open
Open daily for lunch and dinner

Pricing
Dinner for one, without tax, tip, or drinks: $20-$42

Dress Code
Casual

Reservations
Recommended

Parking
Garage and lot nearby

Features
Private room/parties, seasonal outdoor dining

Credit Cards
AE, VC, MC, DC, DS, JBC, En Route

AWARD WINNER
SINCE 1992

302

Geronimo

Back dining room

2 blocks from The Plaza downtown, 1 hr. from Albuquerque International Sunport

Geronimo, in its celebrated twelve years, has established a reputation as the place to dine in Santa Fe. Tradition and innovation merge at Geronimo, a Canyon Road legend. Owners Cliff Skoglund and Chris Harvey have succeeded in bringing unparalleled sophistication to the 1756 adobe home. The romantic, elegant atmosphere creates a fabulous backdrop for the Global Fusion-Southwest influenced creations of Chef Eric DiStefano. Geronimo, where simplicity and understatement reign within the venerable adobe walls.

Foie gras with apples and barries

Chef Eric DiStefano with owners Cliff Skoglund (left) and Chris Harvey

724 Canyon Road
Santa Fe, NM 87501
PH: (505) 982-1500
FAX: (505) 820-2083
www.geronimorestaurant.com

Owners
Cliff Skoglund, Chris Harvey

Cuisine
Global American/Southwest

Days Open
Open daily for lunch and dinner

Pricing
Dinner for one, without tax, tip, or drinks: $40-$60

Dress Code
Business casual

Reservations
Recommended

Parking
Free on site, garage nearby

Features
Outdoor dining, private room

Credit Cards
AE, VC, MC

AWARD WINNER
SINCE 2001

Villa Fontana

Charming Southwestern setting

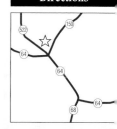

Five miles north of Taos on Highway 522, 2 hr. from Albuquerque International Sunport

A charming atmosphere, sophisticated presentations, and traditional European service make for a memorable experience at Villa Fontana, situated amid the majestic Sangre de Cristo Mountains of northern New Mexico. Local wild mushrooms gathered by Chef/Owner Carlo Gislimberti himself are just one of the house specialties. Expect such exceptional entrées as beef tenderloin with green peppercorns and brandy, and roasted duck with chanterelles, brandy, and cream. A summer garden provides a pleasant spot for outdoor dining.

Regional specialties

Homey interiors

*Chef/Owner
Carlo Gislimberti*

71 Highway 522
Taos, NM 87571
PH: (505) 758-5800
FAX: (505) 758-0301
www.villafontanataos.com
e-mail:villafon@newmex.com

Owners
Carlo and Siobhan Gislimberti

Cuisine
Northern Italian

Days Open
Mon.-Sat. for dinner

Pricing
Dinner for one,
without tax, tip, or drinks:
$20-$40

Dress Code
Casual

Reservations
Recommended

Parking
Free on site

Features
Private room/parties, outdoor dining

Credit Cards
AE, VC, MC, CB, DC, JCB, DS

AWARD WINNER
SINCE 1994

The Summit

Directions

Located at Harrah's Lake Tahoe, 1 hr. 15 min. from Reno/Tahoe International Airport

Highway 50 and Stateline Avenue
Lake Tahoe, NV 89449
PH: (775) 588-6611
www.harrahs.com

Owners
Harrah's Operating Company, Inc.

Cuisine
Contemporary continental

Days Open
Open Wed.-Sun. for dinner

Pricing
Dinner for one, without tax, tip, or drinks: $40-$60

Dress Code
Business casual

Reservations
Recommended

Parking
Free on site

Features
Private room/parties, cigar/cognac events

Credit Cards
AE, VC, MC, CB, DC, En Route, JCB, DS

The Summit

Voted one of the "Top 10 Restaurants" in America, The Summit features contemporary, continental cuisine, and is one of the most prestigious restaurants in the Lake Tahoe region. Located on the 16th floor of Harrah's Lake Tahoe, you'll experience exquisite cuisine in a sophisticated, relaxed townhouse setting with views of Lake Tahoe and the Sierra Nevada. The inviting ambience features classic silver service, intricate wood grain decor, and contemporary artwork and appointments. The Summit is renowned for an uncompromising commitment to impeccable service, and superior cuisine is prepared by a talented culinary staff led by Chef de Cuisine Richard Downer. A salon pianist enhances the dining experience.

AWARD WINNER
SINCE 1999

Andre's French Restaurant

Andre's original downtown location

Directions

Just off the Strip, 25 min. from McCarran International Airport

401 South 6th Street
Las Vegas, NV 89101
PH: (702) 385-5016
FAX: (702) 384-8574
www.andrelv.com

Owners
Andre Rochat and Mary Jane Jarvis

Cuisine
French

Days Open
Open Mon.-Sat. for dinner

Pricing
Dinner for one, without tax, tip, or drinks: $40-$60

Dress Code
Business casual

Reservations
Recommended

Parking
Free on site, valet

Features
Private room/parties, outdoor dining, cigar/cognac events

Credit Cards
AE, VC, MC, CB, DC, JCB

Housed in a 1930 home in a quiet residential neighborhood one block east of the Strip, Andre's is Las Vegas' most honored French restaurant — the best French restaurant and best gourmet restaurant in the city, according to the *Las Vegas Review-Journal* and voted the most popular restaurant in Las Vegas by the Zagat Survey 2000/2001— and has attracted a loyal local following as well as an international clientele. They come for Andre's exquisite classic French cuisine, superior service, and extensive wine list.

Intimate, elegant atmosphere

Owner and Executive Chef Andre Rochat

BEST OF AWARD OF EXCELLENCE

DiRōNA

AWARD WINNER SINCE 1992

Andre's at the Monte Carlo Resort

Main dining room

On Las Vegas Strip across from the MGM Grand, and next door to New York New York, and just minutes from McCarran International Airport

---

Andre's French Restaurant, Las Vegas' most awarded and honored French restaurant, now has a second location within the Monte Carlo Resort Hotel. The intimate main dining room decor is reminiscent of a French Chateau's formal dining room. The tables are magnificent with fresh flowers, Versace china, sterling silver and the soft glow of candlelight. Andre's signature menu is classic French cuisine and changes seasonally. Chef/Partner Norbert Koblitz prepares daily specials which include fresh, top-quality fish, homemade duck foie gras, Provimi veal, and Muscovy duck breast The wine cellar houses more than 950 selections from around the world available to complement your dinner. Voted most popular restaurant in Las Vegas by the Zagat Survey 2000/2001.

Chef/Proprietor
Andre Rochat

Scallop Napoleon with truffles and caviar

3770 Las Vegas Blvd. South
Las Vegas, NV 89109
PH: (702) 798-7151
FAX: (702) 798-7175
www.andrelv.com

Owners
Andre Rochat and
Mary Jane Jarvis

Cuisine
French

Days Open
Open daily for dinner

Pricing
Dinner for one,
without tax, tip, or drinks:
$40-$60

Dress Code
Business casual

Reservations
Recommended

Parking
Free on site, valet

Features
Private room/parties,
cigar/cognac events

Credit Cards
AE, VC, MC, CB, DC, JCB

AWARD WINNER
SINCE 2001

Commander's Palace
Las Vegas

The Garden Room at Commander's Palace

Located on the Strip at the Aladdin Resort and Casino, 5 min. from McCarren Airport

Desert Passage at Aladdin
3663 Las Vegas Blvd. South
Las Vegas, NV 89109
PH: (702) 892-8272
FAX: (702) 892-0052
www.commanderspalace.com

Owner
Brad, Alex, Ti, and Lally Brennan

Cuisine
Haute Creole

Days Open
Open Mon.-Thurs. for lunch, daily for breakfast and dinner. Fri., Sat., Sun. for Jazz brunch

Pricing
Dinner for one, without tax, tip, or drinks:
$40+

Dress Code
Business casual (jackets preferred but not required)

Reservations
Recommended

Parking
Garage nearby

Features
Private room/parties, entertainment (live jazz at brunch), near theater

Credit Cards
AE, VC, MC, CB, DC, En Route, JCB, DS

Commander's Palace Las Vegas, sister to the famed 122 year-old New Orleans original, brings haute Creole cuisine, southern hospitality, and the devilish spirit of the Big Easy to the resort oasis of the Nevada desert. Located at the exotic Aladdin Resort Casino, Commander's Palace Las Vegas is introducing diners to the culinary delights of New Orleans cuisine each day. Don't pass up Commander's Palace mainstays such as turtle soup, shrimp tasso, and Louisiana pecan-crusted fish.

Executive Chef Carlos Guia

AWARD WINNER
SINCE 2004

Ferraro's Restaurant

The home of great Italian cooking

Directions

On W. Flamingo Rd. 2 1/2 miles west of Caesars Palace and the Bellagio, 15 min. from McCarran International Airport

5900 W. Flamingo Road
Las Vegas, NV 89103
PH: (702) 364-5300
FAX: (702) 871-2721
www.Ferraroslasvegas.com

Owners
Gino and Rosalba Ferraro

Cuisine
Regional Italian

Days Open
Open Mon.-Fri. for lunch, daily for dinner

Pricing
Dinner for one, without tax, tip, or drinks: $40-$60

Dress Code
Business casual

Reservations
Recommended

Parking
Free on site

Features
Private room/parties, entertainment, cigar/cognac events

Credit Cards
AE, VC, MC, CB, DC, DS

Since 1985, Gino Ferraro and family have created a unique Italian dining experience. Ferraro's has won many coveted awards over the years including the 2001 DiRōNA Award for our superb Osso Buco, exceptional seafood creations, homemade pastas, and fresh baked bread. The custom wine cellar holds over 500 fine wines and has won the *Wine Spectators* Award of Excellence, and the *Wine Enthusiast* Award. The dining experience is further enhanced with nightly entertainment in the Ferraro's Lounge and Piano Bar.

Award-winning cuisine

The dining room

AWARD WINNER
SINCE 1999

Fiore

Five-star, award-winning dining

At the Rio All-Suite Hotel & Casino, Interstate 15 and Flamingo Rd., 20 min. from McCarran International Airport

Awarded the prestigious Five Star Diamond Award by the American Academy of Hospitality Science, Fiore celebrates culinary delights from the south of France to the northern coast of Italy. Chef Chris Crotty and his team combine the flavors of the Mediterranean with the richness of the wood fired oven, and grille to create the most exquisite dishes. The wine list features over 540 labels. Guests can later escape to the cigar terrace featuring a great collection of fine cigars.

Cigar terrace with views

Distinctive gourmet cuisine

3700 West Flamingo Road
Las Vegas, NV 89103
PH: (702) 777-7702
www.playrio.com

Owners
Harrah's Entertainment, Inc.

Cuisine
Gourmet

Days Open
Open daily for dinner

Pricing
Dinner for one,
without tax, tip, or drinks:
$40-$60

Dress Code
Business casual

Reservations
Recommended

Parking
Free on site, valet, garage nearby

Features
Private room/parties, near theater, cigar/cognac events

Credit Cards
AE, VC, MC, CB, DC

After-dinner conversation

AWARD WINNER
SINCE 1996

Le Cirque at Bellagio

Enter...Le Cirque

At Bellagio hotel, 15 min. from McCarran International Airport

3600 Las Vegas Blvd. South
Las Vegas, NV 89109
PH: (702) 693-7223

Owner
Sirio Maccioni and family

Cuisine
Classic French with contemporary influences

Days Open
Open daily for dinner

Pricing
Dinner for one, without tax, tip, or drinks:
$80+
(or)
Prix fixe:$80
$95 (tasting menu)

Dress Code
Jacket and tie required

Reservations
Required

Parking
Valet

Features
Private parties, near theater

Credit Cards
AE, VC, MC, DS

Ringmaster Sirio Maccioni, long recognized as the "world's most charismatic restaurateur," brought his Four-Star culinary magic to the Las Vegas Strip. Perched aside an eight-acre lake filled with dancing fountains, Bellagio's Le Cirque is a whimsical jewel box of color and detail, from the star-studded entry of polished woods to the sumptuous, swooping silk-tented ceiling. Chef Marc Poidevin matches the surroundings with vibrant French cookery that is by turn rustic and elegant.

Four-star dining in Las Vegas

Credit: Courtney Grant Winston

Le Cirque Bar

Credit: Courtney Grant Winston

Elegant yet playful interior with circus theme

AWARD WINNER
SINCE 2004

Michael's

Intimate dining

For more than two decades, Michael's Restaurant, inside the charming, stained-glass-laden Barbary Coast Hotel & Casino, has provided Las Vegas with elegance and distinction in fine dining. The intimate, 50-seat gourmet room will appeal to the truly enlightened, with an abundance of red velvet and deep mahogany, an Italian marble floor, and an elaborate crystal chandelier. Quite a stage for the cuisine: "We have carefully selected the finest recipes and we use only the highest quality fresh foods available," says Executive Chef Fred Bielak.

At your service

Fine continental cuisine

Chef Fred Bielak

Directions

On the Strip at Flamingo Road, 10 min. from McCarran International Airport

3595 Las Vegas Boulevard S.
Las Vegas, NV 89109
PH: (702) 737-7111
FAX: (702) 369-3055
www.barbarycoastcasino.com

Owner
Michael Gaughan

Cuisine
Continental

Days Open
Open daily for dinner

Pricing
Dinner for one,
without tax, tip, or drinks:
$80+

Dress Code
Business casual

Reservations
Recommended

Parking
Free on site, valet

Features
Private room/parties

Credit Cards
AE, VC, MC, CB, DC, ER, JCB, DS

AWARD WINNER
SINCE 1993

Picasso

Picasso...a dream of country elegance

At Bellagio hotel,
15 min. from McCarran
International Airport

3600 Las Vegas Blvd. South
Las Vegas, NV 89109
PH: (702) 693-7223
www.bellagio.com

Owner
Bellagio

Cuisine
French, with a hint of
Spanish influence

Days Open
Open Thurs.-Tues. for dinner

Pricing
Dinner for one,
without tax, tip, or drinks:
Prix fixe, $79.50
Degustation, $89.50

Dress Code
Jacket required

Reservations
Recommended

Parking
Valet

Features
Private room/parties,
outdoor dining

Credit Cards
AE, VC, MC, DS

Soaring ceilings, intimate nooks, bursts of flowers make Picasso a dream of country elegance. Chef Julian Serrano's Mediterranean cuisine takes flight amidst a profusion of original Picasso artwork. The first Las Vegas chef to be honored with the James Beard Award for "Best Chef, Southwest," Serrano showcases his ingredient-driven, seasonal cuisine in two masterful menus. Picasso is the recipient of the AAA Five Diamond awards of excellence, 2002 and 2003.

Chef Julian Serrano

AWARD WINNER
SINCE 2004

Piero's

Sumptuous decor

Directions

Across from the Las Vegas Convention Center, 10 min. from McCarran International Airport

355 Convention Center Drive
Las Vegas, NV 89109
PH: (702) 369-2305
FAX: (702) 735-5699
www.pieroscuisine.com

Owner
Fred Glusman

Cuisine
Northern Italian

Days Open
Open daily for dinner

Pricing
Dinner for one,
without tax, tip, or drinks:
$40-$60

Dress Code
Business casual

Reservations
Recommended

Parking
Free on site, valet

Features
Private room/parties, entertainment

Credit Cards
AE, VC, MC, DC, JCB, DS

Fine food, an extensive wine list, and caring service that starts at the door make Piero's a consistent winner and a favorite with locals, celebrities, and convention center attendees alike. Executive Chef Gilbert Fetaz's osso buco is world renowned, as are his seafood preparations, notably Florida stone crab (in season) served with a mouthwatering mustard sauce. The delicious desserts are lovingly prepared every morning.

Delicious osso buco

Beautiful presentation

Owner Fred Glusman

AWARD WINNER
SINCE 1995

Pietro's Gourmet Room

Continental cuisine prepared tableside

Located on "The Strip", 10 min. from McCarran Airport

3801 Las Vegas Blvd. South
Las Vegas, NV 89109
PH: (702) 739-2222
FAX: (702) 739-2327
www.tropicanalv.com

Owners
Tropicana Resort & Casino

Cuisine
Gourmet

Days Open
Open Wed.-Sun. for dinner

Pricing
Dinner for one,
without tax, tip, or drinks:
$20-$40

Dress Code
Business casual

Reservations
Recommended

Parking
Free on site, valet,
garage nearby

Features
Private parties

Credit Cards
AE, VC, MC, DC, DS

Pietro's is an intimate gourmet room featuring the finest in tableside, continental cuisine. Our highly dedicated staff provides impeccable service, and unforgettable dining in an elegant, but comfortable ambience. Las Vegas legend, Pietro Musetto, presides as Maître d'. The restaurant has also been named one of America's Top Hundred Restaurants. Pietro's is the Tropicana's top restaurant, and just perfect for a romantic dinner or a special occasion with friends.

Perfectly prepared to tempt every palate

*Master restauranteur
Pietro Musetto*

*The world's most exciting
corner of Las Vegas*

AWARD WINNER
SINCE 1999

Smith & Wollensky, Las Vegas

**Smith & Wollensky, Las Vegas...
the "Big Apple" import**

Directions

On the Las Vegas "Strip",
10 min. from McCarren
International Airport

3767 Las Vegas Blvd.
Las Vegas, NV 89109
PH: (702) 862-4100
www.smithandwollensky.com

Owners
Smith & Wollensky
Restaurant Group

Cuisine
Steakhouse

Days Open
Open daily for lunch
and dinner

Pricing
Dinner for one,
without tax, tip, or drinks:
$40-$60

Dress Code
Business casual

Reservations
Recommended

Parking
Valet

Features
Private room/parties, outdoor dining, near theater,
cigar/cognac events

Credit Cards
AE, VC, MC, CB, DC, JCB, DS

Smith & Wollensky, the Big Apple steakhouse import, shines as a three-story restaurant on the Las Vegas Strip. Featuring its own, private valet for parking, the restaurant is also easily accessible from all major hotels and casinos. Serving USDA Prime beef and excellent seafood with its signature brand of service, the New York steakhouse knows its hometown is not the only city that never sleeps. Wollensky's Grill stays open until 3 a.m. just to prove the point.

*Serving excellent
seafood and steaks*

*Signature steakhouse
atmosphere*

AWARD WINNER
SINCE 1999

Harrah's Steak House

Harrah's Reno Hotel Casino

In downtown Reno, 5 min. from Reno/Tahoe International Airport

219 North Center Street
Reno, NV 89501
PH: (775) 788-2929
FAX: (775) 788-3575
www.harrahsreno.com

Owners
Harrah's Hotel Casino

Cuisine
Steakhouse, Continental

Days Open
Open Mon.-Fri. for lunch, daily for dinner

Pricing
Dinner for one,
without tax, tip, or drinks:
$25-$45

Dress Code
Casual

Reservations
Recommended

Parking
Free on site, valet

Features
Private banquet room, available tableside cooking

Credit Cards
AE, VC, MC, CB, DC, DS

Signature items that will take your breath away, tableside preparation, and attention to the smallest of details have made the award-winning Harrah's Steak House Reno's best restaurant for over 30 years. The commitment to creating an outstanding and elegant dining experience makes Harrah's Steak House the perfect place for an intimate dinner or special celebration. Be sure to experience the Creamy Five Onion Soup, which is baked in a whole Carruso onion and crusted with Gruyere cheese.

Tableside preparation

Continental entrées

Steak House delights

AWARD WINNER
SINCE 1996

Peppermill's White Orchid

1,070 luxurious rooms and jacuzzi suites

The luxurious White Orchid offers Reno's finest dining experience. Chef de Cuisine Roger Morris and his team excel at creating cuisine-as-fine-art, delectable and rich in texture and complexity. To keep the menu fresh, exciting, and in the forefront of modern trends, Chef Morris offers a range of selections from the more traditional to the exotic. The dinner menu and "Chef's Selection" prix fixe menu change monthly, allowing for the inclusion of the season's most flavorful ingredients. With 1,000 labels, the wine list is spectacular, and servers' knowledge is extensive, proven by their "Best of Award of Excellence" from *Wine Spectator* magazine.

Complex, original entrées

The main dining room

Peppermill's award-winning chefs

AWARD WINNER
SINCE 2001

Directions

In the Peppermill Hotel Casino, 10 min. from Reno-Tahoe International Airport

2707 South Virginia Street
Reno, NV 89502
PH: (775) 689-7300
FAX: (775) 689-7189
www.peppermillreno.com

Owners
Peppermill Hotel Casino

Cuisine
Contemporary Continental

Days Open
Open Wed.-Sun. for dinner

Pricing
Dinner for one,
without tax, tip, or drinks:
$40-$60

Dress Code
Business casual

Reservations
Recommended

Parking
Free on site, valet

Features
Private room/parties

Credit Cards
AE, VC, MC, DC, DS

Roxy

The place to see and be seen in Northern Nevada

In the Eldorado Hotel Casino, 10 min. from Reno-Tahoe International Airport

Fourth & Virginia Streets
Reno, NV 89501
PH: (800) 648-5966
FAX: (775) 348-7513
www.eldoradoreno.com

Owners
Eldorado Hotel & Casino

Cuisine
Continental

Days Open
Open daily for dinner

Pricing
Dinner for one,
without tax, tip, or drinks:
$20-$40

Dress Code
Casual

Reservations
Recommended

Parking
Free on site, valet

Features
Private room/parties, entertainment, near theater, wine/cognac events

Credit Cards
AE, VC, MC, CB, DC, DS

Developed in collaboration with San Francisco restaurant designer Pat Kuleto, Roxy is located in the heart of downtown Reno at the award-winning Eldorado Hotel Casino. Roxy offers steaks, prime rib, and seafood entrées, as well as scrumptious soufflés, breads, cakes, and sorbets created in an exhibition bakery. Roxy is famous for its 102 martinis and selection of 900 wines, winning *Wine Spectator's* Award of Excellence. Enjoy live music nightly at Roxy's Bar & Lounge.

Reno's premier destination

Featuring steaks, chops, and seafood

AWARD WINNER
SINCE 1999

Seven unique settings, including the patio

Llewellyn's

On Route 50 on Lake Tahoe's South Shore, 1 hr. 15 min. from Reno/Tahoe International Airport

Harveys Resort & Casino Highway 50 and Stateline Avenue
Stateline, NV 89449
PH: (775) 588-2411
FAX: (775) 588-6643

Owners
Harrah's Operating Co. Inc.

Type of Cuisine
Continental

Days Open
Tues.-Sat. for dinner and Sunday brunch

Pricing
Dinner for one, without tax, tip, or drinks: $25-$40

Dress Code
Business casual

Reservations
Recommended

Parking
Free on site, valet, garage nearby

Features
Private parties, entertainment

Credit Cards
AE, VC, MC, CB, DC, JCB, DS

Scenic dining

I nnovative Continental cuisine, impeccable service, and panoramic views of Lake Tahoe provide a magical and exceptionally memorable dining experience at Llewellyn's, on the 19th floor of Harveys Resort & Casino. Guests who return time and again have voted Llewellyn's view, wine list, and fabulous Sunday brunch as the best in Tahoe. The restaurant is named for Llewellyn Gross, who, with her husband Harvey, established the hotel in 1944.

Tempting cuisine

Panoramic views

AWARD WINNER
SINCE 1997

The River Café

Majestic views

Located under the Brooklyn Bridge on Water Street, 30-40 min. from LaGuardia and Kennedy International Airports

Renowned as one of the world's finest restaurants, The River Café offers exceptional American cuisine accompanied by majestic views of the Manhattan skyline and Statue of Liberty. Executive Chef Brad Steelman's specialties include Maine lobster gratin, Colorado "Cedar Springs" lamb chops, and terrine of duck foie gras. Nestled under the Brooklyn Bridge, The River Café has always been a favorite of New Yorkers. It's award-winning menu and impeccable service has made it a destination for celebrities, statesmen, ambassadors, and well-informed visitors around the world.

Brooklyn Bridge desserts

One Water Street
Brooklyn, NY 11201
PH: (718) 522-5200
FAX: (718) 875-0037
www.rivercafe.com

Owners
Michael D. O'Keeffe

Cuisine
Classic American

Days Open
Open daily for dinner, Mon.-Sat. for lunch, and Sun. for brunch

Pricing
Dinner for one, without tax, tip, or drinks: $80+ (or) Price Fix: $70

Dress Code
Business casual, jacket required for gentlemen, tie optional

Reservations
Required

Parking
Valet

Features
Private room/parties, outdoor dining, piano music nightly

Credit Cards
AE, VC, MC, DC, JCB

Terrace Room

World-renowned dining

Wine Spectator
BEST OF
AWARD OF
EXCELLENCE

DiRōNA
AWARD WINNER
SINCE 1993

The Brewster Inn

The Brewster Inn

Overlooking Cazenovia Lake, on Ledyard Avenue, 40 min. from Hancock International Airport

6 Ledyard Avenue
Cazenovia, NY 13035
PH: (315) 655-9232
FAX: (315) 655-2130
www.thebrewsterinn.com

The Brewster Inn offers gourmet dining in three candlelit rooms adorned with silver and crystal. An expertly trained staff assists you with selections from our award-winning wine list, the perfect complement to a superb menu. The new Terrace Bar, with its panoramic view of Cazenovia Lake, offers casually elegant dining in a room richly appointed with hand-made cherry wine racks and furniture, and which opens onto a large terrace for al fresco dining.

Maryland-style crab cakes

Terrace Bar

Gourmet dining in three candlelit rooms with panoramic views

Owners
Richard A. Hubbard

Cuisine
American/Continental

Days Open
Open daily for dinner.
Sunday for brunch

Pricing
Dinner for one,
without tax, tip, or drinks:
$20-$40

Dress Code
Business casual

Reservations
Recommended

Parking
Free on site

Features
Private parties,
outdoor dining

Credit Cards
VC, MC, CB, DC, DS

AWARD WINNER
SINCE 2004

Friends Lake Inn

Main dining room

E njoy the acclaimed contemporary American cuisine of Chef Stephen Topper, personable service, and an award-winning wine list at this cozy, candlelit dining room with original tin ceiling and chestnut woodwork. Recipient of the AAA Four Diamond Award, the restaurant is located within a historic inn with 17 luxury guest rooms in the foothills of the Adirondacks. Cross-country skiing on premises. Close to lake George and Saratoga. Specialties include an artisanal cheese course, and rabbit cannelloni

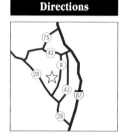

Greg and Sharon Taylor

River Rock Room

Sautéed lobster and scallop crepe, left, and roasted venison loin

AWARD WINNER
SINCE 1998

Directions

20 min. north of Lake George, 1 hr. from Albany International Airport

963 Friends Lake Road
Chestertown, NY 12817
PH: (518) 494-4751
FAX: (518) 494-4616
www.friendslake.com

Owners
Sharon and Greg Taylor

Cuisine
New American

Days Open
Open daily for breakfast and dinner (lunch in winter only)

Pricing
Dinner for one,
without tax, tip, or drinks:
$22–$40

Dress Code
Casual

Reservations
Recommended

Parking
Free on site

Features
Private room/parties,
wine cellar dining

Credit Cards
AE, VC, MC, CB, DC

Salvatore's Italian Gardens

A Buffalo landmark

On Transit Road, 15 min. from Buffalo-Niagara International Airport

6461 Transit Road
Depew, NY 14043
PH: (716) 683-7990
FAX: (716) 684-9229
www.salvatores.net

Owners
Russell and Joseph Salvatore

Cuisine
American and Italian

Days Open
Open daily for dinner

Pricing
Dinner for one, without tax, tip, or drinks: $20-$40

Dress Code
Business casual

Reservations
Recommended

Parking
Free on site, valet

Features
Private parties

Credit Cards
AE, VC, MC, DC, DS

The Italian Renaissance is in full bloom at Salvatore's Italian Gardens. Experience elegant Italian and American cuisine including prime steaks, fresh seafood, lobster, chicken, pasta, and veal dishes. Award-winning Salvatore's offers superior dining in richly decorated rooms and private functions in three grand ballrooms. This gilded gem features live entertainment every Friday and Saturday night for your listening pleasure. Also visit the Garden Place Hotel (dinner packages are available).

Owners Russell and Joseph Salvatore

The Roman Terrace Room

AWARD WINNER
SINCE 2002

Piccolo Restaurant of Huntington

Piccolo's elegant dining room

In Huntington's South Down Shopping Center, 50 min. from Kennedy International Airport

215 Wall Street
Huntington, NY 11743
PH: (631) 424-5592
FAX: (631) 421-5555

Owners
Dean Philippis

Cuisine
Italian Continental

Days Open
Open daily for dinner

Pricing
Dinner for one,
without tax, tip, or drinks:
$40-$60

Dress Code
Casual

Reservations
Recommended

Parking
Free on site

Features
Private parties,
entertainment

Credit Cards
AE, VC, MC, DC, DS

Given the #1 rating for top Italian restaurant on Long Island by the *Zagat Survey* – Piccolo stands out among the best. The décor is elegant with rich dark woods, candlelight and live piano music nightly. The carefully chosen wine list is extensive with more than 400 selections, offering 20 wines by the glass. Signature dishes include crisp Long Island duck, ossobucco, and stuffed veal chop Valdostano. Piccolo also offers catering on and off premises, and take-out.

AWARD WINNER
SINCE 1998

'21' Club

The Upstairs at '21'

Directions

On West 52nd Street, 30 min. from LaGuardia International Airport

21 West 52nd Street
New York, NY 10019
PH: (212) 582-7200
The Upstairs
PH: (212) 265-1900
www.21club.com

Owners
Orient-Express Hotels

Cuisine
American

Days Open
Open Mon.-Fri. for lunch, Mon.-Sat. for dinner (closed mid-August to day after Labor Day)

Pricing
Dinner for one, without tax, tip, or drinks:
Bar Room: $80+
Pre-theater: $37
The Upstairs: Three-course tasting dinner, prix fixe: $70

Dress Code
Jacket and tie required for dinner, jacket for lunch

Reservations
Recommended

Parking
Garage next door

Features
10 private dining rooms including Wine Cellar, near theater

Credit Cards
AE, VC, MC, CB, DC, DS

L egendary '21' offers a la carte dining in its famous Bar Room, and dinner in The Upstairs at '21', it's new 32-seat jewel. It also features ten character-rich private dining rooms, including the unique Prohibition-era Wine Cellar. The spacious Lounge is an excellent spot to rendezvous for cocktails before dinner or after theater. Dining at '21' is best experienced, not described.

Wine Cellar

Lounge

Bar Room

AWARD WINNER
SINCE 1992

Aquavit

Scandinavian chic

On West 54th Street just off Fifth Avenue in midtown, 30 min. from LaGuardia Airport

13 West 54th Street
New York, NY 10019
PH: (212) 307-7311
FAX: (212) 957-9043
www.aquavit.org

Owners
Hakan Swahn, Marcus Samuelsson

Cuisine
Scandinavian

Days Open
Open daily for lunch and dinner

Pricing
Dinner for one,
without tax, tip, or drinks:
$60-$80

Dress Code
Business casual

Reservations
Recommended

Parking
Garage nearby
(on same block)

Features
Private room/parties,
near theater

Credit Cards
AE, VC, MC, CB, DC, JCB

Named for a popular icy neutral spirit (which the restaurant serves in a variety of flavorful incarnations), Aquavit showcases the culinary creations of Co-owner and Chef Marcus Samuelsson, who brings a world of influences and dynamic talent to the bustling kitchen. The distinctive eatery occupies the lower floors of the Rockefeller townhouses across the street from the Museum of Modern Art's sculpture garden. Specialties include gravlax, fois gras ganache, and sorrel-crusted char.

Creative specialties

Hakan Swahn

Marcus Samuelsson

AWARD WINNER
SINCE 1992

Aureole

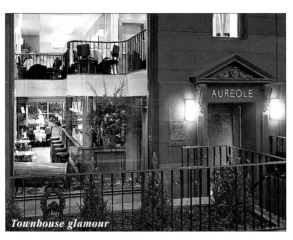

Townhouse glamour

Step into the understated elegance of Aureole, Charlie Palmer's Upper East Side townhouse restaurant. For 14 years, this beautiful establishment has been known for its warm service and distinctive contemporary American cuisine. New features include a six-course tasting menu and a vegetarian menu. Not to be missed are the ever-changing desserts for a grand finale.

Wine bar

Herb-poached guinea fowl

Charlie Palmer

AWARD WINNER
SINCE 1992

Directions

On East 61st Street between Park and Madison avenues, 30 min. from LaGuardia Airport

34 East 61st Street
New York, NY 10021
PH: (212) 319-1660
FAX: (212) 750-3126
www.aureolerestaurant.com

Owners
Charlie Palmer

Cuisine
Progressive American

Days Open
Open Mon.-Fri. for lunch, Mon.-Sat. for dinner

Pricing
Dinner for one, without tax, tip, or drinks: $60-$80

Dress Code
Jacket/tie required

Reservations
Required

Parking
Garage nearby

Features
Outdoor dining

Credit Cards
AE, VC, MC, DC, DS

328

Balthazar Restaurant

Main dining room

Directions

On Spring Street, 35 min. from LaGuardia International Airport

Balthazar is a traditional French Brasserie with a bustling railway station atmosphere serving favorites such as steak frites, duck Shepherd's pie, and chicken Riesling. Balthazar also specializes in seafood dishes, along with a complete oyster and shellfish bar. Balthazar maintains an extensive wine list of over 300 French wines.

Executive Chefs Riad Nasr and Lee Hanson

Oyster bar

80 Spring Street
New York, NY 10012
PH: (212) 965-1414
FAX: (212) 966-2502
www.balthazarny.com

Owners
Keith McNally

Cuisine
French Brasserie

Days Open
Open daily for breakfast, lunch, dinner and late supper, Sunday for brunch

Pricing
Dinner for one, without tax, tip, or drinks: $20-$40

Dress Code
Casual

Reservations
Recommended

Parking
Garage nearby

Credit Cards
AE, VC, MC

French breads from
Balthazar Bakery

AWARD WINNER
SINCE 003

Barbetta

Dining room

On Restaurant Row in the theater district, 30 min. from LaGuardia Airport

321 West 46th Street
New York, NY 10036
PH: (212) 246-9171
FAX: (212) 246-1279
e-mail:barbetta100yrs@aol.com
www.barbettarestaurant.com

Opened in 1906 by Sebastiano Maioglio, and now owned by his daughter, Laura, Barbetta is the oldest restaurant in New York that is still owned by its founding family. In a palatial interior decorated with historic 18th-century Italian antiques, Barbetta serves the cuisine of Piemonte. In summer its romantic garden, flowering and verdant, is one of the city's most sought-after dining sites. Six-time winner of *Wine Spectator's* Best of Award of Excellence.

Owner Laura Maioglio

Owners
Laura Maioglio

Cuisine
Northern Italian

Days Open
Open daily for lunch and dinner

Pricing
Dinner for one, without tax, tip, or drinks: $40-$60

Dress Code
Business elegant, jacket preferred

Reservations
Recommended

Parking
Adjacent lots

Features
Private rooms/parties, outdoor dining, entertainment, near theaters

Credit Cards
AE, VC, MC, CB, DC, JCB, DI

Garden

Quail's nest of Fonduta

AWARD WINNER
SINCE 1997

Bellini Restaurant

Main dining room

Directions

On East 52nd Street, 25 min. from LaGuardia International, and 35 min. from Kennedy International Airports

208 East 52nd Street
New York, NY 10022
PH: (212) 308-0830
FAX: (212) 308-9190
www.bellinirestaurantnyc.com

Owners
Donatella Arpaia

Cuisine
Italian (Neopolitan specialties)

Days Open
Open Mon.-Fri. for lunch,
Mon.-Sat. for dinner

Pricing
Dinner for one,
without tax, tip, or drinks:
$40-$60

Dress Code
Business casual

Reservations
Recommended

Parking
Garage nearby

Features
Private room/parties

Credit Cards
AE, VC, MC, DC, JCB, DS

After three years, Bellini Restaurant, owned by Donatella Arpaia, is distinguishing itself as the best new Italian restaurant in Manhattan. It became a magnet for VIP's and celebrities like Leonardo DiCaprio, Lauren Holly, and Anthony Quinn. Donatella is always there to make sure each customer has an experience to remember. The menu features a variety of homemade pastas, tantalizing antipasti, and delicious cuts of meat and fish, all enhanced by an extensive wine list. Exceptional homemade desserts including gelato, complement the meal.

Owner
Donatella Arpaia

Private dining room

AWARD WINNER
SINCE 2002

Bouley

The dramatic Red Room

At 120 West Broadway, on the corner of Duane Street, 30 min. from LaGuardia International and Newark International Airports

Chef David Bouley cooks French cuisine with world influences at the legendary restaurant, Bouley. Bouley's inspired creative cooking which uses only the best ingredients, delights diners with dishes like phyllo crusted Florida shrimp, baby Cape Cod squid, scuba dived sea scallop and sweet Maryland crabmeat in an ocean herbal broth. Located in the heart of Tribeca, the restaurant is one of the most romantic, and beautiful dining rooms in New York.

The scent of fresh apples will greet you

The elegant White Room

120 West Broadway
New York, NY 10013
PH: (212) 964-2525
FAX: (212) 571-0378
www.bouleyrestaurants.com

Owners
David Bouley

Cuisine
Modern French

Days Open
Open daily for lunch and dinner

Pricing
Dinner for one, without tax, tip, or drinks: $40-$60 (or) $35/lunch tasting menu, $75/dinner tasting menu

Dress Code
Jacket preferred

Reservations
Required

Parking
Garage nearby

Features
Private room/parties

Credit Cards
AE, VC, MC, DC

The intimate bar

DiRoNA
AWARD WINNER
SINCE 2002

Café des Artistes

Directions

Corner of 67th Street and
Central Park West, three
blocks from Lincoln Center,
and 25 min. from LaGuardia
International Airport

1 West 67th Street
New York, NY 10023
PH: (212) 877-3500
FAX: (212) 877-6263
www.cafedes.com

Owners
Jenifer and George Lang

Cuisine
Country French and bistro
European

Days Open
Open daily for lunch and
dinner, Sat.-Sun. for brunch

Pricing
Dinner for one,
without tax, tip, or drinks:
$40-$60

Dress Code
Jacket required for dinner
only

Reservations
Recommended

Parking
Garage nearby

Features
Private room, near theater

Credit Cards
AE, VC, MC, CB, DC, DS

Café des Artistes

The Café des Artistes opened in
1917 and is one of Manhattan's
most historic restaurants. The Café is
world-renowned for its lushly romantic
setting, including the six murals of
wood nymphs painted by Howard
Chandler Christy, and its warm service.
The menu, prepared by Chef Ari
Nieminen, reflects the best of European
bistro cooking, featuring such dishes
as sturgeon schnitzel, pot au feu with
marrow bone, and osso buco with
saffron risotto.

Dining room

Managing Director,
Jenifer Lang

Champagne for two

AWARD WINNER
SINCE 1992

Chanterelle

For over two decades, diners have traveled downtown to Tribeca to experience dinner at one of New York's most critically acclaimed restaurants, Chanterelle. With Karen Waltuck's gracious touch at the front of the house, and David Waltuck's masterful cooking, the couple has quietly set a standard for fine dining in New York City. The serene elegance of the dining room at Chanterelle is a perfect setting to enjoy Chef Waltuck's inspired classic French cuisine.

Serene elegance: the dining room at Chanterelle

Directions

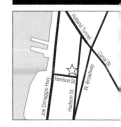

In Tribeca on Harrison St., 45 min. from LaGuardia International Airport

2 Harrison Street
New York, NY 10013
PH: (212) 966-6960
FAX: (212) 966-6143
www.chanterellenyc.com

Owners
David and Karen Waltuck

Cuisine
French

Days Open
Open Tues.-Sat. for lunch,
Mon.-Sat. for dinner

Pricing
Dinner for one,
without tax, tip, or drinks:
Price Fix:
$84 and $95

Dress Code
Business casual

Reservations
Required

Parking
Garage nearby

Features
Private parties,

Credit Cards
AE, VC, MC

AWARD WINNER
SINCE 1992

Cité

Main dining room

This steakhouse with a brasserie accent specializes in succulent steaks, chops, and seafood and luscious home-baked desserts, and features an extensive wine collection of over 9,000 bottles, with nightly wine dinners. Located in the Time-Life Building at Rockefeller Center, the restaurant is filled with hand-painted tiles, marble walkways, and deep leather banquettes. Art deco grillwork and architectural embellishments that once graced Paris' Au Bon Marche department store now give Cité an atmosphere of casual elegance.

The bar at The Grill

The Bacchus Mouth

Directions

At West 51st Street between Sixth and Seventh avenues, 40 min. from LaGuardia Airport

120 West 51st Street
New York, NY 10020
PH: (212) 956-7100
FAX: (212) 956-7157
www.citerestaurant.com

Owners
The Smith & Wollensky Restaurant Group, Inc.

Cuisine
American

Days Open
Open daily for lunch and dinner

Pricing
Dinner for one, without tax, tip, or drinks: $40-$60

Dress Code
Business casual

Reservations
Recommended

Parking
Garage nearby

Features
Private room/parties, prix-fixe wine dinner nightly

Credit Cards
AE, VC, MC, DC, DS, JCB

Wine Spectator
AWARD OF EXCELLENCE

AWARD WINNER
SINCE 1995

Dawat

Dawat

		60th. St.
	Bloomingdales	
Lexington	3rd Ave.	59th. St.
		58th. St.
		57th. St.

On East 58th between 2nd and 3rd avenues, 30 min. from Kennedy International Airport

210 East 58th Street
New York, NY 10022
PH: (212) 355-7555
FAX: (212) 355-1735
www.restaurant.com/dawat

Owners
Sushil Malhotra and
Vinnie Kumar

Cuisine
Indian

Days Open
Open Mon.-Sat.
11:30 a.m. to 3:00 p.m.
and Mon.-Sun.
5:30 p.m. to 11:00 p.m.

Pricing
Dinner for one,
without tax, tip, or drinks:
$20-$40

Dress Code
Smart casual

Reservations
Recommended

Parking
Garage nearby

Features
Private room/parties

Credit Cards
AE, VC, MC, DC, DS

M s Madhur Jaffrey, an internationally renowned Cook Book Author, Actress and Teacher is the driving Force behind Dawat. Her genius for creating Innovative Indian dishes and adapting classic Indian Cooking to contemporary taste has earned her widespread acclaim and positioned "Dawat" amongst the finest Restaurants in New York. Many of the specialty items in the menu are from her personal recipes and are unique to dawat. The service is refined but friendly, ensuring a smooth and pleasurable dining experience.

Succulent and flavorful lamb

AWARD WINNER
SINCE 1994

Gramercy Tavern

Directions

On East 20th Street between Broadway and Park Avenue South, 40 min. from LaGuardia Airport

42 East 20th Street
New York, NY 10003
PH: (212) 477-0777
FAX: (212) 477-1160

Owners
Danny Meyer and Tom Colicchio

Cuisine
Contemporary American

Days Open
Main dining room: Open Mon.-Fri. for lunch, daily for dinner
Tavern: Open daily for lunch and dinner

Pricing
Dinner for one, without tax, tip, or drinks:
Price fix:
Main dining room $68,
Tavern $30

Dress Code
Business casual

Reservations
Required in main dining room; no reservations taken in Tavern Room

Parking
Garage nearby

Features
Private room/parties

Credit Cards
AE, VC, MC, DC, DS

Full of urban and rustic charm, Danny Meyer's Gramercy Tavern was New Yorkers' second-favorite restaurant in the 2000 Zagat Survey. The restaurant is divided into two parts: casual Tavern Room and the pricier main dining room, which presents an ambitious and winning contemporary American menu. Tuna tartare with cucumber and sea urchin vinaigrette; salt-baked salmon with chanterelles, baby spinach, and roast garlic cream; and roasted rabbit with black olives and sherry vinegar are among the specialties than have won over New Yorkers and visiting food cognoscenti alike.

Private dining room

The Tavern

Main dining room

AWARD WINNER
SINCE 1998

Jean Georges

Jean Georges

©Peter Paige

Jean Georges has two dining rooms – Jean Georges and Nougatine (more casual with a sophisticated, hip bar scene, and an exhibition kitchen). The cuisine is based on the deceivingly simple philosophy of using the highest quality ingredients and preparing them to allow their natural flavors to stand on their own. In conceiving this restaurant, Jean-Georges Vongerichten wanted to bring back the elegance of tableside service to accompany his signature style of modern French cooking.

Directions

On Central Park West, 30 min. from LaGuardia International Airport

1 Central Park West
New York, NY 10023
PH: (212) 299-3900
FAX: (212) 299-3914

Owners
Jean-Georges Vongerichten, Phil Suarez and Bob Giraldi

Cuisine
French

Days Open
Open Mon.-Fri. for lunch, Mon.-Sat. for dinner

Pricing
Dinner for one, without tax, tip, or drinks: $87-$118

Dress Code
Casual elegant

Reservations
Required

Parking
Valet, garage nearby

Features
Private room/parties, outdoor Terrace dining (casual menu)

Credit Cards
AE, VC, MC, DC

DiRōNA
AWARD WINNER
2003

Jo Jo

J o Jo's renovation gives a turn of the last century feel to the townhouse with a green and eggplant color scheme, rich velvety and silk fabrics, and XVII century terra cotta tiles. The menu still has the same award-winning signature dishes like goat cheese and potato terrine with olive oil, roast chicken with chickpea fries, or the tuna spring roll with soybean coulis.

Classic Eastside dining

Directions

On 64th Street between Lexington and Third avenues on the Upper East Side, 30 min. from LaGuardia Airport

160 East 64th Street
New York, NY 10021
PH: (212) 223-5656
FAX: (212) 755-9038
www.jean-georges.com

Owners
Jean-Georges Vongerichten,
Jon Kamen

Cuisine
Contemporary French

Days Open
Open Mon.-Sat. for lunch,
daily for dinner

Pricing
Dinner for one,
without tax, tip, or drinks:
$40-$60

Dress Code
Business casual

Reservations
Required

Parking
Garage nearby

Credit Cards
AE, VC, MC, DC

AWARD WINNER
SINCE 1997

La Caravelle

Dining room

On West 55th Street
between 5th and 6th avenues
30 min. from LaGuardia,
50 min. from Kennedy
International Airport

La Caravelle has reigned as one of Manhattan's finest French restaurants since 1960. The elegant hand-painted murals by Jean Pagès evoke charming and colorful Parisian street scenes. La Caravelle's graceful setting is the ideal backdrop for the menu's brilliant integration of classical and contemporary French cuisine by critically acclaimed Chef Troy Dupuy. Guests receive excellent, professional care under the watchful eye of owners Rita and André Jammet. Private dining for parties up to 30 guests is also available.

Black bass with basmati rice, and shrimp broth

Rita and André Jammet, proprietors

Private dining room

33 West 55th Street
New York, NY 10019
PH: (212) 586-4252
FAX: (212) 956-8269
www.lacaravelle.com

Owners
André and Rita Jammet

Cuisine
Classic and contemporary French

Days Open
Open Mon.-Fri. for lunch,
Mon.-Sat. for dinner

Pricing
Dinner for one,
without tax, tip, or drinks:
$60-$80

Dress Code
Jacket required

Reservations
Recommended

Parking
Garage nearby

Features
Private room/parties, near theater, wine-tasting events and fashion show lunches

Credit Cards
AE, VC, MC, CB, DC

AWARD WINNER
SINCE 1994

Le Cirque 2000

The Maccioni family

e Cirque 2000's award-winning cuisine is all its own. Led by the Executive Chef Pierre Schaedelin, Le Cirque 2000 is unlike any other restaurant. The menu features luscious new dishes that bring the enticing flavors and fragrances of France, Italy, and even Cambodia, to the table. Regulars who yearn for old and beloved favorites will be happy to find sautéed foie gras with apple tatin, sea bass wrapped in potatoes with Barolo sauce, and, for dessert, the classic chocolate stove.

The Blue Room

The bar

The entrance

AWARD WINNER
SINCE 1999

Directions

On Madison Avenue between East 50th and 51st streets in midtown Manhattan, 40 min. from LaGuardia Airport

455 Madison Avenue
New York, NY 10022
PH: (212) 303-7788
FAX: (212) 303-7712
www.lecirque.com

Owners
Sirio Maccioni

Cuisine
Modern French

Days Open
Open Mon.-Sat. for lunch, daily for dinner

Pricing
Dinner for one, without tax, tip, or drinks: $60-$80

Dress Code
Jacket and tie required

Reservations
Required

Parking
Garage nearby

Features
Private room/parties, near theater

Credit Cards
AE, VC, MC, CB, DC

Le Madri

Tuscan-style dining

Directions

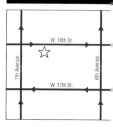

Off Seventh Avenue on 18th Street, 35 min. from LaGuardia International Airport

Opened in 1989 by famed New York chef/restaurateur Pino Luongo, Le Madri continues to collect accolades and maintain a clientele studded with loyal celebrities. Executive Chef Pippa S. Calland turns out such fare as lasagna with béchamel and ragu, and braised beef short ribs with polenta — all pairing perfectly with the wine list, which features the many flavors of Italy. Le Madri is conveniently located between the cultural draws of both downtown and midtown.

Tagliarini

Seafood specialties

Leave room for dessert

168 W. 18th Street
New York, NY 10011
PH: (212) 727-8022
FAX: (212) 727-3168
www.lemadri.citysearch.com

Owners
Pino Luongo

Cuisine
Italian with a Tuscan focus

Days Open
Open Mon.-Fri. for lunch, daily for dinner, Saturday and Sunday for brunch (closed for brunch July, August)

Pricing
Dinner for one, without tax, tip, or drinks: $40-$60

Dress Code
Business casual

Reservations
Recommended

Parking
Garage nearby (validated parking on weekends)

Features
Private parties, outdoor dining

Credit Cards
AE, VC, MC, DC

AWARD WINNER
SINCE 1993

Le Perigord

Private dining room

On East 52nd Street
between First Avenue and
the East River, 25 min. from
LaGuardia Airport

405 East 52nd Street
New York, NY 10022
PH: (212) 755-6244
FAX: (212) 486-3906
www.leperigord.com

Owners
The Briguet family

Cuisine
Contemporary French

Days Open
Open Mon.-Fri. for lunch,
daily for dinner

Pricing
Dinner for one,
without tax, tip or drinks:
$40-$60

Dress Code
Jacket and tie required

Reservations
Recommended

Parking
Garage nearby

Features
Private room/parties

Credit Cards
AE, VC, MC, CB, DC, DS

According to *The New York Times,* "Le Perigord is a survivor among an endangered species in New York: a solid French restaurant in a civilized setting that is conducive to both tranquil socializing and discreet business entertaining." The food is scintillating and the service exemplary at this luxury establishment. Chef Jacques Qualin offers traditional dishes executed with care, including sautéed veal kidneys in Armagnac and mustard.

Fresh lobster

Beef filet mignon

*Georges and Marie Therese
Briguet*

AWARD WINNER
SINCE 1994

Maloney & Porcelli

Main dining room

Madison Ave.

Park Ave.

E. 50th St.

On East 50th Street between Park and Madison avenues in midtown, 30 min. from LaGuardia Airport

37 East 50th Street
New York, NY 10022
PH: (212) 750-2233
FAX: (212) 750-2252
www.maloneyandporcelli.com

Owners
The Smith & Wollensky Restaurant Group, Inc.

Cuisine
Contemporary steakhouse

Days Open
Open daily for lunch and dinner

Pricing
Dinner for one,
without tax, tip, or drinks:
$40-$60

Dress Code
Business casual

Reservations
Recommended

Parking
Garage nearby

Features
Private room/parties

Credit Cards
AE, VC, MC, DC, DS, JCB

This bustling, two-story restaurant reflects Executive Chef/author David Burke's creative approach to food, and its smart menu and dramatic decor draw crowds from the business and entertainment worlds. The classic American fare includes steak and lobsters, but goes beyond the traditional with such innovative dishes as crackling pork shank with firecracker applesauce and thin-crusted Robiola pizza with white truffle oil. Desserts are equally spirited and scrumptious: Try drunken doughnuts or a towering coconut layer cake.

Pork shank with firecracker applesauce

Chef Patrick Vaccariello

Wine Spectator

AWARD OF EXCELLENCE

DiRōNA

AWARD WINNER
SINCE 2001

344

Manhattan Ocean Club

Picasso Room

Set in a sleek, two-tiered dining room, recently remodeled with the help of design consultant Adam Tihany, this classic seafood restaurant has won raves as one of Manhattan's best fish houses, with the day's fresh catch seared, sautéed, poached, or steamed to order. The menu also offers such dishes as seared tuna with applewood smoked bacon, and mahi-mahi marinated in Moroccan spices with eggplant, garlic and parsley-infused olive oil. Scrumptious desserts include the signature Belgian chocolate bags filled with white chocolate mousse with strawberry sauce.

Bounty from the sea

Directions

On West 58th Street between Fifth and Sixth Avenues, 35 min. from LaGuardia Airport

57 West 58th Street
New York, NY 10019
PH: (212) 371-7777
FAX: (212) 371-9362
www.manhattanocean
club.com

Owners
The Smith & Wollensky
Restaurant Group, Inc.

Cuisine
Seafood

Days Open
Open daily for lunch and dinner

Pricing
Dinner for one,
without tax, tip, or drinks:
$40-$60

Dress Code
Business casual

Reservations
Recommended

Parking
Garage nearby

Features
Private room/parties

Credit Cards
AE, VC, MC, DC, DS, JCB

Shellfish bouquet

AWARD WINNER
SINCE 1998

March Restaurant

Dining in an elegant, turn-of-the-century New York townhouse

M arch, celebrated its 12th anniversary in 2002. In recognition of what his cooking has always been, and as a tribute to the city that inspires him, Chef/Co-owner Wayne Nish designates his food as "New York City Cuisine." Specialties include Fricassée of seasonal vegetables with black truffle and fleur de sel, poached lobster with Muscat de beames de venise sauce, and simmered yellowtail with Chinese black beans, bacon, and Brussels sprouts. Wine director/Co-owner Joseph Scalice matches wines, champagnes, sherries, and sakes to compliment Chef Nish's menu.

"New York City" cuisine

Proprietors, Joseph Scalice and Wayne Nish

AWARD WINNER
SINCE 1994

Directions

Off Sutton Place on East 58th Street, 30 min. from Kennedy International Airport

405 East 58th Street
New York, NY 10022
PH: (212) 754-6272
FAX: (212) 838-5108
www.marchrestaurant.com

Owners
Joseph Scalice and
Wayne Nish

Cuisine
New American

Days Open
Open daily for dinner

Pricing
Dinner for one,
without tax, tip, or drinks:
Price fix: $55 - $102

Dress Code
Jacket requested

Reservations
Recommended

Parking
Garage nearby

Features
Private room/parties, outdoor dining, near theater

Credit Cards
AE, VC, MC, CB, DC, JCB, DS

Michael's

Main dining room

Michael McCarty, who opened his acclaimed namesake restaurant in Santa Monica in 1979, brings his experience to bear on Michael's in New York. The comfortable rooms are decorated with Michael's signature collection of original artwork. Chef Robert Ribant utilizes a range of American raw ingredients — including wild cepes, ramps, and morels — in a cuisine that is at once earthy and startlingly original. The menu changes seasonally and might include such unique dishes as pan-roasted durade royal, and fennel potato pureé.

Owner Michael McCarty

Michael's California cuisine

Garden Room

AWARD WINNER
SINCE 1999

Directions

On West 55th Street, 30 min. from LaGuardia and 40 min. from Kennedy International Airports

24 West 55th Street
New York, NY 10019
PH: (212) 767-0555
FAX: (212) 581-6778
www.michaelsnewyork.com

Owners
Michael McCarty

Cuisine
California

Days Open
Open Mon.-Fri. for breakfast and lunch, Mon.-Sat. for dinner

Pricing
Dinner for one, without tax, tip, or drinks: $40-$60

Dress Code
Business casual

Reservations
Recommended

Parking
Garage nearby, local street parking

Features
Private room/parties, near theater

Credit Cards
AE, VC, MC, CB, DC, DS

Montrachet

A Tribeca original

Directions

Located on West Broadway, 30 min. from LaGuardia and Newark and 1 hr. from Kennedy International Airports

239 West Broadway
New York, NY 10013
PH: (212) 219-2777
FAX: (212) 274-9508
www.MyriadRestaurantGroup.com

Owners
Drew Nieporent and Tony Zazula

Cuisine
Contemporary French

Days Open
Open Fri. for lunch,
Mon.-Sat. for dinner

Pricing
Dinner for one,
without tax, tip, or drinks:
$60-$80

Dress Code
Business casual

Reservations
Recommended

Parking
Garage nearby

Features
Private room/parties

Credit Cards
AE, VC, MC, DS

Montrachet is one of New York's most revered and successful French restaurants, with international recognition for excellent cuisine, service, and wine selection. It has consistently received a three-star rating from *The New York Times* and *Forbes Magazine*, and has earned "The Ivy Award" from *Restaurant and Institutions* magazine. Awarded Four Stars and The Grand Award by the *Wine Spectator*, the wine list has been heralded as one of the finest in New York City. Located in Tribeca, Montrachet continues into its second decade as a true restaurant classic on the cutting edge of contemporary French cooking.

Seared foie gras

Award-winning wine selections

GRAND AWARD

DiRoNA
AWARD WINNER
SINCE 1992

Nicola's Restaurant

Manager Pat Rondinelli, Chef Rocco D' Acquaviva and Owner Romano Riccoboni

Nicola's, set in the posh residential area of the Upper East Side, offers the most delectable Italian cuisine. The décor features stained glass of Europe's countryside and autographed frames of its famous clientele including politicians, authors, and movie stars. With the feel of comfort throughout the restaurant, the dinner selections follow suit. Chef Rocco D'Acquaviva's diverse menu includes homemade pastas, chicken, veal, and seafood. Don't forget to leave room for the outrageous desserts!

Wood panel décor

Directions

Between Lexington and Third Avenue on East 84th Street, 20 min. from LaGuardia International Airport

146 East 84th Street
New York, NY 10028
PH: (212) 249-9850
FAX: (212) 772-7564

Owners
Nadia Riccoboni

Cuisine
Italian

Days Open
Open daily for dinner

Pricing
Dinner for one,
without tax, tip, or drinks:
$20-$40

Dress Code
Business casual

Reservations
Required

Parking
Garage nearby

Features
Private parties

Credit Cards
AE, VC, MC, DC

AWARD WINNER
SINCE 1997

Nobu

A visual and culinary delight

In Tribeca on Hudson Street
30 min. from LaGuardia and
Newark International Airports
and 40 min. from Kennedy
International Airport

Nobu is America's most celebrated Japanese restaurant, bringing totally innovative "new style Japanese cooking" to New York City. A partnership of actor Robert DeNiro, Chef Nobuyuki Matsuhisa, and restaurateur Drew Nieporent, Nobu is a visual and culinary delight. The interior design evokes a feeling of the Japanese countryside as tall birch tree columns rise into the ceiling, which is painted copper with open brick patches, along with a wall of Japanese river rocks. The cuisine weds a range of wonderful, zesty sauces with superb raw and cooked ingredients to achieve new levels of taste satisfaction.

Tiradito

Contempory Japanese decor

Black cod with miso

105 Hudson Street
New York, NY 10013
PH: (212) 219-0500
FAX: (212) 219-1441
www.MyriadRestaurantGroup.com

Owners
Drew Nieporent, Robert
DeNiro and Nobu Matsuhisa

Cuisine
New style Japanese

Days Open
Open Mon.-Fri. for lunch,
Mon.-Sun. for dinner

Pricing
Dinner for one,
without tax, tip, or drinks:
$60-$80

Dress Code
Business casual

Reservations
Recommended

Parking
Garage nearby

Features
Private room/parties

Credit Cards
AE, VC, MC, DS

AWARD WINNER
SINCE 2001

ONE c.p.s.

Dining at ONE c.p.s.

Located in the Plaza Hotel, 25 min. from LaGuardia International Airport

1 Central Park South
New York, NY 10019
PH: (212) 583-1111
FAX: (212) 593-7781

Owners
Smith & Wollensky
Restaurant Group

Cuisine
American Brasserie

Days Open
Open daily for lunch and dinner

Pricing
Dinner for one,
without tax, tip, or drinks:
$40-$60

Dress Code
Business casual

Reservations
Recommended

Parking
Garage nearby

Features
Private room/parties

Credit Cards
AE, VC, MC

This stunning restaurant, in the Plaza Hotel, is the combined vision of restaurateur Alan Stillman, Executive Chef David Burke, and restaurant designer Adam Tihany. The idea was to offer cutting-edge food and an old-fashioned, yet fresh atmosphere in what many consider the most quintessential New York location ever created. Tihany was responsible for the physical transformation of the Edwardian Room of the Plaza – installed in 1907 – into a light, and bright new restaurant. His design intent was to highlight the prime location of the restaurant, and to transform the stately room into a contemporary, American eating-place.

Private dinner parties

AWARD WINNER
2003

One if by Land, Two if by Sea

Candlelit dining

Directions

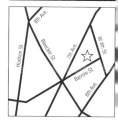

Downtown on Barrow Street near Seventh Avenue, 30 min. from LaGuardia International Airport

17 Barrow Street
New York, NY 10014
PH: (212) 255-8649
FAX: (212) 206-7855
www.oneifbyland.com

This restored 18th century carriage house and stable, formerly owned by Aaron Burr, now houses one of the most romantic spots in New York City. One if by Land, Two if by Sea serves seasonal American cuisine prepared by Executive Chef Gary Volkov, and features such entrees as breast of muscovy duck, and individual Beef Wellington. The diverse dinner menu is accompanied by an award-winning wine list, served in a candlelit setting. A tasting menu is also available. The spacious bar with its two working fireplaces and live piano music is a favorite late-night spot.

Executive Chef Gary Volkov

Rack of Australian lamb

Sesame coated sushi-grade tuna

Owners
Noury K. Goujjane

Cuisine
Seasonal American

Days Open
Open daily for dinner

Pricing
Dinner for one,
without tax, tip, or drinks:
$60-$80 (or) Prix Fixe: $63

Dress Code
Business casual,
jacket suggested

Reservations
Recommended

Parking
Garage nearby

Features
Private room/parties

Credit Cards
AE, VC, MC, CB, DC, DS

AWARD WINNER
SINCE 1996

Park Avenue Cafe

Main dining room

Directions

At Park Avenue and East 63rd Street on the Upper East Side, 30 min. from LaGuardia Airport

The acclaimed Park Avenue Cafe is a fine-dining restaurant showcasing signature dishes of Chef/Partner David Burke and Pastry Chef Richard Leach. Casual, warm, and welcoming, the cutting-edge American fare is served to diners in whimsical presentations. The eatery combines country and contemporary design elements with authentic American crafts. Don't miss such delectable items as the pastrami salmon, salmon tartare, and salmon bacon.

Chef David Burke

The Flag Room

100 East 63rd Street
New York, NY 10021
PH: (212) 644-1900
FAX: (212) 688-0373
www.parkavenuecafe.com

Owners
The Smith & Wollensky Restaurant Group, Inc.

Cuisine
American

Days Open
Open daily for lunch and dinner

Pricing
Dinner for one,
without tax, tip, or drinks:
$50-$70

Dress Code
Business casual

Reservations
Recommended

Parking
Garage nearby

Features
Private room/parties

Credit Cards
AE, VC, MC, DC, DS, JCB

Alan Stillman

Wine Spectator
AWARD OF EXCELLENCE

DiRōNA
AWARD WINNER
SINCE 1997

Picholine

Front dining room

Between Broadway and
Central Park West, near
Lincoln Center and 30 min.
from LaGuardia Airport

At Picholine, Chef-Proprietor Terrance Brennan showcases Mediterranean cuisine, using the best and freshest ingredients from local organic farmers as well as from around the world. His signature dishes include sea urchin panna cotta with lobster consommé and osetta caviar; warm Maine lobster with caramelized endive and vanilla-brown butter vinaigrette; wild mushroom and duck risotto; and tournedos of salmon with horseradish crust, cucumbers and salmon caviar. Picholine is world-renowned for its artisanal cheese cart.

Back dining room

Private dining room

35 West 64th Street
New York, NY 10023
PH: (212) 724-8585
FAX: (212) 875-8979

Owners
Terrance Brennan

Cuisine
Mediterranean

Days Open
Open Tues.-Sat. for lunch,
daily for dinner

Pricing
Dinner for one,
without tax, tip, or drinks:
$40-$60

Dress Code
Gentlemen are required to
wear jackets for dinner

Reservations
Recommended (taken up to
two months in advance)

Parking
Garage nearby

Features
Private dining available,
cheese courses by Fromager
Max McCalman, desserts
by pastry Chef Michael
Moorhouse

Credit Cards
AE, VC, MC, DC

Chef/Proprieter
Terrance Brennan

AWARD WINNER
SINCE 1999

The Post House

Main dining room

At East 63rd Street between Madison and Park avenues, 30 min. from LaGuardia Airport

28 East 63rd Street
New York, NY 10021
PH: (212) 935-2888
FAX: (212) 371-9264
www.theposthouse.com

Owners
The Smith & Wollensky Restaurant Group, Inc.

Cuisine
American

Days Open
Open Mon.-Fri. for lunch and daily for dinner

Pricing
Dinner for one, without tax, tip, or drinks: $40-$60

Dress Code
Business casual

Reservations
Recommended

Parking
Garage nearby

Credit Cards
AE, VC, MC, DC, DS, JCB

Distinctive and dramatic, this award-winning steak and chop-house is a prime cut above the usual, offering a variety of mouthwatering meat entrées seared to juicy perfection. Other specialties include seafood dishes, such as Maryland crab cakes and cornmeal fried oysters, and grilled chicken breast with couscous. The eatery also features a wide variety of seasonal desserts and an extensive wine list and library of rare wines from Bordeaux, Burgundy, and California.

More than just steak

AWARD WINNER
SINCE 1996

Remi

Enter Remi...contemporary Venetian cuisine meets classic Italian architecture

Contemporary. Venetian cuisine defined by Chef Francesco Antonucci, meets classic Italian architecture interpreted by designer Adam Tihany in midtown Manhattan. These talented co-owners have created a restaurant that encompasses the magic of Venice, and incorporates their shared passion for Italian opulence. Enter Remi and embark on a visual odyssey filled with Tihany's enchanting interiors of flying buttress archways, soaring renaissance murals, and colorful, Venetian glass chandeliers. Chef Antonucci salutes his native Venice by dazzling the senses with classic dishes brought to life by his innovative style, including his famous homemade pastas, and creamy risottos that change with the seasons.

Directions

On West 53rd Street, between 6th and 7th avenues, 40 min. from LaGuardia Int'l Airport

145 West 53rd Street
New York, NY 10019
PH: (212) 581-4242
FAX: (212) 581-7182
www.citysearch.com/nyc/remi

Owners
Francesco Antonucci

Cuisine
Italian

Days Open
Open Mon.-Fri. for lunch, daily for dinner

Pricing
Dinner for one, without tax, tip, or drinks: $40-$60

Dress Code
Jacket and tie required

Reservations
Required

Parking
Garage nearby

Features
Private room/parties, outdoor dining, near theater

Credit Cards
AE, VC, MC, DC, JCB

Wine Spectator
AWARD OF EXCELLENCE

DiRoNA
AWARD WINNER
SINCE 1996

356

Ristorante Primavera

Main dining room

Directions

E. 82nd St.

Second Ave

First Ave

On the corner of East 82nd Street and First Avenue, 25 min. from LaGuardia Airport

Ristorante Primavera and its owner Nicola Civetta have been delighting discriminating diners since 1978. This award-winning Italian favorite has a tasteful, stylish look, with walls and ceilings paneled in rich Italian walnut. The crispy zucchini sticks, the delicately fried portabello mushrooms, the phenomenal sea bass crusted in potato with its hint of mustard and horseradish, and for dessert, the perfect raspberry and strawberry custard tart, make for a memorable meal.

Chef Giorgio Bottazzi

Giorgio's favorite dish

1578 First Avenue
New York, NY 10028
PH: (212) 861-8608
FAX: (212) 861-9620
www.primaveranyc.com

Owners
Mr. and Mrs. Nicola Civetta

Cuisine
Northern Italian

Days Open
Open daily for dinner

Pricing
Dinner for one,
without tax, tip, or drinks:
$40-$60

Dress Code
Jacket required

Reservations
Recommended

Parking
Garage nearby

Features
Private room

Credit Cards
AE, VC, MC, CB, DC

Proprietors Peggy and Nicola Civetta

AWARD WINNER
SINCE 2001

San Domenico NY

Main dining room

At Central Park South (59th Street) between 7th Ave. and Broadway, 35 min. from LaGuardia Airport, 45 min. from Kennedy International Airport

A n extraordinary, refined restaurant that reflects the cooking of modern Italy, San Domenico has remained unparalleled in reputation, innovation, and imagination. The cooking is light, incorporating traditional tastes and flavors. Signature dishes—made with the finest and freshest products—include the uovo in raviolo, a homemade soft-egg-yolk filled raviolo with truffle butter, and risotto with beef glaze and parmigiano.

Sea urchin ravioli with tomato, garlic, and peperoncino

240 Central Park South
New York, NY 10019
PH: (212) 265-5959
FAX: (212) 397-0844
www.sandomenicony.com

Owners
Tony May and daughter Marisa May

Cuisine
Contemporary Italian

Days Open
Open Mon.-Fri. for lunch, daily for dinner

Pricing
Dinner for one, without tax, tip, or drinks: $40-$60

Dress Code
Jacket required

Reservations
Recommended

Parking
Garage nearby

Features
Private room/parties

Credit Cards
AE, VC, MC, CB, DC, JCB

Marisa and Tony May with Chef Odette Fada

Private dining room

AWARD WINNER
SINCE 1992

Smith & Wollensky

Third Avenue landmark

The steaks, chops, and seafood here have been highly praised by food critics around the globe. The establishment is also noted for its outstanding wine list, service, and ambience. But steaks are the stars, including double sirloin, chateaubriand (for two), filet mignon, and sliced steak Wollensky. The meat is superbly flavorful and tender; all beef is prime grade and dry-aged in house for 28 days.

Steaks, and then some

Main dining room

At your service

BEST OF
AWARD OF
EXCELLENCE

DiRoNA
AWARD WINNER
SINCE 1992

Directions

At East 49th Street and Third Avenue, 30 min. from LaGuardia Airport

797 Third Avenue
New York, NY 10022
PH: (212) 753-1530
FAX: (212) 751-5446
www.smithandwollensky.com

Owners
The Smith & Wollensky Restaurant Group, Inc.

Cuisine
Steakhouse

Days Open
Open daily for lunch and dinner

Pricing
Dinner for one, without tax, tip, or drinks: $40-$60

Dress Code
Business casual

Reservations
Recommended

Parking
Garage nearby

Features
Private room/parties

Credit Cards
AE, VC, MC, DC, DS, JCB

Sparks Steak House

Hudson Room

On East 46th between Second and Third avenues, 30 min. from LaGuardia Airport

This all-American, robust outpost is everything a popular steakhouse should be. The rosey dry-aged steaks with charred-edge crusts are cooked to mouthwatering perfection. Entrées include jumbo lobster, fresh fish, and veal and lamb chops, plus fresh vegetables cooked to order. The extensive wine list is a consistent *Wine Spectator* Grand Award Winner. Diners also enjoy the restaurant's close proximity to the United Nations.

Victorian Room

Main dining room

210 East 46th Street
New York, NY 10017
PH: (212) 687-4855
FAX: (212) 557-7409

Owners
Michael Cetta

Cuisine
Steakhouse

Days Open
Open Mon.-Fri. for lunch,
Mon.-Sat. for dinner

Pricing
Dinner for one,
without tax, tip, or drinks:
$60-$80

Dress Code
Jacket preferred

Reservations
Recommended

Parking
Garage nearby

Features
Private room/parties,
cigar bar

Credit Cards
AE, VC, MC, CB, DC, DS

AWARD WINNER
SINCE 1993

Swifty's

Swifty's at night

Directions

On Lexington Ave. between 72nd and 73rd streets, 25 min. from LaGuardia, and 35 min. from Kennedy International airports

1007 Lexington Avenue
New York, NY 10021
PH: (212) 535-6000
FAX: (212) 535-1406

Owners
Robert Caravaggi and Stephen Attoe

Cuisine
American with European specialties

Days Open
Open daily for lunch, and dinner

Pricing
Dinner for one, without tax, tip, or drinks: $40-$60

Dress Code
Business casual/jacket recommended

Reservations
Recommended

Features
Private parties

Parking
Garage nearby

Credit Cards
AE, VC, CM, CB, DC

Described by *Forbes Magazine* as "super stylish, low-key, superb", Swifty's attracts a devoted clientele drawn by Chef Stephen Attoe's straight-forward American cuisine. Specialties include grilled filet of beef with foie gras crostini and roasted shallots, jumbo lump crab cakes, classic cheese soufflé and charred twinburgers with fries. House made desserts feature molasses frosted carrot cake, Memphis pecan pie, ice cream and sorbets, chocolate soufflé. Renowned decorator Mario Buatta created the warm atmosphere enhanced by seasonal flowers.

Owners Stephen Attoe and Robert Caravaggi

Sautéed scallops Provençale with fettuccini

AWARD WINNER
SINCE 2003

Terrace in the Sky

The Green House

At West 119th Street and
Morningside Drive atop
Columbia University's Butler
Hall, 25 min. from
LaGuardia Airport

Atop Columbia University's Butler Hall, Terrace in the Sky is one of New York's most romantic restaurants, with full-length windows giving everyone a smashing view of the Manhattan skyline and the city's bridges and rivers. A fireplace, pristine white tablecloths, and red roses decorate the original 1930 terrace floor and

the teak environs of the main dining room. Executive Chef Jason Patanovich combines traditional culinary arts with an eclectic approach. Typical of his skill is dayboat fish en Papillote, with black truffles, Provencal vegetables, and celery root truffle sauce.

Spectacular desserts

French/Mediterranean cuisine

AWARD WINNER
SINCE 1992

400 West 119th Street
New York, NY 10027
PH: (212) 666-9490
FAX: (212) 666-3471
www.terraceinthesky.com

Owners
Morningside Heights
Restaurant Corp.

Cuisine
French, Mediterranean

Days Open
Open Tues.-Fri. for lunch,
Tues.-Sat. for dinner,
Sunday for brunch

Pricing
Dinner for one,
without tax, tip, or drinks:
$60-$80

Dress Code
Business casual

Reservations
Recommended

Parking
Free on site,
valet (evenings only)

Features
Private room/parties, entertainment, wine tasting

Credit Cards
AE, VC, MC

Tribeca Grill

A neighborhood restaurant for the whole world

Directions

On Greenwich Street, on the corner of Franklin, 30 min. from Newark International and LaGuardia International Airport, and 1 hr. from Kennedy International Airport

Entering its second decade, Tribeca Grill, owned by actor Robert DeNiro and noted restaurateur Drew Nieporent, radiates excitement and energy in an unpretentious bar and grill setting. It has become a New York City landmark known for its personable service and Chef Stephen Lewandowski's contemporary American cuisine. "The Grill" has earned many distinctions including the *Wine Spectator, Grand Award 2002* for its 1500-bottle wine list focused on verticals of California cabernet sauvignon, and an extensive list of Zinfandels.

Pan roasted halibut with Peruvian potato puree, warm tomato bacon vinaigrette

Poached Maine lobster

375 Greenwich Street
New York, NY 10013
PH: (212) 941-3900
FAX: (212) 941-3915
www.MyriadRestaurantGroup.com

Owners
Drew Nieporent and Robert DeNiro

Cuisine
Contemporary American

Days Open
Open Mon.-Fri. for lunch, Mon.-Sun. for dinner, Sunday for brunch

Pricing
Dinner for one, without tax, tip, or drinks: $40-$60

Dress Code
Business casual

Reservations
Recommended

Parking
Garage nearby

Features
Private room/screening room, parties, outdoor dining

Credit Cards
AE, VC, MC, DS

GRAND AWARD

DiRōNA
AWARD WINNER
SINCE 2002

Union Square Cafe

An oasis of sophistication

On 16th Street near Union Square, 45 min. from LaGuardia Airport

21 East 16th Street
New York, NY 10003
PH: (212) 243-4020
FAX: (212) 627-2673

Owners
Danny Meyer, Michael Romano, Paul Bolles-Beaven

Cuisine
New American with rustic Italian accents

Days Open
Open daily for lunch and dinner

Pricing
Dinner for one, without tax, tip, or drinks: $40-$60

Dress Code
No dress code

Reservations
Recommended

Parking
Garage nearby

Credit Cards
AE, VC, MC, DC, DS

Since Danny Meyer opened this smart and sophisticated restaurant in 1985, it has maintained its reputation for offering consistent excellence in fine food and service. One of Manhattan's most popular dining spots, Union Square Cafe features New American cuisine with rustic Italian flavors. Executive Chef Dan Silverman dazzles diners with dishes that celebrate both delicate and hearty flavors, such as the appetizer of porcini gnocchi with Swiss chard and parmigiano reggiano.

AWARD WINNER
SINCE 1992

Vong

V ong is Chef Jean-Georges Vongerichten's homage to the exotic spices and flavors of the Far East. Thai-inspired French food is served amid beautiful Thai silks, red paint under gold leaf, and a Buddha altar with bowls of fragrant spices. Signature dishes include sautéed foie gras with ginger and mango, and crisp squab with egg noodle pancake and honey-ginger glazed pearl onions.

Exquisite dining room

Directions

On East 54th Street just off Third Avenue, 30 min. from LaGuardia Airport

200 East 54th Street
New York, NY 10022
PH: (212) 486-9592
FAX: (212) 980-3745
www.jean-georges.com

Owners
Jean-Georges Vongerichten,
Phil Suarez, Bob Giraldi

Cuisine
Thai-inspired French

Days Open
Open Mon.-Fri. for lunch,
daily for dinner

Pricing
Dinner for one,
without tax, tip, or drinks:
$40-$60

Dress Code
Business casual

Reservations
Required

Parking
Garage nearby

Features
Private parties (must rent entire restaurant)

Credit Cards
AE, VC, MC, DC

Wine Spectator
AWARD OF EXCELLENCE

DiRoNA
AWARD WINNER
SINCE 1998

Xaviars at Piermont

The Bully Boy Bar

Off Route 9W in Piermont, 45 min. from New Jersey's Newark International Airport

X aviars is located in Piermont, a picturesque community on the west bank of the Hudson River, 20 minutes north of Manhattan. It is the only restaurant north of Manhattan to have received a four-star "extraordinary" rating from *The New York Times*. Peter X. Kelly's contemporary American cuisine has been roundly applauded, and is served in an intimate, 40-seat dining room adorned with fresh flowers, candlelight, Versace china, and Riedel stemware. The comprehensive wine list has more than 750 selections.

Peter X. Kelly

Hudson Valley foie gras

Crisp crayfish tempura with cucumber jus

506 Piermont Avenue
Piermont, NY 10968
PH: (845) 359-7007
FAX: (845) 359-4021
www.xaviars.com

Owners
Peter X. Kelly

Cuisine
Contemporary American

Days Open
Open Fri. for lunch, Tues.-Sun. for dinner, Sun. for brunch

Pricing
Dinner for one, without tax, tip, or drinks: $40-$60

Dress Code
Jacket and tie required

Reservations
Required

Parking
Free on site, valet

Credit Cards
None accepted

AWARD WINNER
SINCE 1994

La Panetiére

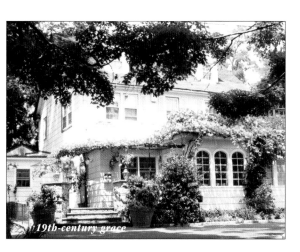

19th-century grace

Jacques Loupiac followed his dreams to the United States, and in 1985 opened La Panetiére in a warm, welcoming 19th-century home. The restaurant's ambience and decor invoke Provence, with the dining room on the first floor separated by hand-painted fresco arches, supported by original beams, and furnished with a working buffet, paintings, and tapestries. The contemporary French menu changes with the seasons and is reflective of the bounty provided by market gardeners, fishermen, free-range poultry farmers, and other quality purveyors.

Charming decor

The Greenhouse (private room)

First floor dining room

AWARD WINNER
SINCE 1992

Short distance off New England Thruway's Exit 19, 15 min. from Westchester County Airport

530 Milton Road
Rye, NY 10580
PH: (914) 967-8140
FAX: (914) 921-0654
www.lapanetiere.com

Owners
Jacques Loupiac

Cuisine
French

Days Open
Open Mon.-Fri. for lunch, daily for dinner

Pricing
Dinner for one, without tax, tip, or drinks: $40-$60

Dress Code
Jacket required

Reservations
Recommended

Parking
Valet

Features
Private room/parties

Credit Cards
AE, VC, MC, CB, DC, DS

The American Hotel

Main dining room

In the Hamptons, 1 hr. from McArthur (Islip) Airport and 2 hrs. from LaGuardia and Kennedy International Airport

This historic brick hotel has been serving vacationers since 1876, and has developed a worldwide reputation for its excellent food. The fruits de mer platter is a revelation — the finest lobster, Petrossian caviar, mussels, clams, oysters, and more. Other menu highlights include Kobe beef and a variety of game. Prepare to spend time perusing the wine list, all 80 pages of it. The American Hotel's eight guest rooms have been enlarged to include modern amenities, and are uniquely decorated with Victorian-era antiques.

Bar area dining room

The Drew Room

Wine Spectator
GRAND AWARD

DiRōNA
AWARD WINNER
SINCE 1992

Main Street
P.O. Box 1349
Sag Harbor, N.Y. 11963
PH: (631) 725-3535
FAX: (631) 725-3573
www.theamericanhotel.com

Owners
Ted Conklin

Cuisine
French/American

Days Open
Open Sat.-Sun. for lunch, daily for dinner

Pricing
Dinner for one, without tax, tip, or drinks: $40-$60

Dress Code
Business casual

Reservations
Recommended

Parking
Free on street

Features
Private parties, outdoor dining, entertainment

Credit Cards
AE, VC, MC, DC, DS

Mirabelle Restaurant

The entrance to Mirabelle Restaurant

On North Country Road, 20 min. from McArthur Airport

404 North Country Road
St. James, NY 11780
PH: (631) 584-5999
FAX: (631) 584-3090
www.restaurantmirabelle.com

Owners
Guy and Maria Reuge

Cuisine
French

Days Open
Open Tues.-Fri. for lunch,
Tues.-Sun. for dinner

Pricing
Dinner for one,
without tax, tip, or drinks:
$40-$60
(or) Price fix: $35

Dress Code
Business casual

Reservations
Recommended

Parking
Valet, Free on site

Features
Private parties, summer
outdoor dining

Credit Cards
AE, VC, MC, CB, DC, DS

Mirabelle Restaurant, opened in December 1983 by Guy and Maria Reuge, is located in a small 19th century farmhouse about an hour from New York City. A simple elegance best describes the modern décor, and the cuisine reflects Chef/Owner Reuge's French background. Fish and seafood are prepared with a light touch, and the duck in two courses is a house specialty.

The simple, yet elegant Mirabelle dining room

Celebrate with the Mirabelle Cocktail

AWARD WINNER
SINCE 1995

Harralds

The main house

Directions

On Route 52 in Stormville, 6 miles east of Taconic Parkway 45 min. from Westchester County Airport and 1 hr. 30 min. from LaGuardia Airport

Harralds, located in a charming Tudor compound in countrified Dutchess County, north of New York City, exemplifies the highest standards of excellence in cuisine and service. For 31 years, Harrald Boerger and his wife, chef Ava Dürrschmidt, have done what perhaps only a dozen or so American restaurateurs have done: They've created a legend, a restaurant whose menu never reflects fads, yet never goes out of style. Come for such specialties as truite au bleu, fresh from the stocked trout tank, and let Harrald and Ava and their devoted staff remind you how joyful life can be.

Bucolic setting

3760 Route 52
Stormville, NY 12582
PH: (845) 878-6595

Owners
Ava Dürrschmidt and Harrald Boerger

Cuisine
Traditional and classic

Days Open
Open Thurs.-Sat. for dinner

Pricing
Six-course price fix dinner for one, without tax, tip, or drinks: $65

Dress Code
Business casual

Reservations
Required

Parking
Free on site

Features
Private room/parties

Credit Cards
None

AWARD WINNER
SINCE 1992

370

Pascale Wine Bar and Restaurant

Beautiful, art-filled dining area

On west Fayette Street, in the historic Armory Square district in the heart of Syracuse, 30 min. from Syracuse/Hancock Airport

Since 1982, brothers Neal and Chuck Pascale have set the standard for fine dining in Central New York with Pascale Wine Bar and Restaurant. Located in the historic Armory Square district, in the heart of downtown Syracuse, the restaurant offers fine dining, an outstanding wine list, and excellent service within a beautiful, art-filled interior. Special features include the wood-burning rotisserie, as well as private dining rooms accommodating parties of various sizes.

One of the private dining rooms

White chocolate pistachio gateau

204 West Fayette Street
Syracuse, NY 13202
PH: (315) 471-3040
FAX: (315) 471-3060
www.pascalesonline.com

Owners
Charles and Neal Pascale

Cuisine
Contemporary American

Days Open
Open Wed. for lunch,
Mon.-Sat. for dinner

Pricing
Dinner for one,
without tax, tip, or drinks:
$20-$40

Dress Code
Business casual

Reservations
Recommended

Parking
Valet

Features
Private room/parties, entertainment, near theater

Credit Cards
AE, VC, MC, DC

AWARD WINNER
SINCE 1992

Ristorante Giovanni's

Picaso Room

Directions

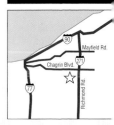

On corner of Chargin Blvd. and Richmond Road in suburban Beachwood, 20 min. from Cleveland Hopkins International Airport

25550 Chagrin Boulevard
Beachwood, OH 44122
PH: (216) 831-8625
FAX: (216) 831-4338

U.S. restaurateurs and food critics regard Giovanni's as one of the Cleveland area's finest restaurants. Carl Quagliata's innovative food techniques and his creative cuisine shine in this elegant setting. Specializing in original pastas and interesting veal, lamb, and seafood dishes, the chef and his eatery have garnered numerous commendations and earned a national reputation.

Grilled Atlantic salmon with citrus beurre blanc

The Foyer   Photo credit: Bill Webb

Owners
Carl Quagliata

Cuisine
Northern Italian, with seafood, and steaks

Days Open
Open Mon.-Fri. for lunch,
Mon.-Sat. for dinner

Pricing
Dinner for one,
without tax, tip, or drinks:
$20-$40

Dress Code
Business casual

Reservations
Recommended

Parking
Free on site, valet

Features
Semi-private room, private parties, wine-tasting events

Credit Cards
AE, VC, MC, CB, DC, DS

AWARD WINNER
SINCE 1992

372

Maisonette

Dining room

In the heart of downtown Cincinnati, 20 min. from Greater Cincinnati-Northern Kentucky International Airport

For more than 50 years, Maisonette has welcomed guests with extraordinary hospitality and dining. This tradition continues under the masterful guidance of Chef Bertrand Bouquin, as he and his international staff prepare remarkable cuisine in an elegant, updated environment. Diners enjoy seasonal specialties created with fresh regional ingredients, turning a meal into a wonderful memory.

**Executive Chef
Bertrand Bouquin**

*Owners Michael E. and
Nat Comisar*

The bar

AWARD WINNER
SINCE 1992

114 East Sixth Street
Cincinnati, OH 45202
PH: (513) 721-2260
FAX: (513) 287-7785
www.maisonette.com

Owners
Michael E. and Nat Comisar

Cuisine
French

Days Open
Open Tues.-Fri. for lunch,
Mon.-Sat. for dinner

Pricing
Dinner for one,
without tax, tip, or drinks:
$60-$80

Dress Code
Business casual

Reservations
Required

Parking
Valet, garage nearby

Features
Private room/private parties,
near theater

Credit Cards
AE, VC, MC, CB, DC, DS

The Palace Restaurant

Dining room

In downtown's Cincinnatian Hotel, 30 min. from Greater Cincinnati-Northern Kentucky International Airport

601 Vine Street
Cincinnati, OH 45202
PH: (513) 381-3000
FAX: (513) 381-2659
www.cincinnatianhotel.com

Long the destination for the discriminating gourmet, The Palace Restaurant features Executive Chef Guy Hulin's seasonal American cuisine, made only with the freshest ingredients. Along with the menu's epicurean delights, the gracious service staff, led by maître d' Scott Jones, meets all diners' expectations, and the setting's understated elegance beautifully complements each culinary creation. With an outstanding list of over 350 wines, one easily finds the perfect companion for any dish.

Splendid times

Executive Chef Guy Hulin

Owners
Brother's Property Management

Cuisine
American-French fusion

Days Open
Open daily for breakfast,
Mon.-Fri. for lunch,
Mon.-Sat. for dinner

Pricing
Dinner for one,
without tax, tip, or drinks:
$40-$60

Dress Code
Business casual

Reservations
Recommended

Parking
Valet available

Features
Private room, entertainment, near theater

Credit Cards
AE, VC, MC, DC, JCB, DS

The Cincinnatian Hotel

AWARD WINNER
SINCE 1992

The Baricelli Inn

The Baricelli Inn

In University Circle area, 20 min. from Cleveland Hopkins International Airport

2203 Cornell Road
Cleveland, OH 44106
PH: (216) 791-6500
FAX: (216) 791-9131
www.baricelli.com

Owners
Paul Minnillo

Cuisine
Continental

Days Open
Open Mon.-Sat. for breakfast (for Inn guests) and dinner

Pricing
Dinner for one,
without tax, tip, or drinks:
$40-$60

Dress Code
None

Reservations
Recommended

Parking
Free on site, valet

Features
Private room/parties, outdoor dining, guest rooms, catering, takeout

Credit Cards
AE, VC, MC

The Baricelli Inn is a turn-of-the-century brownstone in the heart of Cleveland's cultural center. Paul Minnillo's internationally acclaimed restaurant is dedicated to creating fine European and American cuisine. From his larder he creates a seasonal menu reflecting the freshest ingredients available, prepared in a style that is uniquely his own. The restaurant has garnered an unending collection of awards. *Gourmet Magazine* named the Baricelli Inn one of 'America's Best 50 Restaurants'.

Typical guest room

Chef/Owner Paul Minnillo

Dining room

AWARD WINNER
SINCE 1998

Johnny's Bar

Main dining room

On Fulton Road, 20 min. from Cleveland Hopkins International Airport

3164 Fulton Road
Cleveland, OH 44109
PH: (216) 281-0055
FAX: (216) 631-6890
www.johnnyscleveland.com

Since 1952 Johnny's Bar has been recognized for its Northern Italian cuisine, classic, upscale décor, and sophisticated clientele. Johnny's Bar has been named the #1 restaurant in Cleveland form 1996 to 2001. It is listed in the *2001 Zagat Survey Guide* as one of the top restaurants in America. Additionally, the restaurant won *Wine Spectator's* Best of Award of Excellence from 1997 to 2001, and the DiRoNA Award for Fine Dining in 2002. Patrons can expect large portions, a variety of dishes, and a selection of over 850 wines.

Private dining room

Owners
Joseph and Anthony Santosuosso

Cuisine
Northern Italian/Continental

Days Open
Open Tues.-Fri. for lunch,
Mon.-Sat. for dinner

Pricing
Dinner for one,
without tax, tip, or drinks:
$40-$60

Dress Code
Business casual

Reservations
Recommended

Parking
Valet (dinner only)

Features
Private room/parties,
outdoor dining

Credit Cards
AE, VC, MC, DC

AWARD WINNER
SINCE 2002

376

The Refectory

The culinary team

Directions

Near the corner of Bethel and Kenny roads between Routes 33 and 315, 15 min. from Port Columbus International Airport

The culinary creations of Chef Richard Blondin, a native of Lyon, France, are at the heart of the dining experience at The Refectory. His exceptional French cuisine, both classic and contemporary, is complemented by a world-class wine cellar with more than 700 selections. For a quarter-century, The Refectory has been dedicated to presenting each guest with gracious yet unpretentious service.

Executive Chef Richard Blondin

Elegant entrées

1092 Bethel Road
Columbus, OH 43220
PH: (614) 451-9774
FAX: (614) 451-4434
www.therefectoryrestaurant.com

Owners
Kamal Boulos

Cuisine
French

Days Open
Open Mon.-Sat. for dinner

Pricing
Dinner for one,
without tax, tip, or drinks:
$20-$40

Dress Code
Business attire

Reservations
Recommended

Parking
Free on site

Features
Private room/parties,
outdoor dining, business
meetings, wine events

Credit Cards
AE, VC, MC, CB, DC, JCB,

AWARD WINNER
SINCE 1992

L'Auberge

L'Auberge is the piece de resistance

F or a dining experience unsurpassed in elegance and sophistication, L'Auberge is the piece de resistance. For 23 years owner Josef Reif has developed an international reputation for fine dining that encompasses excellence in food, wine, service, and presentation. The luxurious décor is evident throughout the mansion, in the main Dining Room, in the contemporary Bistro with its famous murals, the outside café Le Jardin, the private salons, and in the magnificent wine cellar. Visit L'Auberge, Ohio's only Mobil Four-Star restaurant.

Four-star dining room

The Bistro

Inspired desserts

AWARD WINNER
SINCE 1996

Directions

On Far Hills Ave., 20 min. from Dayton International Airport

4120 Far Hills Avenue
Dayton, OH 45429
PH: (937) 299-5536
FAX: (937) 299-9129
www.laubergedayton.com

Owners
Josef Reif

Cuisine
French continental

Days Open
Open Mon.-Sat. for lunch and dinner

Pricing
Dinner for one, without tax, tip, or drinks: $35-$75
Bistro: $20-$35

Dress Code
Business casual for the Bistro and Le Jardin, jackets after 5 pm in the Dining Room

Reservations
Recommended

Parking
Free on site

Features
Private room/parties, outdoor dining, entertainment

Credit Cards
AE, VC, MC, DC

The Inn at Turner's Mill

Main dining room

B uilt in 1852 as a grist mill, this Hudson landmark has been converted into a family-owned restaurant and has been in operation by the Buchanan family for fourteen years. The seasonal menu stresses traditional American dishes, carefully prepared and beautifully presented. The extensive wine list, concentrating on California varietals, wins awards annually. Service is friendly and impeccable.

Veal chop, and Arctic char with mussels

Downstairs in the E.B. Ellsworth Tavern

The apple tart and chocolate bombe

AWARD WINNER
SINCE 1999

Directions

On Route 303 near Route 91, 30 min. from Cleveland Hopkins and Akron-Canton International Airports

36 East Streetsboro
Street/Route 303
Hudson, OH 44236
PH: (330) 656-2949
FAX: (330) 656-0062
www.turnersmill.com

Owners
The Buchanan Family

Cuisine
Seasonal American

Days Open
Open Mon.-Sat. for lunch, daily for dinner, including most Sundays

Pricing
Dinner for one, without tax, tip, or drinks: $20-$40

Dress Code
Business casual

Reservations
Recommended

Parking
Free on site

Features
Private room/private parties, outdoor dining, entertainment, wine/food pairings

Credit Cards
AE, VC, MC, CB, DC, DS

Alberini's

The Terrace Room

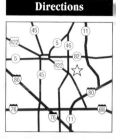

On U.S. 422 in Niles, 15 min. from Youngstown Airport, 1 hr. from Cleveland Hopkins International Airport, and 1 hr. from Pittsburgh International Airport

1201 Youngstown-Warren Road
Niles, OH 44446
PH: (330) 652-5895
and (888) 236-8294
FAX: (330) 652-7041
www.alberinis.com

Owners
Alberini family

Cuisine
Classic and Nuovu Italian

Days Open
Open Mon.-Sat. for lunch and dinner

Pricing
Dinner for one, without tax, tip, or drinks: $20-$40

Dress Code
Business casual

Reservations
Recommended

Parking
Free on site

Features
Private rooms/parties

Credit Cards
AE, VC, MC, DC, DS

The marriage of fine wines and outstanding cuisine consummate the ultimate dining experience. Alberini's atmosphere is sociable and unpretentious, yet maintains a subtle touch of sophistication. Enjoy a variety of pastas enhanced with fragrant Italian spices, succulent seafood, and choice cuts of fork-tender meats. There is a room for every mood, a menu for every occasion, and a wine for every palate. Our wine list is recognized as "world class", with 850 selections from the major wine growing regions of the world.

Ossobuco Milanese

**Owner/Operator/
Executive Chef
Richard Alberini, Jr.**

Wine cellar

AWARD WINNER
SINCE 1995

Polo Grill

Polo Grill of Utica Square

© 2002 Don Wheeler

Known for putting Tulsa on the culinary map, Polo Grill offers a warm, casual but elegant atmosphere that sets the tone for a classic dining experience. Proprietor Chefs Ouida and Robert Merrifield's new southern American cooking brings unique dishes to America's heartland. Menu highlights include Berkshire pork, prime beef, and extensive fresh seafood. Experience the award winning cuisine, and wine list, which boasts over 1,200 selections.

One of five private dining wine cellars

Main dining room

Proprietor/Chef Ouida and Robert Merrifield

AWARD WINNER
SINCE 2003

Directions

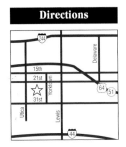

At Utica and 21st Street near Highway 51, 15 min. from Tulsa International Airport

2038 Utica Square
Tulsa, OK 74114
PH: (918) 744-4280
FAX: (918) 749-7082
www.thepologrill.com

Owners
Ouida and Robert Merrifield

Cuisine
New southern American

Days Open
Open Mon.-Sat. for lunch and dinner

Pricing
Dinner for one, without tax, tip, or drinks: $20-$40

Dress Code
Business casual

Reservations
Recommended

Parking
Free on site

Features
Private room/parties

Credit Cards
AE, VC, MC, DC

Joel Palmer House

The Joel Palmer House

Directions

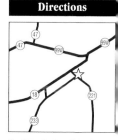

On Ferry Street, 1 hr. from
Portland International
Airport

600 Ferry Street
Dayton, OR 97114
PH: (503) 864-2995
FAX: (503) 864-3246
www.joelpalmerhouse.com

Owners
Jack and Heidi Czarnecki

Cuisine
Northwest – wild mushrooms

Days Open
Open Tues.-Sat. for dinner

Pricing
Dinner for one,
without tax, tip, or drinks:
$20-$40

Dress Code
Casual/business casual

Reservations
Recommended

Parking
Free on site

Features
Outdoor dining

Credit Cards
AE, VC, MC, DS

The Joel Palmer House ranks as one of Oregon's finest historic homes, and is on both the Oregon and the National Historic Registers. Cuisine preparation revolves around wild mushroom that are handpicked by Chef/Co-owner Jack Czarnecki, in addition to locally raised ingredients, and organically produced greens, herbs, and vegetables. Frequently, the Chef will use ingredients found in the cuisines of Mexico, China, Thailand, Poland, and India to create "freestyle" cooking. The owners take pride in   creating dishes which complement the glorious wines of Oregon, especially Pinot Noir, Pinot Gris, and Chardonnay.

"Freestyle" cooking

*Chef/Co-owner,
Jack Czarnecki*

AWARD WINNER
SINCE 2003

Chanterelle

Dining room

Now in its 18th year, this intimate little hideaway — all 13 tables of it — is the loving creation of German-born Ralf Schmidt, who works alone in the kitchen, turning out such delicacies as paillard d'boeuf and dishes using pheasant, buffalo, emu, and other game. "And we are famous for our tiramisu and French silk pie," the chef-owner says, giving credit where credit is due to "the lady who does the desserts" — his wife, Gisela.

Rack of lamb

Lounge

Owner Ralf Schmidt

Directions

5th Ave.
Pearl St.
6th Ave.
High St.
7th Ave.

In downtown, 20 min. from
Eugene Airport

207 East 5th Avenue
Suite 109
Eugene, OR 97401
PH: (541) 484-4065

Owners
Ralf Schmidt

Cuisine
Classical

Days Open
Open Tues.-Sat. for dinner

Pricing
Dinner for one,
without tax, tip, or drinks:
$20-$40

Dress Code
Business casual

Reservations
Recommended

Parking
Free on site

Features
Near theater

Credit Cards
AE, VC, MC, DC, JCB

DiRōNA
AWARD WINNER
SINCE 1994

The Dining Room

The Salishan Lodge

At the Lodge & Golf resort Salishan on Highway 101, south of Lincoln City, 2 hr. from Portland International Airport

7760 Highway 101 North
Gleneden Beach, OR 77388
PH: (800) 452-2300
FAX: (541) 764-3681
www.salishan.com

Owners
The Spring Capital Group

Cuisine
Pacific Northwest

Days Open
June-Sept Tues.-Sat. dinner
Oct.-May dinner Fri.-Sat.

Pricing
Dinner for one,
without tax, tip, or drinks:
$20-$40

Dress Code
Business casual

Reservations
Recommended

Parking
Free on site

Credit Cards
AE, BC, MC, DC, DS

The Dining Room at the Salishan Lodge features Pacific North-west cuisine impeccably served in an atmosphere of quiet elegance. Our culinary staff places special emphasis on seasonal seafood, game, and other regional delicacies. The Dining Room offers guests an intimate culinary experience by candlelight with magnificent views of Siletz Bay.

*Sumptuous entrée
at The Dining Room*

Resort lobby

Wine cellar

AWARD WINNER
SINCE 1992

RingSide Steakhouse Downtown

"Best steaks in town since 1944!"

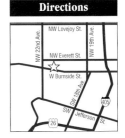

On West Burnside at NW 22nd Ave, 20 min. from Portland International Airport

2165 West Burnside
Portland, OR 97210
PH: (503) 223-1513
FAX: (503) 223-6908
www.ringsidesteakhouse.com

Owners
Peterson Family

Cuisine
American steakhouse

Days Open
Open daily for dinner

R ingSide Downtown is a traditional American steakhouse owned by the same family for 60 years. Consistently ranked as one of America's top ten steakhouses featuring USDA prime beef – custom dry aged, RingSide Downtown also offers fresh seafood. Guests can complement their dinner with a choice from the wine list which features more than 500 labels. Served by an attentive and loyal wait-staff in a cozy and comfortable atmosphere, diners can experience one of America's best steakhouses.

20 oz. bone-in New York steak

Pricing
Dinner for one, without tax, tip, or drinks: $20-$40
(or) Price fix: $35

Dress Code
Business casual

Reservations
Recommended

Parking
Complimentary valet, free on site

Features
Private room/parties, near theater

Credit Cards
AE, VC, MC, CB, DC, JCB, DS

Private dining room

Long time loyal waitstaff

AWARD WINNER
SINCE 2003

RingSide Steakhouse
Glendoveer

Relaxed country club atmosphere

On NE Glisan Street at
Glendoveer Golf Course.
10 min. from Portland
International Airport

14021 NE Glisan
Portland, OR 97230
PH: (503) 255-0750
FAX: (503) 255-9038
www.ringsidesteakhouse.com

Ringside Glendoveer is the sterling sister to the Downtown steakhouse. Celebrating a silver anniversary this year, RingSide Glendoveer has consistently ranked in the top 10 of America's steakhouses. Diners revel in a relaxed and comfortable country club atmosphere served by an attentive and loyal waitstaff. The staff serves from a wine list of more than 700 labels with 30 wines by the glass. The DiRoNA Award of Excellence makes Glendoveer the second steakhouse in Oregon to be so honored. The first was the RingSide Downtown. Diners enjoy USDA prime beef, fresh seafood, and signature sandwiches with service second to none.

16 oz. Prime Rib

Private Cellar Room

Owners
Peterson Family

Cuisine
American steakhouse

Days Open
Open daily for lunch
and dinner

Pricing
Dinner for one,
without tax, tip, or drinks:
$20-$40
(or) Price fix: $35

Dress Code
Dressy casual

Reservations
Recommended

Parking
Free on site

Features
Private room/parties,
on golf course

Credit Cards
AE, VC, MC, CB, DC, JCB, DS

Glendoveer's loyal waitstaff

AWARD WINNER
SINCE 2004

Finelli's Italian Villa

Award-winning fine dining

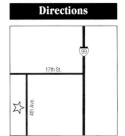
1808 4th Avenue
Altoona, PA 16602
PH: (814) 943-8510
FAX: (814) 943-6800
www.finellis.com

Owners
Frank and Jeanne Finelli

Cuisine
Gourmet Italian

Days Open
Open Tues.-Sat. for dinner

Pricing
Dinner for one,
without tax, tip, or drinks:
$20-$40

Dress Code
Business casual

Reservations
Recommended

Parking
Free on site

Features
Private room/parties, near
theater, cigar/cognac events

Credit Cards
AE, VC, MC, CB, DC, DS

L ocated in the heart of the southern
Allegheny Mountains, Finelli's
Italian Villa has old world charm and
casual elegance that defines the area's
best in award-winning fine dining. The
Finelli family ensures quality service
and attention to detail. Chef Anthony
Finelli is recognized as one of America's
outstanding chefs dedicated to creating
succulent dishes that include a variety
of veal, seafood, steak, and homemade
pastas. Ideal for a romantic evening
or a business function, offering a complimentary limousine for local hotels.

Chef Anthony Finelli

The Finelli family

Succulent dishes

AWARD WINNER
SINCE 2002

Haydn Zug's

Gallery dining room

Near Lancaster on Route 72 north, 25 min. from Harrisburg International Airport

1987 State Street
East Petersburg, PA 17520
PH: (717) 569-5746
FAX: (717) 569-8450
www.haydnzugs.com

Owners
The Lee family

Cuisine
Classic American

Days Open
Open Tues.-Sat. for lunch and dinner

Pricing
Dinner for one,
without tax, tip, or drinks:
$20-$40

Dress Code
Business casual

Reservations
Recommended

Parking
Free on site

Features
Private room/parties

Credit Cards
AE, VC, MC, CB

Haydn Zug's offers a taste of Williamsburg in scenic Lancaster County. The glow of candlelight enhances the tasteful restaurant's fine linen, crystal, and china in an atmosphere of warmth, hospitality, and casual elegance. Relax amid fine art and unique memorabilia while enjoying the diverse menu, which includes such house specialties as lamb tenderloin and lump crab cakes in season. Take your choice from six dining rooms. Winner of the *Wine Spectator* Award of Excellence since 1997.

Grilled lamb tenderloin Dijonnaise

Kate Neira, Restaurant Manager, and Chef Mark Wolownik

AWARD WINNER
SINCE 1997

EverMay On-The-Delaware

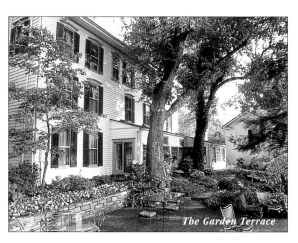

The Garden Terrace

18th-century charm

At this serene hotel, set on 25 acres of gardens and wooded paths, visitors feel like house guests at a country home. Listed in the National Register of Historic Places, EverMay serves an elegant dinner of contemporary American fare in a conservatory garden room or more formal Victorian room. Dinner is one seating, beginning with an aperitif, followed by six courses with a choice of entrée. The wine list is carefully selected, and there is a well-stocked bar.

The Garden Room

The Parlor

AWARD WINNER
SINCE 1992

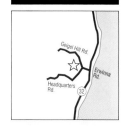

Geigel Hill Rd.
Erwinna Rd.
Headquarters Rd.
32

In Bucks County, 13 miles north of New Hope, 50 min. from Newark International Airport

889 River Road
Erwinna, PA 18920
PH: (610) 294-9100
FAX: (610) 294-8249
www.evermay.com

Owners
William and Danielle Moffly

Cuisine
New American

Days Open
Open Fri.-Sun. for dinner

Pricing
Dinner for one,
without tax, tip, or drinks:
$60-$80

Dress Code
Jacket suggested

Reservations
Required

Parking
Free on site

Features
Private parties,
corporate functions

Credit Cards
VC, MC, AE

Golden Trout

Dining at the Golden Trout

Seafood and steak lovers savor the menu at the Golden Trout, created by Executive Chef Scott Cape and Chef de Cuisine Lewis Cramer. The restaurant, located in the world-class Nemacolin Woodlands Resort & Spa, offers a relaxing meal for both couples and families alike. Diners who prefer seafood will find "Golden Trout" an irresistible dish, while a 22-ounce rib eye steak, grilled over seasoned hickory, will satisfy any hearty appetite. All tempting entrées may be complemented with a selection from the restaurant's award-winning 10,000-bottle wine cellar.

The Wine Cellar

Chateau LaFayette

Executive Chef Scott Cape

AWARD WINNER
SINCE 1992

Directions

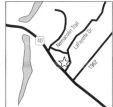

Off Route 40 on LaFayette Dr., 1 hr. and 15 min. from Pittsburgh International Airport

1001 LaFayette Drive
Farmington, PA 15437
PH: (724) 329-8555 or
(800) 422-2736
FAX: (724) 329-6947
www.nemacolin.com

Owners
Joseph A. Hardy and
Maggie Hardy Magerko

Cuisine
Steak and seafood

Days Open
Open daily for dinner

Pricing
Dinner for one,
without tax, tip, or drinks:
$20-$40

Dress Code
Resort casual

Reservations
Recommended

Parking
Free on site, valet

Features
Private room

Credit Cards
AE, VC, MC, DC, DS

Savona

Welcome to Savona

Directions

On Old Gulph Road, 30 min.
from Philadelphia
International Airport

100 Old Gulph Road
Gulph Mills, PA 19428
PH: (610) 520-1200
FAX: (610) 520-2045
www.savonarestaurant.com

Savona serves cuisine inspired by the French and Italian Rivieras, presented in a rich Mediterranean setting. Elegant European service and a wine cellar featuring over 1,000 selections have been acclaimed by AAA, *Wine Spectator, Town and Country,* and *Bon Appetit,* among others. Exquisite private dining is offered for parties of four to forty in six unique dining rooms.

Cuisine of the Riviera

Owners
Dominique Filoni, Evan Lambert, and Sabine Filoni

Cuisine
Inspired by the Riviera, French and Italian

Days Open
Open daily for dinner

Pricing
Dinner for one, without tax, tip, or drinks: $60-$80

Dress Code
Jacket suggested

Reservations
Recommended

Parking
Complimentary valet

Features
Private room/parties (available for lunch and dinner), outdoor dining

Credit Cards
AE, VC, MC, CB, DC, DS

Executive Chef
Dominique Filoni

To create, to invent, to discover...

AWARD WINNER
SINCE 2003

Scatton's Restaurant

Owners Suzie and Larry Dull

One block west of Route 309 N. at 22nd Street, 2 min. from Hazleton Municipal Airport, 50 min. from Wilkes-Barre/Scranton International Airport

1008 North Vine Street
Hazleton, PA 18201
PH: (570) 455-6630
FAX: (570) 384-3230
www.scattons.com
e-mail: suzie@scattons.com

Owners
Lawrence and Suzanne Dull

Cuisine
Classic Northern Italian

Days Open
Open for dinner Mon.-Sat.

Pricing
Dinner for one, without tax, tip, or drinks: $20-$40

Dress Code
Business casual

Reservations
Recommended

Parking
Free on site

Features
Private parties on Sundays, wine-tasting events

Credit Cards
AE, VC, MC, CB, DC, DS

Hazleton area tradition for more than 60 years, this little restaurant is dedicated to the finest quality and consistency of food, service, and comfort. Chef-owners Larry and Suzanne Dull use only the finest quality and freshest products, specializing in veal, seafood, and homemade pasta. The Masters Chef Institute of America declares that "Scatton's is a major destination for gastronomes who especially appreciate Northern Italian cuisine." Each dish is prepared to order and can be varied to suit a diner's taste or special diet. We also offer a large selection of wine.

Scampi Suzanne

Your hosts

Our dining room

AWARD WINNER
SINCE 1997

DiSalvo's Station Restaurant

Dining atrium

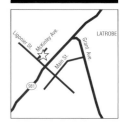

Located in a historic, landmark railroad station on McKinley Ave., 5 min. from Arnold Palmer Airport

325 McKinley Avenue
Latrobe, PA 15650
PH: (724) 539-0500
FAX: (724) 539-1711
www.disalvosrestaurant.com

Owners
Joseph DiSalvo

Cuisine
Authentic gourmet Italian

Days Open
Open Tues.-Sun. for dinner, Sunday for brunch

Pricing
Dinner for one, without tax, tip, or drinks: $20-$40
Private dining car/Prima Classe: $75-$100

Dress Code
Business casual (jacket and tie required for Fri. and Sat. only in private dining car/Prima Classe)

Reservations
Required

Parking
Free on site

Features
Private room/parties, entertainment, cigar/cognac events

Credit Cards
AE, VC, MC, CB, DC, DS

Taste the passion as history and authentic Italian cuisine meet in a nationally registered, historic landmark railroad station in Latrobe. As is the custom, the award-wining Italian cuisine, and service staff of DiSalvo's Station compliment the personal attention of the dynamic father and son duo: CEC-AAC, Gaetano DiSalvo, and exuberantly gracious host, Joseph DiSalvo. Sit back, relax, and enjoy a one-of-a-kind dining and entertainment complex like no other. Buon Appetito!

Joseph DiSalvo and his father CEC Gaetano DiSalvo, AAC

Tunnel entrance

AWARD WINNER
SINCE 2004

La Bonne Auberge

Charming stone farm house

L a Bonne Auberge is a charming, chef-owned, 200-year-old farmhouse serving exquisite food in elegant surroundings. Renowned for its gracious service and attention to detail, it is both a romantic hideaway and a superb location for special occasions. This is a place for all seasons: Cozy fireplaces in winter provide a warm welcome, and cocktails and hors d'oeuvres can be savored in beautifully landscaped gardens in the spring.

Dessert selection

Directions

Off Mechanic Street, 1 hr. from Philadelphia International Airport

Village 2
New Hope, PA 18938
PH: (215) 862-2462
FAX: (215) 862-6350
www.bonneauberge.com

Owners
Gerard Caronello

Cuisine
Classic French

Days Open
Open Thurs.-Sun. for dinner

Pricing
Dinner for one,
without tax, tip, or drinks:
$40-$60

Dress Code
Jacket and tie required

Reservations
Required

Parking
Free on site

Features
Outdoor terrace for drinks
and hors d'oeuvres, open
Tues.-Weds. for corporate
events

Credit Cards
AE, VC, MC

AWARD WINNER
SINCE 1992

The Monte Carlo Living Room

The signature dining room

At South and 2nd streets, 25 min. from Philadelphia International Airport

F ood & Wine magazine has placed The Monte Carlo Living Room among the top 100 restaurants in the United States, and the wine list has received accolades from *Wine Spectator.* Chef Robert Capella's modern European cuisine can be described as haute and earthy at the same time. He views each plate as a canvas and the season's best are his palette. Marinated veal tenderloin with roasted gala apple in a red wine reduction sauce and wild striped bass with braised leeks and sea urchin butter are among menu highlights.

The private wine room

150 South Street
Philadelphia, PA 19147
PH: (215) 925-2220
FAX: (215) 925-9956
www.montecarlolivingroom.com

Owners
Umberto Degli Esposti.
Giorgio Giuliani

Cuisine
Modern European

Days Open
Open Mon.-Sat. for dinner

Pricing
Dinner for one,
without tax, tip, or drinks:
$25-$40

Dress Code
Casual smart

Reservations
Recommended

Parking
Valet

Features
Signature dining room,
private wine room, private
parties Mon-Sun.,
nightclub upstairs

Credit Cards
AE, VC, MC, DC

AWARD WINNER
SINCE 1992

Ristorante La Buca

Established 1980

L a Buca is a below-ground restaurant built around its wine cellar. Owner/chef Giuseppe Giuliani offers an authentic taste of Tuscany with with such regional specialties as ribollita, crespelle all fiorentina, and tagliolini ai porcini. While offering a variety of pasta and meats, La Buca emphasizes fresh grilled seafood. La Buca also offers an extensive wine list, emphasizing "Super Tuscan" wines.

Directions

In downtown Philadelphia, near Independence National Historical Park, 25 min. from Philadelphia International Airport

711 Locust Street
Philadelphia, PA 19106
PH: (215) 928-0556
FAX: (215) 928-1175
www.ristlabuca.com

Owners
Giuseppe Giuliani

Cuisine
Italian and Seafood

Days Open
Open Mon.-Fri. for lunch,
Mon.-Sat. for dinner

Pricing
Dinner for one,
without tax, tip, or drinks:
$40-$60

Dress Code
Casual

Reservations
Recommended

Parking
Validated parking
garage nearby

Features
Private room/parties,
near theater

Credit Cards
AE, VC, MC, CB, DC, DS

AWARD WINNER
SINCE 1997

The Carlton

A favorite restaurant in Pittsburgh

Located located in One Mellon Bank Center on Grant St., 30 min. from Pittsburgh International Airport

500 Grant Street
Pittsburgh, PA 15219
PH: (412) 391-4099
FAX: (412) 391-4240
www.thecarltonrestaurant.com

Owners
Kevin Joyce

Cuisine
American contemporary

Days Open
Open Mon.-Fri. for lunch,
Mon.-Sat. for dinner

Pricing
Dinner for one,
without tax, tip, or drinks:
$20-$40

Dress Code
Casual

Reservations
Recommended

Parking
Free on site

Features
Privat room/parties,
near theater

Credit Cards
AE, VC, MC, DC, DS

In the heart of the downtown business and hotel district, The Carlton has been winning customers since 1984. An inspired culinary team, fresh seasonal ingredients, a daily changing menu and a very ambitious Wine Dinner Schedule continue to keep our cuisine on the cutting edge. The Carlton's *Wine Spectator* Award winning wine list features over 450 selections at prices that are consumer friendly. The service staff is polished and friendly. They work hard to make each dining experience memorable. The Carlton offers complimentary parking after 5 PM and limousine service to Benedum Center, Heinz Hall, O'Reilly Theater, the Byham Theater and PNC Park. The Carlton is the only Dirona Award winning restaurant with a Pittsburgh address.

Dining room

Lobby and Wine Bar

AWARD WINNER
SINCE 2001

Hyeholde Restaurant
AND THE ROUND ROOM

Castle-like charm

Directions

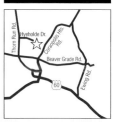

On Coraopolis Heights Road in Moon Township, 20 min. from downtown Pittsburgh and 10 minutes from Pittsburgh International Airport

---

190 Hyeholde Drive
Moon Township, PA 15108
PH: (412) 264-3116
FAX: (412) 264-5723
www.hyeholde.com

Owner
Barbara McKenna

Cuisine
New American

Days Open
Open Mon.-Fri. for lunch,
Mon.-Sat. for dinner

Pricing
Dinner for one,
without tax, tip, or drinks:
$40-$60

Dress Code
Business casual

Reservations
Recommended

Parking
Valet

Features
Private room/parties, outdoor dining, wheelchair accessible

Credit Cards
AE, VC, MC, CB, DC, DS

H yeholde Restaurant is the definition of romance. Located on acres of woodland gardens in a castle with slate-roofed towers, the establishment is the perfect escape. Inside, intimate dining rooms are enhanced with beautiful tapestries, fireplaces, slate floors, and bouquets of fresh flowers. A tunnel leads to a large stone and glass dining room for casual dining and private functions. A chef's table in the kitchen and elegant picnics culminate in a feast for all the senses.

Great Hall

Artistic entrées

The Round Room

DiRōNA
AWARD WINNER
SINCE 1992

The Primadonna Restaurant

Main dining room mural by David Rigo

On Broadway Ave. at Dohrman St., 20 min. from Pittsburgh International Airport

801 Broadway Avenue
McKees Rocks, PA 15136
PH: (412) 331-1001
FAX: (412) 771-8234
www.theprimadonna.com

Owners
Donna and Joseph
Costanzo, Jr.

Cuisine
Italian

Days Open
Open Mon.-Sat. for dinner

Pricing
Dinner for one,
without tax, tip, or drinks:
$20-$40

Dress Code
Business casual

Reservations
None accepted

Parking
Local street parking

Features
Near theater

Credit Cards
AE, VC, MC, CB, DC, DS

The Primadonna Restaurant was voted The Best Italian Restaurant in Western Pennsylvania by the readers of *Pittsburgh Magazine*, *Pittsburgh City Paper*, and *The Pittsburgh Post Gazette*. In *The Pittsburgh Post Gazette's* latest review of The Primadonna Restaurant, Wooden Merriman, dining critic, stated "The Primadonna has food and service that are something to brag about and the Primadonna's walls are covered with the acclaim it deserves." Awarded 2002 America's Top Ten Italian Restaurants by the International Restaurant and Hospitality Rating Bureau.

Spaghetti El Ducé

Owners Donna and Joseph Costanzo, Jr.

Award-winning "wall of fame"

DiRoNA
AWARD WINNER
SINCE 2002

Passerelle Restaurant

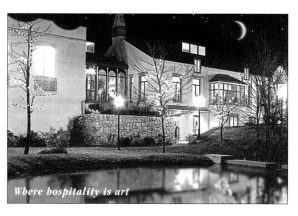

Where hospitality is art

Located a half block off Route 30 (Lancaster Avenue), 20 min. from Philadelphia International Airport

The management and staff of Passerelle Restaurant are truly dedicated to the art of hospitality. The restaurant's contemporary American cuisine encompasses the very freshest ingredients found in the marketplace. From the elegance of the Venetian chandelier to the beautiful garden and swan-filled pond, no detail is overlooked. Come and enjoy the award-winning food and extensive wine selection. Private dining rooms and outside dining are available.

Private dining in Garden Room

Alfresco dining

AWARD WINNER
SINCE 2001

175 King of Prussia Road
Radnor, PA 19087
PH: (610) 293-9411
FAX: (610) 293-0161
www.passerellerestaurant.com

Owners
Martin Grims

Cuisine
Contemporary American

Days Open
Open Mon.-Fri. for lunch, daily for dinner, brunch on Sun.

Pricing
Dinner for one, without tax, tip, or drinks: $40-$60

Dress Code
Business casual

Reservations
Recommended

Parking
Free on site

Features
Private room/parties, outdoor dining

Credit Cards
AE, VC, MC, DC

Dilworthtown Inn

The Dilworthtown Inn

Since 1758, the Dilworthtown Inn has been known for its warm hospitality and wonderful food—an outstanding culinary jewel in a historic setting. Glowing fireplaces and friendly smiles make visitors feel at home as they savor the Inn's delicious gourmet cooking. Weather permitting, the stone wall remains of the original stables offer a unique outdoor dining experience.

Proprietor Jim Barnes welcomes guests

Private meeting facilities

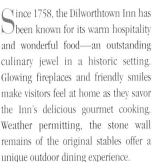

Elegant outdoor dining

AWARD WINNER
SINCE 1998

Directions

In the heart of Brandywine Valley, 20 min. from Philadelphia International Airport

1390 Old Wilmington Pike
West Chester, PA 19382
PH: (610) 399-1390
FAX: (610) 399-1504
www.dilworthtown.com

Owners
Jim Barnes and Bob Rafetto

Cuisine
Continental

Days Open
Open daily for dinner

Pricing
Dinner for one, without tax, tip, or drinks: $20-$40

Dress Code
Jacket required

Reservations
Required

Parking
Free on site

Features
Private room/parties, outdoor dining

Credit Cards
AE, VC, MC, CB, DC, DS

Restaurant Bouchard

Intimate lounge area

Newport, known for its grand mansions and grand yachts, now has another treasure: the grand cuisine of Restaurant Bouchard. Situated in a post-and-beam home, the ambience is created by Sarah Bouchard, complemented by her husband Albert's delectable culinary creations. Whether sitting by the fireplace or in the cozy bar, or even overlooking the action of Thames Street, diners relax and enjoy the marvels of the innovative classic French menu.

Owners Albert and Sarah Bouchard

Superb cuisine

Wild boar, asparagus with morels, and fruit napoleon

AWARD WINNER
SINCE 1999

Directions

Near Waites Wharf on Thames Street, 45 min. from T.F. Green/Providence International Airport

505 Thames Street
Newport, RI 02840
PH: (401) 846-0123
FAX: (401) 841-8565
www.restaurantbouchard.com

Owners
Albert and Sarah Bouchard

Cuisine
Creative classic French

Days Open
Open Wed.-Mon. for dinner

Pricing
Dinner for one,
without tax, tip, or drinks:
$20-$40

Dress Code
Business casual, jacket preferred

Reservations
Recommended

Parking
Lot nearby

Features
Private parties

Credit Cards
AE, VC, MC, DS

Sea Fare Inn

The Inn, circa 1887

The Sea Fare Inn, Rhode Island's only five-star restaurant, is the perfect location for any special occasion. It is set on 10 acres of beautifully landscaped flower gardens and fruit orchards and housed in an elegant 1887 Victorian mansion. Master Chef George Karousos derives his culinary inspiration from Archestratus, the most famous chef in ancient Greece, and uses fresh ingredients in simple presentations.

Seafood symphony

The Garden Room

Chef George Karousos with wife Anna, left, and daughter Kathy

AWARD WINNER
SINCE 1993

Directions

20 min. from Newport, 40 min. from T.F. Green Airport, 1 hr. from Boston's Logan International

3352 East Main Road
Portsmouth, RI 02871
PH: (401) 683-0577
FAX: (401) 683-2910
www.seafareinn.com

Owners
The Karousos family

Cuisine
American regional

Days Open
Open Tues.-Sat. for dinner

Pricing
Dinner for one,
without tax, tip, or drinks:
$20-$40

Dress Code
Business casual

Reservations
Recommended

Parking
Free on site

Features
Private parties

Credit Cards
AE, VC, MC

403

Capriccio

In historic downtown Providence

Directions

Corner of Dyer & Pine street in the Financial District, 15 min. from T.F. Green Airport

2 Pine Street
Providence, RI 02903
PH: (401) 421-1320
FAX: (401) 331-8732
www.capriccios.com

Owners
Vincenzo Iemma

Cuisine
Creative continental with northern Italian accent

Days Open
Open Mon.-Fri. for lunch, daily for dinner

Pricing
Dinner for one, without tax, tip, or drinks: $20-$40

Dress Code
Business casual

Reservations
Recommended

Parking
Valet

Features
Private room/parties, entertainment, near theater, cigar/cognac events

Credit Cards
AE, VC, MC, CB, DC, DS

Carved out of the cellars of a Providence landmark, Capriccio has long been the capital city's renowned mecca for candlelight sophistication where locals, and out-of-towners are deliciously pampered. The restaurant has received over 35 awards for fine dining, wines, and décor. Signature dishes include imported Dover sole, native lobster, prime aged steaks, homemade pastas, and tableside flambé. Revel in one of America's greatest Cognac collections. Piano bar and live entertainment featured nightly.

Master Chef Nino D'Urso

Fresh native seafood

Flambé magic

AWARD WINNER
SINCE 2003

1109 South Main

Restaurant entrance

At South Main and Hampton streets in Anderson, 1 hr. from Greenville-Spartanburg International Airport

1109 South Main Street
Anderson, SC 29621
PH: (864) 225-1109
FAX: (864) 225-3884
www.spa-it.com

Owners
Peter and Myrna Ryter

Cuisine
Continental and sushi bar

Days Open
Open Tues.-Sat. for dinner, other days by special request for groups of 10 or more

Pricing
Dinner for one, without tax, tip, or drinks: $20-$40

Dress Code
Business casual

Reservations
Recommended

Parking
Free on site

Features
Private room/parties

Credit Cards
AE, VC, MC, CB, DC, DS

Revisit the days of *Gone With the Wind* in Anderson, where two exquisitely restored mansions make up 1109 South Main. One mansion houses a plush spa and the other the gourmet restaurant where Swiss-trained Chef/Owner Peter Ryter turns out such specialties as wild mushrooms in puff pastry, duck l'orange, tuna tartare, and lump crab cake with spicy red pepper coulis. Guests can choose from three separate dining rooms and an upstairs sushi bar.

Porchside elegance

Chocolate mousse

The Palmetto Room

AWARD WINNER
SINCE 1993

Circa 1886

Circa 1886 & Gardens

Located in the Wentworth Mansion, 20 min. from Charleston International Airport

149 Wentworth
Charleston, SC 29401
PH: (843) 853-7828
FAX: (843) 720-5290
www.circa1886.com

Owner
Richard Widman

Cuisine
Nouvelle Charleston

Days Open
Open Mon. thru Sat.
for dinner

Pricing
Dinner for one,
without tax, tip, or drinks:
$20-$40

Dress Code
Business casual
(collared shirt required/
jacket suggested)

Reservations
Recommended

Parking
Free on site

Features
Private room/parties,
outdoor dining

Credit Cards
AE, VC, MC, CB, DC, DS

Housed in the elegantly restored carriage house in the rear gardens of the Wentworth Mansion, Circa 1886 offers diners an intimate evening featuring a succulent assortment of dishes which utilize the freshest local produce, savory seafood, and engaging seasonal creations. The enticing menu of Executive Chef Marc Collins reflects Charleston's diverse culinary history.

Lowcountry cuisine

Wentworth Mansion Hotel

Chef Marc Collins

AWARD OF EXCELLENCE

DiRōNA
AWARD WINNER
SINCE 2004

Charleston Grill

Elegant clublike atmosphere

At Charleston Place,
15 min. from Charleston
International Airport

224 King Street
Charleston, SC 29401
PH: (843) 577-4522
FAX: (843) 724-8405
www.charlestongrill.com

Owners
Orient Express Hotels

Cuisine
Contemporary, low country
with French flair

Days Open
Open daily for dinner

Pricing
Dinner for one,
without tax, tip, or drinks:
$20-$40

Dress Code
Elegantly casual

Reservations
Recommended

Parking
Valet, garage nearby

Features
Private room/parties, live
jazz nightly, special events,
wine tastings

Credit Cards
AE, VC, MC, CB, DC, DS

Stellar wines, live jazz, and exciting cuisine create glistening results. Relax and enjoy their tasting menu, or selections from the seasonal a la carte dining menu. Fusing Low country cooking, and his French-influenced technique, Chef Bob Waggoner forms sophisticated new southern haute cuisine. Since his tenure at Charleston Grill, notoriety has been received for the Mobil Four Star and AAA Four Diamond awards, *Wine Spectator's* Best of Award, *Food and Wine's* Reader's Favorite Chef in America Award, as well as being formally knighted by the Government of France with the l'odre du Mérite Agricole.

Maine lobster tempura over lemon grits and fried mini green tomatoes

*Executive Chef
Bob Waggoner*

AWARD WINNER
SINCE 1993

A romantic alcove table

Magnolias

Main dining room

Celebrating a decade of Uptown/Down South, Magnolias combines Old World charm with contemporary excitement. Executive Chef Donald Barickman utilizes the Lowcountry's bounty, creating specialties such as the Down South egg roll, shellfish over creamy white grits with lobster butter, and grilled filet of beef with house-made pimiento cheese. These delicious Dixie classics, an award-winning wine list, and sophisticated atmosphere have won the establishment rave reviews and drawn countless visitors.

Bistro

Executive Chef Donald Barickman

Grouper with artichoke crust

AWARD OF EXCELLENCE

DiRōNA
AWARD WINNER
SINCE 1993

Directions

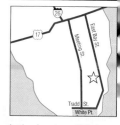

In the downtown Historic District, 25 min. from Charleston International Airport

185 East Bay Street
Charleston, SC 29401
PH: (843) 577-7771
FAX: (843) 722-0035
www.magnolias-blossom.com

Owners
Thomas Parsell and Donald Barickman

Cuisine
New Southern/regional

Days Open
Open daily for lunch and dinner

Pricing
Dinner for one, without tax, tip, or drinks:
$20-$40

Dress Code
Resort casual

Reservations
Recommended

Parking
Free on site evenings and holidays

Features
Private room/parties

Credit Cards
AE, VC, MC, DC

McCrady's

Unity Alley entrance to the restaurant

On Unity Alley, between East Bay and State streets, in the block of Queen and Broad, 20 min. from Charleston International Airport

2 Unity Alley
Charleston, SC 29401
PH: (843) 577-0025
FAX: (843) 577-3681
www.mccradysrestaurant.com

Owner
Tradd Newton

Cuisine
Contemporary American with a French flair

Days Open
Open daily for dinner

Pricing
Dinner for one,
without tax, tip, or drinks:
$40-$60
(or)
Prix fixe: $65

Dress Code
Jacket and tie requested

Reservations
Recommended

Parking
Garage nearby

Features
Private room/parties

Credit Cards
AE, VC, MC

Dazzling flavors, exceptional wines, and unparalleled service in a comfortable, richly detailed and visually sensuous space inspired by Charleston's most evocative architecture. That's McCrady's. Chef Michael Kramer blends contemporary French-American cuisine and classic culinary technique with a modern-day style and presentation. Located in the heart of the historic French Quarter district in Charleston's first tavern, built in 1778. Private dinners in the Longroom are guaranteed to be unforgettable.

Main dining room

*Executive Chef
Michael Kramer*

Tartare of big eye tuna with avocado, soy, fresh wasabi

Wine Spectator
AWARD OF EXCELLENCE

DiRoNA
AWARD WINNER
SINCE 2004

Peninsula Grill

The dining room

L ocated in the historic Planters Inn on the corner of Meeting and North Market streets in Charleston's Historic District, Peninsula Grill is a tasteful blending of traditional Charleston style with contemporary accents. The dining room's walls are covered with rich velvet, antique Cypress woodwork, and local art. The interior combines with views of lush gardens to create an elegant yet relaxed setting for exquisitely prepared and presented local cuisine.

Executive Chef Robert Carter

Alfresco dining

Benne-crusted rack of lamb

AWARD WINNER
SINCE 2001

At Meeting and North Market streets in the Historic District, 20 min. from Charleston International Airport

112 North Market Street
Charleston, SC 29401
PH: (843) 723-0700
FAX: (843) 577-2125
www.plantersinn.com

Owners
Robert Carter

Cuisine
New American with Southern influence

Days Open
Open daily for dinner

Pricing
Dinner for one, without tax, tip, or drinks: $40-$60

Dress Code
Business casual

Reservations
Recommended

Parking
Garage nearby

Features
Private room/parties, outdoor dining

Credit Cards
AE, VC, MC, DC, DS

The Dining Room at Woodlands

Woodlands Resort & Inn

On Parsons Road off West Richardson Avenue, 25 min. from Charleston International Airport

125 Parsons Road
Summerville, SC 29483
PH: (843) 875-2600
and (800) 774-9999
FAX: (843) 875-2603
www.woodlandsinn.com
reservations@woodlandsinn.com

Woodlands Resort & Inn, a beautifully restored 1906 classic revival mansion, is home to The Dining Room at Woodlands and features some of this historic and romantic region's most exciting dining. Serving innovative cuisine with a distinct Low Country flair, the tranquil, romantic atmosphere combined with sophisticated menus assures our guests a true epicurean experience. The Dining Room is proud to be South Carolina's only recipient of the prestigious AAA Five Diamond Award for Culinary Excellence. Member Relais & Chateaux & Relais Gourmand.

The Dining Room

*Executive Chef
Ken Vedrinski*

Owners
Joe Whitmore

Cuisine
New American

Days Open
Open daily for breakfast and lunch, Mon.-Sat. for dinner

Pricing
Dinner for one, without tax, tip, or drinks: $64-$89 (or) Price Fix: $95

Dress Code
Jacket required

Reservations
Recommended

Parking
Free on site, valet

Features
Private room/parties, outdoor dining, entertainment, wine/cigar events, Kitchen tables

Credit Cards
AE, VC, MC, CB, DC, DS

Innovative, new American cuisine

AWARD WINNER
SINCE 2002

411

The Orangery

Old world atmosphere

At Kingston Pike and
Homberg Drive, 25 min.
from McGhee-Tyson Airport

A t The Orangery, diners luxuriate at Knoxville's poshest and most acclaimed restaurant, the recipient of numerous awards over 30 years, including the Best of Excellence Award from *Wine Spectator*. Executive Chef David Pinckney's menu is diverse, ranging from classic French to inspired international. Specialties include Chilean sea bass with red curry sauce, buffalo with fresh foie gras, and elk chop with root vegetable purées and port wine glaze.

Sumptuous cuisine

*Owners Karen Kendrick
and David Pinckney*

AWARD WINNER
SINCE 1993

5412 Kingston Pike
Knoxville, TN 37919
PH: (865) 588-2964
FAX: (865) 588-5499

Owners
Karen and Stuart Kendrick,
David Pinckney

Cuisine
International

Days Open
Open Mon.-Fri. for lunch,
Mon.-Sat. for dinner

Pricing
Dinner for one,
without tax, tip, or drinks:
$20-$40

Dress Code
Business casual

Reservations
Recommended

Parking
Free on site

Features
Private room/parties,
entertainment

Credit Cards
AE, VC, MC, DC

The Georgian Room

Regas Restaurant

A Knoxville landmark

The Regas family has been making memories in Knoxville since 1919. The culinary team uses only hand-carved, heavy aged prime and choice beef, and the finest seafood flown in daily. Specialties include prime steak, prime rib, and New Zealand lobster. A world-class wine cellar offers the perfect complement to any meal. Breads and desserts are prepared fresh daily.

House specialty

World-class wines

Regas Restaurant

Directions

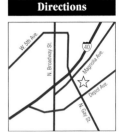

At North Gay Street and Magnolia Avenue, 10 min. from McGhee Tyson Airport

318 North Gay Street NW
Knoxville, TN 37917
PH: (865) 63-REGAS
FAX: (865) 637-7799

Owners
William F. Regas,
J. Michael Connor, and
Kevin W. Thompson

Cuisine
American

Days Open
Open Sun.-Fri. for lunch,
Daily for dinner

Pricing
Dinner for one,
without tax, tip, or drinks:
$20-$40

Dress Code
Business casual

Reservations
Recommended

Parking
Free on site

Features
Private room/parties, entertainment

Credit Cards
AE, VC, MC, CB, DC, DS

AWARD WINNER
SINCE 1995

Chez Philippe

Classic French dining

Directions

At The Peabody Hotel in
downtown Memphis,
15 min. from Memphis
International Airport

149 Union Avenue
Memphis, TN 38103
PH: (901) 529-4188
FAX: (901) 529-3639
www.peabodymemphis.com

Owners
Belz Enterprises

Cuisine
French

Days Open
Open Tues.-Sat. for dinner

Pricing
Dinner for one,
without tax, tip, or drinks:
$40-$60

Dress Code
Jacket and tie required

Reservations
Recommended

Parking
Valet

Features
Private parties, near
Orpheum theater

Credit Cards
AE, VC, MC, CB, DC, JCB, DS

Aclassic French approach to combining ingredients from around the world distinguishes Chez Philippe's cuisine as the best in Memphis. Seafood, exotic spices, Southern specialties, and fine meats by award-winning Executive Chef José Gutierrez—one of only 52 Master Chefs of France working in the United States—are featured at the Mid-South's only Mobil Four Star restaurant. The setting in the fabled Peabody Hotel is opulent and the presentation is classical French.

*Master Chef
José Gutierrez*

AWARD WINNER
SINCE 1992

Folk's Folly
Prime Steak House

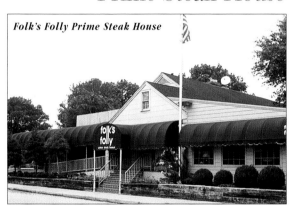

Folk's Folly Prime Steak House

On S. Mendenhall Road, two blocks north of Poplar Avenue, 20 min. from Memphis International Airport

A 25-year Memphis tradition, Folk's Folly Prime Steak House is known for the finest cuts of prime steaks, and seafood that is flown in fresh daily. Folk's Folly Prime Steak House pair's personalized, fine dining service in a warm, comfortable atmosphere. Savor your favorite vintage from the extensive wine list, which received *Wine Spectator's* Award of Excellence. Before dinner, enjoy cocktails while listening to live grand piano music in The Cellar Lounge. Folk's Folly also offers restaurant favorites and customized additions at their Prime Cut Shoppe, open daily.

Prime steaks

Freshest seafood flown in daily

551 S. Mendenhall Road
Memphis, TN 38117
PH: (901) 762-8200 or
(800) 467-0245
FAX: (901) 762-8287
www.folksfolly.com

Owners
Humphrey Jr., Tripp, Michael, Chris, and Carey Folk

Cuisine
Steak and Seafood

Days Open
Open daily for dinner

Pricing
Dinner for one,
without tax, tip or drinks:
$40-$60

Dress Code
Business casual

Reservations
Recommended

Parking
Free on site, valet

Features
Private room/parties, entertainment

Credit Cards
AE, VC, MC, DC

On the grill

AWARD WINNER
SINCE 2001

La Tourelle Restaurant

Fine dining in Memphis

On Monroe Avenue in midtown, 15 min. from Memphis International Airport

E xperience exquisite food in a romantic and intimate setting at Memphis' oldest fine-dining restaurant. La Tourelle, set in a Queen Anne cottage, serves French cuisine under the direction of Executive Chef Justin Young. The menu, which changes seasonally, features rack of lamb, foie gras, and fresh seafood among other standbys. Their list of French and American wines is impressive.

Seasonal French cuisine

2146 Monroe Avenue
Memphis, TN 38104
PH: (901) 726-5771
FAX: (901) 272-0492
www.latourellememphis.com

Owners
Glenn T. Hays

Cuisine
French

Days Open
Open daily for dinner,
Sun. for brunch

Pricing
Dinner for one,
without tax, tip, or drinks:
$40-$60

Dress Code
Business casual

Reservations
Recommended

Parking
Free on site

Features
Private room/parties, near theater

Credit Cards
AE, VC, MC

A romantic setting

Intimate atmosphere

AWARD WINNER
SINCE 1993

Arthur's

Intimate dining

Charlotte Ave.

10th Ave. 7th Ave. 5th Ave.

Broadway

Union Station

Located in the Union Station Hotel at Broadway and 10th Avenue downtown, 20 min. from Nashville International Airport

1001 Broadway
Nashville, TN
PH: (615) 255-1494
FAX: (615) 255-1496
www.arthursrestaurant.com

Owners
James Breuss and
Jaime Camara

Cuisine
Continental

Days Open
Open daily for dinner

Pricing
Dinner for one,
without tax, tip, or drinks:
$50-$75

Dress Code
Business casual

Reservations
Recommended

Parking
Free on site, valet

Features
Private parties, near theater

Credit Cards
AE, VC, MC, CB, DC, DS

Arthur's 24-foot ceilings, Tiffany stained-glass windows, well-spaced tables, and candlelight ensure privacy for romantic and business dinners alike. A verbal presentation of the menu is recited by the captains each evening. Chef Julio Orantes prepares continental fare, including such entrées as roast rack of Colorado lamb and wild game. Fresh fish is flown in daily. Arthur's is near all in downtown Nashville and a short walk from the convention center.

Roast rack of lamb

Captains Romano Allegranti and Dino Buonanno

Chef Julio Orantes prepares tableside entrée

AWARD WINNER
SINCE 1992

Mario's

Owner Mario Ferrari with Chef

On Broadway near
Vanderbilt University, 5 min.
from Nashville International
Airport

Internationally acclaimed for its overall dining experience, Mario's is celebrating its 38th year. The delicious food, elegant atmosphere, and superb service make it perfect for all occasions. Specializing in Northern Italian cuisine, owner and Executive Chef Mario Ferrari prepares such entrées as fresh Dover sole, saltimbocca, ossobuco, and tricolore pastas. The wine list boasts more than 700 selections.

Ossobuco with risotto

Wine cellar

2005 Broadway
Nashville, TN 37203
PH: (615) 327-3232
FAX: (615) 321-2675
www.mariosfinedining.com

Owners
Mario Ferrari

Cuisine
Northern Italian

Days Open
Open Mon.-Sat. for dinner

Pricing
Dinner for one,
without tax, tip, or drinks:
$40-$60

Dress Code
Classy casual

Reservations
Recommended

Parking
Free on site

Features
Private room/parties,
cigar/cognac events

Credit Cards
AE, VC, MC, CB, DC, DS

Banquet room, Dolce Vita

AWARD WINNER
SINCE 1992

Old Hickory Traditional Steakhouse

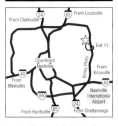

Old Hickory Steakhouse

Directions

In the Gaylord Opryland Resort and Convention Center, 10 min. from Nashville International Airport

2800 Opryland Drive
Nashville, TN 37214
PH: (615) 871-6848
FAX: (615) 871-7872

Owners
Gaylord Entertainment

Cuisine
Traditional steakhouse/American contemporary

Days Open
Open daily for dinnerr

Pricing
Dinner for one, without tax, tip, or drinks: $40-$60

Dress Code
Business casual

Reservations
Recommended

Parking
Free on site

Features
Private room/parties, outdoor dining

Credit Cards
AE, VC, MC, DS

S et in an antebellum style mansion, within the Delta atrium of the Gaylord Opryland Resort and Convention Center, Old Hickory Steakhouse offers a unique indoor yet outdoor setting for exquisite fine dining. Hand selected by Executive Chef Peter D'Andrea, Old Hickory Steakhouse features steaks that are memorable and a true culinary experience. The fresh selection of seafood and lamb complement the eclectic wine list. Old Hickory Steakhouse has elegant private dining rooms that can accommodate up to 100 patrons. Renowned for personalize service; Old Hickory Steakhouse is a requisite when visiting Nashville.

Private venues

A culinary sense of grace

Nightly elegance

AWARD WINNER
SINCE 2004

The Stock-Yard Restaurant

The world-famous Stock-Yard Restaurant

Corner of Second Ave. North and Stockyard Blvd, 15 min. from Nashville International Airport

901 Second Ave. North
Nashville, TN 37201
PH: (615) 255-6464
FAX: (615) 255-9561
www.stock-yardrestaurant.com

The distinctive and historic Stock-Yard Restaurant has been named "One of the Top Ten Steak Houses in America." Award-winning Chef Ahlyege serves only the finest cuts of aged certified Angus beef as well as fresh live Maine lobster daily. Owners Wayne and Linda Fricks are committed to the highest quality food and impeccable service. The 14 unique dining rooms, with seating for up to 700, are elegantly appointed to offer just the right atmosphere for a memorable evening.

Chef Ahlyege

Owners
Wayne and Linda Fricks

Cuisine
Steakhouse

Days Open
Open daily for dinner

Pricing
Dinner for one,
without tax, tip, or drinks:
$20-$40

Dress Code
Business casual

Reservations
Recommended

Parking
Free on site

Features
Private room/parties,
entertainment, cigar/
cognac events

Credit Cards
AE, VC, MC, CB, DC, DS

Entrance foyer

AWARD WINNER
SINCE 2001

Sunset Grill

Patio dining

Directions

On Belcourt in Hillsboro
Village, 10 min. from
Nashville International
Airport

For affordable, casually elegant dining and excellent service, the trend-setting Sunset Grill is a Nashville must. Nestled in historic Hillsboro Village, Sunset Grill's artistic bistro-style ambience and delicious modern American cuisine has earned many fans. The menu stays fresh with delectable seafood, steaks, pastas, low-fat and vegetarian dishes, and daily specials. The wine list offers over 80 top-rated wines poured by the glass, and 300 additional selections by the bottle.

Chef Brian Uhl

Ahai seared tuna

Randy Rayburn and Executive Chef Brian Uhl

2001 Belcourt Ave.
Nashville, TN 37212
PH: (615) 386-3663 (or)
PH: (866) 496-3663
FAX: (615) 386-0495
www.sunsetgrill.com

Owners
Randy Rayburn

Cuisine
Contemporary American

Days Open
Open Tues.-Fri. for lunch,
daily for dinner

Pricing
Dinner for one,
without tax, tip, or drinks:
$30-$50

Dress Code
Casual

Reservations
Recommended

Parking
Free on site, valet

Features
Private room/parties, outdoor
dining, wine tasting events

Credit Cards
AE, VC, MC, CB, DC,
JCB, DS

AWARD WINNER
SINCE 2001

The Wild Boar

Main dining room

On Broadway near Vanderbilt University, 10 min. from Nashville International Airport

2014 Broadway
Nashville, TN 37203
PH: (615) 329-1313
FAX: (615) 329-4930
www.wboar.com

Owners
Brett Allen

Cuisine
Contemporary French

Days Open
Open Mon.-Sat. for dinner

Pricing
Dinner for one,
without tax, tip, or drinks:
$60-$80

Dress Code
Jacket suggested

Reservations
Recommended

Parking
Valet

Features
Private parties

Credit Cards
AE, VC, MC, CB, DC, DS

With a *Wine Spectator* Grand Award wine list and the contemporary French-inspired cuisine of Chef Robert Price, the Wild Boar, which opened in 1993, has established itself as a premier fine dining establishment. Specialties include a five-course degustation menu, and seasonal a la carte menu. We look forward to making your evening an "exceptional experience!"

Red wine cellar

AWARD WINNER
SINCE 1994

Jeffrey's Restaurant

Jeffrey's...Austin, Texas

Nestled in the center of Austin, Jeffrey's is celebrating its 28th anniversary. Jeffrey's has been a mainstay of fine dining because of its constant desire to improve and it's commitment to quality. Chef David Garrido orchestrates the ever-changing menu, using only the freshest of the fresh; wild mushrooms from Oregon, locally grown salad greens, Copper River salmon, and Texas Gulf oysters. Everyone that walks in the door is treated with genuine courtesy and warm, Jeffrey's hospitality. "Our customers are truly wonderful. They appreciate what we've created, and I think that is the ultimate complement." – Ron Weiss, owner.

Crispy oysters on yucca root chips with habanero honey aioli

Owners Peggy & Ron Weiss, with Chef David Garrido

Wine Spectator
AWARD OF EXCELLENCE

DiRoNA
AWARD WINNER
SINCE 2004

Directions

In the center of Austin on West Lynn, 25 min. from Austin-Bergstrom International Airports

1204 West Lynn
Austin, TX 78703
PH: (512) 477-5584
FAX: (512) 474-7279
www.jeffreysofaustin.com

Owners
Ron and Peggy Weiss and Jeffrey Weinberger

Type of Cuisine
Contemporary American

Days Open
Open daily for dinner

Pricing
Dinner for one, without tax, tip, or drinks: $40-$60

Dress Code
Business casual

Reservations
Recommended

Parking
Free on site valet

Features
Private room/parties

Credit Cards
AE, VC, MC

Al Biernat's

Main dining room

In downtown in the Highland Park area, 10 min. from Love Field and 25 min. from Dallas/Ft. Worth Int'l airports

A l Biernat's is much more than a great steakhouse! Incredible seafood such as Nova Scotia lobster, Australian cold-water lobster tail, Beluga caviar, and six types of fresh fish await you daily. The award winning wine list features over 650 rare selections. Enjoy our dry-aged New York strip and see why *Town & Country, Playboy,* and *Wine Spectator* selected Al Biernat's as one of the top steakhouses in the country.

Al Biernat

Chilean sea bass over lobster risotto

AWARD WINNER
SINCE 2003

4217 Oak Lawn Avenue
Dallas, TX 75219
PH: (214) 219-2201
FAX: (214) 219-2093
www.albiernats.com

Owners
Al Biernat

Type of Cuisine
Prime steaks & seafood

Days Open
Open Mon.-Fri. for lunch, daily for dinner

Pricing
Dinner for one, without tax, tip, or drinks: $40-$60

Dress Code
Business casual

Reservations
Recommended

Parking
Valet

Features
Private room/parties

Credit Cards
AE, VC, MC, CB, DC, DS

Executive Chef
Andreas Bautista

Bob's Steak & Chop House

Owner Bob Sambol

Bob Steak & Chop House's award-winning combination of food, service, and atmosphere is the reason it it one of the top steakhouses in the country. An attentive and seasoned waitstaff, prime aged beef, and fresh seafood are just a few specialties you encounter. From the jumbo shrimp appetizer platter to the chophouse salad and bone-in ribeye, only the best is prepared and served. A refreshing atmosphere in which old-world elegance meets modern, business-casual attire welcomes you. Distinguished as one of the country's favorite steakhouses by *Bon Appetit Magazine* and "Hands Down... the Best Steakhouse in Dallas," by *D Magazine*, Bob's keeps patrons coming back again and again.

Sugar-glazed carrot and potato with 28 oz. prime porterhouse

Directions

At Lemmon and Wycliff avenues, 25 min. from Dallas-Fort Worth International Airport

4300 Lemmon Avenue
Dallas, TX 75219
PH: (214) 528-9446
FAX: (214) 526-8159
www.bobs-steakand chop.com

Owners
Bob and Judi Sambol

Cuisine
Steakhouse

Days Open
Open Mon.-Sat. for dinner

Pricing
Dinner for one, without tax, tip, or drinks: $50-$60

Dress Code
Business casual

Reservations
Recommended

Parking
Valet

Credit Cards
AE, VC, MC, DC, DS

Bob's
Steak & Chop House

AWARD WINNER
SINCE 1999

425

Café Pacific

Café Pacific Dining Room

In Highland Park Village off Preston Road, 20 min. from Dallas-Fort Worth International Airport and 10min. from downtown Dallas

Café Pacific, ranked No.1 Seafood Restaurant in Dallas by *Zagat Guide* (1999, 2000, and 2001), inducted into the "Fine Dining Hall of Fame" in (2001) and recipient of the 2003 DiRōNA "Fine Dining Award", caters to many of Dallas' business and social leaders. In the elegant surroundings of Highland Park Village, the second shopping village in America, Chef Brian Campbell features New American cuisine based on classic presentations.

Dining destination for Dallas leaders

24 Highland Park Village
Dallas, TX 75205
PH: (214) 526-1170
FAX: (214) 526-0332

Owner
Jack Knox

Cuisine
Seafood/New American

Days Open
Open Mon.-Sat. for lunch and dinner

Pricing
Dinner for one, without tax, tip, or drinks:
$20-$40

Dress Code
Business casual

Reservations
Recommended

Parking
Valet

Features
Outdoor dining

Credit Cards
AE, VC, MC, DC, DS

Chef Brian Campbell and Dining Room Manager Jean-Pierre Albertinetti

AWARD WINNER
SINCE 1994

The French Room at The Adolphus

Main dining room

Executive Chef William Koval's genius for adapting classic French cooking to contemporary tastes has earned him widespread acclaim and positioned The French Room at The Adolphus as one of the nation's finest dining rooms. No less an authority than *Condé Nast Traveler* has named The French Room one of America's "Top 20" restaurants. A sampling of dishes includes jumbo lump crab cake with a lemon grass lobster sauce and tomato jam, and sweet white miso-marinated Alaskan halibut with baby shiitake, spinach and sweet potatoes in a carrot ginger sauce.

Dinner for two in The French Room

Executive Chef William Koval (right), and French Room Chef Marcos Segovia (left)

At The Adolphus

Directions

In The Adolphus in downtown Dallas, 25 min. from Dallas-Fort Worth International Airport

The Adolphus
1321 Commerce Street
Dallas, TX 75202
PH: (214) 742-8200
FAX: (214) 651-3561
www.hoteladolphus.com

Owners
Noble House Hotels and Resorts

Cuisine
French American

Days Open
Open Tues.-Sat. for dinner

Pricing
Dinner for one, without tax, tip, or drinks: $60-$80

Dress Code
Jacket required

Reservations
Recommended

Parking
Valet

Credit Cards
AE, MC, CB, DC, DS

AWARD WINNER
SINCE 1993

The Old Warsaw

Main dining room

On Maple Avenue, 10 min. from Dallas/Ft. Worth International Airport

2610 Maple Avenue
Dallas, TX 75201
PH: (214) 528-0032
FAX: (214) 871-1965
www.theoldwarsaw.com

Owners
Al Heidari

Type of Cuisine
French

Days Open
Open daily for dinner

Pricing
Dinner for one,
without tax, tip, or drinks:
$40-$60

Dress Code
Jacket required

Reservations
Required

Parking
Valet

Features
Private room/parties, entertainment, near theater

Credit Cards
AE, VC, MC, CB, DC,
En Route, JCB, DS

Ith top-rated cuisine by *Zagat's 2003* survey, The Old Warsaw has continued to serve the finest French continental menu offered for over t50 years. Coupled with classic French service in an elegant old world environment, The Old Warsaw offers a memorable dining experience for romance seekers as well as business professionals. The spacious tables are adorned with fresh flowers, and candlelight. Live music adds sensuality to the refined elegance of the surroundings. The menu and wine list are extensive and exquisite.

Chef Al Heidari

A memorable dining experience

The old world tradition continues

AWARD WINNER
SINCE 1992

428

Rough Creek Lodge

Great Room at Rough Creek Lodge

Directions

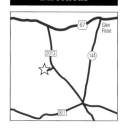

Off US Highway 67, between Glen Rose and Stephenville, 1hr. 30 min from Dallas-Ft. Worth International Airport

M emorable views, elegant settings, and bold menus define the Rough Creek Lodge dining experience that keeps guests returning for more. American regional specialties like sherry maple glazed Texas quail with Parmesan cheese grits are among Chef Gerard Thompson's signature dishes, all complemented by an extensive wine list. From the luxuriously appointed dining room to the star-lit terrace, guests can choose the perfect setting for their mood, and occasion.

Executive Chef
Gerard Thompson

Simple, yet sophisticated American, regional cuisine

P.O. Box 2400
Glen Rose, TX 76043
PH: (800) 864-4705
FAX: (254) 918-2570
www.roughcreek.com

Owners
John Q. Adams, Sr.

Type of Cuisine
American regional

Days Open
Open daily for breakfast, lunch, and dinner

Pricing
Dinner for one, without tax, tip, or drinks: $40-$60

Dress Code
Casual

Reservations
Recommended

Parking
Free on site

Features
Private room/parties, outdoor dining

Credit Cards
AE, VC, MC, CB, DC, DS

A memorable dining experience

AWARD WINNER
SINCE 2003

Brennan's of Houston

Executive Chef Carl Walker serves signature Texas Creole cuisine

Directions

In downtown Houston on the corner of Smith and Stuart, 20 min. from Houston Hobby Airport

3300 Smith Street
Houston, TX 77006
PH: (713) 522-9711
FAX: (713) 522-9142
www.brennanshouston.com

Owners
Alex Brennan-Martin

Type of Cuisine
Texas Creole

Days Open
Open Mon.-Fri. for lunch, daily for dinner, Saturday and Sunday for brunch

Pricing
Dinner for one, without tax, tip, or drinks: $40-$60

Dress Code
Jacket required in main dining room

Reservations
Recommended

Features
Private room/parties, outdoor dining, entertainment, near theater

Parking
Valet

Credit Cards
AE, VC, MC, CB, DC, DS

For 35 years Brennan's has been a preferred choice for those seeking a memorable dining experience in Houston. Bringing its Crescent City flavor to every table, Brennan's exquisitely blends the best of its mixed heritage into its signature Texas Creole cuisine. Transport yourself to New Orleans with fetching courtyard views. Specialties include Gulf of Mexico crab cakes, Louisiana pecan crusted fish, renowned turtle soup, and the mouthwatering bananas Foster.

"Terms of Endearment" Room overlooks New Orleans-style courtyard

Gulf of Mexico crab cakes

Wine Spectator
AWARD OF EXCELLENCE

DiRōNA

AWARD WINNER
SINCE 1994

The Capital Grille

The Capital Grille of Houston

Directions

Two blocks west of the Galleria, on Westheimer Road, 20 min. from George Bush Intercontinental Airport

Located two blocks west of the Galleria, The Capital Grille boasts an atmosphere of power dining, relaxed elegance, and style. Nationally acclaimed for dry aging steaks on premises, The Capital Grille serves classic steakhouse offerings such a chops, large North Atlantic lobsters, and fresh seafood. The restaurant features an award-winning wine list and professional, gracious service. Let the masters of steak provide the perfect dining experience.

Master of steaks

Cold shellfish platter

5365 Westheimer Road
Houston, TX 77056
PH: (713) 623-4600
FAX: (713) 623-4606
www.thecapitalgrille.com

Owners
Rare Hospitality/Cory Graff

Type of Cuisine
Steakhouse

Days Open
Open daily for dinner

Pricing
Dinner for one,
without tax, tip, or drinks:
$40-$50

Dress Code
Business casual

Reservations
Recommended

Parking
Complimentary valet (after 5:00 pm)

Features
Private room/parties

Credit Cards
AE, VC, MC, CB, DC, DS

The Wine room

AWARD WINNER
SINCE 2003

Chez nous

Cuisine Française

In suburban Humble, 10 min. from George Bush Intercontinental Airport

217 South Avenue G
Humble, TX 77338
PH: (281) 446-6717
FAX: (281) 446-8612

Owners
Gerard Brach

Cuisine
French

Days Open
Open Mon.-Sat. for dinner

Pricing
Dinner for one,
without tax, tip, and drinks:
$40-$60

Dress Code
Jacket and tie suggested

Reservations
Recommended

Parking
Free on site

Features
Private room, wine tastings

Credit Cards
AE, VC, MC, DC, DS

The owners are the chefs, as it should be, and they are in the kitchen where they belong. So it is at Gerard Brach and Barbara Farrar's Chez nous, where classic French cuisine is served in a delightful, intimate setting just 20 minutes from downtown Houston. Specialties include fresh foie gras with caramelized apple and honey vinegar, Alaskan halibut with mussels and scallops, and Grand Marnier chocolate mousse in chocolate bag. *The Houston Chronicle* has one word for it: "incomparable."

Incomparable dining

AWARD WINNER
SINCE 1994

La Colombe d'Or Hotel & Restaurant

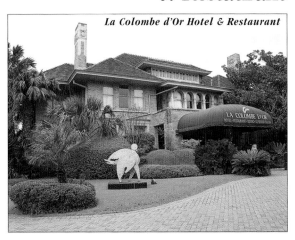

La Colombe d'Or Hotel & Restaurant

Located on Montrose, between W. Alabama and Westheimer, 20 min. from Houston Hobby Airport

3410 Montrose Blvd.
Houston, TX 77006
PH: (713) 524-7999
FAX: (713) 524-8923
www.lacolombedor.com

Owners
Stephen Zimmerman

Type of Cuisine
Modern French

Days Open
Open Mon.-Fri. for lunch, daily for dinner

Pricing
Dinner for one, without tax, tip, or drinks: $40-$60

Dress Code
Business casual

Reservations
Recommended

Parking
Valet

Features
Private room/parties, long term stays, grand salon, near med center

Credit Cards
AE, VC, MC, CB, DC, DS

La Colombe d'Or Restaurant, Hotel and Grand Salon is one of the most unique facilities in the world. Its collection of art, exquisite food, and romantic ambience has attracted patrons worldwide. La Colombe d'Or exudes southern European hospitality, gracious comforts, elegance and warmth, whether you are enjoying an intimate meal, hosting a memorable event, or spending an elegant weekend in the hotel. Specialties include rack of lamb, red snapper, and chateaubriand.

Exquisite food presentation

"Le Grand Salon"

Courtyard villas

AWARD WINNER
SINCE 1992

La Reserve

Main dining room

Just off Highway 610 North, 40 min. from George Bush Intercontinental Airport

---

Omni Houston Hotel
4 Riverway
Houston, TX 77056
PH: (713) 871-8177
FAX: (713) 871-8116
www.omnihotels.com

Grandly elegant and sophisticated, La Reserve, at the AAA Five Diamond Omni Houston Hotel, appeals to the most discriminating diner. Exquisitely prepared contemporary French cuisine is served in a dramatic setting of luxurious fabrics, beveled glass, and crystal chandeliers. Executive Chef Mercer A. Mohr and his talented team use farm-raised fowl, game, and beef and the most exotic fish in concert with the freshest and finest ingredients to create a culinary experience that is second to none.

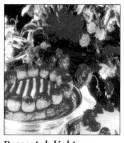

Dessert delights

Owners
Omni Houston Hotel

Type of Cuisine
Contemporary French

Days Open
Open Tues.-Sat. for dinner, Sun. for brunch

Pricing
Dinner for one, without tax, tip, and drinks: $40-$60

Dress Code
Business casual

Reservations
Recommended

Parking
Free on site, valet

Features
Private room/parties, cigar/cognac events, wine dinners

Credit Cards
AE, VC, MC, CB, DC, JCB, DS

Le Pavillion, private room

Le Bar

AWARD WINNER
SINCE 1996

434

Mark's

Owners Lisa and Mark Cox

At the corner of Westheimer and Dunlavy, 30 min. from George Bush Intercontinental Airport

C hef/Owner Mark Cox has given Houstonians an amazing dining experience in Mark's, his innovative namesake restaurant situated in an old church. The food reflects inspirations from many countries, creating a unique melting-pot menu. American regional ingredients are used to create diverse dishes, with taste sensations that echo the authentic food of many different cultures, including Asian and Italian.

Dining room

Cloisters private party room

Sample seasonal entrée

1658 Westheimer Road
Houston, TX 77006
PH: (713) 523-3800
FAX: (713) 523-9292
www.marks1658.com

Owners
Lisa and Mark Cox

Cuisine
American

Days Open
Open Mon.-Fri. for lunch, daily for dinner

Pricing
Dinner for one, without tax, tip, or drinks: $40-$60

Dress Code
Casual

Reservations
Recommended

Parking
Free on site, valet

Features
Private room/parties, near theater

Credit Cards
AE, VC, MC, DC, DS

AWARD WINNER
SINCE 2001

Quattro

Quattro

Accented by jewel-toned velvet, cherrywood veneers, stainless steel beaded curtains, and eclectic lighting; Quattro exudes a warm, yet modern vitality. The wine list offers 250 selections including 25 wines by the glass. Tuck into a cozy booth with a city vista and savor such delights as mushroom risotto or salmon four ways. Portions are both reasonable priced and sized, making ordering dessert a guiltless operation.

Executive Chef Tim Keating

Quattro bar

Relax in the lobby lounge

AWARD WINNER
SINCE 1992

Directions

Located in the east side of downtown Houston, just blocks from the George Brown Convention Center, Theater District and the Downtown Arena. 45 min. from George Bush Intercontinental Airport

1300 Lamar Street
Houston, TX 77010
PH: (713) 276-4700
FAX: (713) 276-4720
www.fourseasons.com/houston/dining

Owners

Type of Cuisine
American-Italian

Days Open
Open daily for breakfast, lunch, and dinner.
Sunday for brunch

Pricing
Dinner for one,
without tax, tip, or drinks:
$20-$40

Dress Code
Business casual

Reservations
Recommended

Parking
Complimentary valet

Features
Private room/parties, near theater, wine events

Credit Cards
AE, VC, MC, CB, DC, JCB, DS

Rotisserie for Beef and Bird

A Houston landmark since 1978

The glories of the Rotisserie for Beef and Bird are well known to Houstonians who have long enjoyed the finest in traditional American cooking, prepared under the watchful eye of proprietor Joe Mannke, who doubles as executive chef. The menu changes seasonally, using the bounties from the forest, the sea, and the rich agriculture of Texas. The wine list is one of the finest in Texas, with more than 950 selections.

Joe Mannke, chef/proprietor

Spit-roasted duck a la orange

Sommelier Vince Baker

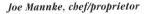

Wine Spectator
GRAND AWARD

DiRōNA

AWARD WINNER
SINCE 1996

Directions

On Wilcrest just north of Westheimer, and 35 min. from George Bush Intercontinental Airport

2200 Wilcrest
Houston, TX 77042
PH: (713) 977-9524
FAX: (713) 977-9568
www.rotisserie-beef-bird.com

Owners
Joe Mannke

Type of Cuisine
Steaks, wild game, lobster

Days Open
Open Mon.-Fri. for lunch,
Mon.-Sat. for dinner

Pricing
Dinner for one,
without tax, tip, or drinks:
$20-$40

Dress Code
Jacket suggested

Reservations
Recommended

Parking
Free on site, valet

Features
Private room/parties

Credit Cards
AE, VC, MC, CB, DC, DS

Tony's Restaurant

Main dining room

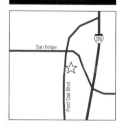

San Felipe

Post Oak Blvd.

On the southern edge of downtown, 20 min. from Hobby Airport and 35 min. from George Bush Intercontinental Airport

1801 Post Oak Boulevard
Houston, TX 77056
PH: (713) 622-6778
FAX: (713) 626-1232

Owners
Tony Vallone

Cuisine
European, Mediterranean

Days Open
Open Mon.-Sat. for dinner

Pricing
Dinner for one,
without tax, tip, or drinks:
$40-$60

Dress Code
Jacket and tie required

Reservations
Recommended

Parking
Free on site, valet

Features
Private room/parties, entertainment, near theater, cigar/cognac events

Credit Cards
AE, VC, MC, CB, DC, DS

Cool and classical meets hot creative ingenuity inside Houston's most favored—and most honored—professional kitchen. For 35 years, Tony's has been a tasteful destination for the world's smartest palates. Owner Tony Vallone and Executive Chef Bruce McMillian have created an innovative, contemporary menu steeped in classical European traditions, guaranteeing extraordinary dining. Professionalism and warm hospitality are the hallmarks of Tony's elegant service. Tony's resonates with perfection.

Poached bosc pear

Executive Chef
Bruce McMillian

Owner Tony Vallone

Wine Spectator

AWARD OF EXCELLENCE

DiRōNA

AWARD WINNER
SINCE 1996

Fig Tree

Patio dining

Directions

Just off the Riverwalk in downtown, 10 min. from San Antonio International Airport

---

The Fig Tree celebrates tradition in a gracious setting just steps from the Riverwalk and near major hotels and the convention center. Fine linen drapes tables set with elegant china, sparkling crystal, and ever-present flowers. Famous for its Continental and eclectic cuisine, The Fig Tree classically prepares chateaubriand, herb-crusted rack of lamb, and bananas Foster tableside. Comfortably elegant areas are available for social and business gatherings.

Memorable entrées

The Crystal Room

515 Villita
San Antonio, TX 78205
PH: (210) 224-1976
FAX: (210) 271-9180
www.figtreerestaurant.com

Owners
Thomas E. Phelps

Cuisine
Global

Days Open
Open daily for dinner

Pricing
Dinner for one,
without tax, tip, or drinks:
$60-$80

Dress Code
Business casual

Reservations
Recommended

Parking
Garage nearby (three-hour validation)

Features
Private room/parties, outdoor dining

Credit Cards
AE, VC, MC, CB, DC, DS

Executive Chef Steve Paprocki

Wine Spectator
AWARD OF EXCELLENCE

DiRoNA
AWARD WINNER
SINCE 1998

Glitretind Restaurant at Stein Eriksen Lodge

Summer dining with breathtaking views

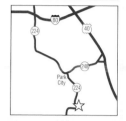

Located mid-mountain at Park City's Deer Valley Resort, in the Stein Eriksen Lodge, 45 min. from Salt Lake City International Airport

The award-winning Glitretind Restaurant presents exceptional New American cuisine with an exquisite alpine, European ambience. Chef Zane Holmquist delights the palate with tantalizing entrées, including his signature tea and Szechuan pepper crusted duck breast. Outstanding wine selections, full bar service, a magnificent jazz Sunday brunch, creative fare, and a memorable mountain setting make the Glitretind an extraordinary dining experience.

Executive Chef Zane Holmquist

Roasted loin of Colorado lamb with salsify

7700 Stein Way
Park City, UT 84060
PH: (435) 649-3700
FAX: (435) 649-5825
www.steinlodge.com

Owners
Stein Eriksen Owners Assoc.

Cuisine
New American

Days Open
Open daily for breakfast, lunch, and dinner, jazz Sunday brunch

Pricing
Dinner for one, without tax, tip, or drinks: $25-$40

Dress Code
Mountain casual

Reservations
Recommended

Parking
Valet

Features
Private dining, outdoor dining, weddings

Credit Cards
AE, VC, MC, CB, DC, JCB, DS

Warm peach dessert with lemon verbena blueberry sauce

AWARD WINNER
SINCE 2003

Grappa Italian Restaurant & Café

Grappa's beautiful façade

Directions

At the top of Main St. in historic Park City, 45 min. from Salt Lake City International Airport

The décor of the award-winning Grappa Italian Restaurant and Café is reminiscent of a Tuscan farmhouse, complete with wood beams, Italian pottery, and baskets of fresh produce. Owner Bill White and his staff are dedicated to culinary excellence, evident in the unique and creative Italian cuisine. Entrées include fresh sea bass, wild mushroom lasagna, plus a favorite salad course, Brie and shaved onions served over a warm spinach salad. The wait staff provides superior service all to create a truly great restaurant experience.

Grappa's rustic ambience

Owner Bill White (right) and Managing Executive Chef John Murcko

Balcony view of dining room

151 Main Street
Park City, UT 84060
PH: (435) 645-0636
FAX: (435) 647-0844
www.grapparestaurant.com

Owners
Bill White

Cuisine
Regional Italian

Days Open
Open daily for dinner

Pricing
Dinner for one, without tax, tip, or drinks: $40-$60

Dress Code
Casual

Reservations
Recommended

Parking
Garage nearby

Features
Private room/parties, outdoor dining

Credit Cards
AE, VC, MC, DS

AWARD WINNER
SINCE 1997

Riverhorse Café

Directions

On historic Main St., 45 min. from Salt Lake City International Airport

Outdoor dining

T he Riverhorse Cafe is located in the former Masonic Lodge on historic Main Street. The unique setting combines turn of the century charm of the Lodge's main dining room with the contemporary ambiance of the new Atrium dining room. The Atrium features floor to ceiling windows and skylights. Since 1987, the Riverhorse Café has set the dining standard for local residents and visitors alike. Chef Hufferd's award-winning cuisine features fresh seafood and USDA Prime steaks. The Atrium features pop and jazz entertainers nightly.

Executive Chef Bill Hufferd and staff

Signature entrées

Entertainment nightly

540 Main Street
Park City, UT 84060
PH: (435) 649-3536
FAX: (435) 649-2409
www.riverhorsecafe.com

Owners
Diversified Restaurant Corp.

Cuisine
American regional

Days Open
Open daily for dinner

Pricing
Dinner for one,
without tax, tip, or drinks:
$20-$40

Dress Code
Casual

Reservations
Recommended

Parking
Local street parking

Features
Private rooms/parties, outdoor dining, entertainment

Credit Cards
AE, VC, MC, DS

AWARD WINNER
SINCE 1995

442

Fresco Italian Cafe

Charming outdoor dining

At South 1500 East and Kensington Avenue, 20 min. from Salt Lake City International Airport

As close as you can get to Italy without a passport, Fresco is an intimate, romantic restaurant and a longtime Salt Lake City favorite. Tucked away in a neighborhood, the cozy cottage houses 13 tables with a roaring fireplace in the winter. In the warm-weather months, the restaurant expands onto a flowering garden patio. The menu is nothing short of exquisite — especially anything with polenta — and there are nightly specials. Attentive service and a great wine list complete the dining experience.

Romantic cottage dining

1512 South 1500 East
Salt Lake City, UT 84103
PH: (801) 486-1300
FAX: (801) 487-5379
www.refectory.com

Owners
David Harries

Cuisine
Northern Italian

Days Open
Open daily for dinner

Pricing
Dinner for one,
without tax, tip, or drinks:
$20-$40

Dress Code
Business casual

Reservations
Recommended

Parking
Free on site

Features
Private parties, outdoor dining

Credit Cards
AE, VC, MC, CB, DC, DS

AWARD WINNER
SINCE 1996

Log Haven Restaurant

Interior foyer with fireplace

L og Haven has forever raised the standards of dining in Utah, offering a sophisticated, exciting menu, and extensive wine list, and attentive service. Surrounded by a national forest, Log Haven's setting is elegant yet comfortable, enhanced by waterfalls, pines, and warm fires. Chef Jones' menus are inspired by the seasons and reflect complex reductions, textures, and presentations. Pictured is one of Log Haven's signature dishes—coriander seared ahi tuna.

Owners Ian Campbell, Faith Sweeten, David Jones, Don Casto

Founders Wayne and Margo Provost

Coriander seared ahi tuna

AWARD WINNER
SINCE 2002

Directions

On Millcreek Canyon, opposite the waterfall, 25 min. from Salt Lake City International Airport

6451 East Milcreek Canyon (4 miles up)
Salt Lake City, UT 84109
PH: (801) 272-8255
FAX: (801) 272-6315
www.log-haven.com

Owners
Margo and Wayne Provost, David Jones, Ian Campbell, Faith Sweeten, and Don Casto

Cuisine
Contemporary

Days Open
Open daily for dinner

Pricing
Dinner for one, without tax, tip, or drinks: $20-$40

Dress Code
Business casual

Reservations
Recommended

Parking
Free on site, valet

Features
Private room/parties, outdoor dining

Credit Cards
AE, VC, MC, DC, DS

Metropolitan

"Utah's culinary jewel"

In downtown Salt Lake City on West Broadway (300 South), 15 min. from Salt Lake City International Airport

Acclaimed by DiRōNA, AAA Four Diamond, and *Zagat*, Metropolitan is famous for exquisite, handcrafted New American cuisine served within stunning, urban surroundings. Signature dishes include seared Hudson Valley foie gras, wild mushroom ragout, and truffle crusted rack of lamb. Try the Chef's nightly tasting menu, or selections from the à la carte, bistro, or vegetarian menus. Featured in *The New York Times*, and recipient of *Wine Spectator's* Award of Excellence, experience why Metropolitan is considered, "Utah's culinary jewel."

Hudson Valley foie gras, toasted brioche carrots vichy

Owner and Gen. Mgr. Karen Olson

Colorado lamb rack with marinated baby artichokes gaufrettes

AWARD WINNER
SINCE 1998

173 West Broadway (300 South)
Salt Lake City, UT 84101
PH: (801) FOIE-GRAS
FAX: (801) 364-8671

Owners
Karen Olson

Cuisine
New American

Days Open
Open Mon.-Sat. for dinner

Pricing
Dinner for one, without tax, tip, or drinks: $40-$60

Dress Code
Business casual

Reservations
Recommended

Parking
Garage nearby

Features
Private room/parties, entertainment, near theater, live Jazz Saturday nights, cyber bar

Credit Cards
AE, VC, MC, DS

La Bergerie

Main dining room

Directions

In the heart of Old Town, 10 min. from Reagan National Airport

218 North Lee Street
Alexandria, VA 22314
PH: (703) 683-1007
FAX: (703) 519-6114
www.La Bergerie.com

Owners
Laurent Janowsky

Cuisine
French and Basque

Days Open
Open Mon.-Sat. for lunch, daily for dinner

Pricing
Dinner for one, without tax, tip, or drinks: $20-$40

Dress Code
Business casual

Reservations
Recommended

Parking
Garage across the street

Features
Private room/parties

Credit Cards
AE, VC, MC, CB, DC, DS

Serving award-winning French and Basque cuisine since 1976, La Bergerie is renowned for its intimate charming atmosphere, professionalism and friendly service. Whether it's an intimate lunch or dinner, a special occasion party, or a business affair, the staff is always on hand to pay close attention to the smallest details and to make sure guests enjoy a wonderful dining experience. "Among the house specialties are lobster bisque fresh foie gras, Dover sole, venison chops and dessert soufflés."

Large banquet room

Seared foie gras

Gold Banquet Room

AWARD WINNER
SINCE 1997

446

Clifton Inn

Arriving at the Clifton Inn

Off Route 729, on North Milton Road, 30 min. from Charlottesville/Albemarle Airport

1296 Clifton Inn Drive
Charlottesville, VA 22911
PH: (999) 971-1800
www.cliftoninn.com

Whether a romantic candlelight dinner on the verandah, or in the elegant historic dining room, guests will savor Executive Chef Christian Kelly's offerings, balancing the flavors of specialty meats -- Black Angus beef, veal and lamb -- with farm vegetables and fruits and berries freshly harvested. Herbs and edible flowers are grown in Clifton's gardens, the bread is baked on the premises, and desserts change to reflect the seasons.

Clifton's historic dining room

Blueberry soup

Lemon tart

Owners
T. Mitchell Willey

Cuisine
Contemporary European with southern influence

Days Open
Open daily for dinner

Pricing
Dinner for one, without tax, tip, or drinks: $40-$60

Dress Code
Business casual

Reservations
Recommended

Parking
Free on site

Features
Private room/parties, outdoor dining, entertainment, near theater, cigar/cognac events

Credit Cards
AE, VC, MC, DS

AWARD WINNER
SINCE 1999

447

L' Auberge Chez Francois

Patio dining

A French country inn situated in the verdant hills of northern Virginia, this gastronomic delight satisfies our secret longings to escape to a peaceful spot to be pampered and revived. The restaurant has received national acclaim for its fine French-Alsatian cuisine, and the accommodating service and homemade pastries and desserts create a harmony to be cherished.

L'entrecôte

Owner François Haeringer

Dining room

At Springvale and Walker roads, 30 min. from Washington Dulles International Airport

332 Springvale Road
Great Falls, VA 22066
PH: (703) 759-3800
www.laubergechezfrancois.com

Owners
François Haeringer

Cuisine
French-Alsatian

Days Open
Open Tues.-Sun. for dinner

Pricing
Dinner for one,
without tax, tip, or drinks:
$40-$60

Dress Code
Business casual

Reservations
Required

Parking
Free on site

Features
Private parties, outdoor dining

Credit Cards
AE, VC, MC, DC, DS

AWARD WINNER
SINCE 1992

Maestro

Maestro's open kitchen

Directions

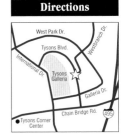

Located in The Ritz-Carlton, Tysons Corner, 16 miles west of Washington, DC, and 20 min. from Dulles International Airport

1700 Tysons Boulevard
McLean, VA 22102
PH: (703) 821-1515
FAX: (703) 821-1520
www.maestrorestaurant.com

Owners
The Ritz-Carlton,
Tysons Corner

Cuisine
Contemporary Italian

Days Open
Open daily for breakfast,
Tues.-Sat. for dinner,
Sunday for brunch.

Pricing
Dinner for one,
without tax, tip, or drinks:
$60-$80

Dress Code
Jacket required

Reservations
Recommended

Parking
Complimentary valet,
garage nearby

Features
Private room/parties

Credit Cards
AE, VC, MC, CB, DC, DS

The critically acclaimed, contemporary Italian cuisine of Chef Fabio Trabocchi combined with gracious service, and an impressive wine selection makes Maestro the ideal restaurant for those celebrating any occasion or simply desiring a night out. With the focal point of the dining room an open kitchen, diners may watch the preparation of signature dishes such as lobster ravioli in a ginger and port wine, wild turbot smoked in hay, and "21st Century" Rossini-style beef.

Table sculptures made from silverware

*Sommelier Vincent Feraud,
Chef Fabio Trabocchi,
Maître d' Emanuele Fissore*

AWARD WINNER
SINCE 2004

Lemaire

The Conservatory

Lemaire, named for Etienne Lemaire, President Thomas Jefferson's maître d'hôtel´, is Richmond's only AAA Five Diamond restaurant. Etienne Lemaire is widely credited with introducing the fine art of cooking with wines, and the restaurant honors its namesake, as well as Thomas Jefferson's own fondness for food prepared with light sauces and garden-fresh herbs. The menu features updated regional Southern cuisine, with classical European and contemporary American influences.

The Library

The Valentine Room

AWARD WINNER
SINCE 1997

In downtown Richmond, near the Convention Center and 20 min. from Richmond International Airport

The Jefferson Hotel
101 West Franklin Street
Richmond, VA 23220
PH: (804) 788-8000
FAX: (804) 649-4624
www.jefferson-hotel.com

Owners
The Jefferson Hotel

Cuisine
Regional

Days Open
Open daily for breakfast, Mon.-Fri. for lunch, Mon.-Sat. for dinner

Pricing
Dinner for one, without tax, tip, or drinks: $60-$80

Dress Code
Jacket and tie required

Reservations
Recommended

Parking
Complimentary valet

Features
Private room/parties, wine events

Credit Cards
AE, VC, MC, DC, DS

The Regency Room at The Hotel Roanoke

The luxurious interior of The Regency Room

Since 1938, The Regency Room at The Hotel Roanoke has been the standard by which other area restaurants are measured. Presidents, rock stars, beauty queens, and dignitaries from around the world have delighted in our signature southern delicacies such as lump crab cakes, peanut soup, and spoon bread – recipes that date to the Hotel's opening in 1882.

Executive Chef Billie Raper displays one of his finest dishes, chicken bourguignonne

Hotel Roanoke & Conference Center, nestled in the Roanoke Valley

AWARD WINNER
SINCE 2003

Directions

Located on Shenandoah Ave. in the heart of downtown Roanoke, 10 min. from Roanoke Regional Airport

110 Shenandoah Avenue
Roanoke, VA 24016
PH: (540) 985-5900
FAX: (540) 853-8290
www.hotelroanoke.com

Owners
Virginia Tech

Cuisine
Continental

Days Open
Open daily for dinner

Pricing
Dinner for one, without tax, tip, or drinks: $20-$40

Dress Code
Jacket and tie suggested

Reservations
Recommended

Parking
Valet, free on site

Features
Private room/parties, outdoor dining, entertainment, near theater

Credit Cards
AE, VC, MC, CB, DC, JCB, DS

Tivoli Restaurant

Main dining room

Just west of the Key Bridge, 5 min. from Reagan National Airport

W ith award-winning wines, fresh-ly made pastas, and daily specials of seafood and game, Tivoli Restaurant offers the finest Northern Italian dining experience in the Washington, D.C., area. The sparkling dining room and personable and attentive service make a meal at Tivoli a memorable affair. A generous pre-theater menu is available for those attending performances at the Kennedy Center, across the Potomac a mere five minutes away.

Ravioli

Chef/Owner Klaus Helmin

AWARD WINNER
SINCE 1992

1700 North Moore Street
Rosslyn, VA 22209
PH: (703) 524-8900
FAX: (703) 524-4971
www.erols.com/tivolirestau-rant

Owners
Klaus Helmin

Cuisine
Northern Italian

Days Open
Open Mon.-Fri. for lunch, Mon.-Sat. for dinner

Pricing
Dinner for one, without tax, tip, or drinks: $20-$40

Dress Code
Business casual

Reservations
Recommended

Parking
Free on site

Features
Private room/parties, near theater

Credit Cards
AE, VC, MC, CB, DC, DS

Sam & Harry's Tysons Corner

Fireplace room

Nestled along northern Virginia's high tech corridor, Sam & Harry's Tysons Corner is a classic American steakhouse featuring prime aged beef, premium seafood, award-winning wines and personalized service. Sam & Harry's has been the "power" restaurant for business executives since its opening in 1998. Handsomely decorated with rich mahogany, sparkling leaded glass windows, portraits of classic jazz musicians, and cozy leather banquettes, Sam & Harry's is the perfect setting for intimate dinner parties, business dinners, and grand celebrations.

Signature steak sauce

Owners Larry Work and Michael Sternberg

AWARD WINNER
SINCE 2002

Lobster and wine

Directions

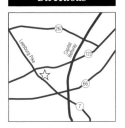

On Leesburg Pike (Route 7), 15 min. from Dulles International Airport

8240 Leesburg Pike
Vienna, VA 22182
PH: (703) 448-0088
FAX: (703) 448-0104
www.samandharrys.com

Owners
Larry Work and
Michael Sternberg

Cuisine
Steakhouse

Days Open
Open Mon.-Sat. for dinner

Pricing
Dinner for one,
without tax, tip, or drinks:
$40-$60

Dress Code
Business casual

Reservations
Recommended

Parking
Valet after 5:30 pm

Features
Private room/parties

Credit Cards
AE, VC, MC, CB, DC, DS

The Dining Room at Ford's Colony

Impeccable service

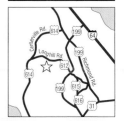

Four miles from Colonial Williamsburg, 35 min. from Newport News/Williamsburg Airport and 1 hr. from Richmond International

240 Ford's Colony Drive
Williamsburg, VA 23188
PH: (757) 258-4107
FAX: (757) 258-4168
www.fordscolony.com

This highly acclaimed restaurant at the Ford's Colony Resort, four miles from Colonial Williamsburg, showcases the modern American cuisine of Executive Chef David Everett. The elegant Georgian-style dining room has intimate seating and a golf course view. Details are important here: The wine list is extensive and fresh local ingredients are mixed with the finest of imports to produce a truly world-class dining experience.

Chef's table

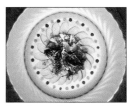

Lobster and green apple salad with sea urchin vinaigrette

Owners
Richard J. Ford

Cuisine
Regional American

Days Open
Open Tues.-Sat. for dinner

Pricing
Dinner for one,
without tax, tip, or drinks:
Price fix:$52 or $86

Dress Code
Jacket required, tie optional

Reservations
Recommended

Parking
Free on site

Features
Private room/parties,
cigar/cognac events

Credit Cards
AE, VC, MC

David Everett in herb garden

AWARD WINNER
SINCE 1993

Regency Room

Directions

45 min. from Norfolk and Richmond Int'l Airports and 20 min. from Newport News-Williamsburg Int'l Airport

136 East Francis Street
Williamsburg, VA 23187
PH: 1-800-361-5261
FAX: (757) 565-1776

An exquisite setting

The Regency Room at the world-renowned Williamsburg Inn was inspired by elements of the royal pavilion at Brighton, England. Palm-leafed columns, crystal chandeliers, silk draperies, and leather furniture create an exquisite setting for a memorable dining experience. Acclaimed for its innovative "new American regional" cuisine, the Regency Room culinary team uses the freshest foods from both around the world and the Virginia Tidewater region. This Award-winning restaurant presents live music nightly and dancing on Friday and Saturday.

Owners
Colonial Williamsburg Foundation

Cuisine
American regional

Days Open
Open daily for breakfast, lunch, and dinner, Sunday for brunch

Pricing
Dinner for one, without tax, tip, or drinks: $60-$80

Dress Code
Jacket and tie required for dinner. Jacket for Sunday brunch

Reservations
Recommended

Parking
Free on site

Features
Private room/parties, outdoor dining, entertainment, food and wine events

Credit Cards
AE, VC, MC, CB, DC

AWARD WINNER
SINCE 1992

River'd Inn

On State Road 663 (Artz Road), 90 min. from Regan National Airport

1972 Artz Road
Woodstock, VA
PH: (540) 459-5369, (800) 637-4561
FAX: (540) 459-8241
www.riverdinn.com

Owners
Diana Lurey and Daniel Fauver

Cuisine
Regional American

Days Open
Open Thurs.-Sat. for lunch, Sunday brunch, Wed.-Sun. for dinner

Pricing
Dinner for one, without tax, tip, or drinks: $20-$40

Dress Code
Nice Casual

Reservations
Recommended

Parking
Free on site

Features
Private room/parties, outdoor dining, wedding receptions, corporate retreats

Credit Cards
AE, VC, MC, CB, DC, DS

The River'd Inn is a luxury country inn offering fine restaurant dining open to the public, and overnight accommodations. The River'd Inn Restaurant offers quiet meals in elegant dining rooms, each with its own distinctive fireplace and intimate seating. Contemporary regional American cuisine utilizing local, fresh ingredients is served in a rich, warm atmosphere. The menu changes seasonally. An extensive selection of beers, wines, and spirits available.

Poached Maine lobster and asparagus salad

Comtemporary American cuisine

AWARD WINNER
SINCE 1999

The Great Room

Hemingway's

Romantic retreat

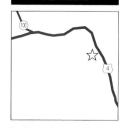

On Route 4, two-and-a-half miles east of the junction of northbound Route 100, 30 min. from Rutland Regional Airport

4988 U.S. Route 4
Killington, VT 05751
PH: (802) 422-3886
FAX: (802) 422-3468
www.hemingwaysrestaurant.com

A warm, gracious evening awaits in this beautifully restored 1860 country home. You can dine fireside, in the old world romance of a stone wine cellar, or regally under a vaulted ceiling. Cited by *Esquire* as "One of the most romantic restaurants in America" and by *Food & Wine* as one of the "Top 25 Restaurants in America." Hand crafted American cuisine features fresh Atlantic seafoods, New England game birds, plus steak and vegetarian specialties. Robert Mondavi Culinary Award of Excellence

Applewood smoked salmon and salmon tartare

Linda and Ted Fondulas

Owners
Ted and Linda Fondulas

Cuisine
International

Days Open
Open Wed.-Sun. for dinner (Closed Mondays and most Tuesdays)

Pricing
Dinner for one, without tax, tip, or drinks: $55-$62

Dress Code
Dressy casual

Reservations
Recommended

Parking
Free on site

Features
Private room/parties

Credit Cards
AE, VC, MC, CB, DC

Fine dining

Wine Spectator
AWARD OF EXCELLENCE

DiRoNA
AWARD WINNER
SINCE 1992

457

The Inn at Sawmill Farm

Dining room

On Route 100, 1 hr. 15 min. from Connecticut's Bradley International Airport

Crosstown Road and Route 100
West Dover, VT 05356
PH: (802) 464-8131
FAX: (802) 464-1130
www.theinnatsawmillfarm.com

Owners
Rodney Williams Jr.

Cuisine
American, Continental

Days Open
Open daily for dinner

Pricing
Dinner for one,
without tax, tip, or drinks:
$40-$60

Dress Code
Business casual

Reservations
Recommended

Parking
Free on site

Features
Private parties, entertainment (weekends only)

Credit Cards
AE, VC, MC, DC

R aves reverberate through the Vermont mountains praising the culinary feats of Chef/Owner "Brill" Williams at his Inn at Sawmill Farm. This fine Relais & Chateaux member and Mobil Four-Star recipient delights guests with selections such as potato-crusted black sea bass on a bed of wild mushrooms, farm-raised squab with a Perigueux sauce, and the ever-demanded rack of lamb. The wine list has garnered *Wine Spectator* magazine's Grand Award.

Smoked salmon with caviar

Chef/Owner "Brill" Williams and Sous-Chef James Hadley

Wine cellar

GRAND
AWARD

AWARD WINNER
SINCE 1992

Hermitage Inn

L ocated just a bit off the beaten path, The Hermitage, with its reputation for good, well prepared food, served with care, has been widely acclaimed throughout the country in newspapers, magazines, and books. Game birds are featured in the Chef's specials including, pheasant, goose, duck, and partridge. Our wine cellar has been the recipient of *Wine Spectator* Magazine's Grand Award every year since 1984, and stocks 40,000 bottles, representing over 2,000 labels.

The Hermitage Inn in summer

Owner James McGovern selects wine

Chef Eric Trites

James McGovern and his wife, Lois

GRAND AWARD

DiRōNA

AWARD WINNER
SINCE 2003

Directions

On Coldbrook Road at Route 100 North, 1¹/₂ hrs. from Albany International, and Bradley Field (CT) airports

Coldbrook Road
Wilmington, VT 05363
PH: (802) 464-3511
FAX: (802) 464-2688
www.hermitageinn.com
e-mail:hermitag@sover.net

Owners
James L. McGovern III

Cuisine
Continental

Days Open
Open daily for dinner,
Sunday for brunch

Pricing
Dinner for one,
without tax, tip, or drinks:
$35-$45

Dress Code
Casual

Reservations
Recommended

Parking
Free on site

Features
Private room/parties,
entertainment, near summer
theater, cigar/cognac
events, wine tasting

Credit Cards
AE, VC, MC, DC

Campagne & Cafe Campagne

Pike Place Market

Located in the heart of Pike Place Market, this cozy establishment serves award-winning French country food in an elegant dining room overlooking Elliott Bay. Drawing inspiration from the sun-drenched cuisine of Southern France, the chef uses only the finest ingredients, many from the Pacific Northwest. Signature dishes include foie gras terrine and grilled lamb loin, and lamb Crepinette with potato galette, niçoise and Picholine olives.

Cafe Campagne

Courtyard

Lounge

AWARD WINNER
SINCE 1992

Directions

At Pike Place Market, 20 min. from Seattle-Tacoma International Airport

86 Pine Street
Seattle, WA 98101
PH: (206) 728-2800
FAX: (206) 448-7562
www.campagnerestaurant.com

Owners
Peter Lewis/Simon Snellgrovel

Cuisine
Country French

Days Open
Open daily for lunch, and dinner, weekends for brunch

Pricing
Dinner for one, without tax, tip, or drinks: $40-$60

Dress Code
Business casual

Reservations
Recommended

Parking
Adjacent lots

Features
Outdoor dining, near theater

Credit Cards
AE, VC, MC, CB, DC

Canlis

Dining room

On Aurora just south of the Aurora Bridge. Two miles outside of downtown, and 30 min. from the Seattle-Tacoma International Airport

For more than 50 years, the Canlis family has made their restaurant an extension of their home. The award-winning Pacific Northwest menu — Pacific king salmon and seared rare ahi are particularly popular — extensive wine list, and elegant surroundings are a Seattle tradition. Enjoy being pampered with impeccable service while enjoying the panoramic views of Lake Union and the dramatic Cascade Mountains.

Alice and Chris Canlis

Blazing hearth in foyer

Exquisite seasonal cuisine

AWARD WINNER
SINCE 1993

2576 Aurora Avenue North
Seattle, WA 98109
PH: (206) 283-3313
FAX: (206) 283-1766
www.canlis.com

Owners
Chris and Alice Canlis

Cuisine
Pacific Northwest

Days Open
Open Mon.-Sat. for dinner

Pricing
Dinner for one,
without tax, tip, or drinks:
$40-$60

Dress Code
Dressy

Reservations
Required

Parking
Valet

Features
Private room/parties, entertainment

Credit Cards
AE, VC, MC, CB, DC, DS

Metropolitan Grill

The Metropolitan Grill "experience"

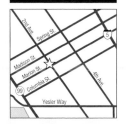

On the corner of Second Ave. and Marion St. in the heart of the financial district, 30 min. from Seattle-Tacoma International Airport

820 Second Avenue
Seattle, WA 98104
PH: (206) 624-3287
FAX: (206) 389-0042
www.themetropolitangrill.com

Nationally recognized as one of the finest steakhouses in the country, "The Met" features 28-day custom aged beef grilled over imported mesquite. The classic steakhouse menu features signature bone-in selections Prime Delmonico, and Porterhouse, as well as Chateaubriand carved tableside. The cellar of premier wines has received national recognition, including *Wine Spectator* Magazine's "Best of Award of Excellence." Bustling with energy, the Metropolitan Grill prides itself on its professional, veteran waitstaff and sommeliers.

Enjoy the best steak in town

The lounge

Owners
Ron Cohn

Cuisine
Prime Steaks

Days Open
Open Mon.-Fri. for lunch, daily for dinner

Pricing
Dinner for one, without tax, tip, or drinks: $40-$60

Dress Code
Business casual

Reservations
Recommended

Parking
Valet

Features
Private room/parties, near theater

Credit Cards
AE, VC, MC, CB, DC, JCB, DS

Cellar of premier wines

AWARD WINNER
SINCE 2003

Place Pigalle Restaurant and Bar

Place Pigalle... a charming bistro

Directions

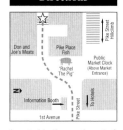

Located in the south end of the Pike Place Market to the left of, and behind, Pike Place Fish ("Flying Fish Company"), 15 min. from SeaTac International Airport

Place Pigalle specializes in seasonal menus combining local ingredients with a variety of culinary traditions. The resulting dishes "always have been artful, always entertaining, always fresh...disarmingly successful." Couple such critical acclaim with a wonderful Elliott Bay and Olympic Mountain view, an award-winning wine list, and a bar that specializes in the unusual and you have the reasons for this Pike Place Market restaurant's success. "Since 1982, this charming bistro has been a romantic destination for diners and drinkers savvy enough to find it." A sunny patio opens in summer.

After dinner selections

Overlooking Elliott Bay

Pike Place Market
81 Pike Street
Seattle, WA 98101
PH: (206) 624-1756

Owner
Bill Frank

Cuisine
Pacific Northwest

Days Open
Open Mon.-Sat. for lunch and dinner

Pricing
Dinner for one,
without tax, tip, or drinks:
$20-$40

Dress Code
Business casual

Reservations
Recommended

Parking
Valet (Thurs.-Sat.), garage nearby (free validation)

Features
Private parties,
outdoor dining

Credit Cards
AE, VC, MC, CB, DC, DS

AWARD WINNER
SINCE 1997

Ray's Boathouse

Ray's Boathouse...a Seattle icon

On Seaview Avenue overlooking the Puget Sound, 30 min. from Seattle-Tacoma International Airport

6049 Seaview Avenue NW
Seattle, WA 98107
PH: (206) 789-3770
FAX: (206) 781-1960
www.rays.com

L ike the red 50-foot "RAY'S" sign near its front door, Ray's Boathouse has become a Seattle icon that has changed the way the northwest eats seafood. Ray's built its reputation on seasonal dishes prepared simply to highlight the flavors of impeccably fresh seafood, and locally grown produce. In celebration of its' 30th anniversary, Ray's has released its first cookbook in April 2003 titled, *Ray's Boathouse: Seafood Secrets of the Pacific Northwest.*

Copper River salmon with Pinot Noir butter sauce

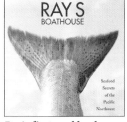

Ray's first cookbook

Seafood Margarita

AWARD WINNER
SINCE 1996

Owners
Elizabeth Gingrich, Earl Lasher, Jack Sikma and Russ Wohlers

Cuisine
Northwest seafood

Days Open
Open daily for lunch and dinner

Pricing
Dinner for one, without tax, tip, or drinks: $40-$60

Dress Code
Business casual

Reservations
Recommended

Parking
Valet

Features
Private room/parties, outdoor dining

Credit Cards
AE, VC, MC, CB, DC, DS

Rover's

A unique dining experience in Seattle

Chef Thierry Rautureau has been honored with the James Beard Award for his unique cuisine. *Zagat* Travel Guide has given Rover's Restaurant its "Highest Food Rating." *Gourmet* Magazine has awarded Rover's "Top Table", "Top Food", "Top Presentation" and *Seattle* Magazine honored Rover's with the title "Seattle's Best Overall Restaurant 2001." Chef Thierry is the recipient of the DiRōNA Ella Brennan "Distinguished Dining Ambassador Award."

Photo credits: Frank Harlan

The Chef in the Hat

Lobster and asparagus martini with white sturgeon caviar

AWARD WINNER
SINCE 1997

Symphony of desserts

Directions

Near downtown Seattle on East Madison, 40 min. from Seattle-Tacoma International Airport

2808 East Madison Street
Seattle, WA 98112
PH: (206) 325-7442
FAX: (206) 325-1092
www.rovers-seattle.com

Owners
Thierry Rautureau

Cuisine
Northwest contemporary with a French accent

Days Open
Open Tues.-Sat. for dinner

Pricing
Dinner for one, without tax, tip, or drinks:
Price fix: $75, $85, $115

Dress Code
Business casual

Reservations
Required

Parking
Free on site

Features
Private room/parties

Credit Cards
AE, VC, MC, DC

The Herbfarm

The Herbfarm Restaurant

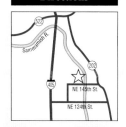

On 145th Street east of the Chateau Ste. Michelle winery, 35 min. from Seattle-Tacoma International Airport

14590 NE 145th Street
Woodinville, WA 98072
PH: (425) 485-5300
FAX: (425) 424-2925
www.theherbfarm.com

Owners
Ron Zimmerman and Carrie Van Dyck

Cuisine
Seasonal Pacific Northwest

Days Open
Open Thur.-Sun. for dinner

Pricing
Dinner for one,
without tax, tip, or drinks:
Price fix: $149-$179
(includes 5-6 wines)

Dress Code
Dressy casual

Reservations
Required

Parking
Free on site

Features
Private room/parties, entertainment, shared tables for single travelers, suites, near wineries, gardens

Credit Cards
AE, VC, MC

E ach week The Herbfarm Restaurant chooses the best from farm, forest, and sea to create thematic 9-course dinners showcasing the culinary glories of the Pacific Northwest. Dinner is one seating, a 9-course chef-created menu including six matched wines. Wine can also be chosen from the 1,400 selections of the award-winning cellar. Dinner begins with a garden tour. The Herbfarm also offers overnight suites with garden views.

Elegant private dining in the Founder's room

Romantic overnight accommodations

Cozy corner in the dining room

AWARD WINNER
SINCE 2003

466

The Immigrant
Restaurant & Winery

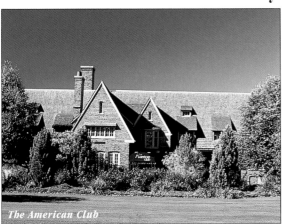

The American Club

South of the junction of Highways 23 and Y, 1 hr. from Milwaukee's General Mitchell International Airport

The American Club
Highland Drive
Kohler, WI 53044
PH: (920) 457-8000 or (800) 344-2838
FAX: (920) 457-0299
DestinationKohler.com

Owners
Kohler Co.

Cuisine
Contemporary

Days Open
Open Mon.-Sat. for dinner (Memorial Day-Labor Day)
Tues.-Sat. for dinner (Labor Day-Memorial Day)

Pricing
Dinner for one, without tax, tip, or drinks: $40-$60

Dress Code
Jacket required

Reservations
Recommended

Parking
Free on site

Features
Private parties, entertainment

Credit Cards
AE, VC, MC, CB, DC, DS, JCB

The Immigrant Restaurant & Winery is located at The American Club, the Midwest's only AAA Five Diamond Resort Hotel and a member of Historic Hotels of America. Contemporary cuisine, fine wines, and exceptional service are the hallmarks of this restaurant. Renovated in 2003, the Immigrant features a signature wine room and a cheese room that focuses on regional, artisan cheeses. A tasting of yellowfin tuna and grilled elk chop are among the award-winning specialties.

Elk chop

The English Room

The Dutch Room

AWARD OF EXCELLENCE

DiRoNA
AWARD WINNER
SINCE 1992

467

Bartolotta's Lake Park Bistro

A Milwaukee landmark

Housed in a landmark building overlooking Lake Michigan, Bartolotta's Lake Park Bistro was an instant classic upon its opening in 1995. Owner Joe Bartolotta and his brother Paul, a James Beard Award-winning chef, brought in Chef Adam Siegel to oversee Milwaukee's most authentic French bistro. Specialties include foie gras, filet au poivre, and the ethereal crème brulée. The *Milwaukee Journal* named Bartolotta's Lake Park Bistro the city's Best New Restaurant of 1995 and has awarded it a four-star rating ever since.

Dining room

Zinc bar

The Bistro, by Guy Buffet

3133 East Newberry Boulevard
Milwaukee, WI 53211
PH: (414) 962-6300
FAX (414) 962-4248
www.bartolottas.com

Owners
Joe Bartolotta

Cuisine
French bistro

Days Open
Open Mon.-Fri., for lunch,
Mon.-Sun. for dinner, Sun. for brunch

Pricing
Dinner for one,
without tax, tip, or drinks:
$20-$40

Dress Code
Business casual

Reservations
Recommended

Parking
Free on site

Features
Private room/parties

Credit Cards
AE, VC, MC, DC

AWARD OF EXCELLENCE

DiRōNA
AWARD WINNER
SINCE 1999

Eddie Martini's

Warm Welcome

The experience is a fine-dining approach unequalled in Milwaukee. The aesthetics and menu are classic 1940's era steakhouse — filet mignon, NY strip, straight up or au poivre, Porterhouse, creamed spinach, garlic mashed potatoes, and sautéed wild mushrooms. Eddie Martini's is classic tradition personified by white tablecloths and service of an era gone by. Napkins float into your lap; ice cubes clink against polished glass…life is good. Eddie Martini's is a throwback to a time when restaurants were known for art, style, elegance, wine, and creative thinking.

Older vintages

Ocean Martini

Intimate dining

Directions

On Watertown Plank, 20 min. from General Mitchell International Airport

8612 Watertown Plank
Wauwatosa, WI 53226
PH: (414) 771-6680
FAX: (414) 771-5034

Owners
Joseph M. DeRosa

Cuisine
Contemporary American

Days Open
Open Mon.-Fri. for lunch,
daily for dinner

Pricing
Dinner for one,
without tax, tip, or drinks:
$40-$60

Dress Code
Business casual

Reservations
Recommended

Parking
Free on site

Features
Semi-private room

Credit Cards
AE, VC, MC, CB, DC, DS

AWARD WINNER
SINCE 2004

The Granary
at Spring Creek Ranch

Spring Creek Ranch

Atop East Gros Ventre Butte just outside of town and 15 min. from Jackson Hole Airport

1800 Spirit Dance Road
Jackson Hole, WY 83001
PH: (307) 733-8833
FAX: (307) 733-1524
www.springcreekranch.com

Owners
Stephen Price

Cuisine
Regional American

Days Open
Open daily for dinner

Pricing
Dinner for one,
without tax, tip, or drinks:
$40-$60

Dress Code
Casual

Reservations
Recommended

Parking
Free on site

Features
Outdoor dining,
entertainment

Credit Cards
AE, VC, MC, CB, DC, DS

Perched atop the Gros Ventre Butte overlooking the Teton Mountains, The Granary is, to say the very least, an unforgettable dining experience. Part of Spring Creek Ranch, Wyoming's award-winning resort, The Granary offers superb cuisine and views that elevate fine dining to unprecedented heights. Elk tenderloin with black bay sauce, lamb loin with garlic flan, and garlic-and-sesame-encrusted rainbow trout are among the memorable specialties.

Fireside dining

Priceless Teton views

Wine Spectator

AWARD
OF
EXCELLENCE

DiRōNA
AWARD WINNER
SINCE 1997

La Chaumière Restaurant

Patio area

On 17th Avenue SW three blocks from Stampede Park, 15 min. from Calgary International Airport

La Chaumière Restaurant serves French market cuisine in an elegant dining room or comfortable patio overlooking Rouleauville Square. Executive Chef C. Bob Matthews prepares an imaginative menu with entrées such as ahi tuna with bok choy and spinach, sesame beurre blanc with sweet chilies, and veal medallions and foie gras with Madeira sauce. The extensive wine list has 750 selections from around the world.

Main dining room

Banquet room

The wine cellar

139 17th Avenue SW
Calgary, Alberta
Canada T2S 0A1
PH: (403) 228-5690
FAX: (403) 228-4448
www.lachaumiere.ca

Owners
Joseph DeAngelis

Cuisine
French Market

Days Open
Open Mon.-Fri. for lunch,
Mon.-Sat. for dinner

Pricing
Dinner for one,
without tax, tip, or drinks:
$20-$40

Dress Code
Business casual

Reservations
Recommended

Parking
Free on site

Features
Private room/parties, outdoor dining, cigar/cognac
events

Credit Cards
AE, VC, MC, DC, ER

AWARD WINNER
SINCE 1993

The Owl's Nest Dining Room

4 Diamonds-*The Owl's Nest* celebrates its 39th year with award winning International and French cuisine, impeccable first-class service, and an extensive top-flight wine list. Tableside prepared lobster bisque or Kobe beef tartare and extravagant entrées of free-range poultry, exotic game, seafood, and naturally grown galloway beef adorn the menu. Alberta producers provide premium ingredients for Executive Chef Martin Heuser. Signature chocolate-covered cherries and sumptuous, delicate soufflés are a voluptuous finale.

Rack of lamb

Signature chocolate-covered cherries

Tempting desserts

Wine Spectator

AWARD OF EXCELLENCE

DiRoNA

AWARD WINNER
SINCE 1993

Directions

In The Westin Calgary, near entertainment/shopping districts, 30 min. from Calgary International Airport

320 4th Avenue SW
Calgary, Alberta,
Canada T2P 2S6
PH: (403) 266-1611
FAX: (403) 233-7471
www.starwoodhotels.com

Owners
The Westin Calgary

Cuisine
International with French accents

Days Open
Open Mon.-Fri. for lunch,
Mon.-Sat. for dinner

Pricing
Dinner for one,
without tax, tip, or drinks:
$20-$40

Dress Code
Business casual

Reservations
Recommended

Parking
Valet, underground garage

Features
Private parties

Credit Cards
AE, VC, MC, CB, DC, ER,
JCB, DS

Post Hotel Dining Room

Dining room

In the Canadian Rockies, 2 hrs. from Calgary Int'l Airport

Set amidst the natural wonders of Banff National Park in the majestic Canadian Rocky Mountains, the Post Hotel Dining Room offers a menu of fresh market cuisine complemented by an award-winning wine list. With over 1,690 selections and an inventory of 28,500 bottles, the wine list has been recognized by achieving *Wine Spectator* Magazine's highest honor, the Grand Award. Fine cognacs and hand-rolled cigars are also available in an adjacent smoking room.

Chef Wolfgang Vogt

Post Hotel
200 Pipestone Road
Lake Louise, Alberta
T0L 1E0 Canada
PH: (403) 522-3989
FAX: (403) 522-3966
www.posthotel.com

Owners
André and George Schwarz

Cuisine
Fresh market cuisine

Days Open
Open daily for breakfast, lunch, and dinner; closed mid-Oct. to mid-Dec.

Pricing
Dinner for one, without tax, tip, or drinks: $50-$75

Dress Code
Smart casual

Reservations
Required

Parking
Free on site

Features
Private room/parties, entertainment, cigar/cognac lounge

Credit Cards
AE, VC, MC

Alberta rack of lamb

GRAND
AWARD

DiRōNA

AWARD WINNER
SINCE 1993

Sooke Harbour House

Stunning views from the dining room

Sooke Harbour House Restaurant is located in a 28-room, luxurious seaside hotel. The romantic candlelit dining room, warmed by a wood-burning fireplace, features spectacular views of the ocean, and towering mountains. The West Coast Canadian cuisine emphasizes seafood, and much of the produce is fresh from the inn's organic vegetable, edible flower, and herb gardens. The restaurant has been rated "2nd Best Country Inn in the World" by *Gourmet Magazine*, and its wine cellar, classified as one of the two best in Canada, received *Wine Spectators* Grand Award.

Owner Frederique Philip lights the dinner candles

Organic hubbard squash and lemon verbena ice cream

Owner Sinclair Philip in the award-winning wine cellar

AWARD WINNER
SINCE 1993

Directions

On Whiffen Spit Rd., 60 min. from Victoria International Airport

1528 Whiffen Spit Road
Sooke, British Columbia
Canada V0S 1N0
PH: (250) 642-3421 or
1-800-889-9688
FAX: (250) 642-6988
www.sookeharbourhouse.com

Owners
Frederique and
Sinclair Philip

Cuisine
West coast Canadian

Days Open
Open daily for dinner (lunch and breakfast for Hotel guests only)

Pricing
Dinner for one,
without tax, tip, or drinks
$40-$60

Dress Code
Casual/business casual

Reservations
Recommended

Parking
Free on site

Features
Private room/parties

Credit Cards
VC, MC, DC, ER, JCB,

C restaurant

Oceanfront dining

Set on Vancouver's scenic waterfront, 30 min. from Vancouver International Airport

1600 Howe Street
Vancouver, British Columbia
Canada V6E 1S3
PH: (604) 681-1164
FAX: (604) 605-8236
www.crestaurant.com

Owners
Harry Kambolis

Cuisine
Contemporary seafood

Days Open
Open daily for dinner (open Mon.-Fri. for lunch, May-Sept.)

Pricing
Dinner for one,
without tax, tip, or drinks:
$60-$80
(or)
Prix fixe: $90

Dress Code
Business casual

Reservations
Recommended

Parking
Valet

Features
Private room/parties, outdoor dining

Credit Cards
AE, VC, MC, DC, En Route

Elegantly set on Vancouver's scenic waterfront, C restaurant is the definitive seafood restaurant in Canada. Executive Chef Robert Clark, and owner Harry Kambolis set the standards by using the best quality seafood available, sourcing products from fishermen and producers. The wine program compliments those standards, with an array of the best of BC, and around the globe selections. Diners revel in the variety of fresh wild BC salmon, oysters, halibut, and yes, steak is available as well.

Setting the standard

Welcome to C restaurant

Private dining in the wine attic

AWARD WINNER
SINCE 2004

Caffé dé Medici

Private dining room

On Robson Street between Burrard and Thurlow, 30 min. from Vancouver International Airport

1025 Robson Street, #109
Vancouver, British Columbia,
Canada V6E 1A9
PH: (604) 669-9322
FAX: (604) 669-3771
e-mail: yourhost@
caffedemedici.com
www.caffedemedici.com

Owners
Steve Punzo and Dean Punzo

Cuisine
Italian/West coast flair

Days Open
Open Mon.-Fri. for lunch,
daily for dinner

Pricing
Dinner for one,
without tax, tip, or drinks:
$20-$40

Dress Code
Business casual/
casual for patio

Reservations
Recommended

Parking
Garage nearby

Features
Private room/parties, out-door dining, near theater, themed dinner events

Credit Cards
AE, VC, MC, DS, and Debit cards

Caffé dé Medici has gained renown for its superb service, outstanding cuisine, and extensive wine list. Executive Chef Aron Zipursky infuses traditional Italian taste and modern variety into all the entrées. The seafood, unique pasta dishes, and antipasto are all prepared fresh. Specialties include ravioli filled with wild mushrooms and ricotta cheese topped with carmelized pears and walnuts, and grilled milk-fed veal chop with mushroom ragout and sage sauce. Attention to detail makes Caffé dé Medici ideal for important luncheons or candlelight dinners.

Roasted rack of lamb in basil jus

Front dining room

AWARD WINNER
SINCE 1993

Cioppino's Mediterranean Grill & Enoteca

Main dining room

Chef Pino Posteraro

Cioppino's Mediterranean Grill & Enoteca's patios

AWARD WINNER
SINCE 2003

Cioppino's wood beamed ceilings and terracotta-tiled floors provide the ideal Mediterranean setting. The menu offers guests a variety of selections designed to entice all appetites. Cold and hot appetizer dishes include tuna and smoked trout tartare with apples and char broiled calamari with lemon marinated tomatoes, capers and Ligurian olives. Main course items include Chef Pino Posteraro's special Cioppino of sea bass, scampi, scallops, prawns, and mussels in a spicy bouillabaisse broth.

Directions

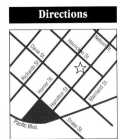

On Hamilton Street, 30 min. from Vancouver International Airport

1129-1133 Hamilton Street
Vancouver, British Columbia
Canada, V6B 5P6
PH: (604) 688-7466
FAX: (604) 688-7411
www.cioppinosyaletown.com

Owners
Pino Posteraro

Cuisine
Italian/Mediterranean

Days Open
Open Mon.-Fri. for lunch,
Mon.-Sat. for dinner

Pricing
Dinner for one,
without tax, tip, or drinks:
$40-$60

Dress Code
Business casual

Reservations
Recommended

Parking
Valet

Features
Private room/parties, outdoor dining, near theater

Credit Cards
AE, VC, MC, DC, En Route

The Five Sails Restaurant

Stunning views

In Pan Pacific Hotel on Canada Place, 30 min. from Vancouver International Airport

999 Canada Place
Suite 300
Vancouver, British Columbia
Canada V6C 3L5
PH: (604) 662-8111
FAX: (604) 891-2864
www.dinepanpacific.com

Owners
Pan Pacific Hotel

Cuisine
Pacific Northwest/Seafood

Days Open
Open daily for dinner

Pricing
Dinner for one,
without tax, tip, or drinks:
$50-$70

Dress Code
Business casual

Reservations
Recommended

Parking
Valet, free on site

Features
Private room/parties

Credit Cards
AE, VC, MC, DC, En Route

L ocated in the Pan Pacific Hotel with a spectacular setting overlooking Vancouver's harbour and mountains. The Five Sails is the recipient of numerous awards: including the prestigious AAA/CAA Five Diamond for the past 8 years. Executive Chef Ernst Dorfler creates his own unique cuisine with a touch of European and Asian influence. An expansive wine list perfectly complements the menu and is expertly advised by our Sommelier. The Chef's weekly tasting menu offers the best of local seasonal cuisine.

Garlic and almond-crusted rack of lamb

Crispy sea bass

The Five Sails Restaurant

AWARD WINNER
SINCE 1993

Imperial Chinese Seafood Restaurant

Main dining room

At the award-winning Imperial Restaurant in the art deco Marine Building, Executive Chef T. Ip's superb Chinese cuisine is combined with classic French service. The dining room, with floor-to-ceiling windows, offers a magnificent view of the North Shore and its snowcapped mountains. Come for the imaginative dim sum lunch, for which the Imperial Chinese Seafood Restaurant is justly famous.

Main dining room

Variety of succulent courses

Dim sum lunch

AWARD WINNER
SINCE 1993

Directions

In the Marine Building on Burrard Street, 30 min. from Vancouver International Airport

355 Burrard Street
Vancouver, British Columbia,
Canada V6C 2G8
PH: (604) 688-8191
FAX: (604) 688-8466
www.imperialrest.com

Owners
K.L. Wong

Cuisine
Seafood and dim sum

Days Open
Open daily for lunch and dinner

Pricing
Dinner for one,
without tax, tip, or drinks:
$20-$40

Dress Code
Casual

Reservations
Recommended

Parking
Valet after 5:30 p.m.

Features
Private room/parties

Credit Cards
VC, MC, DC

Joe Fortes Seafood & Chop House

Foyer with balcony seating above

Located 50 paces north of Robson Shopping Street, 35 min. form the Vancouver International Airport

Joe Fortes Seafood & Chop House is a classic, turn of the century-styled American Brasserie featuring a soaring two-story high Grande Oyster Bar. The second floor balcony seating overlooks the activity below, and leads to the Roof Garden, resplendent with a diamond-shaped herb garden, and surrounding a heated/covered dining area, with a fireplace, and smoking lounge. Grilled fresh fish is a specialty, with over 100 species of seafood, and 42 types of oysters. The wine cellar boasts 450 labels, predominantly American.

3 tiered Seafood Tower in roof garden

Owner Bud Kanke

777 Thurlow St. at Robson
Vancouver, British Columbia
Canada V6E 3V5
PH: (604) 669-1940
FAX: (604) 669-4426
www.joefortes.ca

Owners
Bud Kanke

Cuisine
American seafood
and chops

Days Open
Open daily for lunch and dinner, Sunday for brunch

Pricing
Dinner for one,
without tax, tip, or drinks:
$40-$60

Dress Code
Business casual

Reservations
Recommended

Parking
Valet

Features
Semi-private rooms/parties,
near Financial District,
and hotels

Credit Cards
AE, VC, MC, DC, JCB, DS

Crab & lobster salad

AWARD WINNER
SINCE 2003

Lumière

One of Canada's "best restaurants"

Directions

10 mins. from downtown on West Broadway at Larch and Trafalgar, 20 min. from Vancouver International Airport

S mall and elegant, Lumière is considered one of Canada's best restaurants, and is the only freestanding restaurant in Canada to receive the prestigious Relais Gourmand designation from Relais & Chateaux. A master of subtle tastes, Chef/Owner Robert Feenie's contemporary Canadian cuisine uses classic, light French techniques with regional ingredients incorporatng Asian influences. The wine program offers a perfect range of both Old World and New World selections, including some of the region's best British Columbia wines. Service is delightful yet formal, and the meal creates a lasting impression.

Tasting Bar

Chef/Owner Rob Feenie

RELAIS & CHATEAUX

AWARD WINNER SINCE 2001

2551 West Broadway
Vancouver, British Columbia, Canada V6K 2E9
PH: (604) 739-8185
FAX: (604) 739-8139
www.lumiere.ca

Owners
Robert Feenie

Cuisine
Modern French with Asian influences

Days Open
Dining room and Tasting Bar open Tues.-Sun. for dinner

Pricing
Dinner for one, without tax, tip, or drinks:
Dining Room $80-$110 (Cdn)
Tasting Bar $25-$40 (Cdn)

Dress Code
Jacket and tie suggested

Reservations
Dining room–recommended
Tasting Bar–not required

Parking
Complimentary valet

Features
Outdoor dining, Tasting Bar

Credit Cards
AE, VC, MC

Raincity Grill

Raincity Grill in Vancouver's West End

Directions

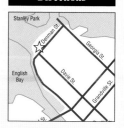

On Denman Street, overlooking English Bay, 30 min. from Vancouver International Airport

Open since 1992, Raincity Grill has been at the forefront of defining regional cuisine in Vancouver. Overlooking English Bay and a parade of ever-changing vistas, Raincity Grill uses local, seasonal ingredients from the Pacific Northwest. Menus are based on availability, changing with the seasons. The wine list reflects the same dedication to the region with an outstanding "by-the-glass" selection. Sample such BC treats as heirloom tomatoes, BC lamb and hand-raised duck, while enjoying the glorious Vancouver sunset.

Defining Pacific Northwest cuisine

1193 Denman Street
Vancouver, BC
Canada V6G 2N1
PH: (604) 685-7337
FAX: (604) 685-7362
www.raincitygrill.com

Owners
Harry Kambolis

Cuisine
Contemporary Regional

Days Open
Open daily for dinner.
Saturday and Sunday
for brunch

Pricing
Dinner for one,
without tax, tip, or drinks:
$40-$60

Dress Code
Casual/Business casual

Reservations
Recommended

Parking
Valet

Features
Private parties, outdoor dining

Credit Cards
AE, VC, MC, DC, En Route

Celebrate all things

Saucy birds...

Wine Spectator
BEST OF
AWARD OF
EXCELLENCE

DiRōNA
AWARD WINNER
SINCE 2004

Restaurant Dubrovnik

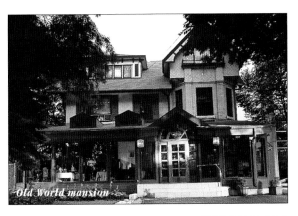

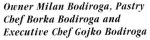
Old World mansion

On Assiniboine Avenue near the Manitoba Legislative Building, 15 min. from Winnipeg International Airport

A part of Winnipeg's fine-dining community for 27 years, Restaurant Dubrovnik is famed for its exquisite international cuisine and sophisticated elegance. Step into the mansion on the Assiniboine River and find yourself in an Old World environment that backdrops Executive Chef Gojko Bodiroga's innovative fare. Dishes include seared foie gras with sweet apple chips and port wine, and fresh salmon coated with cashew nuts in a chardonnay reduction with quince.

Owner Milan Bodiroga, Pastry Chef Borka Bodiroga and Executive Chef Gojko Bodiroga

Elegant entrées

Main dining room

390 Assiniboine Avenue
Winnipeg, Manitoba
Canada R3C 0Y1
PH: (204) 944-0594
FAX: (204) 957-7750

Owners
Milan Bodiroga

Cuisine
French, Continental

Days Open
Open Mon.-Fri. for lunch,
Mon.-Sat. for dinner

Pricing
Dinner for one,
without tax, tip, or drinks:
$40-$60

Dress Code
Business casual

Reservations
Recommended

Parking
Free on site

Features
Private room/parties,
entertainment, near theater

Credit Cards
AE, VC, MC, DC

DiRoNA
AWARD WINNER
SINCE 1998

Langdon Hall
Country House Hotel & Spa

Dining terrace

Langdon Hall, a member of Relais & Chateaux, was a country house built for a descendant of the legendary financier John Jacob Astor. Executive Chef Andrew Taylor prepares contemporary Canadian cuisine. He incorporates vegetables, and edible flowers grown on the property into the menu to create fresh, seasonal Canadian flavors. Guests may choose to dine indoors by soft candle light or outdoors under the arbor.

Creative entrées

Luxurious appointments

Elegant desserts

Directions

At Blair Road and Langdon Drive in Cambridge, near Highway 401 and 40 min. from Toronto's Pearson International Airport

R.R. 33
Cambridge, Ontario
Canada N3H 4R8
PH: (519) 740-2100
FAX: (519) 740-8161
www.langdonhall.ca

Owners
William Bennett and Mary Beaton

Cuisine
Modern country house

Days Open
Open daily for breakfast, lunch, and dinner

Pricing
Dinner for one, without tax, tip, or drinks: $40-$60

Dress Code
Casual

Reservations
Recommended

Parking
Free on site, valet

Features
Private room/parties, outdoor dining, entertainment

Credit Cards
AE, VC, MC, CB, DC, ER

AWARD WINNER
SINCE 1993

Inn on the Twenty

Main dining room

I nn on the Twenty is Ontario's premier estate winery restaurant. The culinary team, led by Executive Chef Roberto Fracchioni, are champions of regional cuisine, committed to the flavors of Niagara's bountiful harvest. Ingredients are carefully selected from the best local producers. Among the exciting regional foods that make their way to Inn on the Twenty's kitchens are fabulous tree fruits and berries, quail, trout, and organically grown vegetables, greens, and herbs. A panoramic view of Twenty Mile Creek enhances the dining experience.

Pan-fried salmon

Restaurant entrance

**AWARD WINNER
SINCE 1997**

Elegant guest accommodations

In the Niagara Escarpment village of Jordan, 1 hr. from both Toronto's Pearson International Airport and Buffalo (N.Y.) International Airport

3836 Main Street
Jordan, Ontario
Canada LOR 1S0
PH: (905) 562-7313
FAX: (905) 562-3348
www.innonthetwenty.com

Owners
Helen Young

Cuisine
Regional wine country

Days Open
Open daily for breakfast, lunch and dinner

Pricing
Dinner for one, without tax, tip, or drinks: $40-$60

Dress Code
Business casual

Reservations
Recommended

Parking
Free on site

Features
Private room/parties, near theater, outdoor dining

Credit Cards
AE, VC, MC, DC, En Route

le jardin

le jardin... a Victorian dining setting

In 1976 a beautiful 19th century Victorian home in Lowertown was lovingly transformed into one of North America's finest restaurants. Since then "le jardin" has offered its discriminating patrons superb five star French cuisine in a setting worthy of the 1978 Heritage Ottawa Award. Le jardin enjoys an international reputation. It is recommended by *The New York Times, Town & Country, Canadian Living, En Route, The Gourmet Diners, The Globe and Mail, and The Ottawa Citizen.* Le jardin coveted the CAA & AAA Tour Diamond Award, the prestigious American Express North American Travel Award, DiRōNA, and the gourmet Diners Society of North America Golden Fork Award.

Superb French cuisine

Dining room with fireplace

Tempting desserts

DiRōNA
AWARD WINNER
SINCE 1995

Directions

Murray		
Clarence		☆
York		

In the historic Byward Market on York Street, 30 min. from Pearson International Airport

127 York Street
Ottawa, Ontario
Canada K1N 5T4
PH: (613) 241-1424
FAX: (613) 241-8911
www.lejardin.biz

Owners
Beyhan Tosun

Cuisine
Classical French

Days Open
Open daily for dinner

Pricing
Dinner for one,
without tax, tip, or drinks:
$20-$50

Dress Code
Business casual

Reservations
Recommended

Parking
Garage nearby

Features
Private room/parties,
near theater

Credit Cards
AE, VC, MC, DC,
En Route, JCB

360 The Restaurant at the CN Tower

The dining room

Directions

On Front Street West downtown, just north of Bremner Boulevard, 30 min. from Pearson International Airport

301 Front Street West
Toronto, Ontario
Canada M5V 2T6
PH: (416) 362-5411
FAX: (416) 601-4722
www.cntower.ca

Owners
CN Tower

Cuisine
Regional Canadian

Days Open
Open daily for dinner
(brunch and lunch in summer only)

Pricing
Dinner for one,
without tax, tip, or drinks:
$40-$60

Dress Code
Business casual

Reservations
Recommended

Parking
Garage nearby

Features
Private parties

Credit Cards
AE, VC, MC, DC, ER, JCB

This outstanding restaurant offers fine cuisine, impeccable service, and an internationally recognized wine cellar of over 510 choice labels. Feast on traditional items, such as Canadian AAA prime rib of beef and roasted rack of mustard crusted lamb or savor a selection of seafood. Save room to enjoy such decadent desserts as the dark chocolate tower. Add the spectacular view and you have the perfect setting for a dining experience like no other. Dining at 360 is an absolute must when visiting Toronto.

Executive Chef
Peter George

Wine cellar in the sky

Director, Food & Beverage
Neil C. Jones

AWARD WINNER
SINCE 1997

Biagio Ristorante

Dining room

Historic St. Lawrence Hall forms the backdrop of this classically elegant restaurant with an authentic Italian pedigree. The long menu, expertly executed by Chef Guy Gnadinger-Harris, draws mainly from Northern Italy with risotti and fresh pastas as its specialties. Don't skip dessert — the lineup is delectable and memorable. Choose a selection from Biagio's extensive wine list. The vintages are varied with a predominance of great Italian wines.

Private dining in the wine cellar

Biagio Vinci

Executive Chef Guy Gnadinger-Harris

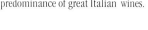

AWARD WINNER
SINCE 1995

Directions

On King Street East at Jarvis, 40 min. from Pearson International Airport

155 King Street East
Toronto, Ontario, Canada
M5C 1G9
PH: (416) 366-4040
FAX: (416) 366-4765
www.biagio.tordine.com

Owners
Biagio Vinci

Cuisine
Authentic Italian

Days Open
Open Mon.-Fri. for lunch,
Mon.-Sat. for dinner

Pricing
Dinner for one,
without tax, tip, or drinks:
$60-$80

Dress Code
Casual

Reservations
Recommended

Parking
Garage nearby

Features
Private room/parties, outdoor dining

Credit Cards
AE, VC, MC, DC

Bistro 990

Bistro 990

Directions

On Bay Street and Wellesley Street West, 30 min. from Pearson International Airport

990 Bay Street
Toronto, Ontario
Canada M5S 2A5
PH: (416) 921-9990
FAX: (416) 921-9497
www.bistro990.com

Owners
Private

Cuisine
Country French/Continental

Days Open
Open Mon.-Fri. for lunch,
Mon.-Sat. for dinner

Pricing
Dinner for one,
without tax, tip, or drinks:
$60-$80
(or) Price fix: $24.90 –
3 courses

Dress Code
Casual

Reservations
Recommended

Parking
Lot nearby

Features
Private room/parties, outdoor dining, near theater

Credit Cards
AE, VC, MC, DC, En Route

A free standing French Country auberge in the heart of Toronto, Bistro 990 has it all…from the lovely, and intimate dining area, to the inviting summer terrace, and a most interesting wine selection to match. Under the watchful, and caring eye of General Manager Fernando Temudo, and with the inspired cooking, and presentations of Executive Chef Ricardo Roque, Bistro 990 continues to be the host restaurant of the Toronto International Film Festival, the Toronto literary community, and visiting celebrities. Ambience abounds here…fresh flowers, tiled floors, French doors, vaulted ceilings, and attentive, unobtrusive service in the European tradition.

*Executive Chef
Ricardo Roque*

*General Manager
Fernando Temudo*

DiRōNA
AWARD WINNER
SINCE 2003

Far Niente

The bar

In financial district two blocks from the Air Canada Centre, 40 min. from Lester B. Pearson International Airport

I n the heart of Toronto's financial district lies Far Niente, an exceptional steak and seafood house. Executive Chef Hugh Kerr offers distinctive California grilled cuisine, award-winning "Living Well" entrées, and decadent desserts created daily from the bakery. Select a wine from the 10,000-bottle cellar to complement the meal. Specialties include grilled ahi tuna steak, served with charred California zucchini, yellow squash, Bermuda onions, sweet peppers, Kalamata olives, and basil-infused olive oil.

The dining room

From the 10,000-bottle wine cellar

187 Bay St., Commerce Court Station, P.O. Box 517
Toronto, Ontario
Canada M5L 1G5
PH: (416) 214-9922
FAX: (416) 214-1895
www.farnientegrill.com

Owners
Hieu Nguyen

Cuisine
California grilled

Days Open
Open Mon.-Fri. for lunch, daily for dinner

Pricing
Dinner for one, without tax, tip, or drinks: $20-$40

Dress Code
Business casual

Reservations
Recommended

Parking
Validated on site after 5:30

Features
Private parties, outdoor dining, near theater

Credit Cards
AE, VC, MC, DC, ER

AWARD WINNER
SINCE 2001

Prego della Piazza

The Enoteca Room

On Bloor Street West between Yonge Street and Avenue Road, 30 min. from Pearson International Airport

150 Bloor Street West
Toronto, Ontario
Canada M5S 2X9
PH: (416) 920-9900
FAX: (416) 920-9949

Owners
Michael E. Carlevale

Cuisine
Continental Italian

Days Open
Open Mon.-Sat. for lunch,
daily for dinner

Pricing
Dinner for one,
without tax, tip, or drinks:
$20-$40

Dress Code
Business casual

Reservations
Recommended

Parking
Garage nearby (2 hours free
at lunch with validation, free
at dinner)

Features
Private room/parties, outdoor dining, entertainment,
near theater, cigar/cognac
events

Credit Cards
AE, VC, MC, DC, ER

Sophisticated, confident, and glamorous, Prego della Piazza looks onto a tented piazza nestled against the Church of the Redeemer. Owner Michael Carlevale has gathered a team of seasoned professionals providing first-rate service and a kitchen founded on the ingredients, style, and techniques of Italian cooking. Located in Toronto's upscale shopping district, the outstanding eatery is enjoying its 14th year.

Owner Michael Carlevale

AWARD WINNER
SINCE 1995

Ristorante La Fenice

The quiet elegance of the main dining room

An elegant candlelit dining room with rosy walls the color of old Roman terracotta: La Fenice's décor is a tastefully subdued tribute to modern Italy. La Fenice serves simply beautiful Italian food, made from the finest ingredients, carefully prepared to show them at their best. Specialties include; grilled fresh fish, flavorful pastas, and risottos, perfectly grilled, succulent veal, and rack of lamb. An extensive wine list complements the classic menu.

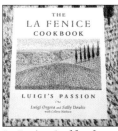
La Fenice Cookbook, co-authored by founder Luigi Orgera

Signature desserts by Alessandra Orgera

House specialty - Mediterranean style whole grilled fish

Directions

On King St. West, at John St., 30 min. from Pearson Int'l Airport

319 King St. West
Toronto, Ontario
Canada M5V 1J5
PH: (416) 585-2377
FAX: (416) 585-2709
www.toronto.com/lafenice

Owners
Orgera Family

Cuisine
Italian

Days Open
Open Mon.-Fri. for lunch,
Mon.-Sat. for dinner

Pricing
Dinner for one,
without tax, tip, or drinks:
$40-$60

Dress Code
Business casual

Reservations
Recommended

Parking
Garage nearby

Features
Private room/parties,
near theater

Credit Cards
AE, VC, MC, DC, En Route

AWARD WINNER
SINCE 1994

Rosewater Supper Club

Main dining room

The Rosewater Supper Club is the quintessential dining experience. Minutes from the heart of Toronto's Entertainment and Theatre districts, this elegantly appointed historic club lends an air of decadence, and romance when dining on the contemporary global French cuisine. The internationally renowned menu, featuring unique items such as caribou carpaccio, and crispy skinned sea bream, is an eclectic combination of culinary styles, and tastes that complement the sophisticated atmosphere.

Main bar

Private dining room

Front lounge

AWARD WINNER
SINCE 2003

Directions

In the heart of Toronto's Entertainment and Theatre districts, 30 min. from Pearson International Airport

19 Toronto Street
Toronto, Ontario
Canada M5C 2R1
PH: (416) 214-5888
FAX: (416) 214-2412
www.libertygroup.com

Owners
Nick Di Donato

Cuisine
Contemporary global French

Days Open
Open Mon.-Fri. for lunch,
Mon.-Sat. for dinner

Pricing
Dinner for one,
without tax, tip, or drinks:
$40-$60

Dress Code
Business casual

Reservations
Recommended

Parking
Valet, garage nearby

Features
Private room/parties, near theater, entertainment (Thurs.-Sat.)

Credit Cards
AE, VC, MC, DC, En Route

Ruth's Chris Steak House

Main dining room

On Richmond St. off University Ave., 35 min. from Pearson International Airport

145 Richmond Street West
Toronto, Ontario
Canada M5H 2L2
PH: (416) 955-1455
FAX: (416) 955-1494
www.ruthschris-toronto.com

Owners
Lana Duke

Cuisine
Steakhouse

Days Open
Open Thurs.-Fri. for lunch, daily for dinner from 5pm

Pricing
Dinner for one, without tax, tip, or drinks:
$40-$60

Dress Code
Dressy casual

Reservations
Recommended

Parking
Free on site from 6pm

Features
Private room/parties, near theater

Credit Cards
AE, VC, MC, DC, JCB

Attention to detail extends beyond food and service to the magnificent décor at the first Ruth's Chris Steak House in Canada. Vaulted ceilings, stained mahogany finishes, and rich carpeting create a warm, and celebratory environment for diners. Ruth's Chris serves generous cuts of the finest corn-fed, USDA Prime midwestern beef available, as well as live Atlantic lobster, fresh seafood, veal, lamb chops, and a vegetarian Portobello T-bone. Our award winning wine list include over 300 labels.

Filet mignon

Owner Lana Duke, Gen. Mgr. Hanne Olesen-Nahman

AWARD WINNER
SINCE 2003

Wine room

Scaramouche

The view of Toronto's skyline

At Benvenuto Place, 30 min. from Pearson International Airport

1 Benvenuto Place
Toronto, Ontario
Canada M4V 2L1
PH: (416) 961-8011
FAX: (416) 961-1922

Owners
Carl Korte, Keith Froggett and Morden Yolles

Cuisine
Contemporary French

Days Open
Open Mon.-Sat. for dinner

Pricing
Dinner for one, without tax, tip, or drinks: $40-$60

Dress Code
Business casual

Reservations
Recommended

Parking
Complimentary valet parking

Credit Cards
AE, VC, MC, DC, En Route

Toronto's benchmark for elegance, the standards at Scaramouche have never wavered. Chef Keith Froggett's innovative creations are grounded in the tenets of classical French cuisine. House specialties like hickory-smoked and roasted Atlantic salmon are seamlessly complemented by an excellent wine list. In a world where the newest and latest are pursued slavishly, the twenty-three years that Scaramouche has spent at the top is all the more remarkable.

"A star for 20 years"
Toronto Life magazine

AWARD WINNER
SINCE 1993

Via Allegro Ristorante

On Queensway, just west of Highway 427, 10 min. from Pearson International Airport

1750 The Queensway
Toronto, Ontario
Canada M9C 5H5
PH: (416) 622-6677
FAX: (416) 622-8306

Owners
Felice Sabatino "President"

Cuisine
Italian with French and California touches

Days Open
Open daily for lunch and dinner

This spectacular room is beyond words, enchanting the senses with both superfine and rustic motifs. Chef Lino Collevecchio's signature dishes include a seafood extravaganza with fresh Nova Scotia lobster, the best Provini veal chops in Toronto, naturally raised prime Canadian steaks aged up to eight weeks, large-eye rack of lamb, and wild mushroom and truffle risotto, prepared tableside. Over 3,000 selections of wine including more than 150 Amarone, 150 Barolo, and such trophies as Bordeaux's 1899, and 1900 Chateau Margaux, as well as 1945 Chateau Mouton-Rothschild. In addition there are 300 different single-malt, and blended whiskeys, and 120 grappa selectaions with five sommeliers to assist you.

Sunburst ba moti

A spectacular selection

Pricing
Dinner for one, without tax, tip, or drinks: $20-$40

Dress Code
Business casual

Reservations
Recommended

Parking
Free on site

Features
Private room/parties, outdoor dining

Credit Cards
VC, MC, DC, En Route

AWARD WINNER
SINCE 2003

Mark Picone at Vineland Estates

Incomparable Zagat review

On Moyer Road, 1 hr. from Pearson International Airport

3620 Moyer Road
Vineland, Ontario
Canada, L0R 2C0
PH: (888) 846-3562
FAX: (905) 562-3071
www.vineland.com

Owner
John Howard

Cuisine
Fine Canadian regional dining

Days Open
Open daily for lunch and dinner (closed Mon. and Tues. from Jan.-April)

Pricing
Dinner for one, without tax, tip, or drinks: $40-$60

Dress Code
Business casual

Reservations
Recommended

Parking
Free on site

Features
Private room/parties, outdoor dining, Winemaker's dinners, tasting menus, pairing menus, Winery events, Wine Club, private and group dining

Credit Cards
AE, VC, MC, DC

Gourmet Magazine, Zagat Review, and the James Beard Foundation have all recognized Mark Picone at Vineland Estates as the quintessential Niagara wine country dining experience with exemplary service and ambience second to none. Executive Chef Mark Picone and his talented team create authentic regional Niagara cuisine with the freshest seasonal ingredients. With fine dining inside or on the patio deck, guests can enjoy the breathtaking view overlooking the vineyards, and Lake Ontario while savoring tantalizing menu creations paired exquisitely with Vineland Estate's award-winning vintages.

Premium wines and exceptional cuisine

Executive Chef Mark Picone C.C.C.

Summing view overlooking the vineyards and patio dining

AWARD WINNER
SINCE 2004

497

Café Henry Burger

Turn-of-the-century charm

In the oldest restaurant in the national capital region and one of the oldest in Canada, a tradition of excellence set by Marie and Henry Burger continues. Refined cuisine, impeccable service, and elegant surroundings ... it's easy to see why Café Henry Burger is still the preferred rendezvous of diplomats, politicians, artists, and connoisseurs. The spring/summer menu offers the scents and flavors of Provence; the autumn menu features a variety of game and foods of the harvest; and wintertime brings light and hearty fare from Quebec and France. The establishment is near the Parliament buildings and Hull Casino.

At your service

Elegant four-course dinner

*Chef-Proprietor
Robert C. Bourassa*

AWARD WINNER
SINCE 1993

Directions

Adjacent to the Canadian Museum of Civilization, 25 min. from Ottawa (Macdonald-Cartier) International Airport

69 Rue Laurier
Hull, Quebec
Canada J8X 3V7
PH: (819) 777-5646
FAX: (819) 777-0832
www.cafehenryburger.com

Owners
Robert C. Bourassa

Cuisine
French seasonal

Days Open
Open Mon.-Fri. for lunch, daily for dinner

Pricing
Dinner for one, without tax, tip, or drinks: $20-$40

Dress Code
Business casual

Reservations
Recommended

Parking
Free on site

Features
Private room/parties, outdoor dining

Credit Cards
AE, VC, MC, DC, ER, JCB

Restaurant Le Mitoyen

Owner Richard Bastien and his staff

Directions

In Laval on Place Publique, 20 min. from Montreal's Dorval International Airport

652 Place Publique
Ste-Dorothée, Laval,
Quebec, Canada H7X 1G1
PH: (450) 689-2977
FAX: (450) 689-0385

For more than 20 years, this award-winning restaurant, ensconced in the owner's ancestral home, has offered its guests quality service and a generous, varied menu. Owner and Executive Chef Richard Bastien prepares such specialties as roast rack of Quebec lamb with fennel puree, and medallions of caribou with raspberries and cranberries. The charm of Restaurant Le Mitoyen will enhance both an intimate dinner or a business gathering.

Award-winning French cuisine

Owners
Richard Bastien

Cuisine
French

Days Open
Open Tues.-Sun. for dinner
(open for lunch for groups
of 10 or more with
a reservation)

Pricing
Dinner for one,
without tax, tip, or drinks:
$40-$60

Dress Code
Casual

Reservations
Recommended

Parking
Free on site

Features
Private room/parties,
outdoor dining

Credit Cards
AE, VC, MC, DC, ER

Front entrance

AWARD WINNER
SINCE 1992

*Owner Richard Bastien is
also the executive chef*

The Beaver Club

Elegant
surroundings

In The Queen Elizabeth
Hotel, 30 min. from Dorval
International Airport

Recognized as one of Canada's very best tables, the legendary and fully renovated Beaver Club offers a culinary adventure you won't soon forget. Taste a legend. Experience the unique and innovative gourmet cuisine promoting the culinary richness of Canada that has earned this storied establishment the Five-Star Mobil Travel Guide rating for many years.

Executive Chef
Alain Pignard

900 René-Levesque
Boulevard West
Montreal, Quebec, Canada
H3B 4A5
PH: (514) 861-3511
FAX: (514) 954-2873
www.fairmont.com

Owners
Fairmont The Queen
Elizabeth Hotel

Cuisine
Haute cuisine highlighting
Canadian products

Days Open
Open Mon.-Fri. for lunch,
Tues.-Sat, for dinner

Pricing
Dinner for one,
without tax, tip, or drinks:
$60-$80

Dress Code
Jacket suggested

Reservations
Recommended

Parking
Garage nearby

Features
Private parties

Credit Cards
AE, VC, MC, CB, DC, ER, DS

AWARD WINNER
SINCE 1993

Chez La Mère Michel

Wine cellar dining room

Since 1965, Montreal denizens and visitors have enjoyed the best in classic French cooking at Chez La Mère Michel. The exceptional quality of its cuisine and service has won rave reviews from restaurant critics everywhere, and garnered the Mobil Four Star rating, one of the highest gastronomic awards. For special dining events, a private room is available, and the wine cellar can be reserved for receptions and wine tasting.

Les crêpes Suzette flambée

The spring is back

Decanting good wine

AWARD WINNER SINCE 1993

Directions

On Rue Guy between Ste. Catherine and René-Levesque, 15 min. from Dorval International Airport

1209 Rue Guy
Montreal, Quebec
Canada H3H 2K5
PH: (514) 934-0473
FAX: (514) 939-0709

Owners
Micheline and
René Delbuguet

Cuisine
Classical French

Days Open
Open Mon.-Sat. for lunch and dinner

Pricing
Dinner for one,
without tax, tip, or drinks:
$60-$80

Dress Code
Business casual

Reservations
Recommended

Parking
Lot nearby

Features
Private room/parties, near theater

Credit Cards
AE, VC, MC, DC, ER, JCB

Le Muscadin

10,000 bottles of Italian wine

The Iacono family has relocated its prestigious fine Italian cuisine restaurant to 639 Notre Dame West in Old Montreal. In its newly renovated location, Le Muscadin has retained its charm of old and has added a touch of class to its ambience. Patrons and their guests are treated like family in surroundings that are reminiscent of the Italian chateaux that produce the fine selection of wines found it its renowned wine cellar.

Le Muscadin of Montreal

Private dining room

The "Sala da Pranzo"

Directions

On Notre Dame West in Old Montreal, 20 min. from Dorval International Airport

639 Notre Dame West
Montreal, Quebec
Canada H3C 1H8
PH: (514) 842-0588
FAX: (514) 842-5347
www.lemuscadin.com

Owners
Leonardo Iacono

Cuisine
Fine Italian

Days Open
Open Mon.-Fri. for lunch,
Mon.-Sat. for dinner

Pricing
Dinner for one,
without tax, tip, or drinks:
$40-$60

Dress Code
Required

Reservations
Recommended

Parking
Free on site (evenings only)

Features
Private room/parties

Credit Cards
AE, VC, MC, DC, En Route

AWARD WINNER
SINCE 2002

Le Parchemin

Le Parchemin

On rue University, 5 min. from major downtown hotels, and 30 min. from Dorval International Airport

1333 rue University
Montreal, Quebec
Canada H3A 2A4
PH: (514) 844-1619
FAX: (514) 844-7873
www.leparchemin.com

Owners
Mario Degioanni

Cuisine
French

Days Open
Open Mon.-Fri. for lunch,
Mon.-Sat. for dinner

Pricing
Dinner for one,
without tax, tip, or drinks:
$40-$60

Dress Code
Casual/business casual

Reservations
Recommended

Parking
Garage nearby

Features
Private room/parties,
near theater

Credit Cards
AE, VC, MC, CB, DC, ER, JCB

An original cuisine which has given Le Parchemin a reputation for pleasing the most demanding gourmet is served in a dignified and unique setting. If you have an urge for deer medallions with fricassee of wild mushrooms, Lac Brôme duck with orange and green peppercorn sauce, or fresh scallops on the shell with four sauces, you'll be rewarded at this splendid restaurant, ensconced in a former presbytery in the heart of Montréal.

Gracious dining and fine wines

AWARD WINNER
SINCE 2004

Le Passe-Partout Restaurant

An authentic taste of French food in Quebec

Two blocks north of Sherbrooke Street, 10 min. from Dorval International Airport

Since 1981 Chef James J. MacGuire and his wife, Suzanne Baron-Lafreniére have served French cuisine in intimate, elegant surroundings. "Gracious" characterizes the service provided by the owners. Every item from breads to ice cream is made fresh, on-premises, and James carefully selects the wines. Chef MacGuire is respected in North America as the great French bread expert, and is the technical editor for the internationally acclaimed book, *"The taste of bread"* by Ramond Calvel, and is assisted in the kitchen by Chef Walter Kuntz. Le Passe-Partout Restaurant has been featured in *The New York Times, Gourmet* reader's poll, *The Financial Times,* London, and is said to have "The best French food in the country" by Joanne Kates, *Globe and Mail.*

Elegant atmosphere

Intimate dining

3857 Boulevard Décarie
Montreal, Quebec H4A 3J6
PH: (514) 487-7750
FAX: (514) 487-5673

Owner
James J. MacGuire and
Suzanne Baron-Lafreniére

Cuisine
French market

Days Open
Open Tues.-Fri. for lunch,
Thurs.-Sat. for dinner

Pricing
Dinner for one,
without tax, tip, or drinks:
$40-$60

Dress Code
Business casual

Reservations
Recommended

Parking
Free on site

Features
Private room/parties,
art gallery, bakery-boutique
open Tues.-Sat.

Credit Cards
AE, VC, MC, DC, ER, JCB

AWARD WINNER
SINCE 1993

Les Caprices de Nicolas

A romantic, evening setting

Les Caprices de Nicolas offers modern French cuisine using the best Quebecois ingredients. The sophisticated, romantic atmosphere features formal service, exquisite china, three low-lit dining rooms, and pillow-lined banquettes. Attention is given to details such as homemade bread and an elaborate cheese course. Connoisseurs can choose from the predominately French wine list (a *Wine Spectator* Best Award of Excellence) that also offers a wide range of selections from the world over.

Dining in the garden

Owner Dan Medalsy

Alaskan Black cod

AWARD WINNER
SINCE 2002

Directions

On Rue Drummond, 20 min. from Dorval International Airport

2072 Rue Drummond
Montreal, Quebec
Canada, H3G 1W9
PH: (514) 282-9790
FAX: (514) 288-0249
www.lescaprices.com

Owner
Dan Medalsy

Cuisine
Modern French

Days Open
Open daily for dinner

Pricing
Dinner for one,
without tax, tip, or drinks:
$60-$80 (Canadian dollars)

Dress Code
Business casual

Reservations
Recommended

Parking
Garage nearby

Features
Private room/parties,

Credit Cards
AE, VC, MC, DC, ER

Les Remparts Restaurant

Les Remparts dining room

Located in the heart of Old Montreal, 20 min. from Dorval Airport

93, rue de la Commune East
Montreal, Quebec
Canada H2Y 1J1
Phone: (514) 392-1649
Fax: (514) 876-8923
www.restaurantlesremparts.com

In his five years at Les Remparts, Janick Bouchard has made his mark with a seasonal "cuisine du marché". Using only the highest quality Quebec produce, fish, and meats, he alters his menus with the changing seasons to ensure the freshness of his ingredients. The result is an exquisite menu of mouth-watering dishes that, along with its elegant décor and polished ambience, have earned the restaurant consecutive Tourisme Montréal "Prix Ulysse" awards in the "Gastronomy" category.

Chef Janick Bouchard

Fine French market cuisine

Owners
Dina Antonopoulos

Cuisine
Fine French cuisine with local market-fresh products

Days Open
Open Mon.-Fri. for lunch, open daily for dinner

Pricing
Dinner for one, without tax, tip, or drinks: $40-$60

Dress Code
Business casual

Reservations
Recommended

Parking
Valet

Features
Private parties, outdoor dining

Credit Cards
AE, VC, MC, DC, ER, DS

elaborate French wine collection

AWARD WINNER
SINCE 2004

Nuances

Nuances restaurant, awarded a Five Diamond rating by the CAA/AAA

On the fifth floor of the Casino de Montreal, 15 min. from Dorval International Airport

Perched on the fifth floor of the Casino de Montreal, Nuances restaurant, awarded a Five Diamond rating by the CAA/AAA, offers breathtaking views overlooking the St. Lawrence River. This award-winning restaurant features an inventive gourmet cuisine, recognized for its freshness, quality, originality, and refinement. The unparalleled gastronomic experience is rounded out with a select wine list, attentive service, and sumptuous décor.

*Executive Chef
Jean-Pierre Curtat*

Elegant dining

A feast for the eyes and the palate

1, Avenue du Casino
Montreal, Quebec
Canada H3C 4W7
PH: (514) 392-2708
FAX: (514) 864-4951
www.casinos-quebec.com

Owner
Loto-Quèbec

Cuisine
Gastronomic

Days Open
Open daily for dinner

Pricing
Dinner for one,
without tax, tip, or drinks:
$40-$60

Dress Code
Jacket required

Reservations
Recommended

Parking
Valet

Features
Private room, near theater

Credit Cards
AE, VC, MC, DC, ER

AWARD WINNER
SINCE 2002

Montreal • Quebec

Opus II

Opus II captures the essence of Montreal and its "joie de vivre". Chic, with simple lines in its design, it is surprisingly seductive. In Montreal's Golden Square Mile, the urban atrium creates a cachet of sophistication. Mediterranean scents, seasonings and colours are the featured attraction in the lunch, dinner and brunch menus.

Dining in an atmosphere of sophistication

AWARD WINNER SINCE 2002

Directions

In the heart of Montreal, 20 min. from Dorval International Airport

1050 Sherbrooke West Montreal, Quebec Canada H3A 2R6
PH: (514) 985-6252
FAX: (514) 284-1162
www.omnihotels.com

Owner
Omni Hotels

Cuisine
Mediterranean

Days Open
Open daily for breakfast, lunch, and dinner

Pricing
Dinner for one, without tax, tip, or drinks: $40-$60

Dress Code
Business casual

Reservations
Recommended

Parking
Valet

Features
Private parties, cigar events

Credit Cards
AE, VC, MC, CB, DC, ER, JCB, DS

508

Ristorante Da Vinci

Ristorante Da Vinci

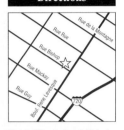

Located in a restored, Victorian home in the heart of Montreal, 25 min. from Dorval International Airport

1180 Rue Bishop
Montreal, Quebec
Canada, H3G 2E3
PH: (514) 874-2001
FAX: (514) 874-9499
www.davinci.qc.ca

Owner
Salvatore Mazzaferro

Cuisine
Italian

Days Open
Open daily for lunch and dinner

Pricing
Dinner for one, without tax, tip, or drinks: $40-$60

Dress Code
Business casual

Reservations
Recommended

Parking
Garage nearby

Features
Private room/parties

Credit Cards
AE, VC, MC, DC, En Route

Ristorante Da Vinci, a Mazzaferro family tradition since 1960. Under the management of Salvatore, the reputation of Da Vinci's stems from the fine dining philosophy of its owners. Located in a beautiful, restored Victorian home, in the heart of Montreal, Da Vinci offers its guests elegant surroundings without being pretentious. Da Vinci livens up its traditional Italian menu with plenty of contemporary daily specials. Da Vinci is truly a feast for both the palate and the eyes.

A tempting vegetable and seafood antipasto bar

Italian cuisine with a contemporary flair

A feast for the palate and the eyes

AWARD WINNER
SINCE 2004

TSIRCO Restaurant Jazz

Third floor dining

On rue Drummond, 20 min. from Dorval International Airport

1075 rue Drummond
Montreal, Quebec
Canada H3B 4X4
PH: (514) 939-1922
FAX: (514) 939-7329
www.tsirco.ca

Owners
John D'Angelo and Luigi Passarelli

Cuisine
Italian influenced Mediterranean

Days Open
Open Mon.-Fri. for lunch, Mon.-Sat. for dinner

Pricing
Dinner for one, without tax, tip, or drinks: $40-$60

Dress Code
Business casual

Reservations
Recommended

Parking
Valet

Features
Entertainment

Credit Cards
AE, VC, MC, DC

TSIRCO Restaurant Jazz blends exquisite food, the best wines and liquors, magnificent romantic décor, and a lively atmosphere enhanced by the melodies of jazz. Our Mediterranean influenced cuisine offers fresh pasta, thick milk-fed chops, fresh fish, and exotic vegetables. The *Wine Spectator* Award of Excellence and recognition by the *Debeur* guide attest to the fact that our team satisfies even the most demanding palate! Wonderful dinners, business lunches, special menus and group reservations are our specialties.

Lobster ravioli

Live Jazz

AWARD WINNER
SINCE 2004

Auberge Hatley

Country inn

Directions

On Virgin Hill in North Hatley, 20 miles north of the Vermont border and 1 hr. 30 min. from Montreal's Dorval International Airport

325 Virgin Hill
North Hatley, Quebec
Canada J0B 2C0
PH: (819) 842-2451
PH: (800) 336-2451
FAX: (819) 842-2907
www.aubergehatley.com
e-mail: hatley@relaischateaux.com

Owners
Groupe Germain

Cuisine
French

Days Open
Open daily for breakfast and dinner

Pricing
Dinner for one, without tax, tip, or drinks: $40-$70

Dress Code
No dress code

Reservations
Required

Parking
Free on site

Features
Private rooms/parties, wine tasting room, chef's table

Credit Cards
AE, VC, MC

With its sensational surroundings, spectacular views of Lake Massawippi, and quiet, serene atmosphere, Auberge Hatley is love at first sight. From the first smile at the front desk, to the inviting warmth of the lounge room with its fireplace, and the unique charm and appeal of each room, everything is designed to please. Honored since 1996 with *Wine Spectator's* prestigious Best of Award of Excellence, Auberge Hatley's wine cellar is nothing short of exceptional: 12,000 bottles, and over 1,200 labels. Chef Alain Labrie and his team draw upon the French tradition to create innovative cuisine where every ingredient expresses its authentic character, masterfully enhanced by a remarkable array of aromatic and herbs.

Poached lobster with grilled vegetables and a watercress emulsion

Patio dining

Living room

AWARD WINNER
SINCE 1993

Manoir Hovey

Dining room with garden view

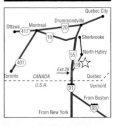

Just outside North Hatley on Hovey Road, 1 hour and 30 min. from Dorval International Airport

575 Hovey Road
North Hatley, Quebec
Canada J0B 2C0
PH: (800) 661-2421
FAX: (819) 842-2248
www.manoirhovey.com

Owners
Stephen, Kathryn, and Jason Stafford

Cuisine
Innovative Quebec

Days Open
Open daily for breakfast, lunch, and dinner

Pricing
Dinner for one, without tax, tip, or drinks: $40-$60

Dress Code
Business casual

Reservations
Recommended

Parking
Free on site

Features
Private rooms

Credit Cards
AE, VC, MC, DC, En Route, JCB

This five-star lakeside inn, famed for its luxuriously appointed rooms as much for its exquisite cuisine, is a delightful setting in which to taste Quebec cuisine at its finest. Chef Roland Menard is passionate about regional specialties, and showcases the freshest veal, duck, wild mushrooms, and raw-mild cheese in this menu. Classic French technique and the best Quebec ingredients strike a perfect match in dishes such as the Caribou with foie gras ravioli.

Chef in herb garden

Caribou with foie gras ravioli

AWARD WINNER
SINCE 2004

Le Champlain

Attentive wait staff

Directions

In the Chateau Frontenac,
20 min. from International
Airport Jean-Lesage

I nside the renowned Chateau Frontenac, this stately dining room overlooking the St. Lawrence River is steeped in Canada's illustrious French heritage. Under the enlightened direction of world-renowned Master Chef Jean Soulard, the freshest of local ingredients marry the flavors of the past with the sophistication of the present. Wait staff, dressed in delightful period costumes, take guests a step back in time and offer gracious service. On weekends the soft tones of harp music enhance the atmosphere. Chef Soulard, who has his own TV show, has just published his third cookbook.

Master Chef Jean Soulard

The historic Chateau Frontenac

Chateau Frontenac
1 Rue des Carrieres
Quebec City, Quebec,
Canada G1R 4P5
PH: (418) 266-3905
FAX: (418) 692-4353
www.fairmont.ca

Owners
Legacy Hotels Corporation

Cuisine
Classic French

Days Open
Open daily for dinner (Tues.-
Sat. in winter), Sun. brunch
year-round

Pricing
Dinner for one,
without tax, tip, or drinks:
$40-$60

Dress Code
Business casual

Reservations
Recommended

Parking
Valet

Features
Private room/parties, near
theater

Credit Cards
AE, VC, MC, CB, DC, ER,
JCB, DS

AWARD WINNER
SINCE 1993

Hotel Restaurant L' Eau a la Bouche

Hotel L' Eau a la Bouche

In the village of Sainte-Adèle, 60 min. from Montreal's Dorval International Airport

3003 BD Ste.-Adèle
Sainte-Adèle, Quebec
Canada J8B 2N6
PH: (450) 229-2991
FAX: (450) 229-7573
www.
relaischateaux.fr/eaubouche

Owners
Anne Desjardins and
Pierre Audette

Cuisine
French

Days Open
Open daily for breakfast
and dinner

Pricing
Dinner for one,
without tax, tip, or drinks:
$70-$145

Dress Code
Business casual

Reservations
Required

Parking
Free

Features
Private room/parties, entertainment, near theater

Credit Cards
AE, VC, MC, DC, ER

At L' Eau a la Bouche, Relais & Chateaux, Relais Gourmand nestled in the Laurentian Mountains, co-owner and Executive Chef Anne Desjardins prepares delicious regional French cuisine in a beautiful setting. Tuna, quail, pork, rack of lamb, beef fillet, and venison loin are among the freshly made entrées. The wine selection is outstanding.

The dining room

A superior room at the inn

Chef/Owner Anne Desjardins

AWARD
OF
EXCELLENCE

AWARD WINNER
SINCE 1993

Ristorante Michelangelo

Exquisite gardens

Located near city access bridges, 10 min. from International Airport Jean-Lesage

3111 Chemin Saint-Louis
Sainte Foy, Quebec
Canada G1W 1R6
PH: (418) 651-6262
FAX: (418) 651-6771
www.restomichelangelo.com

Owners
Nicola Cortina

Cuisine
Italian

Days Open
Open Mon.-Fri. for lunch,
Mon.-Sun. for dinner

Pricing
Dinner for one,
without tax, tip, or drinks:
$60-$80

Dress Code
Business casual

Reservations
Recommended

Parking
Valet

Features
Private room/parties,
outdoor dining,
complimentary limo service

Credit Cards
AE, VC, MC, DC, ER

Located near the bridges that access the city, the Michelangelo's first-class dining room charms guests with its intimate, elegant atmosphere and Art Deco style. The extensive wine list (1,000 selections), high-quality food, and excellent service are a must for visitors. It has won *Wine Spectator's* Award of Excellence since 1997 and has been named one of the few genuine Italian restaurants outside the country by the Italian government.

Main dining room

Lounge

Lobby

AWARD WINNER
SINCE 1999

515

Ristorante CasaNova

Ristorante CasaNova

On Scenic Drive overlooking Acapulco Bay, 15 min. from Acapulco International Airport

Perched on a cliff side with the Pacific Ocean below, Ristorante CasaNova offers a spectacular view of the Bay of Acapulco, and the sparkling lights of Las Brisas. This elegant dining spot, owned by Arturo and Patricia Cordova, became an instant "success" when it opened in 1990. Daughter, and Executive Chef Lorelay Cordova created the innovative "Tuscan Kitchen" which features northern Italian cuisine. Specialties include fresh fish, veal, and lamb, along with fresh pasta, and risotto. Desserts are not to be missed as the Cordova's other daughter, Maria Elisa, prepares beautiful, tempting after meal treats. The "Positano Bar" offers guests live piano music, and a chilled "Mango CasaNova", the house favorite!

The Cordova family, at your service

Italian cuisine from the "Tuscan kitchen"

Ristorante CasaNova
5256 Avenida Escenica
Acapulco, Guerrero
Mexico 39868
PH: 011-525-446-6237 to 39
FAX: 011-525-482-0147
www.hamacas.com.mx

Owners
Arturo Cordova

Cuisine
Italian

Days Open
Open daily for breakfast, lunch and dinner (closed Tuesday in summer and fall)

Pricing
Dinner for one, without tax, tip, or drinks:
$20-$40
(or)
Prix Fixe: $35

Dress Code
Elegant resort wear, jacket not required

Reservations
Recommended

Parking
Free on site, valet

Features
Private room/parties, outdoor dining

Credit Cards
AE, VC, MC

Welcome to elegant dining

AWARD WINNER
SINCE 1994

Blue Bayou

Lush, Bayou setting

Offering elegant dining, featuring Cajun and Creole specialties from New Orleans, Blue Bayou is the only restaurant in Cancun claiming the DiRōNA Award since 1998. The Blue Bayou has been selected to receive the AAA Diamond Award for 2004, making it one of the few restaurants in Cancun with double recognitions.

Cajun and Creole specialties

Award-winning restaurant

Elegant and romantic

Directions

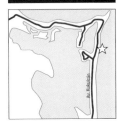

Located in the Hyatt Cancun Caribe, 30 min. from Cancun International Airport

Blvd. Kukulcan KM 10.5
Cancun, Quintana Roo
Mexico, 77500
PH: 011-52-998-848-7800
FAX: 011-52-998-883-1514
www.cancuncaribe.
resort.hyatt.com

Cuisine
Cajun and Creole

Days Open
Open daily for dinner

Pricing
Dinner for one,
without tax, tip, or drinks:
$40-$60

Dress Code
Evening casual

Reservations
Recommended

Parking
Free on site

Features
Cigar/cognac events,
live jazz music

Credit Cards
AE, MC, DC, VC

AWARD WINNER
SINCE 1998

La Dolce Vita

Owners Juan J. Casal, Jorge Kaufer and George Savio

With a loyal, local following for over 20 years, La Dolce Vita boasts beautiful views of the Nichupte lagoon, and one of the most spectacular sunsets in Cancun. Patrons receive the personal attention of owners Juan, Jorge or George as they dine on selections from the menu including freshly made Italian pastas and fresh seafood – Boquinete Dolce Vita is one of the signature dishes. Guests may choose to dine outside on the terrace, or in the main dining room that features a romantic atmosphere with candlelit tables and lace tablecloths. Live, soft jazz plays nightly, Monday through Saturday.

Outside terrace

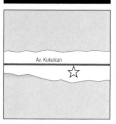

Directions

Located at Av. Kukulcan across from the Marriott Hotel, on the lagoon side, 15 min. from Cancun International Airport

---

Av. Kukulcan Km. 14.6
Cancun, Q.Roo
Mexico, 77500
PH: 011-52-998-8850150 (or)
PH: 011-52-998-8850161
FAX: 011-52-998-8840461
www.cancun.com/dining/dolce

Owners
George and Tim Savio,
Jorge and Susana Kaufer,
and Juan J. Casal

Cuisine
Italian

Days Open
Open daily for lunch and dinner

Pricing
Dinner for one,
without tax, tip, or drinks:
$20-$40

Dress Code
Casual

Reservations
Recommended

Parking
Free on site

Features
Private parties, outdoor dining

Credit Cards
AE, VC, MC

AWARD WINNER
SINCE 2001

518

La Habichuela Restaurant

A Cancun legend

L ocated in a Yucatecan-style house in a quiet residential neighborhood near the Hotel Zone, La Habichuela features fresh-caught Caribbean seafood and Mexican specialties that Executive Chef Juan Rodriguez Medina prepares in his own distinctive regional style. The romantic Mayan sculpture garden is a favorite setting for special events. A Cancun legend since 1977, La Habichuela was certified ISO-9002 in 2001, and received Mexico's Best Restaurant Award in 1997. La Habichuela remains a family operation with the personal touch of the Pezzotti family.

The Mayan sculpture garden

Candlelit dining

The famous Cocobichuela

AWARD WINNER
SINCE 2001

Directions

Downtown, off Av. Tulum on Margaritas, 15 min. from Cancun International Airport

Margaritas 25 SM 22 MZ 20
Cancun, Q. Roo
Mexico, 77500
PH: 011-52-998-884-3158
(or) 011-52-998-887-1716
FAX: 011-52-998-884-0940
www.lahabichuela.com

Owners
Armando Pezzotti Renteria

Cuisine
International, Mexican, Caribbean

Days Open
Open daily for lunch and dinner

Pricing
Dinner for one,
without tax, tip, or drinks:
$20-$40

Dress Code
Casual

Reservations
Recommended

Parking
Free on site

Features
Private parties, outdoor dining, cigar/cognac events

Credit Cards
AE, VC, MC

Pancho's Backyard

Beautiful colonial setting

Avenida Rafael Melgar

2 St. North | 4 St. North | 6 St. North | 8 St. North

On the waterfront at Rafael Melgar and 8 Norte, 5 min. from Cozumel Airport

Avenida Rafael Melgar #27 N.
Cozumel, Quintana Roo
Mexico 77600
PH: 011-52-98-72-21-41
FAX: 011-52-98-72-11-06
www.loscincosoles.com

Owners
Francisco Morales

Cuisine
Gourmet Mexican

Days Open
Open Mon.-Sat. for lunch, daily for dinner

Pricing
Dinner for one, without tax, tip, or drinks: $20-$40

Dress Code
Casual

Reservations
Recommended

Parking
Free on site

Features
Private parties, outdoor dining, entertainment during lunch

Credit Cards
AE, VC, MC

L ocated inside Los Cinco Soles Department Store, at the waterfront, Pancho's Backyard serves extraordinary Mexican food. The famous tequila bar serves awesome margaritas, and there are over 200 tequilas to choose from. Executive Chef Facundo Febles prepares delicious Mexican gourmet cuisine, featuring Steak al Chipotle. Dine on the lush patio of one of Cozumel's most beautiful colonial buildings, amid splashing fountains and tasteful décor. You can enjoy marimba music during lunch, and don't forget your camera—the views are worth capturing.

The famous Tequila Bar

Gourmet Mexican fare

Maître d' Manuel Hernández and Chef Facundo Febles

AWARD WINNER
SINCE 2001

Las Mañanitas

Garden surroundings

Mexico City
Cuernavaca

In Cuernavaca, 1 1/2 hr. from Mexico City International Airport

Ricardo Linares 107
Col. Centro
Cuernavaca, Morelos,
Mexico 62000
PH: 011-52-777-314-1466
FAX: 011-52-777-318-3672
www.lasmananitas.com.mx

Owners
Margot Krause

Cuisine
International

Days Open
Open daily for lunch and dinner

Pricing
Dinner for one, without tax, tip, or drinks: $20-$40

Dress Code
Casual

Reservations
Required

Parking
Valet

Features
Private room/parties, outdoor dining, entertainment

Credit Cards
AE, VC, MC

Exquisite gardens populated with exotic birds set the scene for this beloved restaurant in Cuernavaca, called "the city of eternal spring" by the Aztecs. For more than four decades, Las Mañanitas–a member of the Relais & Chateaux collection of luxury hostelries–has been the worthy recipient of various awards. The menu, featuring Mexican and international cuisine, offers a wide selection of culinary delights, and the staff of over 170 are trained to satisfy the customer's every whim.

Filet with marsalla sauce

View of private garden and pool

AWARD WINNER
SINCE 1993

La Cava

Cross streets: Altamirano and Avenida Insurgentes Sur, 40 min from Aeropuerto Benito Juarez

A dining tradition since 1954

L a Cava is a palatial yet inviting restaurant with breathtaking vistas and exciting international fare. Some of the most famous Mexican cuisine is impeccably created and served here. Tantalizing Spanish, French, Italian, and Mediterranean cuisine are also offered. Specialties of the house include flaming skewered quails and roast duckling in aged wine sauce. The wait staff is personable, knowledgeable, and willing to assist in any way to make your visit a memorable one.

Flaming skewered quails

Wine selections

Avenida Insurgentes Sur, 2465
Mexico, D.F.   01000
PH: 011-5255-55-50-08-52
or, 011-5255-55-50-11-06
FAX: 011-5255-55-50-38-01

Owners
Jordi Escofet

Cuisine
Mexican and Continental

Days Open
Open daily for lunch,
Mon.- Sat. for dinner

Pricing
Dinner for one,
without tax, tip, or drinks
$20-$40

Dress Code
Business casual

Reservations
Recommended

Features
Private room/parties,
entertainment, cigar/
cognac events

Credit Cards
AE, VC, MC, DC

Private room

AWARD WINNER
SINCE 1993

522

La Hacienda De Los Morales

El Patio

Directions

Located on Avenue Vazquez de Mella, 30 min. from Benito Juarez International Airport

Housed in a 16th-century hacienda, La Hacienda de Los Morales features an international cuisine with Mexican specialties, served in an elegant and relaxed atmosphere. Executive Chef Alejandro Heredia prepares authentic dishes such as flor de Calabaza, crepas de Huitlacoche, and pato a la Zarzamora. Presidents, celebrities, and dignitaries all continue to enjoy the hospitality and service that La Hacienda de Los Morales offers, which has distinguished it as a "must visit" when traveling to Mexico.

Courtyard fountain

Main dining room

Chef Alejandro Heredia

La Hacienda De Los Morales
Vazquez De Mella 525
Del Bosque Polanco,
Mexico City, Mexico 11510
PH: 011-52-50-96-3054 to 56
FAX: 011-52-52-82-13-42
www.haciendadelosmorales.com

Owners
Operadora Los Morales SA de CV.

Cuisine
International with Mexican specialties

Days Open
Open daily for lunch and dinner, closed for Easter and Mexican holidays

Pricing
Dinner for one, without tax, tip, or drinks: $20-$40

Dress Code
Jacket and tie required

Reservations
Recommended

Parking
Free on site, valet

Features
Private room/parties

Credit Cards
AE, VC, MC, DC

AWARD WINNER
SINCE 1995

Restaurante Antiguo San Angel Inn

Classic hacienda

Directions

45 min. from Benito Juarez International Airport

Diego Rivera No. 50
Mexico D.F. 01060
PH: 011-52–56-16-14-02
FAX: 011-52-56-16-09-77
www.sanangelinn.com

Owners
Partnership

Cuisine
International

Days Open
Open daily for lunch and dinner

Pricing
Dinner for one,
without tax, tip, or drinks:
$20-$40

Dress Code
Jacket and tie required

Reservations
Recommended

Parking
Free on site, valet

Features
Private room/parties, outdoor dining, entertainment

Credit Cards
AE, VC, MC, DC, JCB

G uests at Antiguo San Angel Inn, housed in an old Carmelite monastery, dine on delicious Mexican gourmet food and international cuisine amid beautiful gardens set with flowers and fountains. Specialties include sea bass Veracruz style, chicken with mole poblano, and roast duckling in blackberry sauce. Often a favorite of celebrities, the establishment is an ideal choice for special occasions.

Jumbo shrimp with Pernod

Dining by fountain

Relaxing patio

AWARD WINNER
SINCE 1994

524

Saint-Honoré

Soft, elegant dining

Situated in Polanco, next to Campos Eliseos, 45 min. from Mexico City Airport

Ave. Presidente Mazarik 341-A
Polanco, Mexico City
Mexico, 11560
PH: (525) 280-9695
FAX: (525) 281-4048
www.saint-honore.com.mx
e-mail:
Saint-honore@mail.insoft.com.mx

Owners
Ernesto Pérez-Rea

Cuisine
French

Days Open
Open Mon.-Sat. for lunch and dinner

Pricing
Dinner for one, without tax, tip, or drinks: $60-$80

Dress Code
Business casual

Reservations
Recommended

Parking
Free on site

Features
Private parties, outdoor dining, cigar/cognac events

Credit Cards
AE, VC, MC, CB, DC

Since 1990, Sainte-Honoré has been offering guests the best of gourmet cuisine such as French foie gras (liver, goose, or duck), Iranian caviar, Norwegian and Scottish salmon, as well as other French dishes all served on French Limoges china in a soft and elegant atmosphere. The wine list has a wide variety of the best vintages in France that can be savored with one of the restaurant's fine cigars.

Iranian caviar

Owner Ernest Pérez-Rea

Gourmet cuisine

AWARD OF EXCELLENCE

AWARD WINNER
SINCE 1998

Restaurantes Suntory
Del Valle Branch

Suntory offering fine Japanese cuisine since 1970

Located on Torres Adalid near Insurgentes Sur, 30 min. from Benito Juarez International Airport

Torres Adalid 14
Col. Del Valle
Mexico City, Mexico 03100
PH: 01-55-5536-9432
FAX: 01-55-5543-0031
www.restaurantesuntory.com.mx

Owners
Restaurantes Suntory, S.A.

Cuisine
Japanese

Days Open
Open daily for dinner

Pricing
Dinner for one,
without tax, tip, or drinks:
$40-$60

Dress Code
Business casual

Reservations
Recommended

Parking
Valet

Features
Private rooms/parties

Credit Cards
AE, VC, MC

One of Suntory's Restaurants in Mexico, which is located in Colonia Del Valle, is the flagship restaurant of 11 Restaurants Suntory in the world. Since its debut in 1970, it has built up an enviable reputation as one of the finest Japanese restaurants in Mexico City. Pioneers in Japanese cuisine in this country, Suntory offers an elegant yet friendly dining atmosphere, while offering high quality menu selections such as Sashimi, Shabu Shabu, Sukiyaki, a variety of fresh Sushi, plus traditional favorites such a steaks, pastas, and chicken. Sake is the beverage of choice with dinner, but there is also an extensive wine list.

The Bar

Shabu Room

Japanese gardens at Suntory

AWARD WINNER
SINCE 1994

El Asador Vasco

Your table is ready

Located on "El Zocalo" (Main Square Park) in downtown Oaxaca, 20 min. from Oaxaca International Airport

Portal de Flores 10-A
Oaxaca, Mexico 68000
PH: 011-529-51-4-47-55
FAX: 011-529-51-4-47-62
www.vasco.com.mx

Owners
Ugartechea Brothers

Cuisine
International, Regional, Basque

Days Open
Open daily for lunch and dinner

Pricing
Dinner for one, without tax, tip, or drinks: $20-$40

Dress Code
Casual

Reservations
Recommended

Parking
Garage nearby

Features
Private room/parties, entertainment

Credit Cards
AE, VC, MC, DC, DS, JCB, En Route

Established in 1978 in an 18th-century colonial home, El Asador Vasco was the first restaurant in Oaxaca to offer formal à la carte service, regional and international cuisine, and dishes of the Basque country, all of outstanding quality. Customers can dine on The Terrace, while enjoying the magnificent view of the Zócalo (Oaxaca's central square) or, in The Tavern with its congenial and informal atmosphere. A vast selection of wines and spirits complements this varied menu.

Grouper green sauce Basque style

Founder Luis Ugartechea

Chapulines con guacamole, an exotic entrée

AWARD WINNER
SINCE 1993

Villa Jacaranda

Colonial charm

San Miguel de Allende

Mexico City

In the town of San Miguel de Allende in central Mexico, 90 min. from Leon International Airport and 3 hr. from Mexico City

Aldama 53
San Miguel de Allende,
Guanajuato, Mexico 37700
PH: 011-52-41-52-10-15
FAX: 011-52-41-52-08-83
www.villajacaranda.com

Owners
Donald Fenton

Cuisine
International

Days Open
Open daily for breakfast, lunch, and dinner

Pricing
Dinner for one, without tax, tip, or drinks: $20-$40

Dress Code
Casual

Reservations
Recommended

Parking
Free on site

Features
Private room/parties, outdoor dining, entertainment, near theater

Credit Cards
AE, VC, MC, JCB

On the high plateau of central Mexico, Villa Jacaranda is a converted Colonial mansion on a quiet cobblestone street, where the discerning traveler will find serenity and impeccable dining reminiscent of a fine European inn. For more than 25 years, Villa Jacaranda's chefs have created international gourmet fare and authentic Mexican specialties from fresh, organically grown ingredients and the finest meats and seafoods available. Poblano chilies stuffed with meats, pecans, and raisins and covered with pecan sauce is one unforgettable dish.

Intimate dining

International cuisine

Serene surroundings

DiRoNA
AWARD WINNER
SINCE 1993

Index of Recipients

'21' Club (New York, NY), 326

21 Federal (Nantucket, MA), 237

23 Page Restaurant
  (Asheville, NC)

30 Degree Blue (Panama City, FL)

45 South at the Pirate's House
  (Savannah, GA)

75 Chestnut (Boston, MA), 226

95 Cordova Restaurant and
  Cobalt Lounge
  (St. Augustine, FL), 161

103 West (Atlanta, GA)

208 Talbot
  (St. Michaels, MD), 253

302 West (Geneva, IL)

360 Restaurant at the CN Tower
  (Toronto, Ontario), 487

510 Restaurant, The
  (Minneapolis, MN)

701 Restaurant
  (Washington, D.C.), 94

801 Steak & Chop House
  (Des Moines, IA), 188

1109 South Main
  (Anderson, SC), 405

1789 Restaurant
  (Washington, D.C.), 95

A

A Pacific Café (Kapaa, HI)

Abbey, The (Atlanta, GA), 172

Acquerello
  (San Francisco, CA), 25

Alan Wong's Restaurant
  (Honolulu, HI), 183

Alberini's (Niles, OH), 380

Al Biernat's (Dallas, TX), 424

Al Forno (Providence, RI)

Alice's at La te da
  (Key West, FL), 133

Al's (St. Louis, MO), 270

Ambria (Chicago, IL), 191

American Hotel, The
  (Sag Harbor, NY), 368

American Restaurant
  (Kansas City, MO)

Anaheim White House
  (Anaheim, CA), 42

Andrea's (Metairie, LA)

Andre's at the Monte Carlo
  (Las Vegas, NV), 307

Andre's French Restaurant
  (Las Vegas, NV), 306

Angus Barn, The
  (Raleigh, NC), 288

Anthony's in the Catalinas
  (Tucson, AZ), 10

Anthony's Pier 4
  (Boston, MA), 227

Antrim 1844
  (Taneytown, MD), 256

Anuenue Dining Room
  (Maui, HI)

Aqua (San Francisco, CA)

Aquavit (New York, NY), 327

Aquellos Tiempos
  (Guadalajara, Mexico)

Arabelle (New York, NY)

Armani's (Tampa, FL), 165

Arnaud's Restaurant
  (New Orleans, LA), 215

Arthur's (Nashville, TN), 417

Arthur's 27 (Orlando, FL), 148

Arturo's Ristorante Italiano
  (Boca Raton, FL), 116

Arun's Restaurant
  (Chicago, IL), 192

Ashley's At the Capital
  (Little Rock, AR), 5

Astor International
  (Miami Beach, FL)

Atlanta Grill (Atlanta, GA), 173

Atlantic's Edge at Checca Lodge
  & Spa (Islamorada, FL), 129

Atlantis (Orlando, FL), 149

Auberge Du Pommier
  (Toronto, Ontario)

Auberge du Soleil
  (Rutherford, CA), 22

Auberge Hatley
  (North Hatley, Quebec), 511

Auberge La Camarine
  (Beupre, Quebec)

Aujourd'hui (Boston, MA)

Aureole (New York, NY), 328

Au Tourant de las Riviere
  (Caregan, Quebec)

Avalon (Toronto, Ontario)

Azzura Point (Coronado, CA)

B

Bacchanalia (Atlanta, GA)

Bali by the Sea
  (Honolulu, HI), 184

Balthazar Restaurant
  (New York, NY), 329

Barbetta (New York, NY), 330

This is a listing of all DiRōNA Award recipients. Only recipients participating in the guide will have a page number next to their name.

Index of Recipients

Baricelli Inn, The
(Cleveland, OH), 375
Bartolatta's Lake Park Bistro
(Milwaukee, WI), 468
Bayona (New Orleans, LA), 216
Bay Tower, The (Boston, MA), 228
Beach Walk Café (Destin, FL), 123
Beano's Cabin
(Beaver Creek, CO), 78
Beaver Club, The
(Montreal, Quebec), 500
Bedford Village Inn
(Bedford, NH), 289
Bellini Restaurant
(New York, NY), 331
Benedetto's Ristorante
(St. Louis), 271
Bernards Inn, The
(Bernardsville, NJ), 292
Bernard's Inn at Ridgefield
(Ridgefield, CT), 93
Bern's Steak House
(Tampa, FL), 166
Beverly's Restaurant
(Coeur d'Alene, ID), 189
Biagio Ristorante
(Toronto, Ontario), 488
Biba (Sacramento, CA), 23
Bishops
(Vancouver, British Columbia)
Bistro 110 (Chicago, IL)
Bistro 990
(Toronto, Ontario), 489
Bistro AIX (Jacksonville, FL), 130
Bistro at Maison de Ville
(New Orleans, LA), 217

Bistro Jeanty (Yountville, CA)
Black Pearl, The
(Dunedin, FL), 126
Blue Bayou
(Cancun, Mexico), 517
Blue Door at Delano
(Miami Beach, FL), 138
Bob's Steak & Chop House
(Dallas, TX), 452
Bombay Club
(Washington, D.C.), 96
Bone's Restaurant
(Atlanta, GA), 174
Bouley (New York, NY), 332
Brass Elephant, The
(Baltimore, MD)
Brasserie La Coze (Atlanta, GA)
Brennan's of Houston
(Houston, TX), 430
Brewster Inn, The
(Cazenovia, NY), 322
Bridges (Danville, CA)
Brigsten's (New Orleans, LA)
Broker Restaurant
(Denver, CO), 80
Brooks Restaurant
(Deerfield Beach, FL), 121
Broussard's Restaurant
(New Orleans, LA), 218

C

C restaurant (Vancouver, British
Columbia), 475
Café 36 (LaGrange, IL), 205
Café Abbracci
(Coral Gables, FL), 124

Café Annie (Houston, TX)
Cafe Cellini
(Palm Beach, FL), 155
Cafe Chardonnay
(Palm Beach Gardens, FL), 159
Café de France
(St. Louis, Mo)
Café del Rey (Marina Del Rey)
Café de Paris (Montreal, Quebec)
Café des Artistes
(New York, NY), 333
Café du Soir (Vero Beach, FL), 170
Café Elan, Chateau Elan
(Braseton, GA)
Café Henry Burger
(Hull, Quebec), 498
Café L'Europe
(Palm Beach, CA), 156
Café L'Europe (Sarasota, FL), 163
Café Margaux (Lake Charles, LA)
Café Marquesa (Key West, FL)
Café Pacific (Dallas, TX), 426
Cafe Pacifica (San Diego, CA), 65
Café Pierre (New York, NY)
Cafe Portofino (Lihue, HI), 187
Caffe de Medici (Vancouver,
British Columbia), 476
Campagne & Cafe Campagne
(Seattle, WA), 460
Campania (Charlotte, NC), 283
Campanile (Los Angeles, CA)
Campiello (Minneapolis, MN)
Canlis (Seattle, WA), 461
Cape Cod Room (Chicago, IL)
Capital Grille, The
(Charlotte, NC), 284

Index of Recipients

Capital Grille, The
(Houston, TX), 431

Capriccio (Providence, RI), 404

Capriccio Ristorante
(Pembroke Pines, FL)

Carlos' Restaurant
(Highland Park, IL), 204

Carlton, The
(Pittsburgh, PA), 397

Carlucci Rosemont
(Rosemont, IL), 209

Carnelian Room
(San Francisco, CA), 26

Casa de Sierra Nevada
(San Miguel de Allende, Mexico)

Casa Vecchia (Coral Gables, FL)

Cascadia Restaurant (Seattle, WA)

Castle Restaurant (Leicester, MA)

Caucus Room, The
(Washington, D.C.), 97

Cavey's Restaurant
(Manchester, CT), 92

Cellar, The (Fullerton, CA), 51

Centro Grill and Wine Bar
(Toronto, Ontario)

Champs Elysees
(Mexico City, Mexico)

Chanterelle (Eugene, OR), 383

Chanterelle (New York, NY), 334

Chanticleer, The
(Siasconset, MA), 241

Chaparral Supper Club
(Scottsdale, AZ)

Chardonnay Restaurant
(Naples, FL), 142

Charles Court
(Colorado Springs, CO), 79

Charles Nob Hill
(San Francisco, CA)

Charleston Grill
(Charleston, SC), 407

Charley's Steak House
(Orlando, FL), 150

Charley's Steak House and Market
Fresh Fish (Tampa, FL), 167

Charlie Trotters (Chicago, IL)

Chartwell
(Vancouver, British Columbia)

Chateau Souverain Café
(Greystone, CA)

Chef Allen's (Aventura, FL), 115

Chez Delmo (Montreal, Quebec)

Chez La Mère Michel
(Montreal, Quebec), 501

Chez nous (Houston, TX), 432

Chez Panisse (Berkeley, CA)

Chez Philippe
(Memphis, TN), 414

Chicago Chop House
(Chicago, IL), 193

Chillingsworth
(Brewster, MA), 235

Chop & Lobster Bar (Atlanta, GA)

Chopstix (Atlanta, GA), 175

Christian's Restaurant
(New Orleans, LA), 219

Christini's Ristorante Italiano
(Orlando, FL), 151

Christy's Restaurant
(Coral Gables, FL), 119

Cioppino's Mediterranean Grill &
Enoteca (Vancouver,
British Columbia), 477

Cité (New York, NY), 335

Circa (Philadelphia, PA)

Circa 1886 (Charleston, SC), 406

Cite Elegant Dining
(Chicago, IL), 194

City Grill (Atlanta, GA), 176

Clay Hill Farm (York, ME), 258

Cliff House Dining Room, The
(Manitou Springs, CO), 85

Clifton Inn
(Charlottesville, VA), 447

Clio's (Boston, MA)

Club XIX (Pebble Beach, CA), 21

Coco Pazzo (Chicago, IL), 195

Colonnade, The
(Manchester Village, VT)

Colony Dining Room, The
(Longboat Key, FL), 136

Columbus Inn
(Wilmington, DE), 112

Commander's Palace
(New Orleans, LA), 220

Commander's Palace
(Las Vegas, NV), 308

Couveron (Portland, OR)

Covey, The (Carmel, CA), 11

Coyote Café (Santa Fe, NM), 302

Criolla's (Grayton Beach, FL)

Crow's Nest, The
(Anchorage, AK), 1

D

Dakotah 624
(Delray Beach, FL), 122

Index of Recipients

Dal Baffo (Menlo Park, CA), 17

D'Amico Cocina
(Minneapolis, MN)

Da Mimmo Finest Italian Cuisine
(Baltimore, MD), 237

Daniel (New York, NY)

Dan'l Webster Inn, The
(Sandwich, MA), 240

Darrel & Oliver's Cafe Maxx
(Pompano Beach, FL), 160

Dawat (New York, NY), 336

DELLA NOTTE Ristorante of Little
Italy (Baltimore, MD), 247

Destin Chops (Destin, FL)

Deux Cheminees
(Philadelphia, PA)

Diaghilev (West Hollywood, CA)

Diamond's (Trenton, NJ), 297

Different Point of View
(Phoenix, AZ)

Dilworthtown Inn
(West Chester, PA), 401

Dining Room, The
(Gleneden Beach, OR), 384

Dining Room, The
(Naples, FL), 143

Dining Room, The
(Short Hills, NJ), 296

Dining Room at Ford's Colony,
The (Williamsburg, VA), 454

Dining Room at Mount Washington
Hotel, The (Bretton Woods, NH)

Dining Room at the Ritz-Carlton
(Chicago, IL), 196

Dining Room at the Ritz-Carlton,
The (Rancho Mirage, CA)

Dining Room at the Ritz-Carlton,
The (San Francisco, CA)

Dining Room at the Ritz-Carlton,
The (Atlanta, GA)

Dining Room at the Ritz-Carlton,
The (Boston, MA)

Dining Room at the Ritz-Carlton,
Laguna Niguel, The
(Dana Point, CA), 50

Dining Room at Woodlands, The
(Summerville, SC), 411

Dining Room, Regent Beverly
Wilshire, The (Beverly Hills, CA)

Di Salvo's Station Restaurant
(Latrobe, PA), 393

Diva as the Met
(Vancouver, British Columbia)

Domaine Chandon
(Yountville, CA), 40

Dominic's (St. Louis, MO), 272

Donatello (Tampa, FL), 168

Doug Arango's
(West Hollywood, CA), 73

Downey's (Santa Barbara, CA)

Duane's Prime Steaks & Seafood
Restaurant (Riverside, CA), 64

DUX (Orlando, FL), 152

E

Eddie Martini's
(Wauwatosa, WI), 469

Eduardo de San Angel (Fort
Lauderdale, FL), 127

El Asador Vasco
(Oaxaca, Mexico), 527

El Bizcocho (San Diego, CA), 66

Elephant Walk (Destin, FL), 124

Elizabeth on 37th
(Savannah, GA), 181

Elizabeth's Café & Winery
(Duck, NC), 285

Elysium (Alexandria, VA)

Emeril's (New Orlean's, LA)

Emeril's at city Walk
(Orlando, FL)

Emile's Restaurant and Cooking
School (San Jose, CA), 36

Empress (Houston, TX)

English Room at the Deer Path
Inn, The (Lake Forest, IL), 206

Erna's Elderberry House
(Oakhurst, CA)

Estoril (Mexico City, Mexico)

Euphemia Haye
(Longboat Key, FL), 137

Everest (Chicago, IL), 197

EverMay On-The-Delaware
(Erwinna, PA), 389

F

Fairbanks Steakhouse
(Robinsonville, MS), 280

Fandango (Pacific Grove, CA), 20

Farallon Restaurant
(San Francisco, CA), 27

Far Niente
(Toronto, Ontario), 490

Faust's (Saint Louis, MO)

Fearington House, The
(Pittsboro, NC), 287

Felida Ristorante (New York, NY)

Index of Recipients

Fenix (West Hollywood, CA), 74

Ferraro's Restaurant
(Las Vegas, NV), 309

Fig Tree (San Antonio, TX), 439

Finelli's Italian Villa
(Altoona, PA), 387

Fior d'Italia
(San Francisco, CA), 28

Fiore (Las Vegas, NV), 310

Five Crowns
(Corona del Mar, CA), 49

Five Sails Restaurant, The
(Vancouver, British Columbia), 478

Flagler Steakhouse, The
(Palm Beach, FL), 157

Flagstaff House Restaurant
(Boulder, CO)

Fleur de Lys (San Francisco, CA)

Folk's Folly Prime Steak House
(Memphis, TN), 415

Forge Restaurant, The
(Miami Beach, FL), 139

Fountain Restaurant
(Philadelphia, PA)

Four Seasons, The (New York, NY)

Fournou's Ovens
(San Francisco, CA), 29

Fox & Hounds, The
(Hubertus, WI)

French Laundry Restaurant, The
(Yountville, CA), 41

French Poodle Restaurant, The
(Carmel, CA), 12

French Room at The Adolphus,
The (Dallas, TX), 427

Fresco Italian Café
(Salt Lake City, UT), 443

Fresh Cream Restaurant
(Monterey, CA), 18

Friend's Lake Inn
(Chestertown, NY), 323

G

Galatoire's Restaurant
(New Orleans, LA), 221

Galileo (Washington, D.C.), 98

Gallagher's (New York, NY)

Gallatin Gateway Inn
(Gateway, MT)

Gardens, The (Los Angeles, CA)

Gene & Georgetti
(Chicago, IL), 198

Geneva (Scottsdale, AZ)

Gennaro's Ristorante
(Glendale, CA), 52

George's at the Cove
(La Jolla, CA)

Georgian Room (Seattle, WA)

Gerard's Downtown
(New Orleans, LA)

Gerard's Place (Washington, D.C.)

Geronimo (Santa Fe, NM), 303

Giovanni's
(Jacksonville Beach, FL), 132

Giovanni's Little Place
(St. Louis, MO), 274

Giovanni's on the Hill
(St. Louis, MO), 275

Giovanni's Ristorante
(Detroit, MI), 259

Giulio Cesare Ristorante
(Westbury, NY)

Glass Chimney, The (Carmel, IN)

Glitretind Restaurant at
Stein Eriksen Lodge
(Park City, UT), 440

Golden Trout
(Farmington, PA), 390

Goodfellows (Minneapolis, MN)

Gotham Bar & Grill
(New York, NY)

G. P. Agostino's
(St. Louis, MO), 273

Gramercy Tavern
(New York, NY), 337

Granary at Spring Creek Ranch, The
(Jackson Hole, WY), 470

Granita (Malibu, CA)

Grant Grill (San Diego, CA), 67

Grappa Italian Restaurant & Café
(Park City, UT), 441

Greenbrier Main Dining Room, The
(White Sulfur Springs, WV)

Grill, The (Los Angeles, CA)

Grill, The
(Amelia Island, FL), 114

Grill, Ritz-Carlton, The
(Manalapan, FL)

Grill, Ritz-Carlton, The
(Clayton, MO)

Grill 23 & Bar (Boston, MA), 229

Grill on the Alley, The
(Beverly Hills, CA), 45

Grill Room, The
(New Orleans, LA), 222

Index of Recipients

Grill Room on Las Olas, The
(Fort Lauderdale, FL)

H

Hamersley's Bistro
(Boston, MA), 230
Hampton's (Baltimore, MD), 248
Harrah's Steak House
(Reno, NV), 317
Harralds (Stormville, NY), 370
Harris' Restaurant
(San Francisco, CA), 30
Haydn Zug's
(East Petersburg, PA), 388
Heathman Hotel Restaurant, The
(Portland, OR)
Hemingway's
(Killington, VT), 457
Herbfarm, The
(Woodinville, WA), 466
Hermitage Inn
(Wilmington, VT), 459
Highlands Bar & Grill
(Birmingham, AL), 3
Highlawn Pavilion
(West Orange, NJ), 298
Hi Life Kitchen & Cocktails
(Norcross, GA), 180
Hobbit, The (Orange, CA), 61
Hogan's Inn at Four Corners
(King City, Ontario)
Horizons at The Grove Park Inn
Resort & Spa (Ashville, NC), 282
Hotel Restaurant L'Eau a la Bouche
(Sainte-Adéle, Quebec), 514
Hyeholde Restaurant and The Round
Room (Pittsburgh, PA), 398

Hy's Encore
(Vancouver, British Columbia)

I

Icarus (Boston, MA), 231
Il Capriccio Ristorante e Bar
(Waltham, MA), 244
Il Fiorentino (Buffalo, NY)
Il Nido (New York, NY)
Il Terrazo Carmine (Seattle, WA)
Il Toscano Ristorante
(Douglaston, NY)
Immigrant Restaurant & Winery,
The (Kohler, WI), 467
Imperial Chinese Seafood Restaurant
(Vancouver, British Columbia), 479
Inn at Little Washington, The
(Washington, VA)
Inn at Manitou, The
(McKellar, Ontario)
Inn at Sawmill Farm, The
(West Dover, VT), 458
Inn at Turner's Mill, The
(Hudson, OH), 379
Inn on the Twenty
(Jordan, Ontario), 485

J

Jack Binion's Steakhouse
(Robinsonville, MS), 281
Jackson's Steakhouse
(Fort Lauderdale, FL), 128
Janos (Tucson, AZ)
Jasper's (Kansas City, MO), 268
Jean Georges (New York, NY), 338
Jeffrey's Restaurant
(Austin, TX), 423

Joe Fortes Seafood & Chop House
(Vancouver, British Columbia), 480
Joel Palmer House
(Dayton, OR), 382
John Mineo's Italian Restaurant
(St. Louis, MO), 276
Johnny's Bar
(Cleveland, OH), 376
Jo Jo (New York, NY), 339
Jo's Restaurant of Palm Beach
(Palm Beach, FL)
Joseph's Table
(Ranchos de Taos, NM)
Juliano's (Billings, MT)
Julien Restaurant Bar & Grill
(Boston, MA)
JW's Steakhouse
(Anaheim, CA), 43

K

Kaspars (Seattle, WA)
Keystone Ranch, The
(Keystone, CO)
Kinkead's, An American Brassiere
(Washington, D.C.), 99

L

La Bergerie (Alexandria, VA), 446
La Bonne Auberge
(New Hope, PA), 394
La Cachette (Los Angeles, CA), 56
La Caravelle (New York, NY), 340
La Cava
(Mexico City, Mexico), 522
La Chaumiére Restaurant
(Calgary, Alberta), 471

Index of Recipients

La Chronique (Montreal, Quebec)

La Colombe d'or Hotel and
    Restaurant (Houston, TX), 433

La Coquina (Orlando, FL), 153

La Cote Basque (New York, NY)

La Dolce Vita
    (Cancun, Mexico), 518

La Embotelladora Vieja
    (Ensenada, Mexico)

La Famiglia (Philadelphia, PA)

Lafite (Naples, FL), 144

Lafitte's Landing Restaurant at
    Bittersweet Plantation
    (New Orleans, LA), 223

La Folie (San Francisco, CA), 31

La Grande Table de Serge Bruyère
    (Quebec City, Quebec)

La Grenouille (New York, NY)

La Grotta Ristorante Italiano
    (Atlanta, GA), 177

La Habichuela Restaurant
    (Cancun, Mexico), 519

La Hacienda De Los Morales
    (Mexico City, Mexico), 523

La Joya (Cancun, Mexico)

La Mer (Honolulu, HI), 185

Langdon Hall Country House
Hotel & Spa
    (Cambridge, Ontario), 484

La Panetiére (Rye, NY), 367

La Parisienne
    (St. Augustine, FL), 162

La Provence (Lacombe, LA), 214

La Reserve (Houston, TX), 434

Lark, The
    (West Bloomfield, MI), 265

Lark Creek Inn, The
    (Larkspur, CA), 15

Larkspur Restaurant
    (Vail, CO), 86

Las Mañanitas
    (Cuernavaca, Mexico), 521

La Strada Ristorante
    (Chicago, IL), 199

Latilla, The (Carefree, AZ), 6

La Tourelle Restaurant
    (Memphis, TN), 416

L'Auberge (Dayton, OH), 378

L'Auberge Chez Francois
    (Great Falls, VA), 448

L'Auberge de Sedona
    (Sedona, AZ), 9

La Vie en Rose (Brea, CA), 47

La Vieille Maison
    (Boca Raton, FL), 117

Lawry's The Prime Rib
    (Beverly Hills, CA), 46

Lawry's The Prime Rib
    (Chicago, IL), 200

Le Bec-Fin (Philadelphia, PA)

Le Bernadin (New York, NY)

Le Bistro a Champlain
    (du Lac Mac, Quebec)

Le Café De Paris (Omaha, NE)

Le Central Bistro
    (San Francisco, CA), 32

Le Champlain
    (Quebec City, Quebec), 513

Le Cirque 2000
    (New York, NY), 341

Le Cirque at Bellagio
    (Las Vegas, NV), 311

Left Bank Restaurant
    (Vail, CO), 87

le jardin (Ottawa, Ontario), 486

Le Latini (Montreal, Quebec)

Le Madri (New York, NY), 342

Lemaire (Richmond, VA), 450

Le Mas des Oliviers
    (Montreal, Quebec)

Le Mistral
    (North Palm Beach, FL), 146

Le Muscadin
    (Montreal, Quebec), 502

Lenox Room (New York, NY)

Le Papillon (San Jose, CA), 37

Le Parchemin
    (Montreal, Quebec), 503

Le Parvenu Restaurant
    (Kenner, LA), 213

Le Passe-Partout Restaurant
    (Montreal, Quebec), 504

Le Perigord (New York, NY), 343

Le Petit Chateau
    (North Hollywood, CA), 60

Le Piment Rouge
    (Montreal, Quebec)

Le Relais (Louisville, KY)

Le Saint Germain
    (Indian Wells, CA), 53

L'Escalier (Palm Beach, FL), 158

Les Caprices de Nicolas
    (Montreal, Quebec), 505

Les Chenets (Montreal, Quebec)

L'Espalier (Boston, MA), 232

Lespinasse (New York, NY)

Index of Recipients

Les Remparts Restaurant
(Montreal, Quebec), 506

Le Titi de Paris
(Arlington Heights, IL), 190

L'Etoile (Madison, WI)

Le Vallauris (Palm Springs, CA)

Le Vichyssois (Lakemoor, IL), 207

LG's Prime Steakhouse
(Palm Desert, CA), 62

Library, The (Roanoke, VA)

Lilly's Restaurant (Louisville, KY)

Llewellyn's (Stateline, NV), 320

Log Haven Restaurant
(Salt Lake City, UT), 444

L'Olivier (San Francisco, CA), 33

L'Orangie (Los Angeles, CA)

Lord Fletcher's Old Lake Lodge
(Spring Park, MN), 267

Louie's Backyard (Key West, FL)

Ludwig's
(Vail, CO), 88

Lumière
(Vancouver, British Columbia), 481

M

Maderias (Acapulco, Mexico)

Maestro (McLean,VA)

Magnolia Grill (Durham, NC)

Magnolias (Charleston, SC), 408

Maison & Jardin
(Altamonte Springs, FL), 113

Maisonette (Cincinnati, OH), 373

Maison Robert (Boston, MA)

Malmaison (St. Albans, MO)

Maloney & Porcelli
(New York, NY), 344

Manhattan Ocean Club
(New York, NY), 345

Manoir Hovey
(North Hatley, Quebec), 512

Manor, The (West Orange, NJ), 299

Mansion on Turtle Creek, The
(Dallas, TX)

Manuel's on the 28th
(Orlando, FL), 154

Maple Drive (Beverly Hills, CA)

Marcel's (Washington, D.C.), 100

March Restaurant
(New York, NY), 346

Marie-Michelle's Restaurant
on the Bay (Naples, FL), 145

Marina Café (Destin, FL)

Marine Room, The
(La Jolla, CA), 54

Mario's (Nashville, TN), 418

Mark Picone at Vineland Estates
(Vineland, Ontario), 497

Mark's (Houston, TX), 435

Marquesa (Scottsdale, AZ), 8

Martha's Restaurant
(Hollywood, FL)

Mary Elaine's (Scottsdale, AZ)

Masa's (San Francisco, CA)

Matsuhisa (Beverly Hills, CA)

Maxwell's Chophouse
(Boca Raton, FL), 118

Mayflower Inn
(Washington, D.C.)

McCrady's (Charleston, SC), 409

Mecca (San Francisco, CA)

Melrose (Washington, D.C.), 101

Melvyn's Restaurant
(Palm Springs, CA)

Metropolitan
(Salt Lake City, UT), 445

Metropolitan Grill
(Seattle, WA), 462

Michael's (Las Vegas, NV), 312

Michael's (New York, NY), 347

Michael's (Santa Monica, CA), 71

Michael's on East
(Sarasota, FL), 164

Michel Richard Citronelle
(Washington, D.C.), 102

Michel's Christiana
(Ketchum, ID)

Michel's on the Beach at the
Colony Surf (Honolulu, HI), 186

Mille Fleurs
(Rancho Santa Fe, CA), 68

Mill River Inn (Oyster Bay, NY)

Milton Inn, The
(Sparks, MD), 255

Mirabelle Restaurant
(Saint James, NY), 369

Mirabelle Restaurant at Beaver
Creek (Avon, CO), 77

Montagna Restaurant
(Aspen, CO)

Monte Carlo Living Room, The
(Philadelphia, PA), 395

Montrachet (New York, NY), 348

Morrison-Clark Historic Inn
(Washington, D.C.), 103

Mr. Stox (Anaheim, CA), 44

Index of Recipients

N

Nava (Atlanta, GA)

Nick's Fishmarket (Chicago, IL)

Nick's Fishmarket (Rosemont, IL)

Nicola's Restaurant
(New York, NY), 349

Nikolai's Roof (Atlanta, GA), 178

Nobu (New York, NY), 350

Nola (New Orleans, LA)

Nora (Washington, D.C.), 104

Norman's (Coral Gables, FL), 120

North 44 Degrees
(Toronto, Ontario)

North Beach Restaurant, The
(San Francisco, CA)

Northwoods (Annapolis, MD), 245

Nuances (Montreal, Quebec), 507

O

Oakroom at the Seelbach Hilton,
The (Louisville, KY), 211

Oceanaire Seafood Room, The
(Washington, D.C.), 105

Old Angler's Inn
(Potomac, MD), 252

Old Hickory Traditional
Steakhouse (Nashville, TN), 419

Old Warsaw, The
(Dallas, TX), 428

Olde Pink House Restaurant &
Planters Tavern, The
(Savannah, GA), 182

ONE c.p.s. (New York), 351

One if by Land, Two if by Sea
(New York, NY), 352

One sixtyblue (Chicago, IL)

Opus II (Montreal, Quebec), 508

Opus One (Detroit, MI), 260

Orangery, The
(Knoxville, TN), 412

Òran Mór (Nantucket, MA), 238

Oval Room, The
(Washington, D.C.), 106

Owl's Nest Dining Room, The
(Calgary, Alberta), 472

P

Pacific's Edge (Carmel, CA), 13

Pahu i' a (Kailua Kona, HI)

Palace Arms at the Brown Palace
Hotel (Denver, CO), 81

Palace Restaurant, The
(Cincinnati, OH), 374

Panama Hatties (Station, NY)

Pancho's Backyard
(Cozumel, Mexico), 520

Panico's
(New Brunswick, NJ), 294

Pano's and Paul's (Atlanta, GA)

Paolo's Restaurant
(San Jose, CA), 38

Park Avenue Cafe
(New York, NY), 353

Pascale Wine Bar and Restaurant
(Syracuse, NY), 371

Passerelle Restaurant
(Radnor, PA), 400

Patina (Los Angeles, CA), 57

Patroon (New York, NY)

Pavilion (Newport Beach, CA), 59

Peninsula Grill
(Charleston, SC), 410

Pepercorn Duck Club, The
(Kansas City, MO), 269

Peppermill's White Orchid
(Reno, NV), 318

Peregrines'
(Atlantic City, NJ), 291

Periyali (New York, NY)

Petrossian (New York, NY)

Picasso (Las Vegas, NV), 313

Piccolo Restaurant of Huntington
(Huntington, NY), 325

Picholine (New York, NY), 354

Pierce's 1894 Restaurant
(Elmira Heights, NY)

Piero's (Las Vegas, NV), 314

Pietro's Gourmet Room
(Las Vegas, NV), 315

Pinons Restaurant (Basalt, CO)

Place Pigalle Restaurant and Bar
(Seattle, WA), 463

Plumed Horse, The
(Saratoga, CA), 39

Polo Grill (Tulsa, OK), 381

Port House (Biloxi, MS), 279

Post Hotel Dining Room
(Lake Louise, Alberta), 473

Post House, The
(New York, NY), 355

Postrio (San Francisco, CA), 34

Prego della Piazza
(Toronto, Ontario), 491

Pricci (Atlanta, GA)

Primadonna Restaurant, The
(Pittsburgh, PA), 399

Prime Rib, The
(Washington, D.C.), 107

Index of Recipients

Prime Rib, The (Baltimore, MD)

Printer's Row (Chicago, IL)

Profusion (Montreal, Quebec)

Pump House, The
(Fairbanks, AK), 2

Pump Room, The (Chicago, IL)

Pyramid Grill (Dallas, TX)

Q

Quattro (Houston, TX), 436

R

Raincity Grill
(Vancouver, British Columbia), 482

Rainwater's on Kettner
(San Diego, CA), 69

Ram's Head Inn
(Galloway, NJ), 293

Ranchers Club of New Mexico
(Albuquerque, NM), 301

Rattlesnake Club, The
(Detroit, MI), 261

Ray's Boathouse
(Seattle, WA), 464

Rebeccas (Greenwich, CT), 91

Refectory, The
(Columbus, OH), 377

Regas Restaurant
(Knoxville, TN), 413

Regency Room
(Williamsburg, VA), 455

Regency Room at The Hotel
Roanoke, The (Roanoke, VA), 451

Remì Restaurant
(New York, NY), 356

Renaissance (Aspen, CO), 75

Renoir (Las Vegas, NV)

Restaurant, The
(Palm Beach, FL)

Restaurant at Hotel Bel-Air, The
(Los Angeles, CA), 58

Restaurant at Meadowood, The
(St. Helena, CA), 24

Restaurant at the Canterbury
(Indianapolis, IN), 210

Restaurant Bouchard
(Newport, RI), 402

Restaurant Dubrovnik
(Winnipeg, Manitoba), 483

Restaurant Jean-Louis
(Greenwhich, CT)

Restaurant La Maree
(Montreal, Quebec)

Restaurant Le Mitoyen
(Laval, Quebec), 499

Restaurant Les Halles
(Montreal, Quebec)

Restaurant Picasso
(Edwards, CO), 84

Restaurant St. Michel
(Coral Gables, FL)

Restaurante Antiguo San Angel
Inn (Mexico City, Mexico), 524

Restaurantes Suntory
(Mexico City, Mexico), 526

Rialto (Cambridge, MA)

RingSide Steakhouse Downtown
(Portland, OR), 385

RingSide Steakhouse Glendoveer
(Portland, OR), 386

Ristorante Café Cortina
(Farmington Hills, MI), 263

Ristorante Casanova
(Acapulco, Mexico), 516

Ristorante Da Vinci
(Montreal, Quebec), 509

Ristorante Giovanni's
(Beachwood, OH), 372

Ristorante i Ricchi
(Washington, D.C.), 108

Ristorante La Buca
(Philadelphia, PA), 396

Ristorante La Bussola
(Coral Gables, FL)

Ristorante La Fenice
(Toronto, Ontario), 492

Ristorante Michelangelo
(Sainte Foy, Quebec), 515

Ristorante Paradiso
(Lake Worth, FL), 135

Ristorante Primavera
(New York, NY), 357

River Café, The
(Brooklyn, NY), 321

River'd Inn (Woodstock, VA), 456

Riverhorse Café
(Park City, UT), 442

Rosewater Supper Club (Toronto,
Ontario), 493

Rotisserie for Beef and Bird
(Houston, TX), 437

Rough Creek Lodge
(Glen Rose, TX), 429

Rover's (Seattle, WA), 465

Rowe, The (ellsworth, MI)

Roxsand (Reno, NV)

Roxy (Reno, NV), 319

Roy's Restaurant (Honolulu, HI)

Index of Recipients

Rudy's 2900 Restaurant
(Finksburg, MD), 250

Rundles Restaurant
(Stratford, Ontario)

Ruth's Chris Steak House
(New Orleans, LA), 224

Ruth's Chris Steak House
(North Palm Beach, FL), 147

Ruth's Chris Steak House
(Toronto, Ontario), 494

Ruth's Chris Steak House
(Winter Park, FL), 171

Ryland Inn, The
(Whitehouse, NJ), 300

S

Saddle Peak Lodge
(Calabasas, CA), 48

Saddle River Inn, The
(Saddle River, NJ), 295

Saint-Honoré
(Mexico City, Mexico), 525

St. Paul Grill, The
(St. Paul, MN), 266

Salish Dining Room, The
(Snoqualmie, WA)

Saloon Restaurant
(Philadelphia, PA)

Salvatore's Italian Gardens
(Depew, NY), 324

Sam & Harry's
(Washington, D.C.), 109

Sam & Harry's Tysons Corner
(Vienna, VA), 453

San Domenico NY
(New York, NY), 358

Sanford Restaurant
(Milwaukee, WI)

Santacafé (Santa Fe, NM)

Sardine Factory, The
(Monterey, CA), 19

Savona (Gulph Mills, PA), 391

Sazerac Bar & Grill
(New Orleans, LA)

Scaramouche
(Toronto, Ontario), 495

Scatton's Restaurant
(Hazelton, PA), 392

Scheherazade (Atlantic City, NJ)

Sea Fare Inn
(Portsmouth, RI), 403

Seagar's (Destin, FL), 125

Seasons (Boston, MA), 233

Seasons (Chicago, IL)

Seventh Inn, The
(St. Louis, MO), 277

Sherwood's Landing at
the Inn at Perry Cabin
(St. Michaels, MD), 254

Shintaro, Bellagio Resort and
Casino (Las Vegas, NV)

SideBern's (Tampa, FL), 169

Signatures Restaurant
(Toronto, Ontario)

Sign of the Vine (Naples, FL)

Silks (San Francisco, CA)

Silks at Stonehedge Inn
(Tyngsboro, MA), 243

Simon & seafort's
(Anchorage, AK)

Sky Room, The (La Jolla, CA)

Smith & Wollensky
(Miami Beach, FL), 140

Smith & Wollensky
(Chicago, IL), 201

Smith & Wollensky
(Las Vegas, NV), 316

Smith & Wollensky
(New York, NY), 359

Smith's Louis XVI Restaurant
Français (New Orleans, LA), 225

Snake River Grill (Jackson, WY)

Sonoma Restaurant
(Princeton, MA), 239

Sooke Harbour House
(Sooke, British Columbia), 474

South City Kitchen
(Atlanta, GA), 179

Sparks Steak House
(New York, NY), 360

Spiaggia (Chicago, IL)

Square One Restaurant
(Key West, FL), 134

Star Canyon (Dallas, TX)

Star of the Sea
(San Diego, CA), 70

Stars (San Francisco, CA)

Stars Waterfront Café
(Ocean Isle Beach, NC), 286

Station Grille (Saint Louis, MO)

Sterling's of Avondale
(Jacksonville, FL), 131

Stock-Yard Restaurant, The
(Nashville, TN), 420

Stonehenge Inn (Ridgefield, CT)

Stone Manor
(Middletown, MD), 251

Index of Recipients

Strings (Denver, CO), 82

Striped Bass (Philadelphia, PA)

Summer House Restaurant
(Siasconset, MA), 242

Summit, The (Juneau, AK)

Summit, The
(Lake Tahoe, NV), 305

Sun Mountain Lodge
(Winthrop, WA)

Sunset Grill (Nashville, TN), 421

Susanna Foo Chinese Cuisine
(Philadelphia, PA)

Swan Court (Lahaina Maui, HI)

Sweet Basil (Vail, CO)

Swifty's (New York, NY), 361

Syzygy (Aspen, CO), 76

T

Taberna Del Alabardero
(Washington, D.C.), 110

Tack Room, The (Tuscon, AZ)

Tallgrass (Lockport, IL), 208

Tante Louise (Denver, CO), 83

Tantra Restaurant and Lounge
(Miami Beach, FL), 141

Tapawingo (Ellsworth, MI)

Terra (St. Helena, CA)

Terra Bistro (Vail, CO), 89

Terrace in the Sky
(New York, NY), 362

Theo's (Souix Falls, SD)

Tivoli Restaurant
(Rosslyn, VA), 452

Tommy Toy's Cuisine Chinoise
(San Francisco, CA), 35

Tony's (St. Louis, Mo), 278

Tony's Restaurant
(Houston, TX), 438

Top of the Cove (La Jolla, CA), 55

Top of the Hub (Boston, MA), 234

Topper's at the Wauwinet
(Nantucket, MA)

Toque! (Montreal, Quebec)

Trader Vic's (Emeryville, CA), 14

Tragara Ristorante
(Bethesda, MD), 249

Tribeca Grill
(New York, NY), 363

Tribute
(Farmington Hills, MI), 264

Troutdale Dining Room, The
(Bristol, TN)

Truffles (Toronto, Ontario)

TSIRCO Restaurant Jazz
(Montreal, Quebec), 510

Tuscany at Lowe's Giorgio, The
(Denver, CO)

Tyrolean (Vail, CO)

U

Union Square Cafe
(New York, NY), 364

V

Valentino Restaurant
(Santa Monica, CA), 72

Vallozzi's (Greensburg, PA)

Va Pensiero (Evanston, IL), 203

Veni Vidi Vici (Atlanta, GA)

Ventana Room (Tuscon, AZ)

Via Allegro Ristorante
(Toronto, Ontario), 496

Victoria & Albert's (Orlando, FL)

Villa Fontana (Taos, NM), 304

Villa Jacaranda (San Miguel de
Allende, Mexico), 528

Vincent Guerithault on
Camelback (Phoenix, AZ)

Vincenzo's (Louisville, KY), 212

Vivere (Chicago, IL), 202

Vong (New York, NY), 365

W

Wally's Desert Turtle
(Rancho Mirage, CA), 63

Wente Vineyards Restaurant
(Livermore, CA), 16

Wheatleigh (Lenox, MA), 236

White Barn Inn, The
(Kennebunkport, ME), 257

Whitney, The (Detroit, MI), 262

Wild Boar, The
(Nashville, TN), 422

Wildflower (Vail, CO), 90

Willard Room, The
(Washington, D.C.), 111

Winston's at the Wynfrey
(Birmingham, AL)

Wright's (Phoenix, AZ), 7

X

Xaviars at Piermont
(Piermont, NY), 366

Y

Yahooz (Leawood, KS)

Yoshi's Café (Chicago, IL)

Z

Zinfandel (Chicago, IL)